the children of chinatown

WENDY ROUSE JORAE

the children of chinatown

GROWING UP

CHINESE AMERICAN

IN SAN FRANCISCO,

1850–1920

THE UNIVERSITY OF

NORTH CAROLINA PRESS

CHAPEL HILL

Designed by Courtney Leigh Baker and set in
Dante and The Sans by Keystone Typesetting, Inc.
Manufactured in the United States of America

The paper in this book meets the guidelines for permanence
and durability of the Committee on Production Guidelines
for Book Longevity of the Council on Library Resources.

The University of North Carolina Press has been a
member of the Green Press Initiative since 2003.

Library of Congress Cataloging-in-Publication Data
Jorae, Wendy Rouse.
The children of Chinatown : growing up Chinese American
in San Francisco 1850–1920 / Wendy Rouse Jorae.
    p. cm.
Includes bibliographical references and index.
ISBN 978-0-8078-3313-1 (cloth: alk. paper)
ISBN 978-0-8078-5973-5 (pbk.: alk. paper)
1. Chinatown (San Francisco, Calif.)—History.
2. Chinatown (San Francisco Calif.)—Social life and customs.
3. Chinatown (San Francisco, Calif.)—Social conditions.
4. Chinese Americans—California—San Francisco—History.
5. Chinese American children—California—San Francisco—
History. 6. Children—California—San Francisco—History.
7. Chinese American families—California—San Francisco—
History. 8. San Francisco (Calif.)—History. 9. San Francisco
(Calif.)—Social life and customs. 10. San Francisco (Calif.)—
Ethnic relations. 1. Title.
    F869.S36C474 2009
    305.23089'951079461—dc22
    2009011633

CLOTH   13 12 11 10 09   5 4 3 2 1
PAPER   13 12 11 10 09   5 4 3 2 1

to the

CHILDREN OF

CHINATOWN,

PAST, PRESENT,

AND FUTURE

CONTENTS

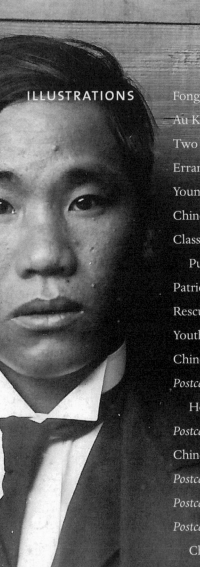

ILLUSTRATIONS

TABLES

ACKNOWLEDGMENTS

I have accumulated many debts through-out this project, and there are numerous individuals and institutions whose support was instrumental in the completion of the final manuscript. I wish to thank Eric Rauchway for all of his support during the early stages of research and writing. I am also extremely grateful to Cecilia Tsu for her insightful comments and expertise on the subject matter. Lisa Materson, Louis Warren, and Kathy Olmsted also provided excellent advice and encouragement dur-ing the early process.

I am especially indebted to Lois Smith for her extensive editorial assistance. I also wish to thank the other colleagues who listened to my ramblings and offered feed-back on my initial findings: Judy Walker, Jean More, and Ben and Sarah Symkowick. I extend a special thank you to Stephanie Chen Wu for her assistance in translating some of the Chinese-language sources.

I am deeply grateful for the help of the numerous individuals who pointed me in the right direction with my research, includ-ing Judy Yung, Colleen Fong, Lucy Salyer, Timothy Fong, Erika Lee, Bill Hing, Mar-lon Hom, Jeanie Low, Sue Fawn Chung,

Laverne Dicker, Charles Egan, Ron Fillon, Marcia Bell, Kathryn Gin, Lynette Choy Uyeda Gin, Miroslava Chavez-Garcia, Lewis Baer, and Jack Hudson. David Garton provided access to his family documents. Jeffrey Staley shared his excitement for the subject and his research findings, and he graciously opened up his home to me. Financial assistance was made possible by Betsy and Roland Marchand, the California State University Chancellor's Doctoral Incentive Program, and the University of California, Davis, Institute of Governmental Affairs. I am also indebted to the following people and institutions: William Greene of the National Archives and Records Administration, Pacific Region, San Bruno; Jeannie Woo and Anna Naruta of the Chinese Historical Society of America; Erika Gee of the Angel Island Immigration Station Foundation; Wei Chi Poon of the Asian American Studies Library, University of California, Berkeley; Tami Suzuki of the San Francisco History Room; Verne Deubler of the California Genealogical Society; Ronald Lee of the Boy Scout Troop Three Alumni Association; Father Daniel McCotter of St. Mary's Chinese School; William Jorae of the Photographic Archives, California State Parks; the California State Library; the California State Archives; the Bancroft Library; the California Historical Society; Stanford Special Collections; the Hoover Institution on War, Revolution, and Peace, Stanford University; the University of Oregon Special Collections; the San Anselmo Theological Seminary; and the Holt-Atherton Library at the University of the Pacific. I continue to be inspired and moved by conversations with several people presently working to improve the lives of the children of Chinatown. These include Marlene Callejas, principal of Gordon Lau Elementary School; Helen Joe-Lew at San Francisco Unified School District Multilingual Programs; Ben Wong, deputy director of Community Education Services; and Christina Wong at Chinese for Affirmative Action.

The anonymous readers for the University of North Carolina Press helped me clarify my points and strengthen the overall argument, and their insightful comments improved the flow of the manuscript. I am also grateful to Chuck Grench, Sian Hunter, Jay Mazzocchi, and the UNC Press staff for believing in this project and guiding it through publication.

On a personal note, I am eternally grateful for the loving support of my husband, Wil Jorae, who is both my most honest critic and best friend. My father, Denis Sweeney, has provided a constant model of integrity and inspired in me a love of learning since I was a young child. My mother, Sherry Sweeney, has taught me the value of hard work while demonstrating the most generous spirit of anyone I have ever met. My grandmother, Lina

Rouse, has been with me every step of the way and has provided a foundation of unconditional love and stability for the entire family.

the children of chinatown

INTRODUCTION

CONSTRUCTING CHILDHOOD IN EARLY CHINATOWN

IMAGE VERSUS REALITY

When one imagines San Francisco's nineteenth-century Chinatown, Chinese children do not usually figure prominently in the picture. Scholars of Chinese American history have focused primarily on the story of male Chinese immigrants; only within the last two decades have significant studies examining the stories of Chinese American females emerged. Chinese children appear only sporadically in the histories. Yet an examination of the historical record reveals important evidence of the existence of Chinese children in America and offers scattered glimpses into their daily lives. The narrow designation of San Francisco's early Chinatown (1850–1920) as a "bachelor society," or more recently as a "split-household" community, ignores the variety of family structures and the small but significant presence of Chinese children. It is important to recognize the presence of children in early Chinatown, not only because it changes the way we conceptualize Chinese American history, but also because the presence of these children and the formation of families impacted the larger controversy surrounding the Chinese in America. This book challenges prevailing scholarly notions of early Chinatown by positioning Chinese children and their families at the center of efforts to combat American anti-Chinese policies. My research reveals the heretofore untold story of child life in early Chinatown while also unraveling the various myths surrounding Chinese American childhood.

I have defined two major objectives for this work. First, I will examine how various groups constructed contrasting images of childhood and family life in Chinatown that significantly influenced the debate over Chinese immigration and the future of the Chinese American community. Second, and most importantly, I will recover the voices and experiences of Chinese American children in early Chinatown and reveal their efforts to circumvent policies of exclusion and segregation in American society.[1] I am most concerned here with reconstructing the lived experience of Chinese children in America by examining their immigration experiences and exploring their daily lives at home, at work, at school, and in the missions and court system.

The persistence and dominance of the bachelor-society paradigm has contributed to the difficulty of recovering the voices and experiences of children in early Chinatown. The success of anti-Chinese propaganda in painting the Chinese in America as a bachelor society in the mid- to late nineteenth century reinforced a social hierarchy that placed Chinese American children at a severe disadvantage. Facing obstacles of immigration exclusion, cultural dislocation, child labor, segregated schooling, and crime and violence in Chinatown, Chinese American children struggled for recognition in a society that increasingly resented their presence. Nineteenth-century anti-Chinese propaganda denied the existence of normative family life as a way of illustrating the deviant culture of San Francisco's Chinatown and contrasting the lifestyle of Chinese immigrants with a middle-class domestic ideal.[2] The perception of a "familyless" Chinese community has pervaded the historical scholarship even into the modern era and has rendered the presence of children in early Chinatown largely invisible. In recent years, the designation of early Chinatown as a split-household community has attempted to move scholars beyond the narrow definition of a bachelor society to examine the unique nature of family life in early Chinatown. The split-household model considers the structural dynamics of Chinese families separated by the Pacific Ocean. In split-household families, men migrated to America while their wives remained in China to raise the children and contribute to the husband's family economy.[3]

The designation of San Francisco's early Chinatown as a split-household community, however, remains problematic in its failure to acknowledge the family life that did exist in Chinatown during this period of Chinese American history. Children in general remained relatively rare in San Francisco compared to similar-sized American cities. As late as 1910, only 19 percent of San Francisco's population was age fourteen and under. This was significantly lower than the 32 percent of children age fourteen and under in the total U.S. population.[4] Decades of anti-Chinese hostility and harsh immigration laws hindered, but did not completely prohibit, the immigration of Chinese children and the growth of Chinese American families in California.

Chinese children (sixteen and under) constituted on average about 11 percent of the Chinese American population in San Francisco from 1860 to 1920.[5] These children attempted to break through segregated barriers while building a world for themselves on the margins of two cultures. Through an analysis of manuscript census data, I have traced the development and diversity of family life in early Chinatown. I am also concerned here with reconstructing the reality of the lives of these children and have presented that reality in their own words. I have combed through autobiographies, oral histories, newspaper articles, missionary reports, photograph collections, and a variety of local, state, and federal records to locate, in many cases, the only remaining documentary evidence of the existence of the children of Chinatown.

This book explores how four major interest groups working in Chinatown during the period under study constructed and reconstructed images of Chinese American childhood in an effort to sway popular opinion and garner support for their individual causes. I have broadly categorized these groups as anti-Chinese politicians and labor leaders; missionaries and social reformers; a loosely associated collection of writers, artists, and photographers; and Chinese American community leaders. Anti-Chinese politicians and labor leaders constructed images of filthy, diseased, and inherently inferior Chinese children to support their efforts to restrict the immigration of Chinese laborers into the United States. In addition, images of deviant Chinese domesticity justified policies of segregation specifically targeting Chinese American children in the school districts of San Francisco. Missionaries and social reformers, believing in the malleability of youth, constructed more favorable images of family life and childhood in Chinatown that reflected their emphasis on the power of reform. Writers, photographers, and artists created exotic and romanticized images of Chinese children that catered to the tourist's ideal of Chinatown. These images tended to portray children as culturally static or foreign and, ironically, only further isolated Chinatown at a time when American-born Chinese children were attempting to define themselves as "Chinese American." The Chinese American community presented a number of diverse images of Chinese childhood, utilizing strategies from accommodation to resistance as they tried to combat anti-Chinese hostility and establish a safe haven for their families in San Francisco. Although I have organized this work thematically to examine various aspects of the daily lives of Chinese children, these caricatures of Chinese childhood emerge again and again throughout the text.

The second major argument of this book is that Chinese children, though rare in early Chinatown, were extremely important, not just as pawns in the games of adults but as active participants in the formation of a uniquely Chinese American community. In their daily lives, the children stood on the frontlines of the battle against exclusion and segregation. The vast majority of this book is concerned with how the children themselves struggled to adapt to a reality far removed from the images created by competing adult interests. Chinese children and their families adopted a number of strategies to circumvent and undermine exclusionary immigration laws and segregation at school, on the job, and on the playground. American-born Chinese children, in particular, helped lay the foundations of a Chinese American community by staking a claim to their due rights as American citizens. Born, raised, and educated in America, native-born Chinese children struggled with problems common to all second-generation immigrant children but were burdened with the additional problems posed by growing up in a segregated and racist society. These children felt compelled to justify their claims to American citizenship, even though they were legitimate citizens by birth. This pioneer generation of Chinese children forged a path through exclusion and segregation for successive generations to follow. In the process, Chinese children and their parents often formed uneasy alliances with Protestant missionaries, Progressive reformers, and law-enforcement agencies to achieve their ultimate goals. At other times, they found themselves engaged in direct combat with these same groups. Change emerged not only as a result of the efforts of middle-class American and Chinese progressive reformers, but also in response to the demands of working-class Chinese parents and their children.[6] Historians have only just begun to document the dilemmas of the first and second generation of Chinese American children who, beginning in the nineteenth century, surmounted substantial social barriers.[7]

Perhaps the biggest challenge to this study is the problem of historical invisibility. Scholars of the history of childhood have repeatedly argued that children remain one of the most invisible groups in history. Historians agree, however, that it is important to look not only at how societies view childhood but also at the unique experiences of the children themselves. Children were actively shaping their own futures, sometimes in cooperation with but often in direct disregard of the intentions of adults. Yet, as Elliott West and Paula Petrik assert, historians have written very little "of the children's own motivations, goals, and acts—and, by extension, of their role as shapers of our past."[8] Research into the history of childhood has resulted in a restructuring of the historical narrative to document the role of children in significant historical moments. West and Petrik recognize that the experiences of children often reflect a reality different from adults, and that these unique viewpoints can illuminate aspects of the historical experience absent from the recollection of most adults. In recent years, scholars have increasingly emphasized the diversity of childhoods in an effort to transcend the ethnic, racial, class, and regional boundaries that have limited the study of childhood predominately to the northeastern, white middle class.[9]

The first histories of Chinatown fixated on the image of the bachelor society and predominantly focused on the stories of Chinese men. More recent research by Asian Americanists has helped to reestablish the role of Chinese women and families in early Chinatown.[10] Much work remains in examining the significance of children and the development of family life in early Chinatown. Yong Chen, in an article on Asian American youth in 2004, asserts that children remain "one of the most invisible groups in Asian American history" and that historians "have yet to make adequate efforts to understand children of early Asian America in a comprehensive and comparative manner."[11] Chen argues that in bridging that gap between the past and the future, Chinese children determined the fate of the Chinese American community. Chen's article is an important contribution in its declaration of the primacy of children in Asian American history.

Each chapter of this book seeks to recover the experiences of these children by exploring various aspects of Chinese childhood. Chapter 1 details the immigration experiences of Chinese children both before and especially after the passage of the 1882 Chinese Exclusion Act. Using autobiographies, oral histories, Immigration Bureau statistics, and evidence from the National Archives Chinese Arrival Case Files, the chapter considers how immigration laws impacted children's immigration experiences, and how some children's efforts to bypass exclusion differed from their parents' attempts to circumvent the immigration laws. Although primarily male children initially immigrated with their fathers as laborers, whole families increasingly immigrated with the intention of educating their children and establishing a home in America. The Chinese American elite recognized that the presence of child immigrants and families in America challenged the images of the parasitic Chinese sojourner perpetuated by anti-Chinese politicians and labor leaders.

Chapter 2 examines family life in early Chinatown in all its various forms. This chapter relies heavily on manuscript census data to reveal the number and variety of family arrangements in early Chinatown. It also continues with the theme of the previous chapter in exploring how various groups promoted images of Chinese family life that perpetuated a political agenda. Oral histories and autobiographies show how families adapted Chinese rituals and child-rearing models to the American environment and struggled to cope with the poverty and disease that plagued inhabitants of San Francisco's urban, industrial society.

The next two chapters focus on the experiences of Chinese children at work and at school. Chapter 3 relies on census data, autobiographies, oral histories, newspapers, and missionary reports to explore the world of child labor in San Francisco's Chinatown. Chinese children increasingly played important roles in the family economy at the same time that a national debate erupted over child labor. This chapter also examines the various factors that led to a decline in child labor in Chinatown and the shift to an emphasis on education. Chapter 4 emphasizes the role of Chinese children in the campaign against segregated education while exploring the various strategies that children and their families employed to combat the inequities of the public educational system. In an effort to achieve equitable educational opportunities and to counteract the negative stereotypes of Chinese children created by anti-Chinese politicians, the Chinese American community and white missionaries, educators, and sociologists constructed new images of Chinese children as model students that highlighted the work ethic and the academic potential of Chinese children in contrast to other immigrant youth.

Chapter 5 examines exceptional cases of Chinese children in the missions and the courts. This chapter relies extensively on newspaper accounts, missionary records, police reports, and court and penitentiary records to explore the uneasy alliance between the Chinese community, missionaries, and social reformers in fighting prostitution, child abuse, and juvenile delinquency in Chinatown. Chinatown's vice endangered not only the safety and security of Chinese children but also threatened to undermine the public image of middle-class domesticity that Chinese community leaders and their allies had promoted. This chapter examines how Chinese parents sometimes used the courts to battle missionaries and child-protective societies for custody of their children. Youth courts also proved to be useful allies in parental efforts to discipline especially unruly juveniles. Children often turned the tables, using the courts to realize their own desires when they had no other voice. Increased state intervention into Chinese family life eventually resulted in public efforts to enforce an American middle-class ideal of domesticity on members of the Chinese working class. To protect their own families, improve social conditions, and establish a more positive image of Chinatown, the Chinese American elite sought to purge Chinatown of prostitution, child abuse, and crime. The goals of reformers and those of the Chinese American elite once again coalesced, and a tentative alliance formed in the effort to establish a safe, family-friendly Chinatown.

Chapter 6 explores the role of children in the emergence of a new Chinatown, both immediately before and after the 1906 earthquake. The chapter focuses specifically on the emergence of a tourist Chinatown and the mass production and marketing of images of Chinese childhood. By examining the material culture of Chinatown tourism, it considers how images of Chinese children in the form of photographs, paintings, sculpture, postcards, and travel narratives came to play an important role in reimagining Chinatown. Meanwhile, the real-life children of Chinatown witnessed the district's historical transformation. Oral histories and autobiographies reveal how Chinese children endured the 1906 earthquake and contributed to the 1911 Chinese Revolution. These events spurred important changes in Chinese American life. Chapter 6 also explores how Chinatown's children coped with challenges both on the global and familial level while struggling to define themselves as Chinese Americans.

MY RESEARCH COMPLICATES the story of early Chinatown and the creation of a Chinese America. The lives of Chinese children, in particular, have been buried and distorted by a history of exclusionary American immigration policy and institutionalized segregation. This work represents the first comprehensive, full-length study of the history of Chinese American childhood. Through an in-depth analysis of Chinese children in San Francisco, the largest community of Chinese in America, we can begin to understand the process of family formation during the earliest period of Chinese American history. By examining perceptions of Chinese childhood, we gain greater insight into the political, social, and economic motivations of the key players in the debate over the "Chinese question." Ultimately, this book uncovers the many ways that Chinese American children negotiated the boundaries of two cultures, challenging the injustices of their era while struggling with their own feelings of cultural dualism.

THE IMMIGRATION OF CHINESE CHILDREN AND THE CHINESE QUESTION

I was eight years old when I went to China. Never was in the Plaza. Never seen a [streetcar].
I do not remember anything at all about San Francisco. But this is an American hat and
pants. I had them when I went to China in 1881. When I was eight years old.
—LEE HIM, *age fourteen*

Lee Him arrived in San Francisco on the Steamer *Rio De Janeiro* on January 7, 1888.[1] The boy was only one of thousands of Chinese children who had passed through the port of San Francisco since the 1850s. Immigrants arriving from China in the 1850s and 1860s easily gained entry into the country. However, with the passage of the Page Act in 1875 and the Chinese Exclusion Act in 1882, the government erected substantial barriers to try to stop the immigration of Chinese prostitutes and laborers into the country. According to the 1882 law, only teachers, travelers, students, diplomats, and merchants qualified for entry under Section 6 of the Exclusion Act. In a series of cases in the years immediately following the passage of the Exclusion Act, the circuit court reinterpreted the law to allow the sons and daughters of natives and merchants access into the United States. In 1884 the circuit court also confirmed *In re Look Tin Sing*, which held that Chinese children born in the United States were American citizens under the law and therefore entitled to their right to reenter the country.[2] Although he claimed to have been born in San Francisco, Lee Him told the customs inspector that he had departed for China with his father in 1881, just prior to the passage of the Exclusion Act. He now desired reentry as a native-born citizen. However, customs officials were inclined to doubt the boy's testimony since hundreds of other children had similarly claimed native status in an attempt to circumvent the exclusion law. The burden of proof lay with the children, who had to conclusively demonstrate their status as American citizens. Regardless of their birth in America, Chinese children aroused the suspicion of immigration officials simply on account of their race. Lee Him's reference to his Western style hat and pants was not only an attempt to demonstrate his prior residence in San Francisco; it was also an effort to seize his fundamental rights as an American citizen in a society that had come to deeply resent its Chinese members.

JOURNEY TO AMERICA

The vast majority of Chinese immigrants to the United States in the nineteenth century came from the Guangdong province in southeastern China. In the mid-nineteenth century, this region of China experienced the ravages of the Opium Wars, internal rebellions, and natural calamities such as droughts, floods, typhoons, and crop failures. In addition, an increase in population of 79.5 percent from the late eighteenth century to the mid-nineteenth century in Guangdong created a crisis in the availability of cultivable land. Farmers also faced oppressive taxation from the struggling Qing government.[3] These combined pressures encouraged the mass migration of individuals from China to various regions of the world during the latter half of the nineteenth century.[4] Still, we must examine individual narratives fully to understand the motives behind Chinese emigration. Individuals weighed the substantial risks and costs of emigration and developed strategies that provided the most benefit for the entire family. The experiences of child immigrants prove especially useful in helping to understand why families would sacrifice the labor and risk the lives of their younger members in a journey halfway around the world.

Individual motivation for immigrating to the United States varied, although most child immigrants admitted that, like their adult counterparts, the lure of a living wage remained their primary motive. Young children listened attentively as neighbors returning home from the United States boasted of their newfound wealth. Lee Chew was inspired to come to America by a man who returned from Gold Mountain and hosted a big feast for the village to share his good fortune. He dreamed of attaining such wealth and sought his father's consent to journey to America in pursuit of his dream. He joined the rush, as thousands of other immigrants journeyed to California in the hope of making their fortune.[5]

Although Lee Chew enjoyed the luxury of choosing to travel to America, not all children exercised the same degree of freedom in determining their future. Ng Shui Cheuk and his brother decided they had to split up and travel to different parts of the world after their father's death had left the family struggling to make ends meet. The boys agreed to stay abroad for two to three years; the first one to find success would return home to care for their mother.[6] Poverty also limited the choices of Yee Loon, whose farming parents did not earn enough money to feed the children. Debt forced his family to sell his brother, and his sister died from lack of medicine. The sixteen-year-old had to try to find work in America to help support his family in China. His father borrowed $1,000—$200 more than the value of the family farm—to buy a birth certificate and cover the travel expenses.[7] Yee Loon bore a heavy burden on his shoulders as he made his way to the United States. The journey to America forced many children into adult responsibilities.

Chinese girls generally had little say in their futures. The patriarchal cultural values of Chinese society discouraged the immigration of Chinese women. Confucian ideology dictated that women limit their activities to the domestic sphere. In addition, the hierarchical social structure positioned women as subordinate to men, requiring a woman to obey her father at home, her husband after marriage, and her eldest son after the death of her husband.[8] Daughters of merchants sometimes traveled to the United States to join their fathers. However, impoverished Chinese girls, like their working-class male counterparts, had very few choices. Poor families sometimes sold their daughters into domestic service or prostitution to help supplement the family income. The Chinese considered the *mui tsai* (domestic servant) system as a form of charity for lower-class children. Parents signed a contract agreeing to sell their children into service for a limited period of time. Chan Fung Chun recalled the sobs of her heartbroken mother as poverty forced her to sell her youngest daughter as a *mui tsai*. Fearing for her daughter's future, the mother begged the slave dealer not to sell the girl into prostitution. Chan Fung Chun's new owner shipped her off to America. The child remembered the long, tearful journey to San Francisco and the cruelty of the slave dealer, who punished her for thinking about home. Although she did work for several years as a domestic servant, her mistress ultimately decided to sell her into prostitution at age fourteen.[9] Unscrupulous men and women sometimes lured girls to America with promises of gold, marriage, jobs, or education, only to sell them into prostitution.[10]

Although they had little choice in the matter, some girls tried to fight back. The father of six-year-old Lilac Chen (Wu Tien Fu) told her that he was taking her to meet her grandmother. However, on the steamer she discovered that her father had sold her: "[He] locked me in the cabin while he was negotiating my sale. And I kicked and screamed and screamed and they wouldn't open the door till after some time, you see, I suppose he had made his bargain and had left the steamer. Then they opened the door and let me out and I went up and down, up and down, here and there, couldn't find him." Despite her objections, Chen was transported to San Francisco and resold as a servant to a brothel.[11] Chinese child immigrants, especially female children, were vulnerable to exploitation by adult relatives and slave traffickers interested only in making a profit from the labor of children.

Whether children immigrated to the United States by force or of their own free will, departing from home was a traumatic experience. Family and friends often offered gifts and bittersweet farewells to departing immigrants. Relatives showered some child immigrants with new clothing and supplies of special foods in preparation for their journey.[12] Huie Kin did not have the luxury of new clothes and sweetmeats. His baggage consisted of bedding and a basket with shoes, a hat, and some homemade biscuits that his mother had baked for him. He recalled his final emotional moments at home: "We said good-by at the doorsteps, and a minute later darkness closed around us and we could not see the folk standing there."[13] Children like Huie Kin experienced fear and uncertainty as they left behind parents and siblings, took on adult responsibilities, and embarked on their journey to California.

Although merchants' families could afford to travel in style, the journey to America was far from pleasant for the majority of Chinese passengers. In 1867 the Pacific Mail Steamship Company began to run ships from San Francisco to China that carried approximately 250 first-class passengers and between 1,200 to 1,400 passengers in steerage. The trip took about a month, with a third-class ticket costing about $50.00. Steerage-class passengers were generally prohibited from frequenting the upper-class compartments. Ben Woo remembered that on his trip to San Francisco in 1911, third-class passengers ate in a mess hall, while first-class passengers enjoyed the luxury of a formal dining room. Third-class travelers packed into the holds of the steamers, where they slept on canvas bunk beds and had to supply their own bedding. The food was generally poor and bland, with water in short supply. Overcrowding and poor ventilation contributed to the uncomfortable conditions. Even children recognized the class distinctions.[14]

Historical studies of immigrant children have described the trauma associated with moving to a foreign land. The harsh conditions of travel, difficulties in finding basic sustenance, exposure to dangerous illnesses, and fear of death all combined to create a deep sense of loneliness.[15] Pangs of seasickness, disease, and homesickness transcended class boundaries. Unfamiliar surroundings and food made the experience especially uncomfortable. Child immigrants traveling alone described a dreadful solitude that sometimes brought them to tears.[16] In addition to the usual hardships of travel, poor children often suffered from the gnawing pains of hunger. Twelve-year-old Fong Sec remembered: "On board, we noticed fellow passengers about our own age whose baskets were brimful with fruits and cakes given by relatives and friends. As my family was poor, I had none. When I saw them eat the fruit and cakes, it made my mouth water. . . . [S]easick and unable to eat any rice, I longed all the more for fruits and cakes, and even became bold enough to beg others to give me some to eat."[17] Heightened in part by their young age and sense of homesickness, the realities of poverty made the trip even more traumatic for working-class Chinese children.

The realities of life and death were always close at hand on board the steamer. The close quarters of the ship encouraged the spread of a variety of contagious diseases, some of which proved deadly. Very young children and the elderly were especially vulnerable, although even healthy young men found themselves the victims of disease. Huie Kin described the death of his relative, Huie Ngou, who became sick with fever on board the steamer. Huie Kin and other boys watched as the body was wrapped in a sheet and lowered into the sea: "For hours afterwards, we stood by the side of the ship, gazing into the darkness, scarcely knowing what to think." They wondered what was to become of them, and "there was an uneasy feeling that his death could not but cast an evil shadow upon our venture."[18] The children expressed anxiety and wondered about their future as the death proved a harsh reminder of human mortality.

For the most part, child travelers described the long days aboard the ship as excruciatingly boring. They spent the time gambling, playing, learning English, and memorizing their coaching books. Children immigrating as "paper" sons or daughters (those carrying false documents that identified them as children of exempt-class Chinese) often spent the time surreptitiously rehearsing the story they would have to communicate to immigration officials. Coached by adult companions, illiterate children simply repeated the story over and over again until they had committed it to memory.[19] Ng Cheng and Ng Kay carried none of these burdens, since their status as first-class passengers and the sons of a prominent merchant practically guaranteed their admittance into the United States. The boys, therefore, used their leisure time and freedom to roam the ship. To alleviate the tedium of the trip, the boys teased and played pranks on seasick passengers. They fondly recalled these pranks as "harmless child mischief."[20] By turning the ship into a playground, some children found a way to cope with the fears and uncertainties of immigration. However, during this early period of immigration, most Chinese children did not enjoy these freedoms. Most traveled as third-class passengers in steerage and suffered the harsh conditions of the voyage.

Despite the hardships of the trip, a child's sense of wonder may have helped to ease his or her adaptation to the dramatic changes inherent in the immigration experience. Young immigrants marveled at the sights on their journey and expressed excitement upon arrival in San Francisco. Lee Chew was awestruck by the power of the steamships: "The engines that moved the ship were wonderful monsters, strong enough to lift mountains."[21] Wen Bing Chung recalled "gazing at the blue expanse or watching a school of flying fishes disporting themselves. Occasionally, a whale spouting a column of water skyward would cause a flutter of excitement on board."[22] Chinese immigrants remembered overwhelming and indescribable feelings as they first set eyes on San Francisco.

Prior to the passage of the exclusion laws, customs officials searched Chinese immigrants for contraband and allowed them to go into town shortly after the steamer landed.[23] Albert S. Evans describes with great literary flourish the arrival of the steamer *Great Republic* from China in the early 1870s. Merchants' wives and their children left the ship with no trouble. Customs agents, however, stopped male Chinese laborers and searched their luggage for opium. Agents of the Six Companies (an organization composed of representatives of Chinese District Associations that formed in San Francisco to assist Chinese immigrants, later known as the Chinese Consolidated Benevolent Association) then separated the men into groups, most likely based on district or family association. Policemen shouted orders and frantically attempted to organize the crowd. Evans describes the arrival of fifteen to twenty Chinese slave girls: "As they land, they are searched in no delicate manner by the officers, and then received by their purchasers, and delivered into the charge of the sallow old hags in black costume, with bunches of keys in the girdles of their waists, who are called 'old mothers,' and who will hold them in horrible bondage and collect the wages of their sin." The girls endured heckling and jeers from the crowds as they passed and boarded express wagons to carry them to their destination.[24] Although Evans's account of these girls is tainted by the prejudices of his time, his description of the rough manner of the customs officials toward laborers and "slave girls" in contrast to the merchant class suggests the inherent class biases of these early immigration procedures. The exploitation of women and children proved an especially volatile issue in the debate over Chinese immigration. Anti-Chinese politicians drew parallels between the Chinese prostitution trade and African slavery and pointed to the sale of women and children as evidence to support the exclusion of the "heathen" Chinese. Over time, anti-Chinese rhetoric would culminate in restrictive laws designed to keep these girls from entering the country.

Immigrants, believing that the hardest part of the journey was behind them, soon discovered the reality of anti-Chinese hostilities. On arrival in San Francisco, Fong Sec hopped on top of the baggage wagon for the trip to Chinatown. He was amazed by the bustling sights of the city and especially enjoyed watching the streetcars. However, his moment of wonder and joy was cut short by a group of angry Americans. The white mob that gathered expressed their frustration at the arriving Chinese laborers by throwing street litter at their wagons.[25] Such receptions became more commonplace as anti-Chinese hostilities increased in the 1870s and 1880s. Chinese children, like Fong Sec, often found themselves in the midst of the fray.

RESPONDING TO ANTI-CHINESE RHETORIC

Although the Chinese American community remained predominantly male into the early twentieth century, Chinese children and families were crucial to the debate over Chinese immigration. A powerful anti-Chinese labor coalition began to exercise considerable sway in both state and national politics in the 1870s, and the family life of the Chinese immigrant became its target. Labor organizations and political parties repeatedly pointed out the devastating economic effects of Chinese immigration on white families and critiqued the sojourner mentality of the Chinese immigrant. In an 1878 speech before the U.S. House of Representatives, Horace Davis testified to the nomadic existence of the typical familyless Chinese immigrant. Davis contrasted the behavior of the Chinese immigrant with his European counterpart, who often brought his wife and children with him, adopted the English language, interacted with American citizens, and ultimately became American.[26] In an 1893 effort to garner support for a strict registration law that targeted Chinese immigrant laborers, Congressman Thomas J. Geary of California argued that Chinese men "bring no families with them, and do not become permanent residents, but are mere birds of passage, whose labor earnings represent no increase of wealth in the State. They establish no domestic relations here, found no homes, and in no wise increase or promote the growth of the community in which they reside."[27] Anti-Chinese politicians perpetuated a popular conception of Chinese immigrants as sojourners who sent their earnings back to China rather than contributing to the wealth of the nation. Although the argument was primarily economic, anti-Chinese rhetoric often pointed to the failure of the Chinese to establish families in the United States as evidence of the unassimilability of Chinese immigrants.

Chinese community leaders recognized the importance of the family issue to the debate over Chinese immigration. As early as 1876, they wrote a letter to President Ulysses S. Grant that offered an explanation for the small number of women and children in Chinatown. Chinese community leaders pointed to Chinese cultural prohibitions against the travel of women and the fierce anti-Chinese violence as factors contributing to the small numbers of Chinese families in America. Despite these barriers to the growth of Chinese families, some Chinese men and women did create a family life in America, and the Chinese community countered exclusion efforts by highlighting these Chinese American families: "It is charged against us, that not one virtuous Chinawoman has been brought to this country, and that here we have no wives and children. The fact is, that already a few hundred Chinese families have been brought here. These are all chaste, pure, keepers at home, not known on the public street. There are also among us a few hundred, perhaps a thousand, Chinese children born in America."[28] Women and children, though rare, were thus crucial to the Chinese community's effort to establish a more respectable image of Chinese family life in America. Their arrival and the gradual growth of an American-born Chinese population partially countered the claims of the anti-Chinese movement.

Although anti-Chinese politicians pointed to the failure of the Chinese to establish families as evidence for exclusion, fear of economic competition remained the primary motive of the working-class Americans who pushed for the passage of laws specifically targeting Chinese laborers. Ironically, these laws further hampered the development of Chinese family life in America. In 1875 Congress passed the Page Act, which was specifically designed to prevent the immigration of contract Chinese laborers and prostitutes. Congress authorized the collector of customs to examine the documents of

Chinese passengers to determine which immigrants were legitimate. The law imposed a fine of up to $2,000 and a maximum jail sentence of one year for anyone found guilty of transporting Chinese laborers and binding them to terms of service without their "free and voluntary consent." The act further restricted the importation of Chinese prostitutes by imposing a maximum fine of $5,000 and five years in prison. The strict enforcement of the Page Act severely restricted the free immigration of all Chinese females. The act failed to significantly reduce the number of Chinese laborers, but it did lead to a decline in the number of Chinese women entering the United States.[29] In 1876 Congress appointed a special joint committee to investigate Chinese immigration. The committee concluded that the Chinese represented an economic and moral threat to the United States and demanded the passage of a strict Chinese Exclusion Act.[30] In an effort to resolve the deficiencies of the Page Act and to limit the continued influx of Chinese laborers, Congress passed the 1882 Exclusion Act, suspending the entry of Chinese laborers for ten years. Congress renewed the Exclusion Act for an additional ten years in 1892 and 1902 and made it indefinite in 1904. With these acts, the federal government established a basic bureaucratic structure to enforce the nation's first restrictive immigration laws.[31]

DETENTION AND EXAMINATION

The Chinese Exclusion Act created substantial hurdles for Chinese men, women, and children desiring to enter the United States. Following the passage of the 1882 legislation, immigration officials would board every arriving ship and carefully examine the documents of each Chinese immigrant to determine if he or she would be detained for further investigation. The Pacific Mail Steamship Company housed Chinese men, women, and children in their company shed on Pier 40 in San Francisco, a crowded and unsanitary room with six windows and only one exit. Although the company had equipped the building for 200 immigrants, over 400 individuals stayed there at times.[32] Luella Miner, a teacher in the North China College near Peking, described the detention shed following a trip to San Francisco in 1902: "Small, barred windows admit a little light and air, but not enough to conquer the darkness and stench of this small place, where over two hundred human beings are herded, with no facilities for bathing or washing their clothes, and with the fumes of opium and tobacco poisoning the heavily-laden atmosphere. . . . Kind treatment from their jailers is the exception;

open contempt, a rude jostle or a kick are more frequently their portion. No callers are allowed, no papers, letters or messages can greet them from the outside world."[33] The *Hong Kong Telegraph* of October 2, 1909, reported the various sanitary violations at the Pacific Mail Company's detention shed. A young boy named Low Suey Sing had arrived on the steamer *Siberia* on the 14th of August. The boy, sick with tuberculosis upon arrival, was refused landing by the inspector and sent to the shed to await further questioning. Despite the pleas from his relatives to land him, immigration officials refused and also initially denied requests for hospital treatment. Although the boy was eventually allowed to go to the hospital, he died within a few days.[34] Reflecting on the conditions of the detention shed, the *Chinese World* on January 22, 1910, reported that "the walls were covered with poems; traces of tears soaked the floor. There were even some who could not endure the cruel abuse and took their own lives. The ropes they used to hang themselves are still visible. Those seeing this cannot help but feel aggrieved and gnash their teeth in anger."[35]

Children waited with their adult counterparts at the Pacific Mail Company shed while immigration officials examined their cases. Typical lengths of detention ranged from one day to over ten months, depending on the nature of the case and the backlog of the courts. Inability to produce the proper paperwork or establish exempt status resulted in delays and sometimes an order of deportation. Discrepancies in testimony attributed either to faulty memories or falsified records could also be detrimental to an immigrant's ability to gain entry. Parents and guardians often hired lawyers to facilitate the entry of their children into the country. Children denied admission by the customs officials remained in the detention shed until their habeas corpus hearing. Some children rebelled against their confinement. Eleven-year-old Chea Ham remained in the detention shed on Pier 40 for about one month and then escaped in the middle of the night.[36] This was one way of expressing discontent over the United States' restrictive immigration policy.

Responding to concerns from immigration inspectors about security and complaints from the local Chinese American community about the sanitary deficiencies of the detention shed, the federal government approved the construction of an immigration station on Angel Island. The station officially opened in January 1910. Angel Island came to symbolize the era of Chinese exclusion and in no way exuded the welcoming presence of the Statue of Liberty and Ellis Island. Architects designed the station primarily as a long-term detention center and noted that impeding communication between immigrants and relatives on the mainland, isolation of contagious Asian diseases, and the prevention of escapes were primary concerns.[37] Twelve-year-old Wong Wing Ton was one of the first detainees at the new immigration station. During his three-month stay there, he and his father slept on government-supplied metal bunks. He remembered that the guards only allowed them to exercise in the yard about once a week, and he described the food as "terrible and unfit to eat."[38] Inmates had little to do but wait for the bureau to decide their cases. Angel Island became the physical symbol of America's racist immigration policies. Chinese children directly experienced the harsh realities of this racism.

The period of detention on Angel Island could range from a few days to several months, depending on the individual case. The barracks were segregated by sex, except that children under twelve usually remained with their mothers. Immigration officials allowed the detainees to get items from their bags about once a week. Missionaries from various Protestant churches visited the detainees, passing out Bibles, helping them compose letters, and providing basic lessons in the English language. Women and young children apparently had more freedom on Angel Island than adult males. Officials allowed them to walk the grounds in small groups. Children read books and played shuttlecock, ball games, and dominoes. A visiting minister's son remembered teaching the children to play marbles, jacks, and hopscotch.[39] Older boys and men remained mostly confined to their quarters, although they did have the use of the exercise yard. Many wrote poetry on the walls, expressing feelings of anger, resentment, and frustration over their internment on the island. Although they could not express their anxieties quite as articulately as older detainees, children nevertheless attempted to express their fears and alleviate their boredom in a number of ways. In addition to the poems, drawings of boats, houses, guns, flags, birds, horses, chickens, rabbits, and fish also illustrate the walls of the men's barracks.[40] Younger boys, lacking the literary skills of their elders, may have carved these naïve drawings on the walls. By defying authorities and damaging Immigration Bureau property, the children also communicated their discontent over their detainment.

Shortly after their arrival in America, Chinese immigrants, including children, received a comprehensive medical exam. During the pre–Angel Island period, the law required shipmasters entering San Francisco harbor to report all cases of Asiatic cholera, smallpox, yellow fever, typhus, and "ship fever." By 1884 the San Francisco Board of Health instituted a process of inspecting,

fumigating, and disinfecting all ships arriving from Asia. Immigrants underwent medical exams to determine the presence of contagious diseases. Officials used their fingers or buttonhooks to pull back a patient's eyelids and
examine for signs of trachoma, which was grounds for exclusion. In 1903
immigration officials adopted the Bertillon system, which included a detailed
examination and measurement of body features, including forearms, feet,
fingers, ears, head, teeth, hair, and genitalia in order to provide future identification markers. Responding to complaints about the intrusiveness of this
procedure, the government ceased using the Bertillon system in 1905. However, many features of the system remained, and the Immigration Bureau
adopted new procedures to search for disease and verify the age of child
immigrants.[41]

With the construction of a hospital on Angel Island, officials hoped to
isolate contagious diseases and streamline the examination process. In the
1890s a Quarantine Station on Angel Island disinfected ships and screened
passengers for contagious diseases such as cholera, smallpox, typhoid, and
the bubonic plague. After 1910 physicians examined stool and blood sam-
ples provided by the immigrants to determine the presence of hookworms
(uncinariasis), roundworms (filariasis), or liver fluke (clonorchiasis). Hookworms and roundworms became grounds for exclusion, and in 1917 immigration officials added liver fluke to the list. The immigrant was entitled to
request medical treatment for conditions such as hookworm if he or she had
the money to do so. After treatment, the immigrant could then be admitted
into the United States.[42] A group of students who arrived at Angel Island in
1912 described the medical exams and treatments as particularly frightening
experiences. Some children claimed to not understand why they were taking
the medicine, and they sensed that the nurses were angry or impatient with
them when they hesitated to follow directions.[43] The new medical treatments succeeded in preventing the spread of contagious diseases. However,
language barriers and the young ages of the applicants most likely impeded
communication and added to the frustration of both nurses and patients.

As historian Erika Lee has argued, the intensive interrogations and medical exams revealed the race, class, and gender biases of American immigration policy.[44] By the early twentieth century, American concerns with white
slavery prompted increased government efforts to identify suspected prostitutes in an attempt to halt the traffic of Chinese women into the United
States. Procurers often went to great lengths to coach these young women in
order to ensure their entry into the country. Although the vast majority of

white slaves in the United States were probably American-born, xenophobic attitudes and the extensive publicity surrounding the influx of foreign prostitutes prompted immigration officials to carefully scrutinize young, family-less, foreign-born women. The scapegoating of foreigners emerged from nativist fears of race suicide. Officials, influenced by late nineteenth-century racial theories of medicine and science, believed that Chinese women presented a particular medical threat to American society because of their less moral and more animalistic tendencies. Chinese prostitutes especially posed a threat to the vitality of American families and the monogamous model of Christian marriage. Immigration officials at both Angel Island and Ellis Island frequently detained single women more than other immigrants for further questioning on the assumption that they sought entry to the United States for purposes of prostitution.[45] Chinese children were not exempt from these interrogations and examinations.

In order to gain admission, Chinese women and girls had to prove they were not prostitutes by demonstrating their sexual respectability.[46] Those who failed to behave or dress properly faced a greater chance of deportation. White slave narratives frequently associated improper conduct (such as gaudy clothing, garish behavior with men, frivolous conversation, and staying out late) with sexual immorality.[47] When sixteen-year-old Lai Ah Kew arrived in San Francisco in 1906, the Chinese interpreter insisted that the girl's association with Chinese men on the steamer led him to doubt her respectability. Carrie G. Davis of the Oriental Home in Berkeley (with the help of an interpreter) talked to Lai Ah Kew on the boat and expressed her opinion of the girl's character in a letter to the Chinese Bureau:

> My firm belief is that she is ignorant of being brought for any other purpose than that of a wife. The man has been smart enough to keep everything from her in every respect. In my own mind I am fully convinced that she has been brought for no other purpose than an immoral life. We are so familiar with the clothing and contents of these girls' boxes that they cannot deceive us. We had the temerity to ask us [her] to show us some of her Chinese clothes. Poor child! When she unlocked the box there was little or none to show. I asked her where her jewelry was and she said: "we were too poor to get any." Meaning her mother. She said her mother was very poor.[48]

Davis's description of Lai Ah Kew demonstrates the tendency of female reformers to view prostitutes as innocent victims of both male exploitation and the sexual double standard. This idea stood in stark contrast to the opinions expressed by male antivice crusaders, who tended to depict prostitutes as vengeful women intent on destroying the innocence of young men.[49] Bay Area mission homes often offered to house women and female children in an effort to shield them from the conditions and influences of the shed. Davis intervened on the girls' behalf: "I regret exceedingly that the other little girl has had to stay there so long with those older ones who have been in vile lives. They cannot help learning much that will contaminate them."[50] This statement reflected the belief on the part of missionaries that Chinese children were more malleable and therefore more capable of reform than their adult counterparts. Missionaries initiated efforts to rescue and reform Chinese girls whom they believed were destined for a life of prostitution. The Bureau of Immigration eventually approved Lai Ah Kew's landing.

As the exclusion laws reveal, American laborers especially despised working-class Chinese because of the perceived economic and moral threat that their presence in the American West signified. Medical exams sought to identify laborers posing as merchants by carefully noting the applicants' hands and feet. Darker skin color or calloused hands and feet indicated that an individual had performed manual labor and was not, therefore, a merchant.[51] Immigration officials expected the wives and female children of merchants to exhibit physical markers of status such as bound feet or jewelry, while automatically suspecting that women and girls without such markers were prostitutes. Inspectors regarded fine clothing, jewelry, good written and verbal communication skills, and even a first-class steamer ticket as indicators of respectability and merchant status. Inspectors usually examined first-class passengers on board the ship, allowing them to bypass Angel Island, while detaining steerage passengers and suspected laborers for more intensive examinations. Immigrants learned to appeal to the preconceived notions of the immigration officials.[52] In 1885 Ching Sow Sing, testifying on behalf of his wife and daughter's right to enter the country, insisted that Custom House officials note the compressed feet of his wife and daughter as a mark of respectability.[53] Children could bypass the immigration restrictions by demonstrating visible markers of their parents' class status.

Chinese children arriving in the United States after 1882 had to establish their exempt status under the Exclusion Act. The only labels specifically mentioned in the law that could apply to children were "student" or "traveler." In 1883 northern California district court judge Ogden Hoffman heard the case of a merchant's son who was denied entry under the exclusion laws.

Hoffman expanded the scope of the law, ruling that the Exclusion Act did not apply to the children of Chinese merchants. The courts consistently ruled that wives and children of Chinese merchants could freely enter the United States. In 1884 the San Francisco Circuit Court heard the case of Look Tin Sing, who was born in Mendocino, California, but returned to China at age nine to seek an education. When he returned to the United States at age fourteen, immigration authorities denied him admission to the country under the exclusion law. The boy's parents hired an attorney and challenged the deportation decision with a writ of habeas corpus. The boy's attorneys argued that, under the Fourteenth Amendment of the Constitution, Sing was a citizen of the United States and therefore entitled to enter the country. The circuit court ruled that Chinese children born in the United States were citizens and therefore also exempt from exclusion. In 1898 the U.S. Supreme Court, in *United States v. Wong Kim Ark*, reaffirmed the Sing decision by concluding that anyone born in the United States could not be stripped of his or her citizenship rights.[54] These children and their parents challenged the legality of exclusion, and although they were unable to eliminate the law completely, their efforts expanded the categories of exempt-class immigrants.

In addition to overcoming the hurdles of race, class, and gender, children applying for admission also had to prove their age both to confirm paternity and to qualify for admittance as the minor children of merchants or U.S. citizens.[55] Physicians designed medical exams specifically to determine the actual age of a child. Doctors examined the child's teeth, skin, genitals, hair, and overall physical development. W. W. King, a physician at Angel Island, described the medical examination of Fong Sun Moon in a 1910 letter to the San Francisco commissioner of immigration: "Applicant has 26 teeth. He is a small boy and looks young. Skin smooth and fresh. He has not passed the age of puberty. Genitals very small. I should say that this applicant is about 12 years of age, and not over 13 years of age."[56] Although the Bertillon system was abandoned in 1905, some doctors apparently continued to use intrusive examinations to authenticate the age of male children claiming exempt status.[57] Such examinations were no doubt embarrassing and frightening, especially for solitary children.

Deterred in part by the exclusion laws and anti-Chinese hostility, Chinese children immigrated in smaller numbers than their European counterparts. Child immigrants to the United States were generally rare, regardless of their country of origin. Between 1873 and 1890, only 21 percent of immigrants from all countries were children; between 1899 and 1920, the percentage of

TABLE 1: Admittance Rates for Chinese Child Immigrants at the Port of San Francisco, 1880–1920 (All Figures Percentages)

DECADE	MALES	FEMALES	AGE <10	AGE 11–14	AGE 15–16
1880s	90	79	68	83	94
1890s	86	95	97	100	76
1900s	80	100	100	83	74
1910s	71	100	93	69	68

Source: Based on a random sample of the files of 320 Chinese child applicants to the Port of San Francisco from 1880 to 1920. Chinese Arrival Files, San Francisco, Immigration and Naturalization Service, Record Group 85, National Archives, San Bruno, California.

child immigrants had declined to 13 percent. Chinese children, however, constituted only 6 to 7 percent of all Chinese immigrants from 1873 to 1920.[58] Young Chinese boys often immigrated with older male relatives who came to the United States to find work to help support their families in China. While American immigration laws and anti-Chinese violence may have dissuaded Chinese women from immigrating, concern for the preservation of the patrilineage and the maintenance of the family homestead and altar ultimately proved a more significant factor in encouraging Chinese men to leave their wives and children in China.[59] Despite these limitations, however, a number of young girls still immigrated to America legally as the daughters of merchants or illegally as prostitutes.

Although the intensive investigation was intended to identify and prevent illegal immigrants from entering the United States, younger children and females generally enjoyed higher admission rates than older male children. Even in cases where discrepancies existed, immigration officials tended to give young children the benefit of the doubt. According to a sample of the Chinese Arrival Files of 320 children, immigration officials at the port of San Francisco between 1880 and 1920 admitted female children at a rate of 91 percent—slightly higher than male children's 81 percent admission rate (Table 1). Age also mattered: immigration officials were much more likely to deny entrance to older children on the assumption that they were potential laborers. Children under age ten enjoyed a 91 percent admission rate, while the admission rate for children over age fifteen was 79 percent.[60] A breakdown by decade reveals that after the turn of the century, female children enjoyed increasingly higher rates of admission, while male children witnessed overall declines in their rates of admission. The lower admission rates for females during the 1880s may have resulted from increased agitation and efforts to restrict the influx of Chinese prostitutes. Age-based breakdowns suggest once again that children under age fourteen enjoyed the highest rates of admission after 1890. The lower rate of admission for children under age ten in the 1880s is a striking anomaly; the vast majority of children arriving during that decade sought admission as natives, and their young age may have limited their ability to recall the necessary details to gain readmission into the United States. Following the passage of the exclusion laws, Chinese children had to definitively prove their exempt status as either native-born citizens, the children of natives or merchants, or students in order to gain admission into the United States.

NATIVE-BORN AMERICANS

The majority of children who sought admission into the United States in the 1880s and 1890s claimed "native" status. Many of these children claimed to have left the country as a young child prior to the 1882 law and therefore could produce no certificate that would prove their nativity. To establish evidence of birth or prior residency in San Francisco, immigration inspectors often asked immigrants the following types of questions:

Have you ever ridden on a streetcar?

Does it snow here in winter?

Do you know of any Chinese restaurants or joss houses in this city?

Have you ever seen a fire engine?

Which store was opposite the one in which you lived?

Do Jackson Street and Dupont Street run in the same direction?

Both adults and children faced these types of questions. Some children simply claimed that they did not know the answers or were too young at the time to remember.[61] Although few children could recall any of their former neighbors due to their young age at departure, the inspectors frequently asked children to name playmates or other children who lived in their neighborhood. Lum Ah Yung testified: "My father never would let me go out into the streets. I do not know the name of any Chinese children in San Francisco. I never went out into the street and didn't play with any white or Chinese children."[62] This inability to recall facts may have hampered their efforts to regain admission. Sometimes white schoolteachers, missionaries, ministers, and merchants helped facilitate the landing of a child by attesting to their birth in the United States. George Van Voorhis, special watchman in the Chinese quarter, testified on behalf of several families in 1885 to verify the exempt status of their children.[63] During this early period of Chinese exclusion, children especially benefited from the testimony of white witnesses. These alliances between the Chinese community and their white neighbors proved crucial to successfully navigating the immigration process.

Although difficulty in recalling details from early childhood reflected unfavorably on a child's testimony, providing too much detail upon investigation could also be detrimental. In *Quock Ting v. United States*, the Supreme Court sustained the immigration commissioner's decision to deny admittance to a sixteen-year-old petitioner who claimed to be a native of San Francisco. The court determined that the applicant's ability to recall vivid details of the city of his childhood was improbable and therefore indicated that the boy had been coached.[64] The child may have prepared in advance for the strict interview, but this did not conclusively prove that he was attempting to gain entry illegally. Parents sometimes produced copies of birth certificates and baptismal records to ensure readmission into the United States.[65] Although American citizens by birth, children had to provide conclusive evidence to immigration officials of their exempt status as native-born Americans.

CHILDREN OF NATIVES AND MERCHANTS

After 1900 fewer Chinese children applied for admission as natives, and more children claimed to be the sons and daughters of merchants or the children of native-born citizens. As such, children's exempt status depended on their father's status. A child had to first reconfirm the exempt status of the father and then prove paternity. Although the procedures varied over time, white witnesses, inspections of the father's mercantile establishment, and partnership lists generally attested to the merchant status of the father.[66] Children born in China of American-born Chinese fathers were citizens of the United States under American law. Children of natives had to provide evidence of their alleged father's citizenship. However, immigration officials frequently denied entry to adult children of citizens, preferring to limit entry to dependent children.[67] To establish paternity, inspectors closely questioned father, child, and witnesses about return trips to China in order to establish a time of conception consistent with the applicant's age. Officials

Fong Bow and his father (File 10329/63, box 322, Chinese Arrival Files, San Francisco, Immigration and Naturalization Service, Record Group 85; courtesy of the National Archives, Pacific Region, San Bruno, California)

also examined the physical features of the father and child to find resemblances that would suggest a genetic relationship. In 1909 attorneys for Fong Bow submitted four photographs of the boy and his father in an attempt to show the resemblance between father and son. Immigration officials carefully examined these photographs in an attempt to verify the claims of the applicant. Despite the effort, officials denied Fong Bow's claim for admittance based on inconsistencies in the testimony of the witnesses.[68] Still, inspectors considered physical resemblance an important method of establishing paternity.

In addition to physical resemblance between father and child, inspectors also observed the behavior of the alleged family members in an attempt to confirm the claimed relationships. This sometimes worked to the applicant's advantage. In February 1909 Commissioner of Immigration Hart Hyatt North denied admission to Chew Gim, an alleged son of a native. However, North changed his opinion after observing "the unaffected grief displayed by the alleged father" when informed of the boy's denial. In a letter to the commissioner general of immigration in Washington, D.C., North recommended that the appeal be sustained and the child be admitted as the son of a native.[69] This public display of paternal affection moved officials to ignore the discrepancies in the testimony and allow Chew Gim to join his father in the United States.

Data collected by the commissioner general of immigration from 1904 to 1920 suggests that children of merchants generally had a harder time gaining admission to the country than any other category of exempt-class Chinese immigrants. Whereas immigration officials admitted 95 percent of merchants and 97 percent of merchants' wives, they admitted only 81 percent of merchants' children.[70] The age of the child also influenced the bureau's decision to admit or deport merchants' children. Gradually, the bureau adopted regulations that favored the testimony of younger sons and daughters of merchants. According to the department regulations of 1915, male children under fourteen were presumed to be members of the father's household. The same rule applied to sons between the ages of fifteen and eighteen, although such cases were subject to rebuttal by inspectors. Sons between the ages of eighteen and twenty-one had to provide conclusive proof of their membership in the father's household. With regard to females, the regulations insisted that "in the absence of evidence to the contrary, it shall be assumed that a wife or unmarried daughter is a member of the household of the husband or father."[71] Immigration officers were less likely to subject especially young children to intensive interrogations or detain them for an extended length of time. In 1913 a Chinese woman, Lum Shee, her thirteen-year-old boy, and a five-year-old girl arrived on the *Chiyo Maru*. Despite discrepancies in the testimonies of both the husband and wife, Inspector W. H. Wilkinson recommended admission for the woman and her children: "There is a very good resemblance between the children . . . and the alleged father, also between these children and the alleged mother; and the latter has every appearance of respectability. It is most unlikely that this woman would seek admission to the United States for an immoral purpose, accompanied by two children, 13 and 5 years of age, respectively, both of whom are undoubtedly her own."[72] Immigration officials granted the children permission to enter the country and reunite with their father, noting familial resemblances, the young age of the children, and how closely the family conformed to respectable standards of domesticity. The effect of these combined attributes could overcome restrictive barriers that made admission for children of merchants generally difficult.

Adopted children of Chinese merchants and of white American citizens presented a special dilemma for immigration officials. Missionaries in China

who adopted abandoned Chinese children wrote letters to the U.S. government requesting information about proper procedures for acquiring visas for
these children. The children's status remained questionable, although officials generally concluded that only those born in the United States or the
blood children of merchants qualified for admission under the law. In 1907
Jung Ah Mook, his wife Lee Ying, and their adopted eleven-year-old son, Jung
Luen Piu, applied for admission at the port of San Francisco. As an American
citizen, Jung Ah Mook immediately qualified for admission into the country.
Because Lee Ying's status derived from her husband's, she also easily gained
admittance. However, the boy's case was a bit more complicated. Immigration officials noted the favorable features of the case: "The man apparently is
fairly well Americanized, and the couple seem to be respectable, simple-
minded, well-deserving people, with quite a deal more than usual of the
romantic partly hidden between the lines of their simple but frank recital of
the circumstances attending the entrance by them into the marital relation.
Their story contains all the elements of truth, and it is quite clear that this is
not properly to be classed among the fictions which the Bureau encounters
daily."[73] However, the Immigration Bureau recommended the appeal be
dismissed since the law failed to authorize the boy's admission. The Office of
the Solicitor, however, disagreed with the bureau's decision, citing an earlier
court case and stating that an adopted Chinese child held the same status as a
natural child.[74] The commissioner general of the Bureau of Immigration and
Naturalization expressed his reservations about the solicitor's policy on admitting adopted Chinese children. He explained that his fear was that this
precedent would "open wide the door to fraud." He recommended that
inspectors require the most conclusive proof and take the greatest care in
such cases.[75]

CHINESE STUDENTS

Although Chinese students were explicitly mentioned in the 1882 law as
members of the exempt class, the definition of "student" changed over time.
Immigration officials determined that individuals coming to study English
did not qualify as "students" under the law. In 1900, according to the solicitor
of treasury, a student was an individual pursing the "higher branches of
study" or preparing for a profession in which the opportunities for study did
not exist in the home country. In addition, the student had to have an
independent means of support and the intent to return home after the

Au Kai Yung (File 12796/
02–20, box 707, Chinese
Arrival Files, San Francisco,
Immigration and Natural-
ization Service, Record Group
85; courtesy of the National
Archives, Pacific Region,
San Bruno, California)

completion of his or her studies.[76] An admitted student also could not become a laborer after arriving in the United States. By 1907 the secretary of
commerce and labor had liberalized and broadened the definition of "student" to admit those who wished to pursue elementary studies.[77] By 1914,
however, the rules required a student to request permission from the immigration officer in his district if he or she intended to pursue any occupation
other than studying.[78]

In order to qualify as a student, the applicant had to show the appropriate Section 6 paperwork, but a respectable manner, Western-style clothing,
references, and money could greatly facilitate the immigration process.[79]
Au Kai Yung arrived in San Francisco in July 1913 and applied for admission as a student. Immigration officials noted that his father was a merchant and the manager of the Shun Shing Bank of Canton and that the
"applicant has attended the schools in Canton for five years and reads readily
from the Four Books and the Book of Poetry, and also writes a very good
letter in Chinese. He presents a good appearance."[80] Au Kai Yung easily
gained admittance.

If the immigration officials suspected that an individual was merely claiming to be a student to gain illegal entry into the country, the interrogation process could become more detailed and intense. Inspectors required Chinese students to demonstrate their degree of education through literacy tests. Officials asked students to read or write a passage from the Chinese classics, and inspectors denied admittance to students who failed to demonstrate sufficient literacy at a level defined by immigration officials.[81] In 1909, when Ng Niebong proposed bringing twenty students to America to educate them and then return them to China, the consul general in Canton, Leo Bergholz, suspected a plot to illegally import laborers into the country. During the examination, the interpreter held copies of Chinese schoolbooks on his lap and pointed to characters with his pencil. The students read the characters as required. However, the interpreter also insisted that the students demonstrate their literacy by writing several characters. Bergholz refused Section 6 certificates to a number of the boys and justified his decision in a letter to the assistant secretary of state. His comments included brief summaries of the reading abilities of individual students and a tally of the number of mistakes each student made in his effort to write Chinese characters.[82] His decision to deny certificates to the students resulted in complaints from missionaries involved in the project and a full investigation. The secretary of commerce and labor overruled the decision, concluding that the consul general in this case had been "unduly exacting" and allowing the students admission to the United States.[83] For others, the literacy tests resulted in orders of deportation.

Nevertheless, Chinese students generally enjoyed high rates of admission compared to other exempt-class Chinese immigrants. From 1906 to 1920, the Immigration Bureau admitted 97 percent of all students who applied for admission to the United States; the admittance rate for all Chinese immigrants was 92 percent.[84] The higher rate of admission for students was no doubt influenced by political factors. In 1906 fifteen young Chinese students at Berkeley testified before Immigrant Commissioner North, criticizing immigration officials' treatment of Chinese student immigrants. The young men complained about discourteous treatment, the conditions of detention, and the brutality of the officers.[85] This testimony (combined with a number of controversial and highly publicized cases, such as the Ng Niebong case discussed above) aroused the anger of government officials in China, missionaries, and the Chinese American community. This negative publicity no doubt influenced the bureau's decision to adopt less-stringent standards in admitting students.

The nature of the exclusion laws did encourage a thriving business in illegal immigration from the late nineteenth century into the twentieth century. Chinese children proved essential players in these efforts to bypass exclusion. Illegal immigration began with individuals simply claiming to be native-born citizens returning from visits to China. Chinese immigrants memorized maps and facts about San Francisco and, under investigation, insisted that they had been born in the city. Witnesses stepped forward to verify their native status. Requirements of birth records and certificates of identification made such claims more difficult to prove. After the destruction of birth records in the 1906 earthquake, however, many immigrants simply claimed to have lost proof of their native birth in the fire. Another means of illegal immigration included the creation of the "paper-son" system. After returning from visits to China, American citizens and Chinese merchants claimed the birth of a son or daughter in China and thus opened a slot for the later immigration of children from China. Young men eager to immigrate to America would simply purchase false papers and pose as the son of a merchant or a native-born citizen in the United States.[86] One boy recalled that his father paid $1,500 to buy entry papers from a fellow villager: "I came over with one of the 'brothers.' Another one had already been admitted into the country. When they interviewed the two younger brothers, the facts were conflicting. That's why I stayed there [Angel Island] three and a half months. I had to appeal the decision."[87] In this case, the boy successfully evaded American exclusion laws by adopting a false identity as a paper son.

Other children became more active participants in evading the exclusion laws by helping smuggle in Chinese immigrants. Henry Moy, a ten-year-old boy, was arrested in Tacoma, Washington, in 1902 for illegally guiding Chinese immigrants from Canada into Washington, Oregon, and California. Several other Chinese boys, ranging in age from ten to twelve, were also involved in the operation. Immigration officials, acting on a tip, investigated the matter and arrested Moy at South Tacoma with three Chinese he had led 130 miles. After his arrest, Moy confessed to the illegal activity and admitted that he and his twelve-year-old brother had led several similar operations.[88] Recognizing that immigration officials were less likely to suspect young children of immigration fraud, the boys' parents or other relatives likely coerced the children into participating in the scheme. Still, Moy's case proves that Chinese children sometimes played a central role in circumventing the exclusion laws.

Enduring public criticism for their failure to stop illegal immigration, officials felt pressure to institute stricter regulations against Chinese immigrants. In 1886 the *San Francisco Call* criticized the immigration commissioners for failing to limit the immigration of prostitutes and laborers: "Human beings are bought and sold for cash, and these slaves are imported into this State, and . . . the Immigration Commissioners have let down the bars to the pseudo wives of pseudo Chinese merchants."[89] San Francisco newspapers began to accuse several immigration officials of actual involvement in the importation of Chinese prostitutes and laborers. San Francisco inspector Carlton Rickards was dismissed in 1899 for his involvement in helping to land illegal immigrants during his employment in Washington State several years before. As late as 1917, an investigation revealed that several top immigration officials had accepted bribes, manipulated or stolen records, and resold these records to attorneys who wanted to coach their clients through the questioning process. The Densmore investigation resulted in the dismissal of twenty-five employees and the indictment of a total of thirty people.[90] Accusations of graft forced the Bureau of Immigration to investigate cases of corruption among their employees while cracking down on the enforcement of the exclusion laws.

The intensive interview and screening process that inspectors had developed by the late nineteenth century was intended to stop the influx of illegal immigration from China. Especially in cases involving children, however, it became extremely difficult to distinguish exempt-class immigrants from those attempting to gain illegal entry. An illicit trade seemed to flourish in the nineteenth century, as traffickers imported women and young girls between the ages of ten and twenty into the country to sell into prostitution.[91] Brokers taught the young girls the appropriate responses to the questions of the immigration officials and told them to claim that they were coming to work as seamstresses.[92] In this manner, young Chinese girls became unwilling participants in extensive illegal immigration schemes.

Many young girls were coerced into giving false testimony but later relented under the pressure of interrogation. Leong Lai Yook arrived on the *Gaelic* in February 1890 and claimed to be native-born and the daughter of a merchant. When questioned by immigration officials, however, the girl failed to recall any streets, churches, joss houses, or gambling houses in San Francisco. Immigration inspectors reported that the father's supposed place of business was actually an empty wood yard, and a witness stated that the alleged father was really a laborer. Under further questioning, the girl admitted that she had lied and that she had been sold by her father: "I was taught in China what to say when I arrived here. I was taught in Hong Kong. I do not know what street. I was taught the day before I went on board the steamer. A man taught me."[93] To avoid such interrogations and the potential loss of profit, some brokers attempted to disguise a girl's identity or physically hide small children in coal bunkers or other concealed areas of the ship.[94]

As the Bureau of Immigration gained greater control over the process, the investigations and questioning of immigrants became more intense. In 1905 the Supreme Court, in *United States v. Ju Toy*, granted the Bureau of Immigration more freedom in the administration of immigration laws by insisting that the decision of the secretary of commerce and labor with regard to immigrant admission was final and conclusive. In effect, the *Ju Toy* decision prohibited Chinese from appealing to the courts in cases where the bureau had determined to deny entry. With the increased authority granted in the *Ju Toy* decision and the expansion of the bureaucratic structure, the Bureau of Immigration exercised tighter control and authority over Chinese immigration. By 1910 the bureau only employed officers who had successfully passed civil service examinations in an effort to improve the overall efficiency in the administration of the immigration laws. Increasing anti-immigrant hostility, coupled with the strong nativist affiliations of the bureau's officers, resulted in more stringent efforts to exclude Chinese immigrants.[95] Inspectors began to ask detailed questions about the immigrant's home village and family. Children drew diagrams for inspectors to illustrate the location of various geographical features of their home village. Although the questions included details about family history and dates that most children would not know, the applicants often recalled very specific details that suggested intense coaching and preparation for the strict interview process. Inspectors examined and reexamined witnesses to verify statements and clarify discrepancies. Immigration Inspector P. B. Jones reported unfavorably on the application of thirteen-year-old Dong Fong in 1914. During an interview with the immigration officials, Dong Fong seemed unable to recognize his alleged brother. The father, speaking in Chinese, informed Dong Fong that the boy was his brother, after which Dong Fong testified, "He is my brother." In addition to this mistake, Dong Fong testified that his house in China had earthen floors, that there was no headstone on his grandfather's grave, and that the family did not own a looking glass. Each of these statements was in direct contradiction to the testimony offered by his alleged brother. For these reasons, the department ordered the boy's deportation.[96]

Immigration officials often declared the applicant too young to testify if the child was under about age ten. Yet, inspectors sometimes questioned children as young as four. Low Shee, a wife of a merchant, arrived in San Francisco in 1915 with her three boys (age nine, seven, and four). Upon questioning, the four-year-old positively identified his mother but seemed to become hesitant and shy when asked his own name. The seven-year-old identified himself and his mother but was silent when asked his age. The nine-year-old brother identified himself, his mother, and his brothers but was unable to state his own age, saying, "I don't know, my mother knows." When asked to state the name of his village, the boy mistakenly provided the district name. The inspector noted the futility of continuing the interrogation. Nevertheless, immigration officials admitted the entire family three days after arrival.[97] Other children were less lucky.

FIGHTING EXCLUSION

The Chinese in America had protested the exclusion laws and their enforcement from the very beginning. Individual Chinese immigrants consistently challenged the decisions of the immigration officials in the courts. Parents filed writs of habeas corpus to challenge the unfair detainment of their children. Between 1882 and 1890, Judge Ogden Hoffman of the U.S. District Court for the Northern District of California heard over 7,000 Chinese habeas corpus cases challenging the denial of entry. At the same time, Judge Lorenzo Sawyer of the U.S. Court of Appeals for the Ninth Circuit also heard thousands of similar cases. Although the two judges generally supported Chinese exclusion, their commitment to legal procedure ensured individual Chinese a fair hearing under the law. Thus, the courts often overruled the decisions of immigration officials favoring the right of the Chinese to enter the country. In the 1890s exclusionists fought to remove the jurisdiction of immigration cases from the courts, transferring power to the Bureau of Immigration. In the 1905 *Ju Toy* decision, the Supreme Court declared that the secretary of commerce and labor had final jurisdiction over the entry of Chinese immigrants into the United States. Shortly thereafter, the Chinese in America demanded that China boycott American goods to protest the treatment of Chinese immigrants. The boycott began in Shanghai and spread to

Canton. The Immigration Bureau responded by relaxing some of their procedures and dropping the Bertillon system of medical examination.[98]

Chinese children proved important to the fight against Chinese exclusion as complaints from the Chinese community increasingly focused on the treatment of child immigrants. Immigration officers were guilty of threatening and intimidating Chinese immigrants of all ages. Henry Cheu arrived at Angel Island at age nine and remembered the harsh actions of the guards, who yelled at the boys and men to hurry as they marched off to the dining room.[99] Chinese immigrants sometimes endured physical abuse by immigration officials. Complaints from the Chinese American community culminated in several investigations. In 1899 an investigation conducted by the Treasury Department found evidence of the use of physical force against detained Chinese.[100]

Incidents involving wives and children proved most offensive to the Chinese American community, which especially protested the abusive treatment of immigrants who were supposed to be exempt from exclusion. Early twentieth-century merchants and Chinese American citizens gradually limited their protests to the treatment of members of their own class.[101] Ng Poon Chew, the prominent publisher of a local Chinese newspaper in San Francisco, published a formal critique of the immigration process as applied to Chinese immigrants. Chew had immigrated to the United States as a child in 1881. Chew's pamphlet specifically demanded a reexamination of the treatment of the exempt classes of Chinese immigrants to the United States by arguing that Chinese merchants and students often underwent unnecessary scrutiny and unfair examinations in an attempt to further limit their numbers in the country. Chew also argued that officials harassed Chinese residents who were attempting to bring their wives and children to America. He detailed the story of the ten-year-old son of a prominent merchant who was unable to enter into the United States because he had trachoma. "Although the American officers at the port of departure had given them a health certificate," Chew observed, "and although Americans on board the vessel testified that the ship's doctor had examined the eyes of all the second cabin passengers without disinfecting his hands," officials refused to reverse their decision to deport the boy.[102] Chew insisted that this case was only one of many examples where immigration officials allowed merchants to land while ordering deportation for merchant wives or children.

The Chinese American community highlighted the experiences of exempt-class Chinese children in their arguments against the exclusion laws. In 1909 the Chinese Consolidated Benevolent Association (CCBA) in San Francisco wrote a letter to President William H. Taft criticizing immigration procedures and specifically referencing their impact on Chinese children. The CCBA complained that American officials certified the health of children before departing China, but upon arrival in the United States, Immigration Bureau doctors found medical conditions that denied the children admission. "These children," the CCBA wrote, "many of whom are of tender years, are refused permission to be removed to recognized hospitals to be there treated by a skilled specialist, under proffer of bonds the amount of which would be prohibitive to other races."[103] The letter further argued that the Immigration Bureau denied women and children the right to communicate with relatives and friends. The merchant community fought back with a class-based argument that exposed examples of injustice and attempted to appeal to the shared middle-class family values of their white audience.

The treatment of children on Angel Island had elicited complaints from the Chinese American community since the immigration station opened in 1910. Chinese residents in America formally complained in a 1910 letter that upon arrival in America, exempt-class wives and children were subject to deplorable conditions. They insisted that even students holding certificates issued by the viceroy and visaed by the American consul endured intense interrogation and were frequently denied admission. The letter also complained that the requirement that students strip naked for medical examinations was particularly demeaning. Chinese merchants objected to the detention of their wives and young children in the same room as prostitutes.[104] When the Downtown Association of San Francisco sent representatives to Angel Island to investigate the complaints of the Chinese American community, they found most of them to be true.[105] While acknowledging the existence of illegal immigrants and prostitutes, Chinese merchants carefully separated themselves and their families from association with this lower class of Chinese immigrant. In this manner, merchants challenged exclusion by highlighting their middle-class status and respectable domesticity.

White missionaries sometimes joined the battle to protect the rights of young exempt-status immigrants. In September 1912 the Immigration Bureau launched an investigation as a result of complaints made by Ida K. Greenlee and a group of young male students from China. Greenlee was associated with the Presbyterian Church, and shortly after observing the diligent study of Chinese students during a 1909 trip to the True Light Seminary in Canton, she was determined to open a school for Chinese boys in the United States. Greenlee first established a school for nineteen Chinese boys in Seattle in December 1909. The school continued for about six months before the students left to live with friends throughout the country. Greenlee, with the assistance of the Reverend Dr. M. A. Matthews in Seattle, decided to organize another trip to China to recruit a new group of students for the school they proposed to open in San Francisco. On June 17, 1912, Greenlee arrived at the port of San Francisco with seventy-seven boys who desired to attend school in the United States. Greenlee proposed once again to educate the boys at the school in San Francisco before housing them with families in various churches throughout the country.[106]

In a typed formal complaint, Greenlee charged officers at Angel Island with rudeness, unfair detainment, slow processing, and harsh treatment toward the boys. In describing the interrogation of twelve-year-old Chan Hing, Greenlee remarked, "This examination was being conducted in such a terrifying tone of voice and manner. . . . [T]he tone of the questioner to the boy was so unkind and harsh that it startled me. When I turned to look at the boy, he was drawing back as in fear from the examiner. . . . He did not understand. He simply saw the man's face, violently contorted, with hand and pencil in the air as if ready to strike and drew back in fear."[107] Greenlee requested written statements from several of the boys in an attempt to substantiate her claims. The letters complained of inappropriate questions, physical and verbal abuse by officers, and the failure of the doctors to explain medical procedures.[108] Although most immigrants to the United States underwent some form of interview prior to gaining entry, Chinese immigrants endured more extensive testimony as a direct result of the Chinese exclusion laws.

The intense interrogations of the boys in this case apparently resulted from immigration officials' suspicions that Greenlee was illegally importing Chinese laborers under the guise of students. Although the Immigration Bureau suspected the motive of Greenlee and her peers, they apparently failed to gather enough evidence to deny admission to the boys. The bureau treated a number of the children for hookworm and trachoma and eventually admitted all seventy-seven. Shortly thereafter, Greenlee submitted her letter of complaint. However, a full investigation, including interviews with a number of employees at Angel Island, failed to substantiate Greenlee's complaints. Inspector Jones dismissed Greenlee's complaints about his harsh examination of the boys: "I believe that Miss Greenlee was to a certain extent under a nervous mental strain, and for that reason has positively, but unintentionally, reported conditions incorrectly as to my demeanor during these examinations."[109] After a meeting at the island in September, Greenlee smoothed over relations with officials and quickly began arrangement for the importation of more students from China the following year.[110] By 1914 the Bureau of Immigration had amended its regulations regarding the admission of students to require that officers at the port of entry confirm the students' school attendance. The rules required immigration officers to contact school officials and request notification if the student withdrew from the school or completed the course work.[111] After the Greenlee case, immigration officials likely passed such rules to detect possible cases of immigration fraud among alleged students. Although the government had admitted them into the country, some child immigrants lived in constant fear of immigration authorities.[112]

The deportation of children became an especially controversial issue between immigration officials and the Chinese community. Discrepancies in testimony, a failure to establish the mercantile status of the father, an inability to demonstrate a relationship between father and child, or the presence of disease were all factors that could result in the deportation of a child immigrant. The commissioner of immigration ordered the deportation of Fong Wing Look and Fong Sou Nam in 1915 when witness testimony failed to establish the relationship between father and sons. In a letter to the commissioner of immigration at Angel Island, the father insisted that he would not appeal the case but begged the commissioner to allow him to say goodbye to his boys and give them some clothing for the trip home.[113] The deportation of children could be especially heart wrenching for both parent and child. In 1911 the Chinese Chamber of Commerce and the Six Companies sent a complaint to the San Francisco Chamber of Commerce that specifically addressed the issue. The letter noted that the Immigration Bureau frequently deported children without notifying friends and relatives. The children were then left stranded in Hong Kong, far from their villages, without money or relatives to meet them. Once again, the experiences of Chinese child immigrants proved important to the efforts to the Chinese American community to challenge American immigration policies and procedures.[114]

In one especially dramatic case highlighting objections to the policy of deporting Chinese children, a white woman kidnapped a young girl from the Methodist mission home to prevent the child's impending deportation. Anna Jones traveled to San Francisco in July 1897 to attend the Christian Endeavor convention. After meeting Ah Lou during a visit to the mission, Jones felt saddened by the story of the girl's forced immigration to America and her impending deportation. Jones personally appeared before the collector of customs to plead against the deportation and offered to adopt the child. However, the collector was unable to grant her request. Jones returned to the mission to find that the director, Margarita Lake, was not there. Jones felt compelled by her Christian faith to do all she could to save the little girl.[115] She kidnapped Ah Lou and fled to Salt Lake City the next day. Jones apparently educated and raised the child as her own. Such desperate measures reveal the extent of opposition against the exploitation of Chinese women and children.

Despite the numerous complaints from both white and Chinese parties, the treatment of immigrants failed to substantially improve. In December 1915 the Native Sons of the Golden State, an organization of Chinese American citizens, sent a petition to the secretary of labor in Washington, D.C., bitterly protesting the treatment of women and children at Angel Island. Among the charges, the Native Sons complained about the severe interrogations and long detentions of women and children, as well as the denial of visitation rights to parents.[116] Once again, Chinese American community leaders hoped to appeal to a common sense of familial values and parental obligation. The Chinese community continued to complain about the unfair treatment and poor conditions faced by immigrants until the repeal of Chinese exclusion in 1943.

CONCLUSION

In many ways, Chinese children's immigration experiences closely mirrored those of adults, although children did face a number of additional burdens. Like their adult counterparts, Chinese children had to overcome race, class, and gender biases. Both boys and girls had to prove their exempt status under the exclusion laws by establishing their nativity, their student status, or the paternity of their exempt-status father. Children also had an additional hurdle in attempting to prove their minor age. By the 1920s immigration officials developed age- and gender-based guidelines that insisted on a greater burden of proof for older, male children. Immigration officials tended to assume that especially young children represented no obvious moral or economic threat. In such cases, these children were admitted with minimal interrogation and little hesitation. Older children readily recognized the injustices and cruelty of the harsh procedures and sometimes openly expressed resentment toward the American government.

Anti-Chinese politicians attempted to negate the presence of Chinese women and children in America by perpetuating an image of the solitary male Chinese sojourner, committed only to earning a large sum of money and returning home. According to anti-Chinese propaganda, the Chinese laborer did not offer any contribution to American society but only devalued the labor of whites while sapping the wealth of America and siphoning it off to China. The Chinese elite pointed to the presence of Chinese children in part to combat the negative sojourner image of the Chinese laborer. They insisted that the immigration of women and children represented the willingness and ability of the Chinese not only to live in America but also to assimilate into American society. At the same time, however, the Chinese in America retained strong ties to China, and many children traveled back and forth between the two countries during their lifetime. Despite the gradual implementation and enforcement of stricter exclusion laws, Chinese children continued to immigrate in small but significant numbers to the United States.

Chinese merchants expressed their discontent with the exclusion laws by directly challenging the legality of the enforcement procedures as applied to their exempt-class children. The experiences of child immigrants provided crucial evidence of the inherent inequalities in the exclusion laws. Ultimately, when legal means were exhausted, individual families turned to illegal means of circumventing exclusion. Children played important roles in the effort to bypass exclusion through the perpetuation of the paper-son system. Decades of exclusion, the creation of the paper-son system, and the stigma attached to illegal immigration have obscured the true identities of thousands of Chinese immigrants. Even today, Chinese American families may know very little about the actual experiences of their ancestors as they struggle to unravel truth from fiction.

However, the journey to America was only the beginning of Chinese children's experience with exclusion and segregation. Shortly after their arrival, Chinese immigrants attempted to deal with the sense of cultural dislocation by building institutions and establishing family relationships in San Francisco that replicated those in China. Exclusion laws created only the first of many barriers to the replication of such traditional family models. As the next chapter reveals, Chinese families in San Francisco adapted to their new environment through a number of unique family arrangements that ensured the continued survival of the Chinese family unit in America.

2 RECENTERING THE CHINESE FAMILY
IN EARLY CHINESE AMERICAN HISTORY

Zona Gale, writing for the *San Francisco Chronicle* in 1903, described her visit to the home of Foo Tai, a Christian Chinese woman and president of the Woman's Society of the Baptist Mission. Curiosity about the home life of Christianized Chinese prompted Gale's visit: "I longed to know Foo Tai, in her own home, and to try to break the silence that hangs over homes like hers. It was possible that, within its walls she simply swept and cooked and gossiped, like the rest of the Christianized world, but I doubted it. For some way there seemed to cling to her the perfume of almond flowers, and the memory of strange worship and strange fabrics, which all possible civilizing could not quite destroy."[1] Gale expressed surprise at the cleanliness of the apartment and frequently commented to that effect throughout her article. Gale noted the parallels between Foo Tai and her white counterparts. Still, Foo Tai and her family remained foreign: "It was a little room in which everything was for use, but it was absolutely clean. About the air clung that indescribable odor of alien flowers and precious wood and of censer smoke which characterizes all the Chinese shops."[2] Even though Foo Tai conformed to American standards of cleanliness and had clearly adopted the teachings of Christianity, the author emphasized her Chinese clothing and food as symbols of her continued foreign status.

As white Americans increasingly agitated against Chinese immigration in the 1870s and 1880s, Chinese families found themselves the object of greater scrutiny, and they became important players in the overall debate over the future of the Chinese in America. By the mid-nineteenth century, the image of the two-parent family was vital to white, middle-class Americans, who envisioned the home as a haven against the corrupting influences of the outside world. Fathers, and especially mothers, played crucial roles in preserving the innocence and malleability of their children. The changes accompanying industrialization, urbanization, and immigration threatened to undermine the sanctity of the middle-class American family and the ideal of the sheltered childhood. The apparently deviant family relations of the Chinese in San Francisco stood in opposition to the ideal two-parent family model of the American middle class. As the debate between American and Chinese leaders illustrates, the controversy over Chinese immigration spilled over into discussions of daily life and ultimately became a dispute over ideal family models. The intent of this chapter is to recenter the Chinese family in the historical narrative by focusing on the significance of Chinese family life within the conflict over Chinese immigration. More importantly, however, this chapter considers how the Chinese surmounted substantial barriers to ensure the safety of their children and establish a uniquely Chinese American family life in San Francisco.

ATTACKS BY THE ANTI-CHINESE MOVEMENT

Without the immigration of thousands of Chinese women and children to the United States beginning in the mid-nineteenth century, Chinese families could never have developed, nor could an identifiably Chinese American community have emerged. Although anti-Chinese politicians and labor leaders sought primarily to limit the influx of male laborers to America, they attacked Chinese family life as well. As we saw in the last chapter, prominent politicians and journalists generated propaganda that attempted to arouse the anger of white voters, not only by highlighting examples of vice and disease in Chinatown but also by criticizing Chinese immigrant men for failing to bring their families to America. The speeches, pamphlets, and promotional literature of politicians and various labor organizations appealed to the sensibilities of American middle-class men and women by emphasizing the unwillingness or inability of Chinese immigrants to establish normal family relations, as well as the possible dangers of intermarriage between Chinese men and American women.

The Chinese in America seemed to represent the most visible threat to the sanctity of the white middle-class household. Anti-Chinese writers argued that the small number of Chinese families in San Francisco served as evidence of Chinese unwillingness and inability to adapt to American society or contribute to the economy. These critics not only denounced the failure of Chinese immigrants to establish families in the United States; they also condemned the few existing Chinese American families for failing to raise their children by the standards of American middle-class society. In 1885 the San Francisco Board of Supervisors counted 722 children in Chinatown and concluded that many of these children were "herded together with apparent indiscriminate parental relations, and no family classification, so far as could be ascertained." The board complained that young children often inhabited brothels, counting eighty-seven Chinese children living with prostitutes. They "live in adjoining apartments and intermingle freely, leading to the conclusion that prostitution is a recognized and not immoral calling with the race, and that it is impossible to tell by a survey of their domestic customs where the family relationship leaves off and prostitution begins."[3] The supervisors identified only fifty-nine children living in a two-parent family setting in what they regarded as legitimate families. Historian Nayan Shah has argued that nineteenth-century politicians and writers labeled Chinatown as an immoral bachelor society that thrived on the very vice that threatened the respectable domesticity and morality of American families. The variety of domestic arrangements in Chinatown, ranging from all-male boardinghouses to women and children living in female-dominated households, directly challenged the two-parent family ideal of middle-class Americans.[4] Anti-Chinese politicians seized on this theme to support their argument that the Chinese represented both an economic and moral threat to American society.

Anti-Chinese politicians in California also raised the specter of interracial marriages and concern over race degeneration to garner support for their cause. In an 1885 report by the San Francisco Board of Supervisors, the authors alluded to the race degeneration that could result from continued Chinese immigration and the birth of an American-born Chinese population: "Will assimilation begin, and race mixture begin, with a mingling of Caucasian and Mongolian blood, and a new addition be thus made to the strain of American blood mixture to add one more thread to the intricacy of the present race problem that is to be worked out on our shores?"[5] The creation of stricter antimiscegenation laws in California in 1880, prohibiting the marriage of a white person with a "Negro, Mulatto, or Mongolian," reflected similar anxieties and fears. These laws severely limited the number of interracial relationships among Chinese and white people in San Francisco.

In 1901 the delegates to the San Francisco Chinese Exclusion Convention also addressed the issue of miscegenation in their memorial to Congress. Although, the memorial admitted that few intermarriages had actually taken place, the document argued that the children of such unions had proven to be "invariably degenerate. It is well established that the issue of the Caucasian and the Mongolian do not possess the virtues of either, but develop the vices of both." The memorial declared, therefore, that "physical assimilation is out of the question."[6] Although middle-class society in the late nineteenth century adopted an image of children as innocent and malleable, some whites viewed Chinatown's mixed-race children as innately corrupted by their parent's "sinful" relationship.[7] Such sentiments reflect the continuing atmosphere of hostility faced by both full-blooded and interracial Chinese children into the early twentieth century and represent the most extreme attacks on the integrity of Chinese American families.

Chinese leaders responded with righteous indignation to these criticisms. Community leaders frequently sought to counter the rhetoric of anti-Chinese writers and defend "respectable" families in Chinatown. Chinese community leaders pointed to both Chinese cultural prohibitions against the travel of women and the fierce anti-Chinese violence as factors contributing to the small numbers of Chinese families in America. By the late nineteenth century, the Chinatown elite increasingly recognized the importance of emphasizing the shared values between the Chinese and the American middle class in an effort to combat the negative stereotypes perpetuated by anti-Chinese politicians. They held up two-parent Chinese families as evidence of normative domesticity in an effort to counter claims of Chinese deviance.

THE REALITY OF CHINESE AMERICAN FAMILY LIFE

The reality of Chinese family life in America was far different from the images constructed by either the Chinese American elite or the anti-Chinese writers. "Family," as defined by middle-class American society in the late nineteenth century, was focused on the ideal of father, mother, and children. Each individual family member played a role in this arrangement based in part on the idea of separate spheres. The primary duty of the mother was to provide moral guidance and loving care for the children, while the father served as wage-earner and disciplinarian. The two-parent family unit was integral to the effort of creating model, Christian citizens. Parents sought to shield their children from the crowding, disease, crime, and immorality of the city. Chinese middle-class parents increasingly moved out of Chinatown while simultaneously organizing efforts to combat vice within Chinatown. Thus, middle-class Chinese children enjoyed a sheltered childhood with an emphasis on moral training and education within the protected haven of the family home. However, this ideal family life did not reflect the reality for most children growing up in America at the time and often came in direct conflict with the needs of working-class families depending on the labor of their children. Differences in class, race, ethnicity, and geographical location contributed to a diversity of child-rearing models.[8] Families in San Francisco's Chinatown rarely conformed to American middle-class visions of domesticity.

Chinese family life in America also differed substantially from the traditional family model in China. Chinese society during the late nineteenth century idealized a patriarchal, patrilocal family model that was multigenerational and included extended family. As many as three generations often lived together in the same household. When a young man married, he would live in his father's house with his wife and children. His brothers likewise would bring their wives and children to live in the family home. Young women in the Canton delta typically married shortly after puberty and immediately assumed the duties of domestic labor, child bearing, and child rearing. The new bride served her husband's family and endured harsh criticism and scrutiny from her mother-in-law. By bearing sons, the wife would eventually assume greater power and authority in the family, ultimately exercising control over the lives of her own sons and their wives.[9]

Although the Chinese immigrants living in San Francisco's early Chinatown attempted to replicate "normal" family relationships, they rarely achieved either the American or Chinese ideal. Prior to the enactment of immigration restrictions, Chinese immigrants sometimes brought women and children with them. However, most immigrants initially intended to remain in America for only a brief period of time before returning home to China. By 1870 at least 1,546 Chinese children under age sixteen were living in San Francisco. According to the census, some 12,022 Chinese individuals lived in the city at the time; therefore, Chinese children constituted about 13 percent of the Chinese population in 1870.[10] These children were predominately male, and the majority had been born in China and had immigrated to the United States. Beginning in the mid-1870s, exclusion laws and anti-Chinese violence discouraged the immigration of women to the United States, thereby hindering the development of Chinese family life in America. Social reformers, concerned about the trafficking of female slaves and fearing

TABLE 2 : Chinese Children in San Francisco Age Sixteen and Under

YEAR	NO. OF CHINESE	NO. OF CHILDREN	CHILDREN AS A PERCENTAGE OF TOTAL CHINESE POPULATION
1860	2,719	106	4%
1870	12,022	1,546	13%
1880	21,745	1,474	7%
1900	13,954	1,435	10%
1910	10,582	1,286	12%
1920	7,744	1,671	22%

Sources: U.S. Bureau of the Census, Eighth Census of the United States, 1860; Ninth Census of the United States, 1870; Tenth Census of the United States, 1880; Twelfth Census of the United States, 1900; Thirteenth Census of the United States, 1910; Fourteenth Census of the United States, 1920.

the moral impact of Chinese prostitution on white boys, fought for the passage of the Page Act (1875), which greatly limited the number of Chinese wives and daughters who immigrated to the United States.[11] Similarly, the 1882 Chinese Exclusion Act had a major impact on the establishment of Chinese families in early Chinatown.

Regardless of these obstructions, families continued to form in Chinatown. Most scholars focus on this period as the era of the split-household family. The vast majority of individuals in San Francisco's Chinatown were males separated from their wives and children in China. This chapter recognizes the split household as the dominant family type but seeks to focus more specifically on the domestic arrangements of the children who lived in Chinatown. This is especially crucial in understanding the process of family formation in early Chinese American history. As the figures in Tables 2 and 3 suggest, the actual number of children in Chinatown remained fairly consistent from 1870 into the early twentieth century, despite significant fluctuations in the total Chinese population. By 1900, though, the demographics of this group had changed significantly. According to the 1900 census, there were 1,435 Chinese children in the city, constituting about 10 percent of the total Chinese American population.[12] However, the numbers of male versus female children had nearly equalized, and the vast majority of children (93 percent) were born in California. The increasing number of two-parent

TABLE 3 : Chinese Children in San Francisco Age Sixteen
and under by Gender and Place of Birth

YEAR	NO. OF MALES	NO. OF FEMALES	NO. CHINA-BORN	NO. CALIFORNIA -BORN
1860	58 (55%)	48 (45%)	80 (75%)	26 (25%)
1870	1,208 (78%)	338 (22%)	1,234 (80%)	310 (20%)
1880	949 (64%)	525 (36%)	957 (65%)	512 (35%)
1900	765 (53%)	670 (47%)	77 (5%)	1,341 (93%)
1910	830 (65%)	456 (35%)	341 (27%)	930 (72%)
1920	901 (54%)	770 (46%)	251 (15%)	1,403 (84%)

Sources: U.S. Bureau of the Census, Eighth Census of the United States, 1860; Ninth Census of the United States, 1870; Tenth Census of the United States, 1880; Twelfth Census of the United States, 1900; Thirteenth Census of the United States, 1910; Fourteenth Census of the United States, 1920.

families in Chinatown accounts for the higher percentage of native-born daughters. By 1920 the number of Chinese children had increased only slightly to 1,671, but they constituted a larger percentage of the Chinese American population (22 percent), in part because of declining numbers of adult Chinese as a result of the exclusion laws. A comparison with the manuscript census data from Sacramento and Oakland reveals similar patterns among Chinese children. The only major deviation is that the number of female children in Sacramento (34 percent) and Oakland (39 percent) remained lower than the number of male children as late as 1920.[13] In adapting to the unique conditions of American laws and society, a variety of family arrangements emerged in late nineteenth-century Chinatown.

Despite the problematic nature of census data, this type of information can assist in examining the realities of family life in early Chinatown. Errors on the part of census takers, Chinese mistrust of government officials, and language barriers all present potential biases that compromise the reliability of census data.[14] However, such data is especially crucial in reconstructing the lives of Chinese children and their families. Census records often provide the only existing documentary record of an individual's life. By examining this data, scholars can reconstruct the stories of otherwise historically invisible people. Nineteenth-century Chinatown included very few families that adhered to either traditional Chinese or American conceptions of family life. I have chosen, therefore, to expand the definition of "family" for purposes of this study to include all domestic arrangements that featured both adults and children living in the same household. Considering children as the essential element to these families, we may begin to unravel the variety of family structures that existed in pre-1920 San Francisco.[15]

Scholars generally recognize that the majority of overseas Chinese operated under a split-household model during the period between 1850 and 1920. In the split-household family, the male earned income overseas while the female managed the household and raised the children at home in China. In San Francisco, males lived in bachelor societies with fictive "families" based on district, dialect, and clan associations. While the split-household family remained the dominant family model among Chinese men living in California, older children sometimes accompanied their fathers to San Francisco.[16] Census records reveal a large number of all-male boardinghouses. The majority of these households included teenage boys (although there were a few teenage girls) living with their fathers, uncles, or cousins and working in laundries or factory settings. Table 4 indicates that in 1870, the number of Chinese children under age sixteen living in all-male households was 573 (37 percent). However, by 1900 this number had dramatically decreased to 54 (4 percent). The added category of "relationship" in the 1880 census more clearly delineates the relationships of the children to the head of the household and allows us to remove single-parent families from the all-male boardinghouse category. After 1880 the numbers reveal a few children living in single-parent households headed by their fathers. Still, the actual number of children living in male-dominated households declined rather dramatically from the late nineteenth century to the early twentieth century. This fact— coupled with the evidence that after 1880 the children in San Francisco's Chinatown increasingly were born in California—suggests the overall effectiveness of the various exclusion laws in limiting the immigration of young Chinese male laborers. A brief, but abrupt, increase in male-dominated households from 1900 (4 percent) to 1910 (19 percent), and an increase in China-born children from 77 (5 percent) in 1900 to 341 (27 percent) in 1910 (Table 3), may suggest the success that some immigrants had in bypassing the exclusion laws through the use of the paper-son system following the 1906 earthquake.

Family types consisting of both children and adults living together in a communal setting were not limited to male households. The 1870 census includes numerous households of predominately female adults living with a

TABLE 4 : Most Common Domestic Arrangements in
San Francisco's Chinatown, 1860–1920

DOMESTIC ARRANGEMENT	1860 NO. OF CHILDREN	1870 NO. OF CHILDREN	1880 NO. OF CHILDREN	1900 NO. OF CHILDREN	1910 NO. OF CHILDREN	1920 NO. OF CHILDREN
Mostly male household	46 (43%)	573 (37%)	387 (26%)	54 (4%)	240 (19%)	58 (3%)
Mostly female household	42 (40%)	336 (22%)	35 (2%)	3 (<1%)	1 (<1%)	3 (<1%)
Two-parent family	1 (1%)	107 (7%)	610 (41%)*	1,037 (72%)*	712 (55%)	1,173 (70%)
Living in non-Chinese household	5 (5%)	388 (25%)	209 (14%)	41 (3%)	47 (4%)	17 (<1%)
Single-parent female	0	15 (1%)	36 (2%)	123 (9%)	94 (7%)	175 (10%)
Single-parent male	0	8 (<1%)	12 (<1%)	20 (1%)	31 (2%)	95 (6%)
Multigenerational family	0	0	28 (2%)	37 (3%)	81 (6%)	78 (5%)

Sources: U.S. Bureau of the Census, Eighth Census of the United States, 1860; Ninth Census of the United States, 1870; Tenth Census of the United States, 1880; Twelfth Census of the United States, 1900; Thirteenth Census of the United States, 1910; Fourteenth Census of the United States, 1920.

Note: Discerning family relationships was difficult, if not impossible, to determine in the 1860 and 1870 census. In the 1870 census, I counted a number of children as living in two-parent families who may have actually been servants to the family rather than biological children. Therefore, the children counted as living in two-parent families in 1870 may be inflated slightly by the presence of these servants. By 1880 the added category of "relation" made it possible to remove servants from the number of children counted as living in two-parent families. In numerous cases, family relationships could not be determined at all as the enumerator apparently listed several families living in one household together. Therefore, I created a separate category in my tally for "mixed" families, which constituted about 11 percent of the children in 1860, 3 percent in 1870, and 2 percent in 1880. Nayan Shah observed that enumerator William Martin in the 1870 census tended to group mixed dwellings of men and women by gender, thereby identifying two families in one dwelling—one of all female prostitutes and one of all male laborers. Enumerator Henry Bennett, however, attempted to identify the numerous family arrangements in each dwelling, thereby recording more Chinese families. Therefore, the biases of individual enumerators have also skewed the data. Nayan Shah, Contagious Divides: Epidemics and Race in San Francisco's Chinatown *(Berkeley: University of California Press, 2001), 83.*

* *I excluded thirty-two children living in households with multiple wives from the 1880 figure and twenty-four children living in households with multiple wives from the 1900 figure.*

number of young boys and girls. In 1870, 336 children (22 percent) lived in this type of setting. Enumerators tended to label these types of households as "brothels." Native-born children living in brothels may have been the unintended progeny of prostitutes.[17] The added category of "relationship" after 1880 reveals a small percentage of children living in single-parent families headed by their mothers and removes these children from the general category of all-female household. Early twentieth-century missionaries, progressive reformers, and Chinese community leaders increasingly demanded an end to prostitution in Chinatown. Media attention focused largely on dramatic cases of young Chinese girls imported as sex slaves. Public denunciations of white slavery forced more stringent laws and efforts to prevent the trafficking of women, and especially children, in the sex trade. Immigration officials focused on limiting the number of suspected prostitutes entering the country. These efforts to clean up Chinatown in part account for the decline in census numbers of children living in all-female boardinghouses. The intense public scrutiny of vice in Chinatown reduced the number of prostitutes and forced the few that remained to move underground. The number of children living in mostly female households began to decline by the turn of the century. By 1900 only three children could be found living in such a setting.

The formation of a significant number of two-parent families had begun in Chinatown as early as 1880. The Chinese exhibited the same tendencies as other immigrant groups in gradually shifting away from the immigration of solely male laborers toward the immigration of some family groups and the gradual increase in American-born children. By 1880, 610 children (41 percent) were living in two-parent families and 512 (35 percent) were American-born. This trend was further accelerated by the passage of Chinese exclusion laws, which greatly limited the immigration of all Chinese while ironically allowing for the immigration of a small elite group of Chinese merchants and their families. By the early twentieth century, fewer children lived in single-sex households, and more two-parent, merchant families began to form in Chinatown. In addition, a number of Chinese laborers living in the United States also married and began producing children. Only 107 Chinese children (7 percent) lived in two-parent family settings in 1870; however, 1,037 Chinese children (72 percent) in San Francisco lived in similar domestic structures by 1900. Although many male immigrants continued to support wives and children in China, the efforts of some Chinese men and women to establish families in San Francisco challenge the characterization of this time period as the era of the split-household. The numbers also suggest the growth of a sizable American-born Chinese population beginning as early as 1880 and rapidly increasing after 1900. The displacement of families as a result of the 1906 earthquake, and the resulting increase in male laborers using the paper-son system, no doubt accounts for the brief decline in the number and percentage of two-parent families in 1910 to 712 (55 percent) and the increase in all-male households. However, by 1920 the figures were again rising, with 1,173 Chinese children (70 percent) living in two-parent families. A few wealthy families included males with two wives, although this type of family arrangement was extremely rare (less than 2 percent in both the 1870 and 1900 censuses).[18] Immigrant families are often stereotyped as unusually large. Yet the vast majority of two-parent Chinese households before 1920 included only one to three children (Table 5). The average number of children per family was 1.8 in 1870, 1.7 in 1880, 2.6 in 1900, 3.0 in 1910, and 3.3 in 1920. Only rarely did families exceed more than five children.

Although households in China tended to be multigenerational, very few children in San Francisco's early Chinatown lived in the same household with their grandparents. While none of the Chinese children in 1870 San Francisco lived in multigenerational families, by 1920, seventy-eight Chinese children (5 percent) lived in families that included one or more grandparent. Efforts to replicate the multigenerational Chinese family structure in America would take several more decades to develop. Judy Yung has noted that since Chinese wives in America did not live under the control of their mother-in-law (as they would have in China), they were able to exercise greater authority in family affairs.[19] The census data suggests that few wives in San Francisco had to submit to the authority of their mother-in-law. Just as multigenerational families remained rare, only 1 to 3 percent of children from 1900 to 1920 lived with an extended family that included aunts, uncles, or cousins. Clearly, a distinctively Chinese American family structure emerged in San Francisco.

In addition to all of the above-mentioned family arrangements, many Chinese boys (ages ten to sixteen) worked as domestic servants in non-Chinese households. Some of these youth participated in the family life of their employer in what may be considered a "fictive" family arrangement. In 1870, 388 Chinese children (25 percent) lived in non-Chinese households, mostly outside of the confines of Chinatown. The fact that Chinese domestic servants employed in these households were almost exclusively male suggests that the Chinese American community attempted to protect female children by confining them to Chinatown. By the turn of the century, fewer Chinese boys were working as servants in white households—decisions no

TABLE 5 : Number of Children of Two-Parent Chinese Families, 1870–1920
(All Figures Percentages)

NO. OF CHILDREN	1870	1880	1900	1910	1920
1 child	53	55	35	26	21
2 children	33	28	26	20	19
3 children	8	11	17	21	19
4 children	2	4	8	11	16
5 children	0	1	5	10	10
6 children	2	0	5	5	9
7 children	0	0	3	3	3
8 children	0	0	<1	2	3
9 children	0	0	<1	0	1
10 children	2	0	<1	0	0

Sources: *U.S. Bureau of the Census,* Ninth Census of the United States, 1870; Tenth Census of the United States, 1880; Twelfth Census of the United States, 1900; Thirteenth Census of the United States, 1910; Fourteenth Census of the United States, 1920.

Note: The calculations for this table are based on two-parent households. Households with more than one wife, or mixed households including multiple adult men and women living together where family relationship seemed unclear, were excluded from my calculations. I excluded two parent households that included more than ten children. Several, because of the ages of the children or mistakes of the enumerator, seemed unlikely to represent an entire family unit. It is possible that male heads of households were absent because they were temporarily living and working apart from the family in the interior mining and agricultural regions of California. I counted all children listed in the family, regardless of age. Therefore, many individuals counted as "children" in each family were over sixteen at the time of the census. These figures obviously do not include children who may have moved out of the family household. Some of the "children" counted in the 1870 census also may have been household servants, but this is impossible to determine until the category of "relation" is added in the 1880 census. According to my calculations, the average number of children per two-parent family was 1.8 in 1870, 1.7 in 1880, 2.6 in 1900, 3.0 in 1910, and 3.3 in 1920.

doubt influenced by the rise of anti-Chinese hostilities and sentiments against child labor. By 1910 enumerators listed only forty-seven Chinese children (4 percent) as servants or boarders in non-Chinese households, and by 1920 this number had dropped to seventeen (less than 1 percent).

A number of interracial families also emerged in early Chinatown, although these families were comparatively rare. The limited number of Chinese women encouraged some Chinese men to seek interracial relationships.[20] California passed an antimiscegenation law in 1880 that specifically prohibited the licensing of marriages of "Mongolians" and whites, but the legislature did not invalidate existing interracial marriages until 1905.[21] While the 1870 census revealed no obvious cases of interracial children, the 1900 census specifically listed sixteen such individuals (about 1 percent). Nine of these families consisted of a Chinese father and a white mother. One household consisted of a Japanese father and a Chinese mother.[22] Enumerators recorded no interracial Chinese families in the 1920 census, although we know that Charles and Tye Leung Schulze, employees of the Immigration Bureau at Angel Island, created a stir when they married and raised a family in San Francisco during the 1920s. Historical studies of interracial children suggest that many biracial children may have more readily identified with their mother's culture (probably as a result of the mother's significant role as purveyor of cultural knowledge). Some biracial children may have self-identified as white. Regardless of their preferred affiliation, however, mixed-race children often encountered discrimination from both the white and Chinese American communities.[23] These families conformed to neither Chinese nor white ideals of the model family.

A study of manuscript census data from Sacramento and Oakland reveals similarly complex Chinese American family arrangements. The majority of Chinese children (61 percent) living in Sacramento in 1870 lived in all-female or all-male households. Although a large number of children also lived in single-sex households in Oakland, Chinese children in that city were much more likely to work as servants in white families in 1870 (66 percent). Some of these children may have originally lived in San Francisco and relocated after finding work with the middle- and upper-class white families in Oakland. By 1920, however, the majority of Chinese children in both Oakland and Sacramento (78–79 percent) lived in two-parent families. Multigenerational and mixed-race families remained extremely rare in both Sacramento and Oakland from 1870 to 1920. The manuscript census data reveals nearly identical patterns of family development among the Chinese American populations of San Francisco, Sacramento, and Oakland, suggesting a general trend in Chinese American history.[24]

Although nontraditional by either Chinese or American standards, the diversity of family arrangements in early Chinatown challenge the myth of a bachelor society. The mere presence of children and the creation of a variety of "fictive" family arrangements suggest attempts to form a Chinese American community. Yet, these unique domestic structures elicited criticism for their failure to live up to white middle-class ideals of "family." By the early twentieth century, Chinese leaders recognized the significance of highlighting the number of two-parent, merchant-class families in Chinatown. While most Chinese were merely attempting to replicate the traditional Chinese family structure in America in an effort to raise their families in a nurturing environment, the Chinese American elite hoped to improve the public image of Chinatown by focusing on its "exemplary" families. Some Chinese parents moved their families away from Chinatown into white American middle-class neighborhoods. Ng Poon Chew, the editor of San Francisco's Chinese newspaper, *Chung Sai Yat Po*, moved his family to a white neighborhood in Oakland after the 1906 San Francisco earthquake. The neighbors expressed obvious anxiety over the presence of a Chinese family in the neighborhood. Chew humorously observed, however, that "it wasn't long . . . till I smoked my cigar harmoniously with the men in the block, my wife talked over the back fence with the ladies and my children played with the other children in the block, and so far as I have been able to learn no one has ever been contaminated by association with the family."[25] Chew's statement not only highlights the similarities between his family and his neighbors but also ridicules the claims of anti-Chinese politicians who argued that the Chinese represented a source of contagion that economically, physically, and morally threatened American families. Discrimination and poverty, however, prevented most Chinese families from moving away from Chinatown. As the battle to improve Chinatown's image raged, both merchant and working-class Chinese parents increasingly struggled with the problem of creating a safe haven for their families despite the poverty, violence, and disease that characterized the district.

GROWING UP IN AN URBAN, ETHNIC ENCLAVE

As the number of Chinese families gradually began to grow in America, parents adapted Chinese cultural practices to their new environment. Between 1901 and 1917, county health officials recorded the birth of 1,907 Chinese babies in San Francisco.[26] This sizable increase in the number of American-born Chinese was crucial to the development of a Chinese American cultural identity. Mothers especially played an important role in transmitting Chinese cultural traditions to their children. At church and school, however, children participated in American and Christian rituals that sometimes challenged their Chinese beliefs. Gradually the influences of Americanization and Christianization altered the basic structure of traditional Chinese rituals, as individuals began to pick and choose from a variety of Chinese and American traditions. The perpetuation and adaptation of these rituals affirms the centrality of the family in the cultural life of Chinese San Francisco.

Important family rituals began with pregnancy and birth. Pregnant Chinese women in America prepared for their new arrival with a variety of Chinese customs. As part of her prenatal diet, the mother consumed herbs to maintain the health of the baby and prepare her body for childbirth. Women generally avoided certain foods, such as shrimp, crab, and fried foods. Following the birth of the baby, Chinese midwives recommended that the mother consume pigs' feet, vinegar wine, chicken broth with wine, eggs, and rice to ensure a quick recovery.[27] A number of superstitions were also associated with pregnancy. Louise Leung Larson's mother believed that if a pregnant woman dreamed of white flowers, she would have a boy, while red flowers indicated a girl. She also believed that eating egg whites was supposed to cause a baby to be born with fair skin. Mothers generally preferred to give birth at home with the assistance of a friend or a midwife. In 1897 eighty-two-year-old midwife Now How Poo claimed to have presided over the birth of over seventy children in San Francisco's Chinatown.[28] Increasingly after 1900, Chinese parents listed American physicians, such as Dr. Edna R. Field and Dr. M. G. Worley, as the attendants at their child's birth.[29] These women provided indispensable assistance and advice for expectant mothers. Over time, mothers adopted a mixture of Chinese and American pregnancy practices and beliefs.

Although Chinese parents typically preferred the birth of a boy, the arrival of a baby, regardless of sex, was always a joyous occasion. Fathers hoped for sons to carry on the family name and provide economically for the household. A daughter, on the other hand, was generally regarded as an economic deficit who would eventually marry into another family. Shortly after birth, the new mother and baby received gifts of clothing, jewelry, and specialty foods. Three days after birth, the infant was ceremoniously bathed. Mother and child typically remained confined to the house for a full month after the birth in an attempt to avoid the unhealthy effects of exposure. At the conclusion of the month-long confinement, the parents held a "full moon" celebration to welcome the new child. In preparation for the occasion, the parents shaved the child's head, leaving only a small tuft of hair in the middle of the skull. The parents dressed the baby in festive clothing, and amulets of silver were hung from his or her wrists and ankles. Family and friends feasted at a banquet held in the baby's honor. The host offered eggs dyed red to commemorate the occasion. Guests brought the baby jewelry, money, and cloth-ing.[30] In October 1914 Look Tin Eli hosted a grand banquet to honor his new granddaughter. As president of the Canton Bank, Look Tin Eli invited over 300 Chinese and white guests, including such distinguished members of the community as the mayor and the chief of police.[31] Although this ceremony was traditionally intended only for male babies, by the early twentieth cen-tury, some Chinese Americans like Look Tin Eli had expanded the custom to celebrate the one-month birthday of girl babies.

Some Chinese families chose to celebrate the birth of their children ac-cording to Christian traditions. The records of several Catholic and Protes-tant churches include a number of Chinese infant and child baptisms. The Reverend Frederic J. Masters baptized six-month-old Bennie Lum in the Methodist Episcopal Church on March 10, 1889. The boy's parents later provided a certificate of baptism to immigration authorities as proof of the child's American citizenship.[32] Although the numerous Protestant missions in Chinatown attracted many Chinese converts, the Catholic Church also succeeded in baptizing a large number of Chinese infants. As members of the church, parents sought to pass on their Christian faith to their children through the sacraments. Beyond baptism, children participated in commu-nion, reconciliation, and confirmation, which signified their education and eventual acceptance as adult members of the church.[33] For some families, Christian baptism may have replaced the Chinese full moon celebration, while other families simply integrated elements of both cultures, creating new and unique Chinese American traditions.

Shortly after the birth, the parents provided the baby with a Chinese personal name believed to bring good luck and ward off evil.[34] The surname carried on the family lineage. Over time, parents began to provide their American-born children with both Chinese and American personal names. Beginning in the early twentieth century, names such as Kathryn, Rosie, Minnie, George, Henry, William, and Edward began to appear in official records. Some parents continued the Chinese tradition of providing their babies with auspicious names by naming them after prominent American leaders. Pardee Lowe's father named him after the governor of California, while his brothers bore the names of Woodrow Wilson and Thomas Riley Marshall. He also had three sisters: Mabel, Helen Taft, and Alice Roosevelt. "Admittedly, we bore 'highfalutin' titles, as our American playmates de-risively put it," Lowe later wrote, "and it cramped our social style. Our lives never seemed to be ours to do with as we saw fit. On the other hand, there is no doubt that it contributed directly to making us better Americans for it brought us sharply to the attention of our public-school teachers, who redoubled their zeal in teaching us. They never forgot the proud American spiritual lineage from which we sprung. Whenever we were naughty they checked us quickly: 'Do not disgrace the proud names you bear!'"[35] Lowe and his siblings felt compelled to live up to the reputation of their names. For their parents, however, the choice of names not only reflected a continuation of Chinese naming traditions but also the conscious decision to speed up the acculturation of their children by adopting American norms and values.

Both Chinese and American families viewed childhood as a period of innocence. Late nineteenth-century Chinese society envisioned children as vulnerable and dependent beings in need of protection and instruction. Prior to about age six, children enjoyed mild discipline and relative freedom.[36] During the same time period, American society began to envision childhood as a distinct period of formation and learning. Parents began to focus less on strict discipline designed to dominate the child's will and turned instead to protecting and guiding the malleable child. Middle-class families viewed the home as a haven from the outside world and a place to nurture their children. The American mother was expected to shape the child's character, inculcating morality through parental love and guidance.[37]

Despite the apparent similarities in conceptions of early childhood, anti-Chinese writers frequently attacked the parenting strategies of Chinese immigrants. Visitors to Chinatown sometimes described Chinese children as peculiar and utterly unlike "Christian" children. In 1896 a reporter for the *Wave* stated: "There is very little in a Chinese child's life that a 'Christian kid' need envy unless it's having a queue to jump rope with."[38] The author described Chinese parents as generally callous and apathetic and insisted that mothers rarely fussed over their babies. Although countless photographs and descriptions of child life in Chinatown may be presented that contradict this image of parental indifference, the author's observations may allude to fundamental deviations in American versus Chinese styles of child rearing and discipline.

Chinese parents often coddled their infants and toddlers, but after age six or seven, parents instituted a strict regimen of discipline and education.[39] American-born children raised in the Chinese style sometimes resented the firm regulation of their later childhood. The emphasis increasingly turned to discipline.[40] China-born mothers and fathers relied predominately on Chinese child-rearing models to correct their children and instill values. Filial piety demanded that children demonstrate appropriate respect and deference to their elders. Edward L. C. recalled that "ever since I was young I was taught not to ask for anything. When I wanted candy once, I was shown an example of a girl who was minus most of her teeth who they said ate too much candy and ever since I never did like candy very much."[41] Parents sought to instill in their children basic ideas of right and wrong while teaching them ideal virtues. Disrespectful or misbehaving children suffered the consequences. Severe disobedience sometimes resulted in corporal punishment.

Chinese parents outlined very different expectations for daughters than for sons. Girls assisted with child care and performed a variety of domestic chores. From an early age, girls learned the "Three Obediences," which positioned women as subordinate to their fathers and later their husbands. Should her husband die, a woman would then obey her son. The "Four Virtues" required women to adopt habits of chastity and obedience, reticence, a pleasing manner, and domestic skills. Fathers expected their sons to acquire an education and take responsibility for the family business.[42] While girls spent their leisure time at home learning to embroider, knit, crochet, and sew, boys often enjoyed the freedom to engage in activities away from home. American-born Chinese girls complained that their fathers neglected them and preferred spending time with their brothers. Esther Wong recalled a sudden change in her relationship with her father after the birth of her younger brother: "When I was 13 my brother was born and then he lost interest in us girls, did not care to bother teaching girls, and seemed to forget what we were like. When we were small he used to work at a machine next to ours, and when we were all busy he would tell us stories as we worked; but later he became very stern and cold and did not try to understand us at all."[43] Chinese children sometimes resented the seemingly more compassionate and intimate relationship that existed between American parents and their children. Most China-born parents attempted to raise their children according to Chinese tradition, and generational conflicts often erupted when their American-born children desired to emulate American families. Families adapted by selectively choosing which Chinese and American traditions and rituals to practice.

Some Chinese traditions were especially subject to scrutiny in America. The practice of foot binding became extremely controversial in San Francisco. As a very real symbol of their bondage to the domestic sphere, gentry- and merchant-class girls at about six years of age had their feet bound. Bound feet represented a sign of wealth, status, and beauty. With tight cloth wrappings, the mother gradually bent her daughter's toes back toward her heel. This process deformed the foot and stunted its growth to a length of a few inches. The smaller the bound feet, the greater the perceived beauty. The process was extremely painful and, once complete, severely hampered the girl's mobility.[44] This debilitating practice offended American middle-class sensibilities. By the late nineteenth century, white missionaries and social reformers began to attack the practice of foot binding among the Chinese merchant class.[45] In 1899 the Reverend Dr. Wilson of the Methodist Church and the Reverend Dr. Locke identified at least twenty girls with bound feet in Chinatown. The clergymen noted the names and addresses of the parents and vowed to take their cause to the courts to stop this cruelty to children.[46] For reformers, the practice of foot binding not only represented an unhealthy and heathen practice; it was also an unacceptable assertion of patriarchal authority and an example of domestic slavery that forcibly confined women and young girls to the home. Foot binding thus represented an affront to emerging feminism and, more importantly, to the central American values of democracy and freedom.[47]

By the early twentieth century, the advance of women's emancipation movements in China and America encouraged women to resist foot binding. Protestant missionaries actively sought to eliminate the practice in San Francisco's Chinatown by educating Chinese mothers in Western traditions and preaching against foot binding. Anti–foot binding societies in China managed to push the Chinese government into outlawing the practice by 1902. Although the tradition died slowly in both China and America, many progressive-thinking parents gladly abandoned the horrific practice. Rose Ow was living in San Francisco at the time, and she remembered that when she was about eight years old, she begged her mother to bind her feet because it was considered fashionable. Rose's mother, who was opposed to foot binding, scolded her and refused to do it.[48] Popular Chinatown newspapers like the *Chung Sai Yat Po* helped influence public opinion against foot binding by publishing editorials condemning the tradition. The *Chung Sai Yat Po* also denounced polygamy, arranged marriages, and slavery, while supporting a woman's right to an education.[49] In China and America, reformers had also begun to challenge traditional approaches to child rearing, identifying them as more harmful than helpful to a child's development.[50] Although the efforts of reformers were far-reaching, traditional Chinese child-rearing practices continued for some time. Increasingly, however, Chinese families in America adapted various parenting strategies to their new environment.

Despite the strict discipline at home, younger girls and boys enjoyed an active imagination and the freedom to play. Through the rituals of play, children frequently participated in imaginary activities that mimicked the realities of their daily life. Lilac Chen grew up in a mission home and recalled organizing a Chinese-style burial for a bird: "So we went out to the backyard. And mourning is all white for the Chinese, so we got bedsheets, and draped ourselves. The chief mourner, Yahoo was her name, knew all kinds of incantations. So she was the chief Buddhist. And she said all these things and we just ducked down one on each side of her with the white bedsheet, and we were the deep mourners. And she would cry out all the sad tones, 'Aiya! Aiya!' You know, it just sounds like a cry."[51] Imaginary play such as this allowed children to act out and cope with their anxieties about life and death. Other forms of imaginary play mimicked the people or animals that children encountered every day.[52] The children of Chinatown also played with a variety of toys, including balloons, dolls, balls, rattles, bicycles, bells, tops, and kites. These toys often reflected the gender biases and underlying intentions of the adults who had given them to the children. Chinese mothers and white female missionaries, for example, often provided girls with dolls in an effort to prepare them for lessons in domesticity.

Young children also took to the streets and organized a variety of games. Visitors to the Chinese quarter captured images of children playing battledore, blindman's buff, hide-and-seek, tag, and shuttlecock.[53] By the early twentieth century, American sports were becoming increasingly popular, and boys played baseball in the street and in empty lots. In 1909 Ella May Clemens, the white wife of Chinese merchant Wong Sun Yue, complained to the police about schoolboys playing baseball in front of her shop on Sacramento Street. The woman insisted that "although she loved the Chinese people very dearly," the boys were frightening away tourists. The boys responded by arguing that "if she really admired the Chinese people as she says she does, then she would have no objection to the boys playing the great American game."[54] Thus, the children recognized the significance of emphasizing their American identity in an effort to assert their basic right to play.

Other street games may have proven more dangerous. Young boys enjoyed playing with firecrackers and building small bonfires.[55] The potential disaster of children playing with fire sometimes became a reality that resulted in serious burns. Teenage girls often bore the responsibility of supervising

Two children pose for the camera (Chinese: Children; Stellman Collection, #10, 835; courtesy of the California History Room, California State Library, Sacramento)

their younger siblings at play. Supervision was necessary because, on rare occasions, play did become extremely dangerous or even deadly. Four days before Christmas in 1905, thirteen-year-old Esther Woo was playing with some of her companions on the roof of the Methodist mission home, as they often did in sunny weather. The girl suddenly lost her balance and fell twenty-five feet off the roof onto the sidewalk below; she fractured her skull and died immediately.[56] Progressive reformers began to focus on creating safe and structured forms of play.

Even at play, Chinese children found themselves the object of reformers' attention. Play reformers of the early twentieth century not only expressed concerns about child safety but also feared the negative influence of street games on a child's character. Progressive beliefs about the influence of the environment on the formation of character lent support to campaigns to construct playgrounds in working-class neighborhoods. Advocates of playgrounds and supervised play insisted that active, character-building recreation could help shape and structure the lives of America's children. By removing poor and immigrant children from the dangers and vices of the streets, reformers hoped to prevent juvenile delinquency and inculcate children with American values.[57]

The Playground Association of America was organized in 1906, and San Francisco established a Playground Commission in 1908 to begin to build playgrounds around the city. The stated objectives of the San Francisco commission were to keep children off the street, provide them with wholesome play, and encourage a "law-abiding spirit." In 1925 the San Francisco Playground Commission began to design the Chinese Playground, which officially opened in 1927. The playground offered a variety of sports, such as basketball, volleyball, and tennis, and activities including dramatics, harmonica bands, marble tournaments, and kite-flying contests. Through organized play and carefully chosen toys, adults hoped to socialize young immigrant children into American racial, class, and gender mores. Reformers believed that organized play was essential to the formation of good citizens by educating them in self-control.[58]

The rise of the Boy Scout movement in America coincided with the evolving Progressive belief in environmental solutions to social problems. The Boy Scouts emphasized character building as a way to combat the perceived problems of the feminization of schools and the overall weakening of masculinity. The organization generally limited their work to the children of the middle class, although by the 1910s organization leaders encouraged working-class immigrant children to join. The Boy Scouts thus became an agency of Americanization by training boys in patriotism and civics. Regardless of the intentions of the movement's founders, however, boys joined the Scouts mostly for recreational reasons.[59]

In 1910 a small group of boys in San Francisco's Chinatown sent for a copy of the Boy Scout handbook and formed an informal group that practiced some of the customs of the organization. In 1914 Chingwah Lee found the old handbook and wrote to the national headquarters about his interest in joining the Boy Scouts. The national Boy Scout organization sent a representative to San Francisco to organize a local council. With the help of their leaders, the boys organized Troop 3 and sent for uniforms. Chingwah Lee's brother, Edwar, remembered that his mother threatened to tear up their uniforms and crush their canteens out of fear that the organization was preparing the boys for a life in the military. Although many Chinese parents, like their white counterparts, were reluctant to allow their boys to join an organization that seemed to mimic military service, they eventually consented to the pleas of the boys.[60] Chinese American community leaders, in direct response to the attacks of critics, sometimes pointed to the participation of Chinese children in such activities as evidence of the Americanness of the Chinese in San Francisco. Yet privately, many Chinese parents worried about the impact of too much Americanization on their children.

Progressive reformers and immigrant parents shared concerns about the behavior of adolescent children. Immigrant parents especially feared the impact of American culture on their female children. By the early twentieth century, young women increasingly pushed the boundaries of domesticity by participating in mixed-sex recreation at dance halls, movie theaters, and amusement parks. This behavior challenged the restrictive role of women defined by both middle-class Victorian standards and immigrant cultures. Chinese parents often objected to their daughters' adoption of American social mores. The newfound freedom of adolescent girls inspired efforts of parents and reformers to protect and police the social and sexual behavior of female adolescents.[61]

Concern over the potentially devastating moral and sexual consequences of such freedom on all working-class children contributed to reformers' efforts to channel adolescent energy into organized recreation. By the early twentieth century, children and adolescents began to join a growing number of organized recreation clubs segregated by race, gender, and age. At school and recreational centers, children learned to play sports such as baseball, basketball, football, and volleyball. Christian organizations especially tried to reach out to Chinese youth. In 1911 the Chinese Young Men's Christian Association (YMCA) opened in Chinatown and provided young men with a variety of recreational and educational opportunities. Boys took classes in English, Mandarin, machine shop, and mechanical drawing. The YMCA sponsored the organization of a Chinese orchestra, as well as athletic teams such as track and field, soccer, and basketball. Children enjoyed summer outings to Lagunitas and Marin County with the YMCA. The Chinese Boys Band organized in 1911 and began to perform at numerous Chinatown and city events. The Chinese Young Women's Christian Association (YWCA) organized in 1916 and provided classes in English, sewing, piano, and cooking for women. The YWCA also offered gymnasium and glee club for high school girls. Recreational activities included marching, folk dancing, table tennis, tap dancing, and badminton. Younger girls enjoyed a variety of clubs, including the Bluebirds.[62] By the 1920s, various churches in Chinatown also organized recreational activities and social clubs for Chinese youth in an effort to redirect their energy into productive and healthy activities.

White and Chinese adults attempted to mold the recreational activities of Chinese children and youth in an effort to instill specific cultural values. However, as historians of childhood have pointed out, children tend to appropriate toys and utilize their imagination to create their own play, regardless of the intentions of adults.[63] Play among Chinese children became a means of self-expression, working through anxieties and fears, and developing a sense of confidence while learning to interact socially with their peers. This was especially important as Chinatown's children struggled to overcome the barriers imposed by exclusion and segregation and negotiate a place for themselves in America. By developing a strong sense of Chinese American identity through play and family ritual, Chinese children were better prepared to confront and fight inequalities at work, at school, and even on the playground.

HOLIDAYS AND RITUALS

The importance of children in the formation of a Chinese American community is perhaps best illustrated in the perpetuation and adaptation of various holiday rituals. At home, parents sought to pass on Chinese culture and traditions as a way of countering the influences of Americanization both on the playground and in the classroom. A number of festivals provided opportunities for Chinese children to enjoy themselves while celebrating Chinese culture. Although the most well-known holiday was Chinese New Year, Chinese Americans also celebrated the Pure Brightness Festival, Lantern Festival, Dragon Boat Festival, Festival of the Seven Sisters, Spirits' Festival, Mid-Autumn Festival, Kite Festival, and Winter Solstice. These occasions usually involved special food, holiday clothing, offerings to the ancestors, visits with relatives, games, and parades. Mothers especially ensured that these traditions passed to the younger generation. Children frequently played a prominent role in perpetuating these rituals, as well as in modifying and adapting them.

By far the most festive holiday was Chinese New Year. Men prepared for the holiday by paying off all debts and meeting all obligations. Women cleaned the house carefully and purchased new clothes. Mothers dressed the children in holiday clothes and visited friends and neighbors. White observers frequently noted the colorful decorations and festive good nature of the Chinese quarter during the weeklong festivities. The New Year's parade included elaborate floats, streamers, banners, and bands. Women and girls freely wandered the streets, enjoying the sights and sounds of the holiday. Men and boys exploded firecrackers far into the night. Children especially looked forward to parades, fireworks, balloons, toys, and collecting li shee, or "good-luck money." Fong Sun Chow, a Presbyterian mission student, wrote a letter to his teacher in 1893 that expressed his delight that Chinese New Year had arrived: "I have new coat and new hat and new red pants and new shoes and have flowers. I have new picture and all Chinese men new year and all stop work, and take walk and plenty orange and good eat breakfast, and good eat dinner, and good eat supper."[64] New Year's food included candied ginger, coconut strips, lichee nuts, sweet-and-sour plums, and tsai (an assortment of Chinese vegetables).[65] Reporters and photographers descended upon the Chinese quarter during the Chinese New Year to record the peculiarities of the occasion for an eager white audience. Descriptions of the clothing and joyful behavior of Chinese children became a common feature of these stories.[66] Chinese children also celebrated variations of other festive occasions. Although reporters tended to focus on the foreign nature of these activities, newspaper accounts demonstrate the significance of these holidays for the Chinese American community and the prominence of children in these celebrations.

The celebration of Chinese festivals in America evolved over time, as individual families altered the celebration of the rituals and incorporated Western traditions into their holidays. Educated in the local mission schools or the city public schools, Chinese children celebrated American holidays at school and encouraged their parents to adopt certain practices at home. Many Chinese families, both Christian and non-Christian, celebrated Thanksgiving, Christmas, Easter, and the Fourth of July.[67] Children learned the significance of gifts from Santa Claus while also enjoying the benefits of li shee at Chinese New Year. Through these unique combinations, children created a distinctive Chinese American identity.

Children also actively participated in the perpetuation and evolution of holidays to remember the dead. For the Chinese, reverence for ancestors was an integral part of daily life, and at least two annual festivals specifically honored deceased relatives. In the spring, during the Pure Brightness Festival (Ch'ing Ming), families visited the local cemetery to clean the graves. Sweeping a grave with a willow branch was believed to repel evil spirits. Relatives laid offerings of food and drink before the graves and burned paper clothing and incense. Firecrackers created a distraction to prevent evil spirits from harming both the living and the dead. During the summer, the family again visited the graves to present offerings to the deceased. On this day, some-times referred to as the Feast of the Hungry Ghosts, the Chinese believed that the gates of the underworld opened to permit the spirits of the discon-tented deceased to wander the earth. These "hungry ghosts" did not have any living family to provide them with offerings of food and clothing. In their effort to find consolation, they wandered the earth, attempting to find suste-nance. Families prepared platforms of cooked food for the ghosts, who returned to earth to feast. The living also offered miniature paper garments (representing clothing) and burned paper money to provide the deceased with earthly necessities in the underworld.[68] Children were vital participants in these activities, as parents attempted to instill in them a sense of filial piety and respect for Chinese beliefs in the afterlife.

Parents also attempted to perpetuate Chinese cultural traditions by recit-ing Chinese myths and legends and practicing Chinese folk religion. Older family members reiterated old Chinese legends, ghost stories, and folktales.[69] These stories sometimes appeared very real. Some parents feared that soul-stealing devils would seek out their children. Sons were especially susceptible to danger, and some parents dressed boy babies in girl's clothing to confuse demons. Families frequently spent money purchasing talismans or consult-ing fortune tellers to protect their children from malignant spirits. Charms or embroidered images of tigers and lions protected children from demons. Children wore bells on their clothing and amulets of various metals around their necks to bring good luck, ward off evil, and bind the child's soul firmly to earth.[70] At his one-month celebration, Lee Ah Chuck wore a gold pendant around his neck that represented a warrior riding astride a lion. His father hoped the charm would give the boy strength and courage.[71] The parents believed that a child was most susceptible within the first 100 days after birth. If a baby became ill, the mother would bathe the child in an attempt to wash away the illness and the demon that had produced it. She then discarded the water outdoors to prevent it from spreading to others.[72] Through the evolu-tion and adaptation of Chinese folk religion in America, parents hoped to perpetuate Chinese traditions and, more importantly, to protect their chil-dren from the dangerous influences of their new environment.

THE REALITIES OF ILLNESS AND DEATH

Despite parents' best efforts to protect children from harmful influences, infants especially were extremely susceptible to illness in the urban, industrialized environment of San Francisco. Illness posed a serious challenge for Chinese families to overcome. Poor children often suffered from the effects of inadequate housing, clothing, and food in an urban slum. Effie Lai remembered that in early twentieth-century San Francisco, crowded conditions contributed to the spread of tuberculosis, the disease that claimed the life of her younger brother.[73] Malnutrition, pneumonia, tuberculosis, smallpox, bubonic plague, typhoid fever, and cholera infantum were also frightening realities of urban life. Chinese children became not only the victims of these illnesses but also the targets of anti-Chinese efforts to incriminate all Chinese in the development and spread of epidemic disease.

Beginning in the mid-nineteenth century, health officers gathered evidence of disease in the Chinese quarter to corroborate the argument that the Chinese represented a health threat to American families. Upon discovery of smallpox in the city in 1876, city health officers ordered every house in Chinatown inspected and thoroughly fumigated. That same year, John L. Meares, the San Francisco health officer, testified about the conditions of Chinatown to a congressional committee organized to investigate Chinese immigration. Meares blamed the smallpox epidemic on the Chinese and their disregard for sanitary laws. Officials accused the Chinese of concealing known cases of smallpox, thereby further endangering the health of the city's white population. Accusations against the Chinese did not end with the smallpox epidemic. In 1900 fear of bubonic plague encouraged city authorities to quarantine Chinatown and to order a house-to-house inspection, searching for evidence of the plague. Guards examined all Chinese attempting to leave the city for symptoms of plague. Officials washed and disinfected houses, basements, gutters, and sewers. Chinatown leaders questioned the legality of the quarantine. A large crowd of Chinatown residents protested inoculation procedures and expressed fear of the potential negative side effects associated with the vaccine. Chinese children often became the victims of this widespread hysteria and fear. On inoculation day at the Presbyterian mission home, one terrified Chinese girl jumped out of a second-story window, breaking her ankle.[74]

The origin of epidemic disease remained a highly controversial topic, and white Americans suspected Chinese children and families as the cause of contagion. The statistical data, however, did not always support the contention of anti-Chinese officials that the Chinese were the source of epidemic disease. For the fiscal year 1873–74, health officers reported that the death rate of Chinese children under age seventeen was 23.3 per 1,000. This rate was slightly lower than the death rate for all other children (27.4 per 1,000).[75] Contrary to the testimony of Meares was that of Arthur B. Stout, who testified before Congress in 1876 that the death rate among whites was comparatively greater than among the Chinese and denied charges that smallpox originated in the Chinese quarter. In reference to Chinese children, Stout insisted that "the number of Chinese children here is very small comparatively, but the children are healthy. I have not seen a case of diphtheria nor a case of typhoid fever among their children."[76] Although twenty-two Chinese children were the victims of variola or smallpox in the 1870s, relatively few cases of infectious diseases such as diphtheria, typhoid fever, plague, or influenza appear in the statistical record. In fact, only seven Chinese child deaths could be directly attributed to bubonic plague from 1900 to 1903. This is especially ironic, given the insistence of health officials that Chinatown was the "source" of the plague.[77] However, inaccurate reporting and poor data-collection techniques make it difficult to compare death rates between white and Chinese children prior to 1900.

Unfortunately, illness and death were an ever-present fact of life for all children growing up in late nineteenth-century American cities. Overcrowding, unsanitary conditions, poor housing, limited nutrition, and inadequate medical care all contributed to infant mortality. City health officials reported frequent outbreaks of cholera infantum among infants, characterized by diarrhea and vomiting that slowly led to dehydration, emaciation, and ultimately death. This illness, transmitted via contaminated milk, water, and food, was responsible for the deaths of tens of thousands of urban infants each year.[78] Chinese mortuary records for San Francisco reveal a total of 1,941 childhood deaths between 1870 and 1918 (Table 6). Infants (children under one year of age) were most susceptible to disease, constituting 48 percent of the number of childhood deaths (Table 7). The most common causes of infant death from the 1870s through the 1890s were gastrointestinal disorders such as gastroenteritis, marasmus, inanition, and cholera infantum. After 1900, however, respiratory diseases such as bronchitis, pneumonia, and bronchopneumonia became the number-one killer of Chinese infants in San Francisco.[79] According to a series of investigations by the Children's Bureau beginning in 1913, the most common causes of death among infants in the United States were related to problems in early infancy, such as prematurity, congenital debility, congenital malformations, or injuries at birth. Gastrointestinal disorders and respiratory diseases, respectively, constituted the second and third major categories of infant deaths.[80] In 1913 the San Francisco

TABLE 6 : Deaths of Chinese Children Residing in
San Francisco by Sex, 1870–1918

DECADE	MALES	FEMALES	TOTAL NO.
1870–1879	214 (60%)	145 (40%)	359
1880–1889	268 (57%)	205 (43%)	473
1890–1899	320 (60%)	215 (40%)	535
1900–1909	156 (55%)	132 (45%)	288
1910–1918	174 (61%)	112 (39%)	286
Total	1,132 (58%)	809 (42%)	1,941

Source: "San Francisco Chinese Mortuary Records, 1870–1933," vols. 1–5, unnumbered microfilm, National Archives and Records Administration, Pacific Region, San Bruno, California.

Note: This data includes all children age sixteen and under. I have excluded all data for children who died in San Francisco but listed a residence outside the city.

TABLE 7 : Deaths of Chinese Children Residing in
San Francisco by Age, 1870–1918

DECADE	<1 YR.	1–4 YRS.	5–9 YRS.	10–16 YRS.	TOTAL NO.
1870–1879*	157 (44%)	104 (29%)	41 (11%)	56 (16%)	359
1880–1889	232 (49%)	154 (33%)	43 (9%)	44 (9%)	473
1890–1899	267 (50%)	156 (29%)	64 (12%)	48 (9%)	535
1900–1909*	149 (51%)	84 (30%)	29 (10%)	24 (8%)	288
1910–1918	137 (48%)	94 (33%)	38 (13%)	17 (6%)	286
Total	942 (48%)	592 (31%)	215 (11%)	189 (10%)	1,941

Source: "San Francisco Chinese Mortuary Records, 1870–1933," volumes 1–5, unnumbered microfilm, National Archives and Records Administration, Pacific Region, San Bruno, California.

Note: I have excluded all data for children who died in San Francisco but listed a residence outside the city.

* *The ages of one individual during the 1870s and two individuals during the 1900s remain unknown.*

Board of Health reported that San Francisco children were less likely to be afflicted with the gastrointestinal disorders that plagued the youth of other cities, and therefore the establishment of milk stations in San Francisco had been given very little serious consideration.[81] Respiratory ailments remained the major cause of infant deaths in turn-of-the-century San Francisco, largely because of unhealthy living conditions.

Limited available data and inaccurate reporting make it difficult to offer a comparison of infant morality based on race. However, data available in the San Francisco Municipal Reports of 1912 to 1917 indicates that the rate of infant mortality among Chinese children did appear to be higher than the rate among white children. The average infant mortality rate for those years was 90.96 per 1,000 live births for Chinese children, compared to 78.43 for all children.[82] Thus, Chinese children appeared to have been more susceptible to childhood illness in the early twentieth century. This was no doubt exacerbated by the unhealthy conditions of overcrowded tenement housing and limited access to quality health care.

Beginning in the mid-nineteenth century, public health reformers nationwide initially sought to reduce infant mortality by focusing on environmental reform to improve urban sanitation. Reformers concentrated first on improving the immigrant home. New York City enacted laws to improve the overall health and sanitation of the city's tenement houses. These reforms inspired a series of similar ordinances in cities across the nation.[83] After 1880 the concern shifted to improving the quality of the urban milk supply and later to educating mothers about infant feeding and care. Some reformers regarded the higher infant mortality rates among the urban, immigrant poor as evidence of racial inferiority and, therefore, increasingly focused their efforts in immigrant communities.[84]

By the mid-1870s Presbyterian women missionaries on the West Coast had begun to conduct home visits in Chinatown to educate Chinese women in acceptable white middle-class hygiene. In what historians have labeled as a form of "imperial domesticity," Protestant women reformers provided domestic management and housekeeping advice to Chinese women to combat "foreign" habits of filth and contagion in San Francisco's Chinatown. Inspired by the belief in the influential impact of environment and the inherent malleability of children, a number of Protestant organizations opened up mission homes and schools for Chinese children while also conducting periodic home visits.[85] Margarita Lake of the Methodist mission noted that with bright picture cards, flowers, music, and stories of Jesus, they could convert the children and then reach the mothers through the children.[86] Thus, Chinese children proved the essential link between the reformers and the Chinese race.

The writings of female reformers emphasize a strong belief in the cleansing power of Christianity. In 1881 Emma Cable described the cramped apartment of a Chinese family: "Setting aside all feelings of loathsomeness born of the repulsive aspect of this filth and darkness, I entered upon the task of illuminating a soul of corresponding degradation, speaking to her of God's love, pure air and sunshine, contrasting these with her present surroundings. Each succeeding visit found a growing appreciation of my words, 'till finally she became as thoroughly nauseated with her surroundings as myself. Today we find her in a cheerful room at 822 Dupont Street, which she has thoroughly cleaned, white-washed and papered."[87] The contrast between light and dark, cleanliness and filth, or heathenism and Christianity is a frequent theme in missionary writing. According to the missionaries, cleanliness was but one step in improving the health of Chinese immigrant families while preparing them for eternal salvation. The children often took these lessons in cleanliness to heart. Mission teachers asked twelve-year-old Ah Choie to explain the biblical words "create in me a clean heart." Ah Choie explained, " 'I ask God to take the *dirt* from my heart, and make clean, all 'e same as wash it?' " They inquired further, asking Ah Choie whether God had done it. The teachers were delighted to hear him reply, " 'He can do it.' "[88] Missionary efforts to reform the Chinese family seemed to offer visible evidence of success. Mrs. Ira M. Condit of the Presbyterian Church noted in 1881 the improvement in a number of homes in Chinatown and attributed these improvements to the efforts of missionaries in educating Chinese women in household management. Condit noted that although the women retained Chinese food customs and styles of dress, "the floors are cleaner, fresh paper and pictures are on the walls, tidies are on the chairs, and pretty little ornaments are on the shelves. And what is better, our English and Chinese Bibles are on the tables, and we know they are read."[89] The emphasis on food, dress, and household management in Condit's account is typical of reformers, who insisted that immigrants conform to a middle-class, white standard of motherhood in order to fully assimilate into American society.[90]

Although missionaries continued their Chinatown crusades, after the turn of the century, a number of nonsectarian, Progressive organizations also formed to combat a variety of problems in the city. Shortly after the 1906 earthquake, Katherine Felton of Associated Charities appealed for public funds to take care of orphaned babies. The Babies' Aid Society developed a system of foster care to support dependent babies until they could be adopted.[91] However, private charities such as the Protestant Chinese missions continued to care for orphaned or abandoned Chinese children, since the new foster programs catered exclusively to white children.[92] The Certified Milk Fund Committee of the Association of Collegiate Alumnae (later the Baby Hygiene Committee) was formed in San Francisco in 1909 to reduce infant mortality by supplying mothers with uncontaminated milk and educating parents on the proper care and feeding of babies. Although Chinese children rarely benefited directly from the charity of these later organizations, overall advances in pediatrics and improvements in urban sanitation contributed to a decrease in infant mortality and better health care. Christian organizations such as the Chinese YWCA and teachers at Presbyterian and Methodist missionary homes continued to minister to Chinese families and attempted to inculcate middle-class standards of cleanliness. In 1928 the Chinese YWCA cosponsored a Well Baby Contest as part of a national campaign to educate mothers on infant hygiene and improve the overall health of the nation's babies.[93]

While cleanliness and child welfare campaigns helped to greatly reduce the number of child deaths related to disease, deaths due to accidents and violence continued. Although these types of deaths occurred relatively infrequently, accidents did happen, as evidenced by the small number of deaths resulting from suffocation, burns, falls, and poisonings that occasionally appeared in the record. The newspapers reference a number of cases of children struck and injured by automobiles and streetcars.[94] These incidents sometimes caused serious injuries, though they rarely resulted in death. Quin Tuck suffered injuries after being struck by a cable car. He wrote to his mission teacher, "I am Quin Tuck. You know me for long time, the cars catch me under, make me sick. I not walk, run or play many months. A man he take me in house, too much sick peoples there, doctor make my arm well." Tuck apparently also suffered additional injuries as a result of a later accident with scissors: "I put scissors in one eye, no see good, very dark, one eye all right."[95] Tuck's accidents, however, were a statistical rarity.

Chinese child deaths resulting from accidents rarely constituted any statistical significance except during the decade of the 1870s, when child deaths resulting from accidental burns occurred fairly frequently. These incidents were often reported in the newspaper. On May 21, 1885, a fire broke out in the home of a laundryman and his family. The mother rushed into the burning building in an attempt to rescue her two children, who were trapped inside. The roof collapsed with the woman and her children still in the building. Although firemen rescued the woman and rushed her to the County Hospital, the two children perished in the fire.[96] Fires posed a significant threat to all urban Americans during this period, and cities later improved efforts to minimize the risk of fire.

Although infrequent, cases of violence against Chinese children did occur. Cases of child abuse appeared in the records of missionary organizations and child-protective societies. These incidents, however, rarely resulted in death. Occasionally, children found themselves in the middle of violent disputes between adults. Fifteen-year-old Jue Do Hong was shot to death by a man who had a disagreement with the boy's father. The assailant, Jue Lin Ong, apparently had an argument with the child's father over some property in China and traveled across the ocean to attain vengeance by murdering the boy. After shooting Jue Do Hong twice in the back with a 44-caliber Colt revolver, Jue Lin Ong fled to Oakland in an attempt to hide from the police. Police captured him in Napa; after his trial, Jue Lin Ong was executed for the crime at San Quentin on July 22, 1904.[97]

Although the data suggests otherwise, anti-Chinese writers frequently argued that the Chinese expressed little compassion toward their sick and dying children. This was part of the effort to emphasize the foreignness of Chinese culture and the unwillingness or inability of Chinese immigrants to conform to American standards of domesticity. In 1876 Ernest C. Stock, a police reporter for the *Morning Call*, testified before a congressional committee about the callous attitude of Chinese parents toward their dying children. Stock related the story of a Chinese man who requested a coffin for his sick boy, desiring to lay the child in the coffin before his death. Stock interpreted this as evidence of a lack of love for the child.[98] G. B. Densmore in 1880 commented that "in San Francisco, the sick and helpless male orphans are often turned out on the street to die. Sometimes they put them into little rooms, without light, bedding or food. There they are left to starve and die. The Chinese have some superstition in regard to persons dying in their houses. They believe to let one die in the house brings bad luck."[99] Chinese cultural beliefs reflecting fear of exposure to death and malevolent spirits may help explain this seemingly callous attitude toward the ill. An absence of family, superstitions about evil spirits, or simply an unwillingness to pay the price of the funeral may have contributed to the abandonment of some individuals during the final stages of a terminal illness.[100]

The facts, however, reveal that Chinese parents were rarely as callous toward their sick children as suggested in the popular press. Although the City and County Hospital restricted the number of Chinese patients beginning in 1881, parents consistently sought the best Chinese and American medical care for their ill children. The mortuary records reveal that parents frequently rushed their sick children to one of the many hospitals in San Francisco or sought the care of Chinese physicians. The Chinese Six Companies opened the Tung Wah Dispensary in 1900, and Chinese parents continued to seek both Chinese and American medical treatment for their ill children.[101] Chinese families thus went to great lengths to overcome segregated policies in order to secure a safe and healthy future for their children. Meanwhile, children quickly learned to adapt to the realities of life and death.

While the death of a child was emotionally devastating for the parents, the death of a mother or father often created a heavy burden for the children. The emotional burden of suffering the loss of a parent was very difficult to bear. With the loss of her mother, a girl had to take on additional household responsibilities. The eldest daughter often took over the parental role by cooking, cleaning, and caring for her siblings. Even younger children shared in the household chores and the responsibility of caring for infants. Upon the death of his father, a boy often took over the role of economic provider. It was generally the custom that after one of their parents died, daughters of marriageable age quickly married to provide the family with some financial relief. Younger children often went to live with relatives or were sent to work as domestics with other families.[102] Unexpected parental deaths prematurely forced children into adult roles.

Children also played prominent roles in the perpetuation of Chinese death rituals in America.[103] Although he was only four years old at the time of his mother's death, Elmer Wok Wai vividly recalled her funeral. Relatives dressed him in all white, the traditional color of mourning. Ritual wailing was an obligatory and essential part of the funeral ceremony, and Wai remembered that he and his eight-year-old sister, Guai Ching, had to show visible signs of their grief by crying. Because she was older, Wai's sister bore more responsibility in the ceremonies and probably better understood the somber requirements of the occasion. The excitement of the funeral procession enthralled the young boy: bands, priests beating cymbals, horses, and mourners paraded down the street, carrying banners and a drawing of his mother. However, the long trip to the cemetery and the behavioral requirements of the day were exhausting for a young child; Wai fell asleep on the ride back to the family home. The mourning continued for a year, and the children played a crucial part in maintaining a solemn attitude to express the family's grief. Wai remembered an empty feeling that persisted for some time afterwards. All of his mother's possessions had been burned at the grave, and the only reminder was her shrine on a shelf on the wall. He recalled burning punk and carrying rice, fish, and tea to the shrine twice a day for months before his memory of her gradually faded.[104] Over time, Chinese Americans adapted traditional Chinese death rituals by including elements of Christian beliefs and ceremonies into their mortuary practices.

CONCLUSION

Anti-Chinese politicians and labor leaders feared the continued influx of unassimilable Chinese and pointed to the slow development of family life in San Francisco's Chinatown as partial evidence to support exclusion and segregation. Images of Chinese children in Chinatown reflected these anxieties and fears. The propaganda generated by anti-Chinese politicians pointed to the scarcity of women and children as evidence of the sojourner mentality of the Chinese immigrant. As the numbers of Chinese women and children grew, critics also attacked the variety of domestic arrangements in Chinatown, contrasting these nontraditional households with the two-parent, middle-class American family. Chinese merchants and community leaders responded to the attacks by holding up their wives and children as examples of legitimate family life in Chinatown and attacking the image of a "bachelor society." Meanwhile, they sought to protect and preserve the sanctity and privacy of their homes. Protestant missionaries often defended family life in Chinatown while attempting to Christianize, Americanize, and mold Chinese women and children into a middle-class ideal of "family." Progressive-era social reformers—firm believers in the influences of the environment—focused on reshaping the immigrant home and community.[105]

Chinese immigrants struggled against overwhelming odds to build a family life in America, and they soon found themselves forced to defend those families against attacks. A variety of unique family structures developed as a means of adapting to the barriers to family formation imposed by American immigration restrictions, antimiscegenation laws, segregation, and anti-Chinese violence. The "families" that emerged conformed to neither Chinese nor American ideals of family life. The mere presence of these nontraditional families challenged the limited, Eurocentric, and two-parent definition of "family" espoused by anti-Chinese writers. Chinese parents sought to protect their children from the dangers of their new urban, industrial environment at the same time that they struggled to survive. Families adapted Chinese child-rearing practices and rituals to their new environment and chose to incorporate select elements of American culture. Personal accounts combined with public records provide an intimate glimpse into family life by describing efforts to overcome poverty, illness, and death that resulted from living in an urban ethnic enclave. Survival often depended upon the support and labor of the whole family. As the next chapter reveals, Chinese children were crucial members of the household economy.

3

FOR THE FAMILY BACK HOME

CHINESE CHILDREN AT WORK

San Francisco journalist and photographer Louis Stellman frequented Chinatown in the early twentieth century and attempted to capture images of daily
life among its inhabitants. One of his photographs shows a young girl walking down the road carrying two pails of dried shrimp, bamboo, and bean-
sprout stew. Stellman wrote in his notes that the girl was carrying dinner to
the Chinese men in the goldsmith shops. She may have worked in the family
restaurant or labored as a domestic servant in the home of a Chinese family.
Included among Stellman's other photographs are images of child domestic
servants weighed down by the burden of babies strapped to their backs.
Many Chinese children worked as domestic laborers in Chinese households
and were responsible for supervising children only slightly younger than
themselves. Census data reveals that a large number of children in early
Chinatown were employed as servants in both Chinese and white households. Many more worked in factories and shops throughout Chinatown.
Initially, the older Chinese children (over age ten) who immigrated to America came for the same purpose as their adult counterparts—to work and earn
money to send home to their families in China. Stellman's photographs offer
a rare glimpse into the reality of child labor for working-class Chinese children in San Francisco's Chinatown.[1]

This chapter examines the contributions and explores the lives of Chinese
child laborers in nineteenth-century San Francisco. As a segment of the larger
labor force, these children played a small but significant role in promoting
California's economy. More importantly, Chinese child workers found them-

selves in the middle of the national conflict over the presence of Chinese laborers in California and the future of child labor. Continuing with the theme of previous chapters, this chapter examines how various forces promoted images of Chinese children at work that furthered political agendas. Using census data, oral histories, and autobiographies, we will explore how child workers coped with anti-Chinese hostility and consider the various factors resulting in the decline of child labor by the early twentieth century.

THE DEMAND FOR CHINESE LABOR

San Francisco in the mid-nineteenth century was a rapidly industrializing city specializing in the manufacture of cigars, clothing, shoes, boots, and slippers. The initial shortage of workers encouraged business owners to support the immigration of cheap Chinese labor. Recruiters hired large numbers of Chinese men to work in the city's factories at rates lower than their white counterparts. Especially after the profits from mining began to dwindle in California's foothills, Chinese men took advantage of the industrial job opportunities in the city. While the Chinese constituted only 8 percent of the population in 1870 San Francisco, they composed 13 percent of the city's total labor force.[2] Money earned in the factories went to support wives and children back in China.

Tables 8 and 9 provide information regarding the work experience of Chinese children from 1860 to 1920. The majority of Chinese children who arrived in San Francisco in the mid-nineteenth century found employment in factories, Chinese laundries, or domestic service. These children constituted 12 percent of the San Francisco Chinese labor force and approximately 2 percent of the city's total labor force in 1870.[3] Young children (under age ten) rarely worked; however, the majority of Chinese children in San Francisco in 1870 were between ten and sixteen years old and employed. During this period of rapid industrialization, child labor was on the increase all over the United States. The demand for workers increased substantially by the early twentieth century, as the United States emerged as the leading industrial nation in the world. Working-class, especially immigrant, children found employment in the nation's factories. In fact, Chinese children were statistically much more likely to work than their white counterparts. In 1870 the federal census recorded that 13 percent of all American children age ten to fifteen were employed. The San Francisco census returns for that year revealed

Errand girl (Chinese: Children; Stellman Collection, #10, 818; courtesy of the California History Room, California State Library, Sacramento)

dramatically higher figures for Chinese children in San Francisco, where 92 percent of children age ten to fifteen were employed.[4] During these early years, Chinese children immigrated to the United States primarily to work.

Although both boys and girls worked, the vast majority of reported child laborers in Chinatown were male. Census enumerators were less likely to record female child labor since many young girls worked from home. According to the census figures for 1870, 80 percent of Chinese boys age sixteen and under had jobs, while only 38 percent of Chinese girls under age sixteen did.[5] Chinese boys worked as domestic servants, laundrymen, and factory workers, while girls worked as servants (*mui tsai*) in Chinese families or as prostitutes. (We will discuss the issue of prostitution in more detail in chap-

TABLE 8 : Occupations of Chinese Children in San Francisco, 1860–1920

OCCUPATION	1860	1870	1880	1900	1910	1920
At home/ none listed	67 (63%)	444 (29%)	708 (48%)	808 (56%)	1,095 (85%)	1,389 (83%)
At school	0	21 (1%)	82 (6%)	479 (33%)	15 (1%)	221 (13%)
Servant/cook/ gardener	4 (4%)	498 (32%)	322 (22%)	49 (3%)	57 (5%)	12 (<1%)
Laundry/ washman	1 (1%)	179 (12%)	89 (6%)	15 (1%)	29 (4%)	6 (<1%)
Cigar maker	0	188 (12%)	60 (4%)	3 (<1%)	2 (<1%)	0
Clothing manufacturer	1 (1%)	5 (<1%)	52 (4%)	44 (3%)	18 (1%)	0
Shoe/slipper factory	0	42 (3%)	23 (2%)	0	0	2 (<1%)
Laborer	20 (19%)	49 (3%)	42 (3%)	6 (<1%)	16 (1%)	0
Prostitute	0	66 (4%)	33 (2%)	1 (<1%)	0	0
Miscellaneous	13 (12%)	54 (3%)	63 (4%)	30 (2%)	54 (4%)	41 (2%)
Total	106	1,546	1,474	1,435	1,286	1,671

Sources: U.S. Bureau of the Census, Eighth Census of the United States, *1860; Ninth Census of the United States, 1870; Tenth Census of the United States, 1880; Twelfth Census of the United States, 1900; Thirteenth Census of the United States, 1910; Fourteenth Census of the United States, 1920.*

Note: This data is based on my survey of all Chinese children age sixteen and under in San Francisco. The category of clothing manufacturer in this table includes all children whose occupations were listed as seamstress, tailor, embroiderer, sewing machine operator, pants and overall maker, shirt maker, button sewer, or underwear maker. The miscellaneous category included a number of children employed in the food-service industry.

ter 5.) A larger, and mostly unrecorded, number of children probably worked from home, assisting their mothers in industrial piecework. These remained the primary occupations of Chinese children into the early twentieth century, although the total number of children reported as working had declined substantially by 1900. Chinese children proved important contributors to the family economy, both in America and China. The next section considers the

TABLE 9 : Occupations of Chinese Children by Gender, 1860–1920

OCCUPATION	1860		1870		1880	
	MALE	FEMALE	MALE	FEMALE	MALE	FEMALE
At home/ none listed	19 (18%)	48 (45%)	236 (15%)	208 (13%)	309 (21%)	399 (27%)
At school	0	0	21 (1%)	0	60 (4%)	22 (1%)
Servant/cook/ gardener	4 (4%)	0	436 (28%)	62 (4%)	266 (18%)	56 (4%)
Laundry	1 (1%)	0	179 (12%)	0	89 (6%)	0
Cigar maker	0	0	187 (12%)	1 (<1%)	60 (4%)	0
Clothing manufacturer	1 (1%)	0	5 (<1%)	0	44 (3%)	8 (<1%)
Shoe/slipper factory	0	0	42 (3%)	0	23 (2%)	0
Laborer	20 (19%)	0	49 (3%)	0	42 (3%)	0
Prostitute	0	0	0	66 (4%)	0	33 (2%)
Miscellaneous	13 (12%)	0	53 (3%)	1 (<1%)	56 (4%)	7 (<1%)
Total	58 (55%)	48 (45%)	1,208 (78%)	338 (22%)	949 (64%)	525 (36%)

work experiences of Chinese children in the most common types of employment in 1870s San Francisco.

DOMESTIC SERVANTS, *MUI TSAI*, AND LAUNDRYMEN

Chinese boys as young as ten years old frequently found work in non-Chinese households as domestic servants, cooks, or gardeners. By the mid-nineteenth century, 15 to 30 percent of all American households included

OCCUPATION	1900		1910		1920	
	MALE	FEMALE	MALE	FEMALE	MALE	FEMALE
At home / none listed	327 (23%)	481 (34%)	660 (51%)	434 (34%)	705 (42%)	684 (41%)
At School	321 (22%)	158 (11%)	10 (<1%)	5 (<1%)	150 (9%)	71 (4%)
Servant / cook / gardener	46 (3%)	3 (<1%)	57 (4%)	0	9 (<1%)	3 (<1%)
Laundry	15 (1%)	0	29 (2%)	0	6 (<1%)	0
Cigar maker	3 (<1%)	0	2 (<1%)	0	0	0
Clothing manufacturer	17 (1%)	27 (2%)	4 (<1%)	14 (1%)	0	0
Shoe / slipper factory	0	0	0	0	2 (<1%)	0
Laborer	6 (<1%)	0	16 (1%)	0	0	0
Prostitute	0	1 (<1%)	0	0	0	0
Miscellaneous	30 (2%)	0	52 (4%)	3 (<1%)	29 (2%)	12 (<1%)
Total	765 (53%)	670 (47%)	830 (65%)	456 (35%)	901 (54%)	770 (46%)

Sources: U.S. Bureau of the Census, Eighth Census of the United States, 1860; Ninth Census of the United States, 1870; Tenth Census of the United States, 1880; Twelfth Census of the United States, 1900; Thirteenth Census of the United States, 1910; Fourteenth Census of the United States, 1920.

domestic servants. Increasingly, middle-class families enjoyed the luxury of hiring domestics to assist in day-to-day housekeeping chores. Servants assumed many of the responsibilities typically assigned to the mother, such as cooking, cleaning, and taking care of the children. Although domestic service was overwhelmingly a female occupation in the United States, Chinese men and boys gradually worked their way into the profession as the shortage of females in California and the aversion of white men toward this work opened up a demand for their services.[6] In 1870 census takers recorded 498

Chinese children (32 percent) working in these positions. By 1880 the number of children employed as domestics had declined to 322 (22 percent). Chinese youth provided cooking, dish-washing, laundry, child-care, and gardening services for mostly middle- and upper-class white families in San Francisco. At the age of eleven or twelve, George Lem arrived in the United States in 1875 with his father and uncles. His father worked in a laundry but helped him find work as a servant with an American family. Trained on the job, Lem mostly helped in the kitchen with food preparation.[7] Domestics, especially child servants like Lem, often lived in the same house with their employers. This unique domestic arrangement presented a number of challenges and opportunities for Chinese children growing up in San Francisco.

Some white families treated their Chinese domestics like members of the family. Christian employers believed that they could have a morally uplifting influence on their servants.[8] Huie Kin recalled that while working as a domestic for the Gardiner family, he was taught by Mrs. Gardiner to read and write along with her own children. The Gardiners also encouraged Kin to attend Sunday school and gave him the time off to attend the classes. Although Huie Kin admitted that initially his goal was simply to learn English rather than religion, he eventually converted to Christianity and was baptized at the Presbyterian church in Oakland.[9] His close personal relationship with the Gardiners contributed to his overall pleasant experience as a domestic servant. While some Chinese servants may have enjoyed this status as pseudo family members, there were many reminders of the employer/employee relationship. Employers reserved the right to dismiss their servants at any time, and Chinese domestics always remained in a subservient relationship to other members of the household. Cultural differences also posed substantial obstacles to the formation of relationships. Problems of cultural adjustment sometimes dampened the overall experience.

Chinese servants struggled to overcome language barriers and cultural dislocation in their new homes. Boys sought domestic-service jobs through an employment agency or advertised their desire for work in the local newspaper. Recognizing that American-style clothing and good English-language skills made them more marketable, many Chinese youth highlighted these qualifications in their advertisements.[10] A large number of servants, however, came directly from China and had little training in the English language or experience with American culture. At the age of sixteen, Lee Chew went to work in the home of an American family that included a husband, a wife, and two children. Although he could not speak English, Lee Chew learned by watching: "I did not know how to do anything, and I did not understand what the lady said to me, but she showed me how to cook, wash, iron, sweep, dust, make beds, wash dishes, clean windows, paint and brass, polish the knives and forks, etc., by doing the things herself and then overseeing my efforts to imitate her. She would take my hands and show them how to do things. She and her husband and children laughed at me a great deal, but it was all good natured."[11] Despite this language barrier, Lee Chew fondly recalled his work as a domestic in California, noting his relative freedom of movement. His employers allowed him to come and go as he pleased, and he remembered frequent visits to the Chinese theater and dinner parties in Chinatown. For Huie Kin, the cultural divide proved particularly frustrating to his culinary desires: his dislike of applesauce, a staple in one of the homes in which he worked, and his craving for a Chinese meal only heightened his homesickness and sense of cultural isolation. For many Chinese youth, language and cultural distinctions prevented full integration into their American pseudo families.[12]

Chinese girl servants encountered a different set of problems. The sixty-two Chinese girls (4 percent) listed as servants in 1870 worked primarily for Chinese families living in Chinatown. These girls cooked, cleaned, shopped, and provided child care for their employers. Quan Laan Fan's parents sold her at a young age as a servant to a Chinese family who later relocated to America. She was responsible for running errands for the family. Although she did not have to cook the meals, part of her chores included picking up the family dinner from the store: "I'd go out by myself at 9 o'clock in the morning to get our daytime meal and at 4 o'clock for the evening meal. . . . I was so short . . . I dragged the pot home every day until I wore a hole in it!"[13] Although she experienced little of the cultural dislocation and isolation of servants situated in homes outside of Chinatown, she faced the frustrations of most workers of her social status. Her memoirs recalled the intense manual labor she daily endured as a *mui tsai*. The labor of these girl servants freed their families from the burden of supporting an additional child.

Although Chinese girls rarely served as domestic servants outside the confines of Chinatown, the Chinese Methodist mission did experiment with placing mission girls in white households to learn domestic skills and build "character, habits of industry, independence and self-reliance."[14] The Methodist mission provided a home for orphaned, abandoned, or abused Chinese girls. Missionaries "rescued" most of the girls from what the reformers perceived as virtual slavery in Chinatown. Working as *mui tsai* and pros-

Young servant girls known as *mui tsai* (Chinese Children, Roy D. Graves Pictorial Collection, 1905.17500 v. 29:340ALB; courtesy of the Bancroft Library, University of California, Berkeley)

titutes under the supervision of Chinese "masters," the girls sometimes endured harsh conditions as well as physical, emotional, and sexual abuse. The mission attempted to educate and reform the girls. Missionaries eventually placed older girls in white, Christian households to learn Western methods of household management. The experiences of these young women no doubt mirror some of the experiences of younger male Chinese domestic servants also working outside of Chinatown. In 1897 Laura Lee, a nineteen-year-old former resident of the Methodist mission, wrote to the mission director, Margarita Lake, to describe her duties in the Reeves household of Alameda:

> I feel like Robinson Crusoe away out here, away from all my kind and loving friends, but I thought I would write to you to let you know that I am alive. I am getting along nicely, and am very much satisfied with my new home, because Mrs. Reeves and her children are all very kind to me. I am learning to cook, and when I come home again to you, I will

show you how nice I can cook. I cooked breakfast last Saturday all by myself, and had it all ready in time for the children to start for school. Wednesday morning I cooked the mush and did not put any salt in it, but the lady said she used to do the same thing herself at one time. Tell Gum that I am having worse troubles than she has. I get up every morning at 6:30 and make the fire and cook the mush and make the coffee and set the table, and wake up Mrs. Reeves to cook the meat.[15]

The mission girls' education and greater familiarity with Euroamerican culture may have helped to ease some of their feelings of isolation. Still, Lee described a longing for home: "I went to church with Mrs. Reeves and her children, but the very minute the preacher commenced to speak I commenced to cry, because I felt homesick for my own church."[16] Although Lee expressed homesickness and seemed to be complaining about her extensive chores, her letter expressed overall satisfaction with the work. She was particularly happy that Mrs. Reeves allowed her to study from the children's books each day after they went to school. Lee praised the kindness of her employer and looked forward to the opportunity to study. Her positive experiences seemed to confirm the missionary belief in the benefits of this method of training young Chinese women in Christian, middle-class domesticity.

Yet, some mission girls resented their work as domestics and longed to be with their family and friends. Marie Chan, another former Methodist mission girl, described her struggle to overcome feelings of loneliness while working in the home of the Edmonds family. Writing to the newly married Margarita Lake (Garton) in 1910, Chan complained about her situation and expressed a desire to return to her former life in the mission home:

> I am not used of working like this, so I am awfully lonesome. I feel as if I had lost all my friends. Because this place that I am working now is between Oakland and Berkeley. Berkeley is just as far as Oak. from here. I am sick and tire [sic] of Oakland and Berk. I wish I could find a job in the city. I am going to the country with the family, for three weeks. We are going next Thursday. I hate to go with them, but in the case of had to. I know I will feel very lonesome, because I don't like countries. I like cities. Countries are too lonesome for me.[17]

The feeling of loneliness expressed by Chan was no doubt a common experience for many domestic servants. Lacking the freedom and comforts of home, servants missed friends, family, and the general sense of community of

Chinatown. Most Chinese domestic servants employed in white households lived in relative isolation from the Chinese American community. Some servants, like Lee Chew, attempted to alleviate this sense of isolation by occasionally taking free time to participate in holidays and activities in Chinatown. A cruel or simply unkind employer could make such loneliness nearly intolerable.

Chinese laundrymen also frequently lived and worked in isolation from the larger Chinese American community. The initial shortage of women in San Francisco created a demand for laundry services. During the early years, Chinese laundrymen found a profitable niche in an industry that most white men considered "women's work." By the 1880s the Chinese owned and operated over three-quarters of the laundries in San Francisco, and about nine-tenths of Chinese laundry workers were located in white neighborhoods, catering to a white clientele.[18] The shop served not only as the physical working space but also converted to sleeping and living quarters as well. Living away from Chinatown, laundrymen felt somewhat isolated from the Chinese community. However, frequent visits to Chinatown prevented complete seclusion, and laundrymen, like domestic servants, maintained an economic and cultural connection to their compatriots in Chinatown.[19]

Chinese children worked alongside their fathers, uncles, and cousins in the laundry business. In 1870 census takers listed 179 children age sixteen and under (12 percent) working in Chinese laundries. The census figures reveal that the laundries employed exclusively male children. Laundry owners typically employed and housed family members, immigrants with the same surname, or clansmen from the same village or district. These men became partners in the business. Fathers sent for their sons or nephews and groomed them to eventually take over the business.[20] Laundrymen formed unique domestic relationships based predominately on kinship.

The work of a laundryman was especially tedious, requiring a great deal of physical exertion. Workers stood most of the day and endured intense heat from the water and the furnace. Frequent contact with hot water and soap damaged the skin. At age sixteen, Yee Loon worked after school in his uncle's laundry, sorting, washing, drying, and pressing the clothes. Yee Loon recalled working seven days a week until midnight and earning a monthly wage of $15.00 in 1920.[21] Despite the harsh conditions of labor, the work provided necessary income for the family back home in China. At the same time that children labored in the Chinese laundries, Chinese child laborers also established a presence in the city's manufacturing industry.

In the 1870s the largest employers in San Francisco were the manufacturers of cigars, clothing, boots, shoes, and slippers. By the 1880s the city had emerged among the top ten centers of industrial production in the United States.[22] Chinese men, women, and children worked in these industries, manufacturing goods for white consumers. An increasing number of Chinese entrepreneurs also owned and operated their own factories, producing similar goods. However, competition with white labor and anti-Chinese sentiment forced many Chinese owners out of business. Still, the manufacturing industry remained a major source of employment for Chinese living in San Francisco.

Chinese children found employment either working directly in the factories or producing piecework from home. In 1870, 250 Chinese children (16 percent) labored in the factories. Initially, employers preferred to hire only Chinese men and boys. Boys endured the same conditions and completed the same work as older males. Children engaged in the manufacture of clothes often sat at sewing machines in dark rooms for twelve to fifteen hours a day, performing sewing work for their employers.[23] Boys working in cigar factories sat hunched over, rolling cigars for hours a day. Such work proved mentally exhausting and could be physically debilitating for all workers. The realities of factory work proved especially dangerous and tedious for child workers.

Piecework provided an avenue for young children to earn income. Relatively few San Francisco manufacturers in the 1870s hired women or younger children to work in the factories. American and Chinese gender roles defined the domestic sphere as the domain of the female and generally denied them entry into the public workforce. Still, many women and children took in homework from the factories. Evidence of the number of children working at home on piecework is not revealed in the census data. However, oral histories and autobiographies suggest that these women and children frequently worked in their tenement apartments, washing clothes, rolling cigars, making slippers, and finishing pants and overalls. In fact, this appeared to be a common practice among many working-class and some merchant-class Chinese families. Women worked for about half the amount paid to Chinese men working in the factories.[24] In 1886 Quin Tuck wrote to his missionary teachers describing his work at home: "My mamma not much money, I sew buttons, buy rice and clothes. My papa's money all gone, too much poor."[25] The family obviously depended on the additional money provided by the boy's work. While a child's labor may have provided much-needed additional income for working-class families, merchant-class families may have used the extra income simply to provide the family with a few additional luxuries while inculcating values of thrift and industry in their children through hard work.

In addition to their regular domestic duties, *mui tsai* also participated in piecework, contributing to the family economy. As a servant for a Chinese family in San Francisco, Quan Laan Fan would roll cigarettes at home. Older girls would bring home clothes from the factories to sew. Quan Laan Fan described her work as exhausting: "While rolling the cigarettes I'd get sleepy . . . really tired. Then, they'd hit me. It was really tedious. I'd roll cigarettes all day long and there was no one to talk with. We'd just sit there rolling cigarettes."[26] The work seemed especially burdensome for a young child.

Children often balanced schoolwork and domestic chores with the piecework necessary to provide extra income for the family. Lily King Gee Won remembered begging for food as a young child and later learning how to shell shrimp at home. The Chinese restaurant owners would bring the shrimp to the tenements in the evenings: "My sisters and I would get our share and bring it home. Then everyone would sit down and begin working. Dawn would see us taking the shelled shrimp back for a paltry sum to supplement our living expenses." The younger girls also picked up and delivered garment pieces for the older girls, who finished the clothing at home. They later learned to embroider slippers: "The surfaces of the slippers were embroidered with glass beads of all colors and sizes. How many reds were used for each pattern, how many whites, how many yellows . . . I had to commit all that to memory. Every time a pattern was changed it would involve a lot of work. But because I had a good memory I could make the changes fast and I managed to make a living despite my tender age."[27] Employers no doubt preferred the smaller and more nimble fingers of the younger workers. Piecework was a less-visible form of child labor that would prove no less controversial than children laboring in the factories.

By the twentieth century, as American women began to challenge traditional gender roles that confined them to the home, Chinese women and girls increasingly took advantage of newfound opportunities to work in factories. In 1922 Elsa Lissner of the Industrial Welfare Commission and Sarah Lee of the University of California examined factories that employed women and children in Chinatown. The visitors observed that most women arrived at work between ten and eleven in the morning, going home at noon and again around three to care for their returning school-age children. Younger children accompanied their mothers to work. Women strapped the babies on their backs, cradled them in the piles of unmade garments, or set them on the shelves to sleep.[28] Older children assisted in the work. Daisy Lorraine Wong Chinn worked in a denim factory with her mother on Saturdays sewing buttonholes. At age twelve, she went to work in her father's garment factory cutting out patterns.[29] Although child labor was becoming very controversial, Chinese children continued to work into the 1920s.

CHARACTERISTICS OF CHILD LABOR IN
NORTHERN CALIFORNIA CHINATOWNS

A comparison of the San Francisco figures with the manuscript census data of Chinese children living in Sacramento and Oakland reveals that child labor was quite common in California Chinatowns during the nineteenth century. Like their San Francisco counterparts, the majority of Chinese children age sixteen and under living in Sacramento and Oakland worked in 1870 and 1880. However, over 90 percent of the Chinese children living in Oakland were employed, compared to an average of about 60 percent of the Chinese children in Sacramento and San Francisco. The higher numbers for Oakland may be partly explained by the presence of large factories there that recruited young male Chinese laborers. For example, in 1880 the Pacific Bag Factory in Oakland employed 121 Chinese boys age sixteen and under (64 percent of the total number of Chinese children living in the city). The early twentieth century witnessed a sharp decline in the numbers of Chinese child laborers. By 1920 census enumerators listed less than 5 percent of Chinese children in San Francisco, Sacramento, and Oakland as being employed.[30] Child labor in general was in decline across the nation after the turn of the century.

The unique family structures of Chinese child laborers make it difficult to compare them with other laboring children in America. Brian Gratton and Jon Moen, scholars of child-labor history, examined the demographics of American child laborers from 1880 to 1920. Gratton and Moen argue that children were more likely to work if they had a large number of siblings, an earlier place in the birth order, or a female or illiterate head of household.[31] Comparing similar data for Chinese children is complicated by the variety of domestic arrangements in early Chinatown. Many of the employed Chinese children in the San Francisco census did not live with their parents, and therefore it is impossible to determine the number of siblings, birth order, or the identity of the head of household. From the available data, it appears that these factors did not significantly increase the likelihood that a Chinese child would work. Additional siblings may have lived in China or separate from the family, which also makes it difficult to determine if birth order had any influence on which children worked. Census enumerators also rarely listed occupations for Chinese children living with their parents. Although children may have assisted the family at home in piecework, census enumerators were unlikely to list children living in two-parent homes as employed. One attribute, however, stands out as a likely indicator that a Chinese child would work: his or her place of birth. China-born Chinese children were much more likely to work than their American-born counterparts. In 1870, 99 percent of Chinese child workers in San Francisco were foreign-born; this figure remained at just over 50 percent by 1920. Chinese children continued to immigrate to the United States with the primary intention of working. Increasingly after the turn of the century, however, the nature of child labor in Chinatown began to change as the debate over Chinese labor, and child labor in general, impacted the work of Chinese children.

The dramatic decline in the number of Chinese child laborers after the turn of the century suggests that social pressures may have influenced Chinese parents' decision to remove their children from the workforce. The percentage of Chinese child laborers in San Francisco declined substantially from 1870 to 1920. Gratton and Moen argue that public criticism of child labor encouraged immigrants to conform to American social norms and remove their children from the workforce. Their findings reveal a higher probability of child labor among recently arrived immigrants.[32] (This partly explains why there was a greater likelihood that China-born children would work.) A number of other factors also influenced the decline of Chinese child labor. The pressures of anti-Chinese politicians, the creation of state and federal laws regulating child labor, and the eventual growth in the number of two-parent families—with their increased emphasis on the importance of education—combined to reduce the number of Chinese children in the workforce by the early twentieth century.

THE ANTI-CHINESE MOVEMENT AND CHINESE LABOR

Anti-Chinese hostilities intensified in the 1870s and 1880s, as white workingmen increasingly identified Chinese laborers as an economic threat. During that same period, Chinese laundrymen and domestic servants became a common sight in white, middle-class neighborhoods. As discussed in the previous chapter, by 1870, 388 Chinese children age sixteen and under (25 percent) lived as domestics in non-Chinese households. An additional 179 (12 percent) worked in laundries in predominately white neighborhoods. By 1870 the Chinese dominated the laundry business, and by 1882 there were 176 Chinese laundries scattered around San Francisco.[33] The location of Chinese laundries in white neighborhoods and the presence of Chinese domestic servants in white families fostered further fears of the potentially contaminating influences of the Chinese. In 1880 the Workingmen's Party of California insisted that Chinese servants and laundrymen carried germs into the households of white families, creating "a perfect network of contagion and infection."[34] The presence of Chinese men and boys in their neighborhoods —often in their very homes—aroused deep-seated racial tensions and fears in some whites. In addition to the economic argument, anti-Chinese rhetoric depicted Chinese laborers as a source of disease and a moral threat to white women and children.

Journalists and public health officials cited examples of Chinese immorality and raised the specters of disease and sexual perversion to discourage the employment of Chinese domestics.[35] In 1876 Sarah E. Henshaw, writing for *Scribner's Monthly*, offered a warning to women who hired Chinese domestic servants: "They come here with a secret sense of superiority to us all as barbarians, and a secret contempt for women in particular as inferior beings, which makes it hard for them to submit to the control of the mistress of a family. Therefore they become 'uppish' quite as readily as other servants." She further warned that Chinese men could not be trusted and argued that "no matter how good a Chinaman may be, ladies never leave their children with them, especially little girls."[36] Such admonitions contributed to the general increasing hostility toward Chinese laborers in the late nineteenth century.

The anti-Chinese movement also frequently cited examples of filth in Chinese factories to substantiate their arguments against Chinese immigration. During the smallpox epidemic of the 1870s, city health officer John L. Meares testified before a congressional committee that the Chinese concealed cases of smallpox among laborers in factories. Meares insisted that he witnessed a smallpox victim working in a slipper factory among hundreds of piles of slippers. Senator Augustus A. Sargent from California asked Meares, "Would those slippers absorb the poison, and going out be worn by people, thus communicate the disease to them?" Meares replied, "It is generally understood among medical men that that is one way of transmitting the disease, especially in woolen goods." Meares's testimony reflected public fears of the spread of contagious disease from Chinatown into white neighborhoods.[37] In 1880 G. B. Densmore complained that Chinese cigar makers "take a cigar in their mouth and put spit on it, in order to get the shine on it—what is called a Chinese polish. The using of spittle on cigars is peculiarly a Chinese creation."[38] Critics similarly charged Chinese laundrymen with unsanitary practices through the use of the mouth blower in ironing laundry. The worker blew air through a brass tube to sprinkle water on the laundry as he ironed. The popular press began to criticize the unsanitary implications of this method of spraying laundry and painted the Chinese laundryman as a health threat.[39]

In response to the demands of a growing anti-Chinese contingent in the city, officials passed a series of ordinances to regulate Chinese labor and harass Chinese workers. In 1870 a local ordinance specifically targeted the traditional practices of Chinese laundrymen by outlawing the use of baskets carried on poles. Next, the San Francisco Board of Supervisors passed a quarterly tax of $15.00 for every person employed in a Chinese laundry.[40] Between 1873 and 1884, the city passed fourteen ordinances designed to regulate these laundries. City officials insisted that the ordinances were necessary to protect the health and safety of the general population. One ordinance required business owners to obtain a license for laundries operating in wooden buildings. The penalty for noncompliance was a $1,000 fine or six months in jail. Although city officials ostensibly intended these laws to apply to all laundry operators regardless of race, the selective enforcement of the new ordinances clearly discriminated against Chinese business owners. In 1885 the board rejected all of the Chinese applications for licenses while granting all but one of the licenses sought by non-Chinese. The Chinese laundrymen decided to challenge this inequality by remaining open for business. The owner of the Yick Wo laundry resisted the law, was arrested by San Francisco police, and challenged the decision in the courts. With the help of the Chinese laundry guild, Tung Hing Tong, he appealed his case all the way to the U.S. Supreme Court. In 1886 the Chinese American community won a major victory with the *Yick Wo v. Hopkins* decision. The court ruled that to arbitrarily discriminate against Chinese laundries was a denial of the Fourteenth Amendment right to equal protection under the law.[41] This victory, however, did not eliminate the image of Chinese laborers as threats to white American families.

Although the ordinances passed after the *Yick Wo* decision tended to be less overtly racist, San Francisco police ultimately determined how these ordinances would be enforced. In 1897 police conducted a number of raids on Chinese laundries, basing their actions on an ordinance that required laundries to cease work after ten o'clock at night and on Sundays. When a clergyman complained that the noise from a Chinese laundry interfered with his Sunday church services, the police responded by arresting the laundry's occupants. The police then moved on to other businesses, arresting ninety-four Chinese laundrymen in a single morning.[42] Although later ordinances failed to specifically mention the Chinese, their intended target was clear. In 1898 the Board of Supervisors passed an ordinance to regulate the sanitary conditions of cigar factories. Several sections of the ordinance targeted the Chinese by prohibiting sleeping, cooking, and the smoking of opium in a factory. The ordinance reflected public health fears by outlawing the placing of cigars in the mouth, the spraying of water from the mouth, and spitting on the floors. The ordinance also prohibited individuals suffering from contagious or infectious diseases from working, sleeping, lodging, or remaining in a cigar factory.[43] While these new laws improved the overall sanitation of such factories, the underlying intent was clearly to drive the Chinese out of business. Attacks on Chinese business practices rarely specified Chinese child or female laborers because of white leaders' tendency to generalize about the Chinese workforce and use homogenous terms that rarely differentiated age or gender. Chinese laborers remained the intended target of the laws.

The success of anti-Chinese labor leaders in eliminating the Chinese as a source of labor and competition is the first factor to consider when examining the decline of child labor. The passage of the Chinese Exclusion Act in 1882 and the creation of a vast array of laws targeting Chinese businesses eventually forced many Chinese immigrants to return home. The Chinese population in San Francisco declined from 21,745 in 1880 to 13,954 in 1900. In 1870, prior to Chinese exclusion, about 70 percent of Chinese children age sixteen and under labored in San Francisco; by 1900 only about 10 percent of children in this age range were working.[44]

A frequent complaint of anti-Chinese writers was that the Chinese contributed little to the economic well-being of the state and only drained the local economy. George B. Morris wrote: "As quick as John Chinaman receives his wages all but what he actually needs for his living he ships back to China so that the money he earns in this country never circulates among us again."[45] James Whitney in 1888 insisted that white men could not compete with the frugal lifestyles of Chinese laborers: "Competition with Chinese labor is simply competition with the conditions under which the Chinese laborer chooses to exist. But the Caucasian can neither eat the food, nor breathe the air, nor sleep in the dens that are opulence and comfort to the Chinese coolie."[46] The popular press often referred to the system of contract labor utilized by the Chinese as "coolie" labor. The use of the term "coolie" indicated a comparison of Chinese labor with African slavery, in part because of the fraud, graft, kidnapping, and generally abhorrent conditions that characterized the coolie trade in the West Indies and South America in the mid-nineteenth century. Chinese immigrants arriving in California came primarily via the credit-ticket system, in which they owed their debt to a broker for the cost of their passage to America, rather than the coolie system, in which immigrants agreed to a term of service. However, the association of all Chinese labor with coolie labor remained a powerful rhetorical tool in California after the Civil War.[47] Just as the term "slavery" indicated the inferior status of black labor, the term "coolieism" was associated with inferior Chinese labor.[48] Chinese child laborers inherited these stereotypical constructions that positioned them as threats to white children and families.

Labor organizations and political parties repeatedly pointed out the devastating effects of Chinese immigration on white children. These groups tended to cite the impact of the growing Chinese labor force on the availability of jobs for America's youth. In an 1888 mass meeting, the Workingmen's Party of San Francisco insisted that the presence of the Chinese reduced white youths to the position of "idle vagabonds" and effectively prohibited their "finding work to make an honest living."[49] In the 1901 debate over the reenactment of Chinese exclusion, the San Francisco Board of Supervisors called a meeting of over 3,000 delegates to the Chinese Exclusion Convention. The members of the convention issued a memorial addressed to the president and Congress that again appealed to the labor issue. This memorial specifically attacked Chinese agricultural laborers and questioned whether "the boys and girls of the fields and of the orchards [should] be deprived of their legitimate work in the harvest?"[50] These appeals clearly represent the anxiety felt by labor leaders about the perceived negative impact that a cheap Chinese labor force had on the economic opportunities available to white working-class men, women, and children.[51]

Despite these pleas, a few ardent defenders of Chinese immigration insisted on the overall efficiency and economic benefits of a Chinese labor force. The Reverend Otis Gibson, a prominent Methodist minister and former missionary to the Chinese, argued that Chinese labor actually benefited the economy by reducing the price of labor and products, therefore making it possible for white families to live and thrive in California.[52] Critics dismissed his testimony as biased by his desire to recruit converts to the church. Yet, business owners who profited from Chinese labor tended to agree with Gibson's conclusions. William H. Jessup, a manufacturer of matches in San Francisco, also testified to the benefits of Chinese labor. When asked by a congressional investigation committee in 1877 to compare Chinese workers with white boys and girls, Jessup said that the Chinese "were more attentive to their business; there was no fooling or leaving of their work. They would stay and work, and they were satisfied with the wages that they made, depending all the while on the facility in getting along faster, turning out more work after a while, and they would learn."[53] Jessup insisted that, unlike white boys, Chinese laborers refrained from talking, fooling, and fighting while on the job. Jessup's Chinese workers were men and boys ranging in age from fourteen to thirty-six. Upon further questioning from members of the committee, Jessup also testified to the honesty and cleanliness of his Chinese workers, responding in part to the frequent accusations of the anti-Chinese contingent.[54] Gibson and Jessup contributed to the creation of a new image of Chinese children and adults as model workers.

The Chinese American community and their white allies also responded to anti-Chinese attacks by criticizing the work ethic of other immigrants. One anonymous Chinese man insisted that "red-handed members of the Italian Mafia—a society of murderers—the most ignorant class in Ireland, Wales, and England, the scum of Russia, and the human dregs of Europe generally are welcome, but the clean, hard-working Chinaman is excluded."[55] Chinese immigrant Lee Chew also resented the prejudice against Chinese workers and noted that the "Irish fill the almshouses and prisons and orphan asylums, Italians are among the most dangerous of men, Jews are unclean and ignorant. Yet they are all let in, while Chinese, who are sober or duly law abiding, clean, educated and industrious, are shut out."[56] The Chinese American community and their allies promoted an alternate image of the Chinese worker as an industrious and superior laborer. In contrasting Chinese laborers with African American and Irish workers, white capitalists also declared the Chinese a more reliable and hardworking labor force. This early strategy of comparing minority groups suggests the nineteenth-century origins of the model-minority myth of the 1960s.[57]

Anti-Chinese labor organizations eventually succeeded in shutting down many Chinese businesses and driving Chinese adults and children out of the labor force. White workers demanded boycotts of Chinese-made goods and factories that employed Chinese labor. In the 1870s the Anti-Chinese Union of San Francisco formed with the goals of ending Chinese labor, discouraging Chinese immigration, and compelling "the Chinese living in the United States to withdraw from the country." The organization's constitution called for each member of the club to pledge to not employ Chinese workers or purchase Chinese goods. The club determined to publish the names of individuals and corporations that employed Chinese and to encourage a general boycott of such businesses. Although the constitution required members to refrain from abusing Chinese men and to discourage "unprovoked assaults" on Chinese residents, the very existence of the organization served to further exacerbate hostilities toward the Chinese.[58] In the 1870s white cigar makers urged a general boycott of Chinese-made cigars and explicitly advertised their own cigars as "Made with White Labor Only."[59] While not completely driving the Chinese from the industry, these businessmen did succeed in greatly reducing the number of Chinese cigar makers in San Francisco. In 1870, for example, 90 percent of the city's cigar makers were Chinese; only a decade later, their ranks made up only 33 percent of the total.[60] Similarly, in shoe manufacturing, the Knights of St. Crispin organized to drive the Chinese from the market. Employers began to replace Chinese workers with white women and children. The Chinese responded by opening their own firms in direct competition with white businesses. However, competition from the East resulted in the decline of the boot and shoe industry in California by the turn of the century, and therefore the number of Chinese children working in these industries also declined.[61]

Although parents may have attempted to protect their children, Chinese youth directly experienced anti-Chinese hostilities.[62] In the summer of 1877, anti-Chinese sentiment erupted into large-scale violence. The trouble began on the night of July 23, when the Workingmen's Party of the United States held a demonstration in support of striking railroad workers in the East. Frustrated by economic depression, unemployment, and the railroad monopoly, the workingmen found a scapegoat in the Chinese. Sometime around 9:00 P.M., someone in the crowd yelled "On to Chinatown!," and a group of rioters launched an attack on over twenty Chinese laundries. In the frenzy of the evening, a number of men pelted the Chinese Methodist mission home with rocks. Although they were badly frightened, none of the Chinese women and children who resided there were seriously injured. The rioting continued for two more nights, resulting in several deaths and hundreds of thousands of dollars worth of property damage. In September of that year, Denis Kearney formed the Workingmen's Party of California.[63] This group united with other anti-Chinese and labor organizations to drive the Chinese out of San Francisco industries.

The inflammatory speeches of Kearney and the Workingmen's Party created a hostile attitude toward all Chinese in San Francisco, and children often could not find a refuge from the violence. George Lem recalled his terrifying experience as a servant working outside of Chinatown: "I was walking along Kearny Street. I had a queue then and had on my round cap and long coat, and a lot of boys knocked off my cap, pulled my queue, and threw rocks at me and bruised my head and made it bleed. I was living with a family there then, the Freemans. . . . I helped in the kitchen, fixing vegetables, and they taught me. . . . I was just a little boy and I ran home crying. They fixed me all up and then gave me a police whistle and told me the next time anything like that happened to blow it and the policeman would come."[64] Some Chinese parents, unnerved by the violence of the period, chose to remove their children safely across the ocean to China. In June 1878 Lee Hee Wah, keeper of a San Francisco joss house, determined to send his five American-born children to China, citing concern about their safety following the Kearney riots. The children, all under age ten, apparently remained with their mother in China while their father returned to the United States.[65] Lee Hee Wah made the difficult decision of breaking up his family in order to better provide for their physical security.

Even after the chaos of the Kearney era died down, Chinese children experienced continued hostility. In 1899, after health officials quarantined Chinatown, Hugh Liang's mother became increasingly concerned about the safety of her children. White boys initiated fights with Liang and his brothers, using taunts such as "Ching Chong Chinamen, go back to China." Mrs. Liang decided to return to China with the younger children.[66] Gradually, anti-Chinese sentiment caused a decline in the number of Chinese child laborers, as parents made the decision to withdraw their children from the labor market.

Although the intensity of the anti-Chinese movement was certainly a major factor in reducing child labor in Chinatown, a second factor was the emergence of state and national efforts to impose limits on all child labor in the early twentieth century. While not directly intended to help Chinese children, these efforts reduced the overall number of child laborers in the United States. California reformers pushed for child-labor laws beginning in the 1870s. As early as 1878, the California legislature made it a misdemeanor for children under sixteen to work in "public musical, dancing, or acrobatic exhibitions; or for any indecent or immoral purposes; or in any mendicant or wandering business; or in any unhealthful or dangerous occupation."[67] In 1889 the state legislature passed a law regulating the hours and employment of minors. This law stated that no child under age eighteen could work more than sixty hours a week in a manufacturing, mercantile, or mechanical establishment and forbade children under ten from working in these industries at all. The law further required employers to keep a careful account of all laborers under age sixteen, recording the number of hours they worked each week.[68] These new laws, however, were only sporadically enforced and did little to help Chinese children employed as domestic servants or working long hours on piecework at home.

Reformers especially objected to child labor because of the dangerous conditions that children often faced on the job. The Chinese mortuary records highlight a few cases of work-related child deaths. In October 1875 Ah Ying, a fourteen-year-old domestic servant working for Captain Batchelder on Clay Street, started a fire in the kitchen stove with coal oil. When the can of coal oil ignited in the boy's hand, an explosion followed. With his clothes on fire, the boy rushed into the street, screaming for help. Although local citizens assisted him, the boy suffered fatal burns. He died the next day at the City and County Hospital.[69]

Missionaries working among the Chinese population in San Francisco were the first to raise the issue of child labor in Chinatown. In the 1880s missionaries called public attention to the presence of Chinese child laborers and the dangerous conditions they faced. Emma Cable referred to the case of a girl laborer in the 1888 annual report of the Woman's Foreign Missionary Society: "I may mention the case of the Little Tobacco Waif whom I found in a cigar factory on Pacific street, at the tender age of four, stripping tobacco leaves, surrounded by fifty or sixty men, in an atmosphere that would poison you. I could only remain a few moments to teach her, and paid her master for the time I had taken her from her work."[70] Although such accounts were often laced with anti-Chinese rhetoric, the missionaries truly desired to help the women and children of Chinatown.

Protestant missionaries openly criticized and condemned the *mui tsai* system as diabolical. Resurrecting images of African slavery and associating the system with coolie labor, missionaries emphasized the coerced and involuntary nature of child domestic servitude in Chinatown. As discussed in more detail in chapter 5, missionaries in San Francisco often battled for custody of Chinese girls on the grounds that they had been forced into an abusive and cruel system of "Chinese slavery." Missionary literature emphasized the lack of freedom of Chinese girl servants and foreshadowed their ultimate fate as sexual slaves. Little girls are "never allowed to step out into God's free sunshine" but instead "are compelled to work hard, often under cruel treatment, until old enough to be sold into a life of shame."[71] Missionaries fought to remove these "slave girls" from their homes in an effort to liberate them from bondage.

In 1901, however, Chinese consul general Ho Yow countered the claims of missionaries and defended the *mui tsai* system. In a public statement, the consul general argued that it "is an apprentice system, not a system of slavery." Ho Yow explained that the system served as a form of protection for poor girls, offering them food, clothing, and shelter rather than a "much more deplorable fate." He further insisted that "it is unjust and unwarranted to class these apprentices with the unfortunates who are forced into real slavery." Faced with no immediate solution to the poverty in China, the consul general argued that "the system is necessary and the good that results therefrom must be apparent."[72] This debate reflected a larger schism in American and Chinese—or perhaps, more accurately, in working-class and middle-class—ideas of the purpose and function of child labor.

Beginning in the mid-nineteenth century, the American middle class increasingly viewed childhood as a period of innocence, during which an individual required protection from the negative influences of the outside world.[73] However, few working-class children experienced the education or sheltered leisure time enjoyed by middle-class children. The labor of working-class children was often essential to the survival of the family. The debate over child labor increasingly became a moral conflict over the economic usefulness of children. While child-labor advocates valued the economic benefits of child labor, reformers defended the sentimental value of the child and childhood.[74] Beginning in the early twentieth century, a number of social reformers began to draw national attention to the issue of child labor. In April 1904 the National Child Labor Committee (NCLC) was formed to combat the problem. Although NCLC members rarely addressed the specific needs of Chinese children, they did recognize the impact of child labor on children in general. According to the 1900 U.S. census, 1,750,178 children between the ages of ten and fifteen were working. By 1910 over 2 million children in the same age group were employed. Reformers battled against popular opinion and a tradition of child labor among agricultural communities. Manufacturers insisted on the benefits of child labor in preventing juvenile delinquency and recognized the profit potential in piecework produced by low-paid women and children. Parents frequently relied on the extra income of their children. Reformers responded to all of these arguments by insisting that child labor threatened the health and limited the educational opportunities of America's youth.[75]

These conflicting ideas are apparent in discussions about a variety of types of child labor in Chinatown. In addition to criticizing the *mui tsai* system, missionaries and social welfare workers also condemned the employment of children in industrial piecework. Marjory White, working for the War Work Council of the YWCA, noted in her observations of children at work in Chinatown that parents frequently forced their children to work long hours to contribute to the family economy. The children worked for minimal wages in unsanitary and unsafe conditions. White observed that the unhealthy conditions in these homes were often "dark, damp, and miserable," with children working in artificial light. The theme of coerced and dangerous labor repeatedly recurred in the missionary literature. Reformers described piecework as a form of slavery imposed by parents desiring to profit from the labor of their children. White condemned piecework by mothers as dangerous to the welfare of the entire family: "Her home duties are neglected and her position as mother ignored for the sake of a paltry bit of silver."[76]

Protestant missionaries often intervened in cases where they believed that parents had forced Chinese children to work. Carrie Davis of the Methodist mission home in San Francisco rescued Helen Lau from her home in 1912 on the grounds that her parents had forced her to labor in an Oakland cannery for $1.50 a day. Davis further questioned whether the girl's father was actually her biological father. Although Lau insisted that the man was her father and expressed a desire to return to her parents and her work, Davis petitioned for legal guardianship, arguing that Lau was practically a slave girl. Alameda superior court judge Frank Ogden returned Lau to the custody of her parents, citing insufficient evidence that the father had mistreated the child. Ogden also believed that there was little evidence to support Davis's contention that the child was not the biological daughter of the Chinese couple.[77] Davis obviously suspected that the child was actually a domestic slave intended for a future life of forced prostitution. Lacking strong evidence for her theory, she had turned to the controversial issue of child labor as a means of garnering support for her cause and gaining custody of the girl.

Protestant missionaries instituted a regimen of domestic chores in the mission homes and often hired out children as agricultural field workers and domestics in white homes. Yet, despite their simultaneous condemnation of child factory labor, industrial piecework, and the *mui tsai* system, they apparently did not consider this to be a hypocritical contradiction of their own ideals. The distinction hinged on the missionaries' conclusion that the labor of mission girls was neither coerced nor intended solely for the profit of others. Instead, the domestic training in the missions, which included sewing for factories, was intended to teach habits of industriousness, thrift, and discipline. After spending their school vacation canning apricots in San Jose, the girls from the Presbyterian mission home bought material to make their own dresses and hats. The *Oakland Tribune* praised the girls for their independence and ambition.[78] Missionary literature often emphasized that the mission girls enjoyed the fruits of their own labor to distinguish this work from other, more dangerous forms of child labor.

The campaign against child labor in California earned a significant victory in 1905 with the passage of a new state law that severely restricted child labor under age eighteen. Compulsory school-attendance laws required children to attend school during the day. Children over the age of twelve could work on school holidays and during summer breaks with a vacation permit. To acquire such a permit, a student had to seek written approval from school authorities. Children between the ages of fourteen and sixteen could apply for "an age and schooling certificate" to authorize work after school. The superintendent of schools could also issue this certificate to grant a child the right to work during daytime school hours if the student could demonstrate competence in reading and writing English or was enrolled in a night school. In exceptional cases, such as illness preventing a parent from working, the law allowed a child over age twelve to work to support the family. Minors could work for no more than nine hours a day or fifty-four hours in a week. The law also strictly regulated the type of work minors could perform. Lawmakers continually redefined these rules, but generally, the law forbade children from work that involved heavy machinery or dangerous conditions.[79] These new laws reflected a shift in public sentiment against child labor.

Social reformers, dominated by members of the middle and upper classes, vowed to continue the campaign to eliminate child labor through both state and federal lobbying efforts. In 1912 the federal government created the U.S. Children's Bureau with the intent of abolishing child labor, reducing infant and maternal mortality, improving child health, and obtaining care for children with special needs. The bureau immediately began to conduct investigations of infant mortality and child labor while pushing for federal legislative reforms. In 1916 Congress finally passed the Keating-Owen Act, which employed the interstate commerce clause to prohibit the interstate shipment of goods produced by child labor. The Supreme Court, however, struck down the act two years later, declaring it an unconstitutional expansion of congressional authority.[80]

By 1920 state and federal laws had succeeded in significantly reducing the number of child laborers. The 1920 census recorded the number of children working as just over 1 million. Considering the 15.5 percent increase in population within that age group, the percentage of working children actually had declined 9.9 percent since 1910.[81] The number of Chinese children employed in San Francisco also drastically declined. Whereas census enumerators found that 70 percent of Chinese children age sixteen and under were working in 1870, only 10 percent of children that age had occupations in 1900, and fewer than 4 percent were working in 1920.[82] These numbers, however, most likely do not include children employed part-time, after school, or working at home in the evenings.

Despite significant success, the NCLC failed to completely eliminate industrial homework.[83] Sewing factories in Chinatown employed Chinese women and children to finish overalls, aprons, shirts, nightgowns, and blouses. Restaurants hired children to shell shrimp. Women and children worked in one-room shops or in their homes. Although not recorded as "laborers" by census enumerators, many children nevertheless worked for hours in the home before and after school.[84] "A Survey of Race Relations," a document composed in the early 1920s, dramatically recounted the story of fifteen-year-old Ah Seen, who worked in a garment factory every day after school. She worked half days on Saturdays before returning home to wash the family

laundry. The child died of tuberculosis in May 1924, just four months after her high school graduation. The anonymous author noted that Ah Seen's parents "were kindly and well-meaning but they did not realize the rights and needs of an adolescent child."[85] The stated intent of the document was to raise awareness about the continued existence of child labor within the Chinese American community.

The third factor that contributed to a reduction in the number of Chinese child workers was an increase in the number of two-parent, merchant-class families in Chinatown. According to the 1920 census, an overwhelming 96 percent of children age sixteen and under in Chinatown listed their primary occupation as "at home" or "at school." This development corresponds with the increase in the number of two-parent families in Chinatown. In 1870, 70 percent of Chinese children worked, and the vast majority (59 percent) lived in apparently fictive family relationships in predominately male or female boardinghouses. Only 7 percent lived in two-parent households. By 1920 enumerators recorded a major reduction in the number of Chinese children at work (4 percent) and a dramatic increase in the number of children living in two-parent families (70 percent). The manuscript census data from Sacramento and Oakland reveals a similar inverse relationship between the percentage of children working and the percentage of children living in two-parent families.

In addition, the affluence of families in Chinatown appeared to be improving, as evidenced by the increase in the percentage of families headed by fathers employed in professional or trade-based occupations. Census data suggests that in 1870, over 60 percent of primary wage earners in two-parent homes worked in agriculture, domestic/personal service, or artisan/manufacturing positions. Only 36 percent of the heads of household in two-parent families could be classified as working in professional or trade-based occupations. However, by 1920 the trend had reversed: over 60 percent of two-parent families were in the professional or trade category and only 27 percent were in agriculture, domestic/personal service, or artisan/manufacturing positions.[86] This reflected the advancing socioeconomic status of Chinese families already living in San Francisco and the stricter enforcement of the exclusion laws, which promoted the immigration of more affluent Chinese families. This demographic change in the Chinese American community served as an additional factor reducing the number of child laborers in Chinatown.

Working-class Chinese families continued to live in Chinatown and depend, in part, on the labor of their children. These families frequently shared crowded tenements with other families, prostitutes, and laboring men. Families packed into tiny rooms, and some even took in additional boarders to help pay the expenses. Several rooms of people shared washing and cooking facilities. Women often found it awkward to live side by side with large groups of laboring men.[87] Working-class children struggled with school and chores and sometimes went to work to help with finances. The children of small business owners often recalled living in the rear of or above the family store, sharing their private space with the public operations of the business. Effie Lai remembered living in the back of her father's garment factory on Clay Street. The long cutting table served as a workspace during the day and converted to the children's bed at night. As many as three children could sleep on the table together.[88] Family life and work life were integrated, and there was little separation of public and private space.

Unlike their working-class counterparts whose families depended upon their labor, children born into educated, affluent Chinese American families enjoyed the sheltered childhood prized by American middle-class society.[89] They could afford to live in single-family dwellings with several rooms for the various members of the family. Wealthier merchants often hired servants to assist their wives with the cooking, laundering, and cleaning. Children of the middle and upper classes enjoyed more privacy and leisure time than working-class Chinese children. A few merchant-class Chinese families chose to move outside the confines of Chinatown, although discrimination and segregation hindered their efforts to move into white neighborhoods.

Some middle-class children did work part-time after school or in the evening hours at home, but these children were less likely to work because of sheer economic necessity.[90] Merchant-class, two-parent households generally provided a more stable economic environment that freed children from the burdens of work, but some parents insisted that their children work at least part-time in order to learn the value of hard work. Edwar Lee's father was a prominent herb doctor who hoped to instill self-reliance and discipline in his boys by requiring them to work. As one of nine children, Lee believed that his father had enough to cope with in providing food, clothing, and shelter for the family. Lee cooked, cleaned, and served meals for a French-Italian family for about $2.50 a week. Throughout his high school years, Lee continued working as a domestic after school. During the summers he also worked as a fruit picker in the Sacramento River Valley.[91] As their numbers grew, middle-class Chinese parents tended to keep their children out of the labor force until adolescence. The main emphasis of childhood had shifted from work to education.

Chinese children growing up in nineteenth-century Chinatown were important contributors to the family economy. Most Chinese child immigrants between the ages of ten and sixteen arrived in nineteenth-century San Francisco with the intention of working and sending remittances home to China. These children worked predominately as domestic servants, *mui tsai*, and laundrymen. A small number of children also worked in factories and at home alongside their mothers doing piecework. Their labor helped to ensure the survival of their families. The work was tedious and part of the grueling reality of growing up an immigrant child in industrial America.

The presence of Chinese laborers on the West Coast aroused intense hostility beginning in the 1870s. These anti-Chinese tensions coincided with the growth of male Chinese domestic servants in white households. Chinese domestic servants and cooks earned good wages as the demand for their services increased among the white middle class. Chinese boys employed as domestics became a visible reminder of the economic threat of Chinese labor. In addition, some middle-class Americans increasingly questioned whether the Chinese presence in white households would have a corrupting moral influence on their own families. Business owners, on the other hand, defended the Chinese as hardworking, essential contributors to the American economy, while the Chinese American community often allied with sympathetic whites in promoting an image of Chinese laborers as model workers. Growing anti–child labor sentiment challenged the presence of children in the workforce. Missionaries and reformers sometimes intervened in Chinese families in an effort to protect children from the negative effects of child labor. These encounters often revealed racial and class tensions, as reformers attempted to impose American middle-class values on working-class Chinese families.

By the early twentieth century, Chinese American families increasingly embraced the middle-class ideal of a sheltered childhood. Child-rearing experts insisted that young children were precious and in need of protection, while older children required careful guidance and education. The dramatic shift from an emphasis on child labor to education in Chinatown reflected not only the success of anti-Chinese leaders in driving the Chinese working class out of the labor force and the triumph of Progressive reformers in limiting child labor, but also the greater financial security achieved by an increasing number of two-parent families in Chinatown. As parents became less dependent on children's contributions to the family economy, they began to emphasize the importance of education and embraced progressive Chinese and American ideals of childhood, which stood in strict opposition to child labor. By 1919 the state permitted probation officers to investigate and enforce both the child-labor and compulsory-education laws.[92] Children of the working class continued to work part-time or perform piecework at home, but most parents insisted on at least an elementary education for their children. Merchant-class children enjoyed both the benefits of an education and the luxury of leisure time. Yet, as the next chapter reveals, Chinese children and their parents often had to battle for the right to an education, which was not always free and was rarely equal to that available to other middle-class American children.

4   CHALLENGING SEGREGATION

CHINESE CHILDREN AT SCHOOL

San Francisco, Feb. 22, 1886

My Dear Friend—

This is a very cloudy and dark day. There are not many children in school, some boys do not know their lessons, some boys are standing on the floor, teacher will punish them because they were lazy. It is pretty near twelve o'clock, now, Ah Took and Ah Tong are playing with their basket.

This is February 22nd, General Washington's birthday. I see many flags on the houses. I see thirty-eight white stars. American boys not go to school to-day. China boys go all time. We have learned from Holy Bible that Jesus love China boys all the same as American boys—when the heart good.

Your Chinese boy, nine years old.

    —AH BENG, IN *Thirteenth Annual Report of the Occidental Branch of the Woman's Foreign Missionary Society*

Ah Beng was a student at the Presbyterian mission school in 1886 and his reference to the Bible and Jesus in this letter reflected the Christian emphasis of his education. At first glance, Ah Beng's letter, written at the request of his schoolteacher, appears as a child's simple recitation of the day's events. However, upon closer examination, this letter reveals the variety of competing interests at work in San Francisco's early Chinatown and hints at the impact of a segregated society on Chinese children. Mission schools arose to meet the Chinese American community's desire for education. Public education for Chinese children in San Francisco was available only sporadically during the 1850s and 1860s. Exclusionists, insisting that Chinese children represented a moral threat and a source of contagion to white children, succeeded in preventing Chinese children from acquiring any public education in San Francisco from 1871 to 1885. Chinese parents took advantage of the mission schools even as they fought for the reopening of a public school in Chinatown. Although they eventually succeeded in securing their right to establish public schools, a policy of segregation prevented Chinese children from receiving an equitable educational experience.

By the late 1880s, children growing up in Chinatown and desiring an American education chose between attendance at one of the private schools or at the segregated Chinese Public School. Ah Beng's reference to the observance of George Washington's birthday reveals the curricular emphasis of both the public and the mission schools in attempting to inculcate foreign-born schoolchildren with patriotic American values. These early efforts foreshadowed twentieth-century Progressive campaigns that promoted Americanization. Chinese parents, although not opposed to American education, attempted to counter some of the negative influences of Christianization and Americanization by sending their children to Chinese-language and Chinese-culture schools in Chinatown. Most Chinese children attended both American and Chinese schools, and Ah Beng probably attended Chinese school in the afternoons or on the weekends. Attendance at both Chinese and American schools contributed to a feeling of dual identity common to many second-generation immigrant children. Ah Beng's letter hints at his struggle to cope with the feeling of living on the margins of two worlds. He points out the unfairness that "American boys not go to school to-day," but "China boys go all time." He concludes his letter with a reminder to himself that "we have learned from Holy Bible that Jesus love China boys all the same as American boys—when the heart good." He appears to be struggling with the contradiction between the Christian teachings of egalitarianism and the segregated realities of his daily existence. Although just a child, Ah Beng at some level felt the impact of segregation and recognized the inequalities of the educational system in San Francisco.

Even as Ah Beng's teachers emphasized the equality of all children in the eyes of God, forced educational segregation denied these children full status as American citizens. This chapter will explore how Chinese families fought for the right to a public education and, soon afterward, sought the end of segregation in the school system. We will also examine the variety of strategies that Chinese children adopted to challenge the injustices of segregation and cope with the realities of racism in their daily lives.

Chinese culture traditionally valued education, and many merchant-class parents sacrificed time and money in order to ensure at least an elementary education for their children. Illiteracy rates of immigrants age fourteen and over (compiled by the U.S. commissioner general of immigration from 1899 to 1910) illustrate the value of education in Chinese culture. Chinese immigrants had a 7 percent illiteracy rate, which was considerably higher than the illiteracy rate for Scandinavian (0.4 percent), Scotch (0.7 percent), English (1 percent), Bohemian and Moravian (1.7 percent), or Finnish (1.3 percent) immigrants. Yet, the 7 percent rate of Chinese illiteracy paled in comparison to other immigrant groups, such as Southern Italian (53.9 percent), Mexican (57.2 percent), Turkish (59.5 percent), or Portuguese (68.2 percent) immigrants. More effective enforcement of the Chinese exclusion laws during the early twentieth century limited immigration primarily to members of the merchant class. This fact, coupled with the heavy emphasis on education in Chinese culture, in part accounts for the lower rate of illiteracy among Chinese immigrants.[1]

Whereas most immigrant parents in the late nineteenth and early twentieth centuries did not associate schooling with upward mobility, some groups placed a higher value on education. Polish, Jewish, German, and Chinese immigrants encouraged their children to attend ethnic schools to learn more about their native language and culture.[2] The predominance of mission schools and private Chinese-language schools in San Francisco's Chinatown in the nineteenth century attests to the value that Chinese parents placed on their children's education. Chinese families first had to overcome substantial prejudices just to obtain the right to an education, however. Anti-Chinese hostilities in the 1870s forced the closure of schools for Chinese children, and Protestant mission schools emerged to fill the gap created by the denial of public education. The legal struggle waged by Chinese parents for educational equality in San Francisco and the numerous private schools established in Chinatown are further evidence of the value of education in Chinese American culture.

Beginning as early as the 1850s, discriminatory state and local school laws hindered efforts to secure an equal education for Chinese children. Shortly after the arrival of Chinese immigrants, many Californians reverted to a tradition of racism to discriminate against the Chinese. Anti-Chinese rhetoric frequently mirrored antiblack rhetoric.[3] These prejudices against Chinese and blacks, combined with an anti-Indian attitude, fueled the movement to segregate California's schools in the mid-nineteenth century. In 1854 San Francisco established California's first separate school for black children; the following year, the state legislature passed a law stipulating that state education funds be used only for white children. In his 1858 report, Andrew J. Moulder, state superintendent of public instruction, insisted on the continued segregation of "inferior races," fearing that mixed schools of whites, blacks, Chinese, and Indians would result in the ruin of the schools. Upon the petition of the Chinese community, the first Chinese Public School opened in September 1859 at Stockton and Sacramento Streets. By June 1860 officials decided to convert the school to an evening school in an effort to attract students who worked during the day. That same year, the California legislature passed a law specifically prohibiting "Negro, Mongolian, and Indian" children from attending schools for white children. John Swett replaced Moulder as state superintendent in 1863 and began a gradual liberalization of the state educational policy. The 1864 school law deleted penalties for schools that admitted nonwhite students and allowed the establishment of separate schools when the parents of ten or more black, Asian, or Indian children made a written request. The 1866 law permitted these children to attend school with whites if a school district could not provide for their education in any other way.[4]

In 1870 a new state segregation law provided for the creation of separate schools for black and Indian children but failed to mention the Chinese at all. This justified the decision of the San Francisco Board of Education to shut down the Chinese Public School and deny Chinese children access to even a segregated education. Black and Indian children continued to attend segregated schools. However, the African American community in San Francisco challenged the constitutionality of school segregation in *Ward v. Flood*. In 1874 the California State Supreme Court upheld the principle of separate schools. The following year, the San Francisco Board of Education abolished separate schools for black children due to the expense of maintaining separate facilities but retained the right to segregate students in the future.[5] Black children were thus integrated into the public school system at the same time that San Francisco denied Chinese children an education of any kind—segregated or integrated.

Although legislators removed all mention of race from the state school law in 1880, school officials continued to justify the exclusion of Chinese children under the law that denied admittance to "children of filthy or vicious habits." From 1871 to 1885, the law deprived Chinese children in San Francisco of any public education. California passed a compulsory attendance law in 1874, but the act was rarely enforced and clearly did not apply to the Chinese. Parents turned to the Protestant missions or private tutors to educate their children, while challenging the injustice by appealing to the state legislature, the newspapers, and the courts.[6] In 1878 over 1,300 Chinese residents in San Francisco and Sacramento signed a petition addressed to the senate and assembly of California. The petition noted that although Chinese residents paid property and poll taxes to support the public schools, more than 3,000 school-age Chinese children were excluded from the system. The petitioners insisted that the state should either admit their children to the public schools or establish separate schools for them.[7] Missionaries echoed these concerns and defended the right of the Chinese to a public education. John G. Kerr, a medical doctor with the Presbyterian mission, spoke before the YMCA in San Francisco in 1877. He argued that "every youth has a right to the benefits of our free schools. The Chinese have this right in common with all others; and they pay into the School Fund of this State, in this city alone, over $42,000 per annum, and a large sum in other parts of the State, while all Chinese youth are excluded from the public schools. We ask, will you unite in securing to them this right, and protecting them in the enjoyment of it?"[8]

San Francisco officials responded to the protests of the Chinese American community and others by citing examples of disease and immorality in Chinatown as evidence supporting the denial of public education to Chinese children. In 1880 G. B. Densmore, a San Francisco writer, expressed fears over the potential threat of disease carried by Chinese schoolchildren. Densmore noted that a white missionary teacher taught a private class of Chinese children at the Globe Hotel: "It would seem this lady, however laudable her object may be, wantonly brings a herd of Mongolians together in their very lair, and afterward walks abroad in our streets, coming hither and going thither, and thus disseminating whatever contagious germs these unclean celestials may carry about with them, and which she must of necessity share by contact."[9] A report issued by the Special Committee of the Board of Supervisors in San Francisco in 1885 argued that Chinese children were "born and nurtured in such conditions of immorality and degradation." According to the board, "the laws of morality, and the law of self-protection, must compel our own people to sternly prohibit them from mingling with our children in the public schools, or as companions and playmates." The board proposed that the ultimate solution was an end to Chinese immigration. The report concluded: "Meanwhile, guard well the doors of our public schools, that they do not enter."[10] Densmore and his contemporaries on the Board of Supervisors resurrected the image of Chinese children as moral threats and used these arguments to deny them access to the public schools.

The Chinese community continued to demand the right to education for their children, even if that education was segregated. City officials were hesitant to finance the construction of separate facilities.[11] Some Chinese parents simply chose to defy authorities and send their children to the regular public schools. In 1884, when the principal of Spring Valley School in San Francisco refused to admit Mamie Tape because of her Chinese heritage, her parents, Joseph and Mary Tape, appealed the case all the way to the California Supreme Court. On March 5, 1885, the court ruled in favor of the Tapes, affirming that Chinese children had a right to a public education since no law specifically prohibited Chinese from going to school with whites. Horrified by the court's decision, Assemblyman William May quickly introduced a bill that required all school districts to establish separate facilities for "Mongolians." The bill passed through both houses of the California state legislature, with only one objection. The San Francisco Board of Education quickly opened a new school for Chinese children in an effort to prevent Mamie from attending Spring Valley, forcing her to attend a segregated school.[12] Mamie's mother, Mary, expressed her anger in a letter to the Board of Education:

> Do you call that a Christian act to compel my little children to go so far to a school that is made in purpose for them. My children don't dress like the other Chinese. They look just as phunny amongst them as the Chinese dress in Chinese look amongst you Caucasians. . . . Her playmates is all Caucasians ever since she could toddle around. If she is good enough to play with them! Then is she not good enough to be in the same room and studie with them? You had better come and see for yourselves. See if the Tape's is not the same as other Caucasians, except in features. It seems no matter how a Chinese may live and dress so long as you know they Chinese. Then they are hated as one. There is not any right or justice for them. . . . I guess she is more of a American then a good many of you that is going to prewent [sic] her being Educated.[13]

Mary Tape's letter expressed the resentment of many in the Chinese American community who felt cheated out of their recent court victory. By emphasizing the family's American, middle-class, and Christian values, the Tape family and their white allies hoped not only to gain support for the fight against segregation but also to gain the acceptance of the Tape children in American society. This was a strategy that some Chinese American families would increasingly rely on after the turn of the century. The Tapes also hoped that the physical remoteness of the family home from Chinatown had distanced them from the negative stereotypes that clung to the Chinese in San Francisco. However, the public outcry against the Tape children at Spring Valley only solidified policies of segregation and exclusion.

The response to the Tape case demonstrated the overt hostility of the San Francisco Board of Education to the Chinese community. In an 1886 circular to San Francisco schools, Superintendent Moulder expressed the continued biases of the board against the Chinese in San Francisco. The board adopted a resolution prohibiting principals and teachers from employing, patronizing, or in any way encouraging the Chinese. Moulder expressed his personal opinion toward the Chinese race and insisted that teachers had the duty to save their white students "from contamination and pollution by a race reeking with the vices of the Orient, a race that knows neither truth, principle, modesty nor respect for our laws. The moral and physical ruin already wrought to our youth by contact with these people is fearful."[14] This attitude on the part of school officials and educators pervaded the entire public school system and obviously influenced the children under their instruction.

By the late nineteenth century, the segregation of the Chinese American community in San Francisco had become as pervasive as the system of Jim Crow laws that segregated African Americans. Following the collapse of Reconstruction, separate-coach laws became the basis for the segregation of waiting rooms, public parks, restrooms, ticket offices, and other public buildings. The 1896 *Plessy v. Ferguson* decision by the U.S. Supreme Court affirmed the doctrine of "separate but equal," thus legitimizing the segregation of African Americans in the South and, in effect, Chinese Americans in San Francisco. The black boycott movement against streetcar segregation in the South had the effect of creating a sense of interdependence and solidarity among the African American community.[15] In a similar manner, the battle against school segregation in San Francisco helped to unify and build a common sense of mission among the families of Chinatown. Still, class divisions remained. Some families, such as the Tapes, attempted to distance themselves from working-class Chinese families and Chinatown itself in order to justify their right to utilize the public school system. Similarly, Chinese and African Americans in San Francisco saw little benefit in organizing a unified campaign against school segregation.

A classroom in the Chinese Primary Public School at 920 Clay Street before the 1906 San Francisco earthquake (Postcard from author's collection)

Although the African American community in San Francisco was much smaller than the Chinese American community (representing less than 1 percent of the population in 1870), black families also organized to demand quality education for their children. Rather than combine efforts with the Chinese and form an alliance against school segregation, though, African American leaders consciously chose to separate themselves from the Chinese. San Francisco's African Americans chose to identify themselves with American culture by adopting nativist rhetoric and opposing the immigration of Chinese. The black community resented the economic competition of Chinese labor and viewed the Chinese as foreign corrupters of American families.[16] Blacks and Chinese, therefore, fought similar but separate campaigns for educational equality in San Francisco. While blacks fought for integrated public education in the 1870s, the Chinese were fighting to regain their access to public education. After the Chinese community finally succeeded in winning the right to a segregated public education in 1885, they slowly began to wage a new battle for integrated education. Whereas blacks had obtained the right to integrated education in San Francisco by 1880, the Chinese would remain legally relegated to segregated schools until 1947.[17]

Chinese Children at School : 117

In 1900 census enumerators reported that 33 percent of Chinese children were attending school, a dramatic increase from the 1 percent reported in 1870.[18] The segregated Chinese school offered only primary curriculum; students desiring to advance their studies beyond the primary level were left with few options. Segregation deterred John Jeong from pursuing further studies. After attending the Oriental School (the name of the Chinese Public School after 1906) for two years, Jeong transferred to a public school on Geary Street: "But after I was there a week someone told me it was not for Chinese. We were only supposed to go to the Oriental School. So after that I just studied at home and worked in my brother's store."[19] The Board of Education never authorized the opening of a separate Chinese high school, in part because so few Chinese students continued their education beyond the primary level. Students who completed all the grade levels at the Chinese school and desired to continue their education applied for admittance to one of the local public high schools. In 1900 the Board of Education attempted to prevent Chinese children from entering the public high schools and suggested instead that they remain at the Chinese elementary school. Chinese American community members forced the school board to capitulate after they threatened to withdraw all of their children from the Chinese Primary School, thereby forcing white teachers and the principal out of their jobs.[20]

In the decades following the *Tape v. Hurley* decision, Chinese parents continued to use the examples of their children to fight segregation in the courts. In 1902 Katie Wong Him attended Clement Grammar School for four months before a number of white parents objected to her presence at the school. The Board of Education ordered Katie to attend the primary school for Chinese children. The *San Francisco Call* seemed to sympathize with Katie's story. The reporter wrote that "Katie was happy and for four months she walked home from school with her white schoolmates and took part in their games. Then one day she went home to her father, and with tears in her eyes told him how she had been summoned to the room of the principal of the school and told that she could not go to the school with the white children any more."[21] Katie's father, Dr. Wong Him, a prominent Chinese herb doctor, applied for a writ of mandate to compel the Board of Education to allow his daughter to remain as a student at the Clement Grammar School. Like the Tapes, Him highlighted his class status and attempted to separate the association of his family with working-class Chinese children in

Chinatown. Him argued that since he did not live in the Chinese quarter, his children should be able to attend the nearest public school. Yet, Him also defended the rights of all Chinese children by claiming that educational segregation was based solely on a hatred of the Chinese race. Despite Him's arguments, the court ruled against Katie, declaring that the state had a right to provide separate schools for the children of different races provided that the schools made no discrimination in educational facilities. The judge ordered Katie to attend the Chinese school.[22] The Chinese American community immediately responded by petitioning the Board of Education and the California state legislature. The Chinese Six Companies issued a statement insisting that, as taxpayers, they deserved their fair share of the benefits of the school system. However, both the Board of Education and the state legislature denied the petition.[23] The legal battles continued.

When state and local action failed to yield results, the San Francisco Chinese community appealed their children's cases to the federal government. In 1903 residents from Chinatown met to discuss the issue of segregation in the school system. Chan Chun Seen, former secretary of the consulate, drew up a petition on behalf of the community to President Theodore Roosevelt. The men claimed that over 2,000 Chinese students in San Francisco received a poor education in an unequal, segregated school: "We are not asking a special privilege or a favor, but an equal chance with other American children to obtain an education which will qualify us to be true, genuine and patriotic American citizens."[24] In an effort to gain the support of the white community, the Chinese elite highlighted their Americanness and argued that integrated public school education would help in the process of Americanizing their children. Roosevelt, apparently, did not respond to their petition. Nevertheless, the Chinese American community continued the campaign against segregated education.

In 1906 the Chinese Public School became the Oriental Public School, accommodating not only Chinese but Japanese and Korean students as well. The Japanese government angrily protested the segregation of Japanese American schoolchildren and threatened retaliation. Fearing political repercussions, President Roosevelt finally intervened in the debate. The federal government initially threatened to force the San Francisco Board of Education to abandon its policy of segregating Japanese students by initiating court action against the board. In an effort to avoid legal conflict, however, Roosevelt decided to invite city officials to Washington, D.C., where he negotiated a compromise that struck at the heart of the real issue: San Franciscans' concern with increased Japanese immigration. The 1907 "Gentlemen's Agreement" agreed to lift the segregation order on Japanese American students in exchange for an agreement that Japan would limit the immigration of laborers into the United States. Although this treaty amounted to a major victory for Japanese schoolchildren in San Francisco, the Board of Education still required Chinese and Korean students to attend the Oriental School.[25]

Inspired in part by the success of the Japanese government in protecting the educational rights of their children, the Chinese Consolidated Benevolent Association (CCBA) in 1909 directly petitioned President Roosevelt. Their petition protested the continued segregation of Chinese schoolchildren and asked for presidential intervention. The Six Companies demanded the same justice rendered to the Japanese, pointing out the favorable treatment of Japanese over Chinese immigrants. They requested that Roosevelt take a stand against California's discriminatory school laws. Roosevelt never responded to this petition, either. The CCBA knew that the Chinese government lacked the military might of Japan, which had been demonstrated in the Russo-Japanese War. Despite repeated examples of similar passionate pleas, school segregation for the Chinese remained officially legal in San Francisco for several decades thereafter.[26]

CIRCUMVENTING SEGREGATION AND BATTLING SEXISM

Living in a segregated society presented a number of challenges to Chinese children growing up in early San Francisco. Individual children reacted to discrimination in a variety of ways. Some avoided confrontational situations or repressed their feelings, while others resisted or fought back against prejudice. Many began to identify more strongly with their Chinese heritage.[27] While some Chinese Americans and their white allies legally challenged segregation orders, others simply deceived school authorities. A Japanese boarder living with Clara Lee's family attended the Washington Grammar School. The boy told school authorities that Lee was his sister. Believing that Lee was Japanese and not Chinese, the principal of the Washington School for boys talked to the principal of the Broadway Grammar School for girls, who agreed to allow Lee to attend school there.[28]

While Lee actively pretended to be a Japanese student in order to attend the white school, other children simply failed to state their ethnicity, hoping to pass as non-Chinese. David Young attended the Chinese Baptist mission school until the fourth grade, when his teacher took him to the local white grammar school. Young recalled that the principal must have mistaken him for a Filipino. About one month before he graduated from grammar school, Young had a conversation with another Chinese boy, who believed that he had been admitted under the same misconception. Some white children overheard their conversation and reported it to the principal. School officials immediately insisted that Young return to the Oriental School in Chinatown.[29] After a brief attendance at the Oriental School, Young transferred to Washington Grammar School. It is not entirely clear whether or not the principal of Washington Grammar was aware that Young was Chinese. However, when the principal of the Oriental School complained to the Board of Education about the transfer, the principal of Washington Grammar defended Young's right to remain at his school. The principal's willingness to retain him as a student and his satisfactory progress reports forced the Board of Education to allow him to remain at Washington Grammar.[30] Evidently, school officials exercised some freedom and flexibility in implementing and enforcing the Board of Education's segregation policies.

Young girls faced segregation from American society while struggling with traditional Chinese beliefs against the education of women. As early as the 1870s and 1880s, missionary women attempted to educate Chinese girls, often encountering resistance. In 1886 missionary Emma Cable described the difficulty in gaining parental consent to teach Chinese girls through her program of house visits. However, she found that by appealing directly to the fathers, she was able to gain access to sixteen new students. By the end of her fourth year, she had 100 pupils on her list.[31] Many forward-thinking Chinese merchants openly sought education for their wives and daughters. In 1876 Dr. Li Po Tai offered to pay Presbyterian missionaries to come to his home and instruct his wife and daughters in fancywork and the English language. These requests for private instruction were becoming quite common in the turbulent 1870s, as parents considered it improper and unsafe for their daughters to be seen in public.[32] As the annual reports of the Presbyterian mission revealed, missionary teachers praised the progress of their female pupils and expressed great pride in their accomplishments. Early twentieth-century changes in the roles of women in both China and America eventually led to changes in the lives of Chinese girls.

Historian Judy Yung has argued that the influences of Christianity, acculturation, and Chinese nationalism combined to gradually erode objections to the education of Chinese girls. Whereas missionaries primarily advocated the education of Chinese women as a means of converting the race,

Chinese reformers advocated the emancipation of women as essential to the modernization of China. Chinese children in San Francisco benefited from the agenda of both groups. By the early twentieth century, the leading Chinese-language newspaper in San Francisco, *Chung Sai Yat Po*, openly supported the education of Chinese women and advertised several Protestant girls' schools in Chinatown. It is no coincidence that the newspaper's editor, Ng Poon Chew, was a Presbyterian minister influenced by Christianity, American middle-class ideology, and Chinese nationalism.[33] Despite these influences, many tradition-minded parents continued to resist education for girls into the twentieth century. One woman remembered that after completing grammar school, she asked her father if she could attend high school. Her father said, "You have enough. Be glad that you got through eighth grade. . . . You don't go to school." Her cousins provided her with American newspapers and mystery novels, and she continued her education on her own.[34]

Chinese American children sometimes spoke out in protest of the injustices of segregation and sexism. In 1905 Yuk Ying Lee, a Chinese girl attending Lowell High School, resisted segregation by writing that "children of any nationality except Chinese, even native-born, have enjoyed admission into public schools freely, and may our friends of justice remedy this unjust exception in the near future." Lee went even further by arguing for the educational rights of all Chinese women. Lee criticized parents who conformed to traditional gender roles and denied their daughters the right to an education.[35]

Other Chinese American girls also took a stand against sexism in both American and Chinese society. In 1905 the *San Francisco Call* interviewed a number of Chinese high school girls, who candidly revealed their hopes for the future. The girls also recognized the societal limitations they faced, both as Chinese and as females. Several of the girls expressed a desire to return to China as missionaries or professionals. Others hoped to remain in America, attempting to bridge the gap between Chinese and American culture. The *Call* reporter commented, "Ignorance has been the bane of Chinese women. Give them an education and they meet us on equal footing, even in one generation."[36] By the 1920s it was quite common for girls in Chinatown to enjoy the benefits of an education. About 65 percent of Chinese girls in San Francisco attended the Oriental Public School in 1920.[37] These educated young women would play an important role in defining the future of the Chinese American community.

Parents recognized the importance of quality education in preparing their children for the future. A typical child in Chinatown attended a combination of private and public, segregated and nonsegregated Chinese and American schools. Edwar Lee attended kindergarten and Sunday school at the First Chinese Baptist Church before transferring to the segregated Oriental Public School. After school, he attended the Sung Yuen Tong Chinese School, switching to the Chinese School at the Chinese Congregational church and later at the Methodist church. Lee transferred to the integrated Polytechnic High School after grammar school.[38] For many Chinese parents, education in both American and Chinese schools was essential to training their children to be productive citizens in a transpacific community.[39] The children themselves, however, struggled to successfully meet the academic demands of two different schools. The following sections will examine the children's experiences in each of the three types of schools in Chinatown.

CHINESE MISSION SCHOOLS

By the 1870s a number of Christian missionary organizations had opened schools in Chinatown. The Presbyterians, Baptists, Methodists, Episcopalians, and Congregationalists all provided English-language classes in San Francisco.[40] These schools were supported and partially funded by Chinese merchants, who sought to provide an education for their children when the public school system denied them one.[41] In the 1870s and 1880s, Marian Bokee conducted a school for Chinese children under the auspices of the Woman's Union Mission. The school met daily in the basement of the Old Globe Hotel at Jackson and Dupont Streets. The promotional literature of the Woman's Union Mission clearly stated their goal of evangelizing Chinese women and children, insisting that "the very best way to gather a harvest for the Heavenly Taskmaster, is to get hold of little children, just as young as possible, and train them into habits of virtuous living." The missionaries insisted that the large number of children in the streets of Chinatown presented an excellent opportunity for missionary work: "If China is ever to be made the kingdom of our Lord and of His Christ, it will be mainly done through work among the children."[42] The mission hoped to educate and return the children to China to serve as missionaries to their own people. George B. Morris visited the school around 1870 and noted about forty to fifty Chinese children in attendance.[43]

An important goal of both parents and mission teachers was to educate the children and prepare them for future integration into the public school system. To that end, the missions standardized their curriculum as much as possible to that of public schools, in part by adopting the California state series of textbooks. Students studied English language, spelling, grammar, arithmetic, geography, history, Chinese language, singing, music, sewing, and cooking. However, the Protestant influence of these schools also stressed evangelization.[44] Weekday, evening, and Sunday school programs offered a Christian education through Bible study, recitation of scripture, prayer, and hymn singing.[45] Some Chinese families converted to Christianity, while others ignored this aspect of the education and enjoyed the access to general education offered by the mission schools.

Most children in Chinatown began their education at one of the kindergartens offered by the mission schools. In 1896 Fred Hackett of the *San Francisco Call* visited the Chinese kindergarten opened by the Baptist Home Missionary Society in the old Baptist church at Sacramento Street and Waverly Place. The school provided Christian and secular training for thirty-five children age two to five. The teacher spoke both English and Chinese and provided lessons in English, counting, primary and secondary colors, form, size, motion, and melody. Hackett noted that the children were stringing beads and singing songs on the day he visited. He recorded the lyrics of one song about the birds in the sky:

> Up, up in the sky the little birds fly;
> Down, down in their nests the little birds rest,
> With a wing on the left and a wing on the right,
> We'll let the dear birdies rest all the long night.
>
> When the round sun comes up and the dew floats away,
> "Good morning bright sunshine," the little birds say;
> How bright are the flowers, how green is the wood;
> Our Heavenly Father, how kind and how good![46]

The children also practiced accompanying gestures as they sang the songs. Hackett described in vivid detail the joy and intensity with which the children participated in these activities. The reporter noted the frenzied excitement created by another song about a baby and his toys. "The pounding, the clapping and the tooting in this song were so spiritedly reproduced, especially by the boys, that several of them tired out before the song was over, put their hands into their pockets, sat down on their stools, crossed their legs and rested in speechless silence."[47] These songs and gestures not only served a recreational function but also reinforced the evangelical goals of the mission school.

By 1920 there were five Protestant day schools in San Francisco, serving 434 students in the Chinese community. The majority of the students in these schools were in either kindergarten or the first grade. With basic education provided in the kindergarten and primary day schools, Chinese children could ultimately transfer into the public school system. In addition to the day schools, nine Protestant night schools operated in Chinatown, providing education to 301 students. The pupils of the evening schools tended to be older men and boys who worked during the day. The primary goal of the operators of the day and evening schools was the Christianization of the Chinese community. For Chinese men, women, and children, however, these schools provided not only religious instruction but also, more importantly, English-language instruction that allowed them to increase their socioeconomic status.[48]

THE CHINESE PUBLIC SCHOOL

The Chinese Public School, which operated throughout the 1860s, closed, and reopened in 1885, offered the same curriculum as the regular public grammar schools. The lower grades emphasized reading, writing, spelling, and arithmetic, while the upper levels focused on language, geography, history, and the biographies of American heroes such as Christopher Columbus, George Washington, and Benjamin Franklin.[49] Nineteenth-century American methods of teaching emphasized memorization, drill, obedience, and discipline. Yet, Americans also valued competition, independence, and individuality. Competitive games and ranking helped reinforce these ideals.[50] An 1867 observer of the Chinese Public School in San Francisco described a typical lesson. The teacher had written various English words on the blackboard and required individual students to correctly spell and pronounce each word. The instructor awarded correct answers by moving the successful student to the head of the class, thereby physically separating the child from his or her peers.[51] This system of rewards and punishments encouraged correct memorization of the spelling and pronunciation of English words while celebrating academic achievement.

By the early twentieth century, teachers in the public schools still employed the same method of rote learning. Monotonous reading, frequent repetition, and drilling encouraged simple memorization of key concepts. A 1917 survey of San Francisco schools conducted by the U.S. commissioner of education criticized this lack of creativity and stimulation in education. The commission recommended efforts to avoid simple formalism by allowing students to express their thoughts through drawing and dramatization. With specific regard to the Oriental School, the commission recommended an adjustment of the general curriculum to meet the unique needs of Chinese children. The commission feared that difficulty with the English language hindered the ability of Chinese students to fully absorb their daily lessons and, ultimately, to appropriately assimilate into American society. They recommended that school officials adapt the curriculum and assessment standards to meet the individual needs of Chinese schoolchildren.[52] Generally speaking, the commission recognized that Chinese children in the public schools lacked access to the resources they needed to succeed academically.

The inherent inequities of segregated education reflected the continued dominance of anti-Chinese attitudes. The San Francisco Board of Education spent considerably less money on the education of Chinese children. Whereas the average cost of education per pupil around 1916 was $31.07 in similar-sized, "all grades" schools, the Board of Education spent only $25.07 per student in the Oriental School. In addition, Chinese children endured larger class sizes, with fifty-one students per teacher compared to an average of forty-one students per teacher in integrated white schools.[53] These factors, coupled with the language difficulties faced by Chinese students, no doubt impacted the quality of education in the Oriental School.

Attendance at the segregated public elementary school generally insulated Chinese children from the overt racist attitudes of white peers. However, reality sometimes intruded into the children's daily lives. School textbooks revealed the prejudices of American society toward the Chinese. Janelle Schlimgen Barlow examined the images of Asian Americans in twentieth-century world history textbooks. Barlow noted that in textbooks dating from 1900 to 1910, the Chinese were presented as weak, arrogant, and hostile to missionaries, the West, and reform. The textbooks expressed a fascination with Chinese culture, while simultaneously condemning the "antiquated ways" of China.[54] A 1910 civics textbook approved by the California State Board of Education specifically addressed the issue of Chinese immigration exclusion: "Our government allows to all equal opportunities and equal rights. Only in the case of the Chinese has the government prohibited the immigration of a nationality; and in this case it is because the Chinese remain foreigners, no matter how long they live here. They fail to become Americanized, fail to adopt as their own the interests and customs of this country."[55] Statements such as this painted Chinese Americans as perpetual foreigners and ensured that yet another generation of white Americans would fail to see Chinese children as "true Americans."

In addition to biased textbooks, Chinese schoolchildren endured the frequent intrusions of white visitors who interrupted the school day to observe the "quaint" sight of white women educating heathen children. In 1896 Principal Rose Thayer of the Chinese Public School expressed her frustration to a reporter from the *San Francisco Evening Bulletin*. The reporter published an article about the school, explaining that "the principal of the school strongly objects to having articles written about her pupils, for she says they do not like it, and then she dislikes having them put on a footing with the inhabitants of a museum." Although the reporter noted these objections, she went on to write about the students in the objectified manner that Principal Thayer had protested: "We considered ourselves especially fortunate in getting a peep at the little yellow men, for she [Thayer] declares that this afternoon she shall see that the Board of Education decrees that writers, artists and tourists are not to be allowed to visit the school."[56] Thayer's point seemed lost on the reporter, who sought to catch "a peep" and write her story before school officials limited access to the children.

Because no segregated Chinese high school existed in San Francisco, the few grammar school students who determined to continue their education attended integrated institutions. The number of Chinese children who continued on to high school was too small to justify the construction of a separate school. In 1908 only eleven Chinese children (4 percent of the total number of Chinese schoolchildren in San Francisco) were attending high school. The percentage of other immigrant schoolchildren, and even native-born white children, attending high school also appeared quite low, fluctuating between 1 and 7 percent of each group's total population of schoolchildren. The notable exceptions were San Francisco's Canadian and German Jewish populations (11 percent and 14 percent, respectively). Even so, Chinese children attending an integrated high school in 1908 were outnumbered by their native-born and foreign-born white counterparts by a count of 2,067 to 11.[57]

Outside the protection of the ethnic enclave, Chinese children often encountered their first instance of overt hostility and racism from their white classmates. Wong Wing Ton entered Polytechnic High School in 1916 and experienced a form of racial discrimination he had not encountered at the

Oriental School. After enduring name-calling and other forms of harassment, however, he chose to fight back. One boy called him "Chink," and Wong retaliated by slamming the boy's arm in the door. Another time, when a boy threw chalk at him as he was standing at the blackboard, Wong turned around and threw an eraser at the boy's head. The class cheered when the eraser hit the aggressor square on the head.[58]

Perhaps more shocking was the hostility that Chinese students endured from encounters with adult school officials. Esther Wong, for example, encountered racism from her French teacher. After she did some sight-reading, Wong waited while the teacher paused and looked her over carefully. Finally, the teacher said, "Well, you read all right, but I don't like you. You belong to a dirty race that spit at missionaries." Unable to move, Wong felt her face grow hot. She was horrified. Although the embarrassing moment passed, Wong would never forget the humiliation. She decided to drop the class rather than to continually endure such verbal harassment.[59]

In addition to enduring racism from their Euroamerican schoolteachers and peers, Chinese students also became the target of white parents. In 1905 the parents of students at the Washington Grammar School complained that four Chinese students had been cheating on exams. These four boys consistently excelled above their peers, earning top scores on tests. Responding to the complaints, school officials separated the Chinese boys, placing them in the four corners of the room during the next exam. Despite these precautions, the boys once again earned the top scores in the class, and white parents took their complaints to the Board of Education. The board acquiesced to the demands of the parents and removed the four boys from the school.[60]

Unresolved racial anxieties sometimes erupted into violence. Hostilities between the Chinese and their white neighbors were frequent, especially as Chinese children clashed with the neighboring Italian children. With the influx of a greater number of Italian immigrants to the city around the turn of the century, tensions between the races grew. The boundary lines between Chinatown and the local white neighborhoods were clearly delineated, and anyone who crossed the line suffered the consequences. Few Chinese children ventured alone outside the confines of Chinatown for fear of facing a volley of stones from white children. Andrew Kan recalled that while he was growing up in San Francisco, the hoodlums would "pull your queue, slap your face, throw all kind of old vegetables and rotten eggs at you. All you could do was to run and get out of the way. Nobody would ever try to stop them."[61] These hostilities sometimes resulted in serious injuries or even death. Riding the cable car home from school could be especially dangerous for high school students. Wong Wing Ton referred to the fighting between rival gangs of Chinese and Italian boys: "Street fighting, complete with rock throwing and 'hell whipping,' was common until one day an Italian youngster was fatally shot."[62] The incident that he was apparently referring to occurred in 1912 in the yard of the Oriental School. A group of white boys, ranging in age from ten to fourteen, launched a volley of stones over the Oriental School yard fence. The resulting battle ended tragically when an adult Chinese bystander, Wong Shee, intervened to stop the assault on the Chinese boys. After a white boy named Jose Aguilar fired an air rifle, Wong Shee retaliated by firing his pistol at Aguilar. The bullet missed its intended target and killed fourteen-year-old James Kane instead. Police arrested Wong Shee and charged him with murder.[63] This incident generated a great deal of negative publicity for the Chinese American community, while the violent culmination of racial tensions posed dangers for children on the playground.

Although this death had a sobering effect on the children, the hostilities did not completely cease. Disputes between Chinese and Italian children continued for years. In 1918 the *San Francisco Call* reported that three Italian boys stabbed an eleven-year-old Chinese boy during a fight over some packages of gum the Italian boys were selling. The Chinese boy apparently survived the attack.[64] It is interesting to note that the conflict between Chinese and Italian immigrant children in early twentieth-century San Francisco coincided with the success of nativist immigration policies that targeted both Chinese and southern and eastern European immigrants. These two groups lived in neighboring ethnic enclaves in the least desirable section of the city. Exacerbated by competition for jobs, violent outbursts between Chinese and Italian children reflected adult ethnic and racial tensions.

CHINESE-LANGUAGE SCHOOLS

Some families, fearing the impact of too much Americanization, determined to send their children to China for an education in Chinese language and culture. Thomas Chinn recalled that "when my father found out we were getting so Americanized, he was worried that we would forget all about our Chinese culture, so he decided for our sakes, and for our future in case we were deported . . . to go back to a larger Chinese community so that we could be sure and learn Chinese."[65] When the children failed to learn enough Chinese from language schools in San Francisco, Chinn's father determined that it was necessary to send the eldest son to China. Although a few families sent their children to China for a Chinese education, most parents simply hired private tutors or contributed to the opening of Chinese schools in the United States. As members of a transpacific community, the Chinese in San Francisco also envisioned Chinese schools in America as a way of preparing their children to become useful citizens of China.[66]

By 1880 at least a dozen Chinese teachers had opened schools in San Francisco. Family associations typically hired teachers to conduct Chinese classes for their clan members. The schools catered predominately to the children of merchants who could afford the $4.00 to $5.00 monthly tuition. In 1888 the Chinese community opened the Gold Mountain School (later known as the Academy of the Great Qing Empire), which offered a traditional curriculum in Chinese classics and language. Most of the children attended evening classes after a full day of American school.[67]

During the early twentieth century, the Chinese imperial government ordered the modernization and Westernization of the Chinese educational system. In 1907 the Chinese government sent Leong Chin Kwai (Liang Qinggui), commissioner of education, to supervise the opening of a Chinese school in the United States. Leong arrived in San Francisco in 1908 to help establish the Chinese Primary Public School of Subjects of the Great Qing Empire on the second and third stories of the Chinese Consolidated Benevolent Association headquarters building. The Chinese government covered the cost of tuition, while students had to pay only the cost of books. The school employed five teachers, and the curriculum focused on teaching the Chinese classics, music, ethics, language, history, geography, mathematics, rhetoric, and calligraphy. In addition, the school offered training in gymnastics and singing. The Chinese Primary Public School of Subjects opened with an initial enrollment of 104 students. The San Francisco Chinese American community proudly supported such Chinese schools as a way to modernize both Chinatown and China.[68] By 1920 the Baptist, Congregational, Cumberland Presbyterian, Episcopal, Methodist, and Presbyterian Churches in San Francisco responded to the high demand for Chinese education by also offering Chinese-language classes.[69]

Children generally entered Chinese school between the ages of five and seven, while simultaneously beginning their education at the mission or public school. The Chinese schools operated on weekends and weekday afternoons so as not to conflict with mission and public school hours. After spending a full day in school, some children dreaded the prospect of spending the afternoon at Chinese school. Edwar Lee resented the children who could leisurely walk from public school to Chinese school and legitimately cut thirty to forty minutes out of Chinese school every day. Lee considered himself unfortunate to live directly across from the Chinese school and half a block away from the Oriental Public School.[70] The number of hours spent in school seemed unnecessary to some children. As Chinese boys and girls advanced to high school and associated more with white children whose parents did not require attendance at afternoon language schools, Chinese children increasingly resented the demands of the Chinese schools.

Chinese schools mirrored the curriculum of schools in China. Textbooks included the *Trimetrical Classic, Thousand-Character Essay, Surnames of the Hundred Families,* and the *Four Books.* Drill and rote memorization was the preferred teaching method. In addition to the Chinese classics, some schools offered education in Chinese music, history, geography, mathematics, and rhetoric.[71] Students demonstrated their mastery of the material by standing before the class and repeating lessons they had memorized from the day before. If a student found himself at a loss for words, the other children would help by mouthing words, using body language, or holding up English sounds for the Chinese words. A student in the front row might help his troubled peer by turning the book upside down and tilting it up slightly for his classmate to read. Lee remembered that some children would cheat by bringing the lesson copied on a small piece of paper cupped in their hand.[72] To escape the drudgery of school life, some children played hooky. Lee enjoyed the feeling of freedom so much that once he took three days off in a row to play. When the teacher discovered the reason for his absence, Lee received sixty lashes on his back with a rattan stick as punishment. However, Lee determined to protest his punishment by refusing to cry. The teacher seemed angry: "So you won't cry, uh? The rattan must not be heavy enough to do a good job." Then he began to whip the boy harder.[73] Such strict discipline contributed to the authoritarian reputation of the Chinese schools.

Not all children dreaded or resisted their Chinese education. Some eagerly desired to learn about their heritage and embraced the challenge of learning to read and write in Chinese. Dr. James Hall attended Chung Wah School from 1909 to 1911 and enjoyed the numerous activities and the sense of community offered by the school. Hall fondly remembered participating in mock military drills and marching down the cobblestones of Stockton Street during his days at Chung Wah.[74] This experience seemed to solidify his identity as a Chinese American.

While Chinese schools were established to counter the negative effects of Americanization, white, middle-class reformers recognized the significant role of mission and public schools in helping to mold immigrant children into model American citizens and Christians. In doing so, teachers often sought to emphasize assimilation, while promoting the eradication of corrupting foreign habits.[75] As early as 1867, a reporter with the *San Francisco Alta* recognized the assimilative benefits of public education for Chinese children: "It is to be hoped that the Board of Education will give attention to this subject, if for no other reason than that of inculcating ideas of Christianity and civilization among Chinese at that time of life which impressions take deepest root in the mind."[76] The mission and public schools discouraged pupils from speaking Chinese at school and emphasized English-language training.[77] The ultimate goal of the teachers was to replace the students' Chinese habits with American practices.

With these goals in mind, the public and mission schools celebrated Christian and American holidays with the Chinese students. In 1897 the Chinese Public School organized a public Christmas program to showcase their students' talents. Some parents actively approved of and endorsed the activities. A group of Chinese merchants purchased a Christmas tree and lent a hall for an evening of singing, exercises, and drills. At the conclusion of the activities, the children received toys. Boys asked for English books such as *Gulliver's Travels* and *Robinson Crusoe*.[78] In 1910 the Christmas program at the Occidental School concluded with a visit from Santa Claus: "The eyes of the children opened wider and still wider as he spoke to them and commenced to reveal the wonders of his bag."[79] The schoolchildren received gifts of dolls, Chinese aprons, and copies of the Gospels. The mission and public schools also observed American holidays rooted in American history, emphasizing patriotic values. By 1920 the schools took holidays for Thanksgiving, Labor Day, California Admission Day, Memorial Day, and Washington's Birthday.[80] The graduation exercises of the Oriental Public School included patriotic songs, recitations, and a procession of American flags.[81] Although many Chinese children eagerly participated in the holidays and activities at school, Chinese New Year remained the most popular holiday in Chinatown. The schools reported a significant drop in attendance during the New Year festivities.[82] The mission and public schools attempted to indoctrinate Chinese children with American values through participation in patriotic holiday celebrations. Yet, as discussed in chapter 2, Chinese children and their families selectively adapted certain American festivities to create uniquely Chinese American traditions.

School cleanliness campaigns offered another means of inculcating immigrant children with American middle-class values. Public and mission schools in lower-class and immigrant communities offered lectures on health and hygiene, medical exams, and home visitations for their students.[83] The San Francisco public school system employed a team of doctors and nurses to routinely visit the schools and conduct medical examinations of the students. The children at the Oriental School grew accustomed to these exams and benefited from the improvements in health.[84]

In a further effort to promote Americanization, educators encouraged children's participation in organizations that embodied American ideals. In 1898 Chinese girls in the Presbyterian mission formed a Red Cross Society. Suey Leen, an eleven-year-old girl, wrote the following letter to the soldiers: "I write These letters for you. I am very Sorry you go to war. I hope God help you. I live These Country. I Give These text for you: 'Be thou faithful unto death. And I will give thee a crown of life.' I was born in These Country. I am native daughter. God bless you, good-bye."[85] Suey Leen's emphasis on her status as a native daughter indicates her self-identification as an American and her desire that the soldiers understand their common connection as both Americans and Christians. This letter attests to the successful Americanization and Christianization efforts of Suey Leen's teachers. Many children internalized the teachings of their public and/or mission school education, even if their families outwardly resisted some of the changes caused by Americanization.

State and national efforts to Americanize immigrants rapidly organized in the early twentieth century. The California State Commission of Immigration and Housing (CSCIH) was formed in 1913 under Governor Hiram Johnson. At the federal level, the Committee for Immigrants in America was organized in 1914 and began advocating the education and Americanization of immigrants. State and federal committee leaders did not distinguish between Asian and non-Asian immigrants but extended their efforts to all immigrant groups, promoting the same course of Americanization for Chinese children as for foreign-born whites. For all non-English-speaking immigrants, however, these organizations stressed the importance of English-language training. On July 4, 1915, San Francisco joined 150 other U.S. cities in celebrating Americanization Day in an attempt to honor the diverse ethnic

Patriotic Chinese American boys (Chinese: Children; Stellman Collection, #10, 858b;
courtesy of the California History Room, California State Library, Sacramento)

heritage of the nation and the contributions of various peoples to the creation of the United States. In 1916 settlement-house workers helped establish the National Conference on Immigration and Americanization and began a unified national effort to assimilate immigrants.[86]

California also continued its efforts at Americanization. A 1919 report by the CSCIH recommended a rather Progressive curriculum that emphasized a multicultural approach. The report recommended that schools adopt a program of study that examined the heroes of the past (including men such as Washington and Confucius) and promoted an educational emphasis on the diverse people, languages, and countries that had contributed to U.S. culture. The report emphasized the importance of teaching that all children are Americans regardless of their country of birth, and that all have the ability to rise from poverty through their own individual efforts. The writers declared that "Democracy is dependent upon freedom from race prejudice and class distinctions."[87]

The process of Americanization and Christianization frequently undermined the authority of Chinese parents and challenged their cultural values. This created substantial generational conflicts. As early as 1888, mission teachers noted the impact of evangelization on Chinese family life. Ms. Baskin of the Occidental School submitted the following letter from one of her students: "Dear Teacher:—I will write a few line to you. My father told me go worship idol, say I, no, won't go. Because you is disobedient me, you is no honor me, then I go. Teacher, please excuse me."[88] Baskin responded, "Here was a thoughtful, conscientious, though not a Christian boy, refusing to worship idols, until convicted of *disobedience* by the word of God. Had he consulted us before he acted, we would have said, 'Obey your parents in the *Lord*,' but as neither father nor son sustained that attitude, our words would have seemed worse than idle."[89] Although reformers intended to strengthen the family and the home, alliances and increased dependency on professionals and outsiders in child rearing at times diminished the authority of the parents and the home.[90]

Yet, this irony was not completely lost on Progressive reformers. Jane Addams, founder of Chicago's Hull House, recognized the problem of intergenerational conflict in the education of immigrant children and suggested that educators should seek to counter the negative effects of Americanization. In 1919 the CSCIH admitted that the process of Americanization contributed to feelings of superiority among the children of immigrants, who sometimes rebelled against the authority of their parents.[91] The commission recommended that teachers encourage children to discuss their schoolwork with their parents to foster respect for the parents and reinforce parental discipline. In addition, reformers emphasized a teaching philosophy that respected, or minimally tolerated, cultural diversity. Addams advocated a pluralist approach that emphasized the unique gifts that each immigrant group carried with them to the United States. She sought to eliminate barriers between immigrants and native-born Americans by preserving native cultures while encouraging a gradual assimilation of immigrants into American culture.[92] The CSCIH adopted a similar philosophy by insisting that teachers must work to educate students about the histories of various nations and model respect for all cultures.[93] Despite these recommendations, reformers generally believed that Chinese cultural practices limited the immigrant child's ability to adjust and assimilate into American society.[94]

Education in the English language and American culture remained the primary goal of the Americanization effort into the twentieth century. In a 1917 report by the U.S. Bureau of Education, investigators noted that the Oriental School in San Francisco seemed handicapped by language barriers. The reporter noted that although the children recited the oath of allegiance and performed the flag salute, they seemed to lack a general comprehension of the ceremony. The investigators recommended that the public school curriculum be adjusted to meet the unique needs of the school's student body and assure successful Americanization of the second generation.[95] After 1920 the California State Department of Education continued the work of the CSCIH by promoting Americanization in the state school system.[96]

Members of the Chinese merchant class recognized the significance of highlighting the academic success and Americanization of Chinese children in order to improve the image of Chinatown. Missionaries and public school-teachers also joined the campaign to improve the image of Chinese American schoolchildren. After interviewing the principal of the Chinese Public School in 1896, a reporter for the San Francisco Call described Chinese students as "quiet and exceedingly docile, showing a profound respect for their teachers. Though many of them are employed in stores and also attend the Chinese school, they thoroughly enjoy the public school work and prove apt students."[97] White teachers and school administrators publicly praised the work of their Chinese pupils in an effort to gain local support for their work. In January 1912 Jennie Cilker's eighth-grade class of boys visited the Museum of Anthropology at the University of California, Berkeley. The boys wrote essays following their visit, and Cilker forwarded the essays to professor Alfred L. Kroeber. Kroeber, impressed by the intelligence and good behavior of the boys, forwarded the essays to Phoebe Hearst, who read them and also commented on the children's intelligence and writing abilities. In October 1912 Kroeber once again complimented the good conduct of the Chinese schoolboys in response to a letter written by Principal Cecelia C. Newhall.[98] Cilker apparently solicited these letters as evidence of the exemplary behavior and academic abilities of her Chinese students, understanding that such examples of scholarly aptitude countered anti-Chinese claims of the intellectual inferiority of the Chinese child.

Others sought to compare and contrast Chinese children with white children to highlight the success of Chinese as students. A teacher at the Chinese Public School remarked in 1896: "I've taught American children for years and I prefer these Chinese. They are so gentle and human and interesting. In anything that is artistic the Chinese boys excel the white children, and especially is this true in penmanship." The principal of the school insisted that the Chinese students especially excelled in math.[99] In 1911 the Reverend John Hood Laughlin of the Presbyterian Church praised the work ethic of Chinese students in America, recognizing that these children were willing to work and sacrifice for their education: "They thus bring into the school room a spirit which would provoke our Anglo-Saxon students to greater diligence, lest they be left behind in a race with a foreign people."[100]

William Greenwell, the principal of the Lincoln School in Oakland, also praised the Chinese as superior students in a 1924 letter written for the Survey of Race Relations: "I have never worked with a group of foreigners whom I would prefer to the Chinese. They are among our very best students and, taken as a whole, do the best work that is done in this school. Their English work, especially written English, is equal to if not superior to that which is done by the American children."[101] Greenwell was a vocal advocate of Chinese schoolchildren and often publicly praised their academic and athletic abilities, insisting that poor discipline was rarely a problem.[102] In this manner, missionaries and educators helped to perpetuate an image of Chinese children as model students. Such praise from teachers and principals stood in stark contrast to the claims of anti-Chinese politicians and school administrators who insisted on the inability of Chinese children to compete with their white peers.

In 1921 Mary Bo-Tze Lee completed a master's thesis in education at the University of California, Berkeley, examining the segregated school in San Francisco's Chinatown. Lee emphasized the eagerness of the children to learn and their dedication to their studies. Her research stood in defense of Chinese children and as a testament to their right to an integrated, or at least equal, education. She argued that Chinese children possessed a strong desire to obtain an education: "They are industrious and are willing to work hard in order to secure an education; for they reverence learning itself. All of these provide stimulating influences for the American children."[103] Lee noted the contradiction between American principles of equality and Christian ideals of brotherly love and the existence of segregation in San Francisco's schools. The results of intelligence tests given to 500 Chinese students in San Francisco seemed to prove that Chinese children were just as intelligent as their American counterparts. Lee also contrasted the test results of the Chinese students with those of southern European students and determined that the former were far superior: "Since the intelligence of the Chinese is found to be almost equal to that of the Americans and superior to the Spanish, Portuguese or Italian, is it not unfair to judge the Chinese so unfairly and segregate them? If the Chinese were found to be lower in intelligence than other races, then it is justifiable to segregate them, but they are not, and therefore should be given the same opportunities of learning as are children of other nationalities."[104] Although Lee's intention was simply to counter over fifty years of anti-Chinese rhetoric, Lee and other writers sympathetic to the plight of Chinese schoolchildren inadvertently contributed to the creation of new stereotypes of Asian Americans as model minorities by contrasting the success of Chinese students with the lesser achievement of other immigrant groups.

CONCLUSION

The struggle for equitable education in San Francisco's Chinatown began with the arrival of Chinese children in the mid-nineteenth century and continued into the early twentieth century. Chinese families valued education and waged countless battles in the courts, in the legislature, and in the classroom for integrated and equal education. When denied a public education, Chinese children attended private, mission schools. After 1885 the segregated Chinese school stood as a visible symbol of anti-Chinese hostility and the barriers of segregation and exclusion that Chinese American children would face throughout their lives. Chinese American community leaders also opened Chinese-language schools in an effort to educate the children about their Chinese heritage, counter the negative influences of Americanization, and prepare the children for a future in either China or America.

However, the stereotypes created by anti-Chinese writers stood as obstacles to the full acceptance of American-born Chinese children as American citizens. Anti-Chinese groups predominately attacked Chinese children as a threat to white children. While some families chose to question the constitutionality of segregation outright through the court system, other families chose to avoid conflict and make the best of a bad situation. Yet another strategy employed by the Chinese American community and their white allies was to emphasize the work ethic and academic achievements of Chinese children and highlight their success in comparison to other immigrant students. In the previous chapter, we saw a similar effort on behalf of capitalists and Chinese immigrants to construct an image of Chinese laborers as model workers. Although the emergence of the stereotype of Asian Americans as model minorities is usually associated with the latter half of the twentieth century, scholars have located the nineteenth-century origins of the myth in the efforts of white capitalists to favorably contrast Chinese laborers with African American and immigrant workers from other countries.[105] This chapter, similarly, locates the early origin of the model-minority myth in the efforts of white missionaries, teachers, and Chinese American community leaders to counter the claims of the inferiority of Chinese schoolchildren. Unfortunately, the perpetuation of this myth would have unforeseen consequences in the mid- to late twentieth century. In the 1950s and 1960s, journalists again proclaimed the high educational and economic achievements of Chinese and Japanese Americans. Political conservatives seized on the model-minority thesis as a confirmation of the attainability of the "American dream" for those minority groups who exhibited the proper work ethic and were more willing to assimilate. It is important to distinguish the differences in intent in the construction of the model-minority image. The goal of the early twentieth-century commentators was simply to defend the abilities of Chinese students against anti-Chinese attacks. The objective of conservatives in the mid-twentieth century, however, was to explain away the achievement gap by blaming African American and Latino students for their academic shortcomings. The continued persistence of this stereotype not only downplays the socioeconomic struggles of Chinese Americans, and indeed all immigrants, but it also shifts the focus from the societal constraints that limit an immigrant's success to an individual's own desire and motivation. The idea of a "model minority" tends to pit minority groups against one another in a battle in which, ultimately, no group emerges as the victor. Instead, this stereotype simply obscures centuries of institutional racism and segregation.[106] The children growing up in San Francisco's early Chinatown struggled with these realities every day. As we will see, not all Chinese children lived up to the model-minority image, as some found themselves in the missions and court system.

5 ARTICLES OF CONTENTION

CHINESE CHILDREN IN THE MISSIONS AND COURTS

Slaves Seared with Hot Irons, While the Stars and Stripes
   Floated Gayly Overhead
Dragged Shrieking to Death, Terrible Fate of a Chinese
   Slave Girl Who Tried to Escape
An American Girl Sold to Slavery: Laura Lee's Narrow Escape
   from Living with Chinese
—HEADLINES IN THE *San Francisco Call*

Sensational articles about urban vice were common journalistic fare in American newspapers during the late nineteenth and early twentieth centuries, and San Francisco's newspapers were no exception. Tales of white slavery, detailing the sexual exploitation of women, proved especially popular.[1] Crime in San Francisco's Chinatown seemed even more lurid and exotic, as articles appeared almost daily with scandalous new details to entice eager readers. This chapter focuses on some of Chinatown's exceptional and rare cases by examining the experiences of Chinese children in the missions and the justice system. Once again, various groups manipulated the facts to further their own agendas. Although entertaining to a white audience, highly publicized and exaggerated stories of opium consumption, gambling, slavery, prostitution, and tong murders tarnished the image of Chinatown and threatened the safety and security of Chinese American families.

The cases presented here help illuminate the dark side of Chinatown to reveal aspects of the Chinese American experience that prove otherwise elusive. In some of these stories, Chinese and white adults fought for custody of Chinese children. The children thus became articles of contention in the much larger political and economic debate over the presence of the Chinese in America. These cases also demonstrate a clash in cultural values, as Chinese and whites not only debated the best methods of caring for these children but also argued about who should be in charge of the process. Yet, Chinese parents and their children sometimes formed alliances with white reformers in their efforts to create a stable and safe environment in which to raise their children.

PROSTITUTION AND DOMESTIC SLAVERY IN CHINATOWN

Beginning in the mid-nineteenth century, reform-minded Americans became increasingly concerned with the moral impact of prostitution on society. Fears of the changing roles of women and the decline of the small-town community as a form of social control were exacerbated by the tensions accompanying industrialization, urbanization, and immigration. The importation of Chinese women became the subject of governmental investigations of white slavery beginning in the 1870s and culminating in the 1875 Page Act, which specifically sought to limit the trade in Chinese prostitutes. The new immigration of the late nineteenth century included Roman Catholic and Jewish immigrants from southeastern Europe as well as a small but steady stream of Chinese and Japanese immigrants from Asia. The "unassimilability" of the new immigrants, and their alleged disregard of sexual morality, threatened the stability of white, middle-class, Protestant family life. Americans believed that immigrants introduced foreign, perverse, and depraved forms of sexuality that would corrupt their own children.[2] As one of the most physically and culturally distinct immigrant groups on the West Coast, the Chinese seemed to represent an imminent threat to families living in cities such as San Francisco. Stereotypical accounts of the Chinese emphasized the importation and exploitation of Chinese women and expressed fears of the use of opium to corrupt and exploit white women. Anti-Chinese writers perpetuated these images and frequently highlighted crime in Chinatown as further evidence for the exclusion of Chinese laborers. Many reformers focused on the regulation of sexuality, and Chinatown became one of the nation's earliest battlegrounds in the fight to eradicate prostitution.

Although the extent of the white slave trade is a controversial subject among historians today, the importation of Chinese women and girls for purposes of prostitution beginning in the mid-nineteenth century is an indisputable fact. Census data, the results of government investigations, and oral history accounts provide evidence of the exploitation of Chinese women and girls. Entrepreneurs saw a lucrative market in the male-dominated China-towns overseas. Impoverished families in China sometimes resorted to selling a daughter into prostitution to provide much-needed income for the family. Brokers negotiated a price and then arranged transportation overseas, where brothel keepers in San Francisco offered competing bids for the girl. The powerful Chinatown tongs owned many of the brothels and controlled the trade by demanding a head tax on every imported prostitute.[3] Brothel keepers often asked the girls to "agree" to the terms of their labor by signing a contract such as the following:

> An agreement to assist a young girl named Loi Yau. Because she
> became indebted to her mistress for passage, food, &c., and has nothing
> to pay, she makes her body over to the woman Sep Sam, to serve as a
> prostitute to make out the sum of $503. . . . Loi Yau shall serve four and
> a half years. . . . When the time is out Loi Yau may be her own master,
> and no man shall trouble her. If she runs away before the time is out
> and any expense is incurred in catching, then Loi Yau must pay that
> expense. If she is sick fifteen days or more, she shall make up one
> month for every fifteen days.[4]

Although the trade peaked in the 1870s and immigration laws such as the Page Act attempted to suppress the importation of Chinese prostitutes, slave dealers continued to successfully smuggle in young girls and women for illicit purposes well into the early twentieth century. San Francisco census enumerators in 1870 listed sixty-six Chinese girls age sixteen and under as prostitutes (20 percent of all Chinese girls in San Francisco). Enumerators recorded a larger number of children (336, or 22 percent) living in mostly female households. Although census takers may have erroneously labeled some of these households as brothels, it is likely that the majority of them actually were, given the prominence of prostitution in early Chinatown. As previously stated, most native-born children living in these brothels were probably the offspring of prostitutes. Since a large percentage of Chinese female immigrants in the mid-nineteenth century were either servants or prostitutes, however, China-born girls living in the brothels were likely servants purchased by brothel owners as future potential prostitutes.[5]

Contemporary observers described two types of brothels in San Francisco's Chinatown. Some brothels offered low prices that attracted racially diverse and predominantly working-class customers; others catered to upper-class Chinese clients. Working-class houses of prostitution were generally located in alleys, where the prostitutes propositioned men from behind wicket screens in the doors. Customers who entered the establishment waited in a small reception room, where the madam of the house greeted them. The house was further divided into several small rooms about five by eight feet in dimension. The rooms included only simple furnishings, the central feature of which was a bunk. Prostitutes frequently worked on piecework during the daytime to provide additional income for brothel owners. As seamstresses, they sewed shirts, undergarments, and shoes for manufacturers. Disease often claimed the lives of these girls, who rarely lived beyond six years in the profession.[6]

Because Chinese men generally viewed women who had sex with white men as degraded, wealthy Chinese preferred parlor houses that catered to an exclusively upper-class Chinese clientele. These prostitutes tended to work for a few regular customers and lived a more lavish lifestyle, receiving gifts of expensive clothing and jewelry. Elmer Wok Wai remembered visiting parlor houses as a boy. He would play with his toy wagon while waiting for his father in the hallway of the Peking Boat, an upper-class Chinese brothel. He recalled the elaborate furnishings of the house: embroidered curtains, mirrors, teakwood furniture, porcelain pillows, and red- or black-lacquered, carved, and gilded beds. Each room was equipped with gold spoons to clean out the ear, ivory back scratchers, and opium pipes made of jade, ebony and gold, or ivory and mother of pearl. The women were elaborately dressed and heavily made-up, their bodies adorned with jade, opal, pearl, and gold jewelry.[7] Some of the women also attended tong banquets and entertained the guests with their singing.

In 1877 Dr. Hugh H. Toland, a member of the health board and founder of Toland Medical College, insisted that numerous young white boys had contracted syphilis from frequenting Chinese brothels. He argued that the low prices and low morals of the Chinese prostitutes attracted the young boys.[8] Toland's views echoed the concerns of reformers of the antebellum period, who had tended to focus on the seductive power and malevolence of prostitutes.[9] But Toland went a step further by indicting Chinese prostitutes in particular, blaming them for seducing boys, spreading syphilis, and, consequently, corrupting American families.

The opinions of Toland and others of his mindset are perhaps better understood by examining the broader context of the national discourse regarding the white slave trade. Concern over the trafficking of Chinese female slaves was part of a national anxiety about the forced sexual exploitation of women of all races. Brian Donovan, in *White Slave Crusades* (2006), argues that by the late nineteenth century, many reformers, including Frances Willard of the Woman's Christian Temperance Union (WCTU), depicted African Americans and new immigrants as sexual predators victimizing native-born white women. The WCTU insisted that the vice districts blurred racial boundaries and undermined the existing racial hierarchy, thereby threatening the Anglo-Saxon family. Donovan argues that stories of yellow slavery in San Francisco's Chinatown "acted as a vehicle for nativist arguments" while also revealing the "threat of 'yellow peril.'" Missionaries relied on these narratives to gain support for their efforts to protect Chinese women and girls from forced slavery. Still, Donovan concludes that "crusades against white slavery helped build racial hierarchies by emphasizing moral and sexual differences between Anglo-Saxons or native-born whites on one hand and new European immigrants, Chinese, and African Americans on the other."[10] The Chinese, depicted by nativists as the most foreign and unassimilable immigrants, clearly found themselves at the bottom of this racial hierarchy. Thus, Toland's attempts to link syphilis, and therefore the corruption of American families, to Chinese prostitutes is, in part, explained by the racialized rhetoric that came to characterize the national discourse on white slavery and was further exacerbated by decades of anti-Chinese rhetoric. Prominent Anglo-Saxon Americans such as Toland perpetuated an image of a vice and disease-ridden Chinatown that clearly contrasted with the purity of the white, middle-class family model.[11]

However, some medical experts disagreed with the racist conclusions of Toland and others regarding the origins of venereal disease in Chinatown. Dr. Arthur B. Stout insisted that syphilis was not a disease specific to the Chinese but was common in large cities and among all populations. In direct response to Toland's statement about syphilis among white youth, Stout testified before the state senate committee that white boys rarely visited Chinese prostitutes for any other purpose but to harass them.[12] Stout's opinions stood in contrast to the social-purity advocates who linked disease with foreign prostitutes and desired to eradicate prostitution. Regulationists adopted a view similar to Stout's, insisting that prostitution was necessary to assuaging the sexual desires of men and maintaining the sanctity of the white, middle-class home. Regulationists argued that instead of abolishing prostitution, the state should attempt to regulate and control it.[13]

When public anxieties flared, city officials responded by cracking down on Chinese prostitution. In 1866 an ordinance culminated in several police raids aimed at removing all Chinese prostitutes from the city. After the tensions subsided, Chinese prostitutes once again took up residence in the area. This pattern of inconsistent and selective enforcement of the law occurred over and over again. Few laws existed in California at the time that specifically protected the interests of minors. Concern over teenage prostitution led to the passage of a state law in 1874 that specifically made it a felony to force girls under eighteen into prostitution. Evidence that a child had willfully consented to become a prostitute effectively impeded enforcement of the law. Two years later, San Francisco passed an ordinance designed to eliminate prostitution among girls under age fourteen. Although police rarely enforced the laws with regard to Chinese prostitutes, the ordinance did provide a legal framework for the rescue activities of mission workers who tried to save girls from a life of sexual slavery.[14]

The Chinese system of indenturing children into domestic service also evoked intense public scrutiny, as critics resurrected images of African slavery in an attempt to associate the two forms of labor. Although the Chinese intended the *mui tsai* system to serve as a form of charity for impoverished children, young girls who worked as domestic servants sometimes found themselves the unfortunate victims of cruel masters. Six-year-old Lilac Chen (Wu Tien Fu) arrived in the United States in 1893. Her owners kept her in a house of prostitution and hid her under a bed during police raids. The girl was sold several times and eventually ended up working as a *mui tsai* for an abusive woman. Wu Tien Fu remembered laboring long hours with the woman's baby tied to her back. As the baby fussed and cried, she grew frustrated: "Oh, I got desperate, I didn't care what happened to me, I just pinched his cheek, his seat you know, just gave it to him. Then of course I got it back. She, his mother, went and burned a red hot iron tong and burnt me on the arm."[15] An anonymous individual reported the abuse to missionaries, who later removed the child from the home. The corporal punishment was reminiscent of the conditions faced by African slaves in the antebellum South.

As property, *mui tsai* retained few rights, and some masters subjected them to emotional, physical, and sexual abuse. Child-protective societies and missionaries often published accounts of cases of child abuse in Chinatown. In 1897 Tsau Kuk, nicknamed "Topsy" by missionaries, arrived at the Methodist mission home. She had been burned by a hot iron, and her legs, feet, arms, and back were covered in various other scars, bruises, cuts, and burns. Chinese neighbors witnessed the abuse and notified the mission workers, who came to her aid. The women of the mission home were deeply moved by the tears and look of terror in the young girl's eyes.[16] Such horrific cases highlighted the extreme cruelties of the *mui tsai* system. Missionary accounts of child abuse tended to paint Christian women as saviors and heathen Chinese as abusers. It can be difficult to discern truth from fiction, especially as newspaper reporters exaggerated the details of these stories. Missionaries also often ignored cultural differences in ideas of child rearing, sometimes erroneously labeling parental discipline as abuse. However, the evidence of extreme physical abuse in the cases of Lilac Chen and Tsau Kuk, and the intervention by Chinese neighbors, suggests that these were legitimate cases of child abuse.

Concern for the welfare of all children led reformers to take up the cause of assisting abused children by petitioning the state for stronger child-protective laws. In 1876 the California state legislature passed an act for the incorporation of societies for the prevention of cruelty to children. These societies investigated cases of child neglect and mistreatment, prosecuted offenders, and applied for guardianship of children when necessary. Replicating the work of its New York predecessor, the California Society for the Prevention of Cruelty to Children (SPCC) pushed for the passage of "An Act for the protection of children, and to prevent and punish certain wrongs to children." This 1878 act banned children from entering saloons without the accompaniment of a parent or guardian. The law also empowered child-protective societies to assume guardianship, with the court's permission, of children found begging, wandering, destitute, orphaned, or frequenting the company of thieves or prostitutes. The act further prohibited children under age sixteen from being imprisoned with adults. "An Act Relating to Children," passed on the same day, regulated the types of employment available to children in an attempt to protect them from dangerous or morally corrupting influences. The law also made it a misdemeanor to physically or mentally abuse a minor.[17] These acts provided reformers with the legal framework to intervene on behalf of the children of Chinatown.

In the nineteenth century, San Francisco also had a number of charitable institutions that catered to the needs of abandoned, abused, or delinquent children. Most of these institutions were supported by one of the many Jewish, Catholic, or Protestant churches in the city. In 1870 California state law provided financially for the organizations by guaranteeing $50 per year for each orphan and $25 per year for each half-orphan assigned to the care of an institution. Within five years, the yearly amount increased to $100 for each orphan and $75 for each half-orphan.[18] Although these societies must be acknowledged for the protection and care they provided abused and neglected children, the attitudes of many child welfare workers in San Francisco reflected the nativist and middle-upper-class orientation of these organizations.

In the tradition of an earlier generation of moral reformers, the leaders of San Francisco's charitable organizations attributed poverty to the character defects and moral flaws of the lower class.[19] While poor children of other races received support from the city's charitable organizations, Chinese youth were often ignored and even turned away by these groups. Methodist and Presbyterian missionaries recognized this deficiency and built mission homes in the 1870s to meet the needs of abandoned and abused Chinese women and children. However, missions supporting Chinese children apparently received no state funding and relied entirely on church support and private donations. According to an 1890 report by M. W. Shinn on charities for children in San Francisco, this severe inequality in funding resulted from community members who were "by no means convinced that it is a matter of any importance to save Chinese children from abuse."[20] Although many Methodist and Presbyterian reformers held, along with their anti-Chinese neighbors, a general disregard for the Chinese lifestyle, missionaries in San Francisco's Chinatown offered a competing image of Chinese children as malleable and capable of reform. Increasingly, reformers recognized the debilitating impact of an improper environment and expressed a firm belief in the ability to reform and mainstream young immigrants into American society.[21]

RESCUE AND REFORM

Efforts to assist Chinese prostitutes and abused or neglected Chinese children began as early as the 1870s. A coalition of Chinese and American mission workers, ministers, child-protective society members, and lawyers cooperated to remove individuals from Chinatown's brothels. In 1870 the Methodists opened a mission home, and in 1874 the Presbyterians followed by also opening a home for Chinese women and children. The missionaries hoped to reform the mind, body, and soul of the Chinese child. However, the children first had to be saved from their oppressive and abusive home environment. Middle-class, white, Christian women vowed to "rescue" the children by forcibly removing them from their parents or guardians. Officers of the SPCC and the Pacific Society for the Suppression of Vice frequently utilized their quasi-police powers to assist the Presbyterian and Methodist missions in the rescue of Chinese children.[22]

Local newspapers dramatized the exploits of Margaret Culbertson, Donaldina Cameron, and Kate and Margarita Lake of the Presbyterian and Methodist missions, turning these women into legendary figures. Journalists retraced the women's steps as they swept through the lurid streets of Chinatown, following leads about the location of enslaved children. In a typical story, reporters described a dark back alley, where the rescuers located a "secret" room with a hidden door that concealed the young victim. Danger awaited the rescuer at every turn. The story continued with the heroic missionary woman scooping up the terrified child and rescuing her from a fate worse than death. Comforted and reassured of her safety, the child gladly fled with her rescuers. The story ended happily ever after, with the child safely at home in the mission. However, real-life rescues did not always have a happy ending, nor were they as romantic as suggested in the newspapers and magazines. These tales of heroic, daring rescues mixed truth with fiction and captured the imagination of a Victorian middle-class audience that sympathized with the fate of "poor Chinese slave girls." Regardless of the age of the rescued female, missionaries tended to label both child *mui tsai* and adult prostitutes as "slave girls" and portrayed both as innocent victims of exploitation. Even though such stories exaggerated the extent of vice in Chinatown, they helped draw attention to the exploitation of Chinese women and children. Ironically, however, the stories also perpetuated an image of deviant Chinese domesticity just when children living in two-parent, middle-class families had become the norm in Chinatown.

A deconstruction of these romantic tales reveals that the reality of such rescue missions was rarely as flawless as suggested by the newspaper accounts. Missionaries usually responded after receiving word from either a concerned Chinese informant or a child desiring to be rescued. In 1902 a girl named Ah Oye penned the following letter to Margarita Lake at the Methodist mission: "I am take time write few lines to you today. I am went you come here Bring me go city you there school all time. My name ah oye. My house Be green and red. You must Be sure and be sure come here Bring me if you know come here bring I Be sure and Die. My mama sclod [scold?] me and went sell me go the Bod [bad?] Place do bod think all. You sure I sure come here. Bring me go you there."[23] In a second letter, Ah Oye explained that it was her stepmother who was beating her and who had threatened to sell her. The child once again begged and pleaded with Margarita Lake to come rescue her.[24] Although the fate of Ah Oye is not known, missionaries attempted to rescue many other girls in similar predicaments. Cooperating with child-protective agents or police officials, missionaries forced their way into private homes and businesses to rescue abused children and underage prostitutes. Rescuers sometimes resorted to breaking down doors or otherwise damaging property to get inside a building. Often the children fled in terror, or their adult captors attempted to hide them behind secret doors or under floorboards.[25]

It was not unusual for rescuers to encounter violent resistance. In 1901 missionaries and law-enforcement officers arrived at the home of fifteen-year-old Yee Yow with the intention of rescuing the girl from a life of sexual slavery. The child kicked, bit, fought, and screamed as policemen Haskins and Anthony forcibly removed her from the house on Sullivan Alley. The woman of the house responded to the intrusion by striking Kate Lake of the Methodist mission. Although the rescuers managed to escape to the mission home with the girl, Yee Yow continued to cry and refused to eat food out of fear of being poisoned by mission workers.[26] Missionaries argued that although slave girls actually wanted to be rescued, they would often act afraid of their rescuers in an effort to avoid potential future retaliation from their owner should the rescue attempt fail. While this seems logical, a number of children like Yee Yow continued to resist well after safely arriving at the mission home, perhaps because Chinese slave owners frequently indoctrinated the girls with antimissionary stories. Regardless of whether these children were genuinely afraid of the missionaries or merely "acting the part," it is clear that not all rescued girls went willingly. Some brothel owners employed guards to protect their possessions and watch over the slave girls.[27] Missionaries determined to wage spiritual warfare against the slave trade in part by physically gaining possession of the girls, and some children, like Yee Yow, had little choice in the matter.

Despite the evidence to the contrary, Chinese children were not always simply passive pawns in the games of adults. Children often sought out opportunities to improve their fortunes and actively seize control of their own future. Some girls did not wait to be rescued; they ran away to the mission home. In 1897 two girl servants, Suey Leen and Dong Ho, planned an escape to the Presbyterian mission. Twelve-year-old Suey Leen helped Dong Ho flee and then bided her time, waiting for another opportunity to escape. Dong Ho arrived at the mission home dirty, starving, and exhausted. A handkerchief contained her possessions: "two broken Chinese toys, a pair of worn-out chopsticks, a cracked bowl and two soiled garments." Although Dong Ho told the missionaries about Suey Leen, the missionaries were unable to locate the girl. Three months later, Suey Leen found her way to the home. Donaldina Cameron remembered the reunion of the two girls: "I never saw anything so affecting as when they saw one another. I thought that they would be broken in two with their hugs. Then we realized that it was Suey Leen. And since then they have always been inseparable."[28] These children took great risks in leaving their homes and venturing into the unknown. They risked their lives in the hope of improving their situation, seizing the opportunity to determine their own fate. However, the difficulties for such girls were far from over. Shortly after their arrival at the mission, these children often found themselves confronted by their parents or former owners as missionaries fought for their custody in the courts.

GUARDIANSHIP DISPUTES

While the children resided temporarily in the mission homes, missionaries attempted to secure guardianship rights through the courts. Court battles typically occurred when parents or Chinatown criminals challenged the guardianship claims of the missionaries. Chinese men and women hired lawyers, filed writs of habeas corpus, and initiated criminal charges in an attempt to regain custody of rescued girls. Brothel keepers sometimes stood before the court and claimed to be the legitimate parents of a girl in an effort to retain custody. In 1895 Charley Hung applied for a writ of habeas corpus, alleging that the Methodist mission was unlawfully detaining seven-year-old Ah Soo. The Chinese consular office and the Six Companies quickly interfered in the proceeding, testifying to the unscrupulous history of the notorious highbinder, opium dealer, and ex-convict. Their efforts prevented Hung from gaining custody of Ah Soo and revealed the undeclared alliance between reformers and Chinese American community leaders in eradicating vice in Chinatown.[29]

Chinese children sometimes found themselves in the midst of fierce custody battles that revealed ideological discord between missionaries and child-saving agencies. In 1901 Chan Ah Ying was rescued by the Society for the Suppression of Vice and placed in the Methodist Chinese mission. Chan Ah Ying's guardianship hearings revealed a developing rift between Margarita Lake of the Methodist mission home and Frank Kane of the Society for the Suppression of Vice. The court initially appointed Kane the guardian and, as usual, Kane turned the child over to the care of the mission home. However, Kane later tried to remove the child from the mission and return her to her reformed mother. Lake desired that the girl remain in the mission home and challenged Kane's guardianship in court. Chan Ah Ying's mother contested the claims of both organizations and fought for custody of her daughter. A year later, a judge denied the claim of the Methodist mission and determined that since the mother had found stable employment with a white family, she was the proper guardian of the child.[30] The court generally preferred to keep children with their biological parents whenever possible. Relations between Kane and Lake were strained thereafter.

Unscrupulous adults sometimes tried to intimidate children into giving false testimony in court to protect themselves from criminal charges. One seven-year-old girl was so intimidated by her master's repeated abuse that, even after she was safe in the mission, she refused to testify against her former owner in court. Police officers were unable to press charges against the abuser.[31] The girl was no doubt haunted by fear and insecurity even as she lived within the security of the mission home. The child may have understood that if the missionaries failed to gain legal guardianship, she would be returned to her former home. Making public statements against her abuser could make the situation worse in the long run. The children in these cases had to negotiate their fate by carefully weighing their options. They feared the unknown of the mission home and may have doubted the sincerity of missionaries and their guarantees of safety. Facing pressures from all sides, the children exercised a limited degree of autonomy in determining their future.

Other children found their voice through the courts and determined to use the court to exercise their own desires. While some chose to return to their homes, others began a new life in the mission. In 1902 Margarita Lake rescued ten-year-old Chen Ha Wau. Although a Chinese merchant claimed the child as his daughter, Lake feared the girl was actually a "slave" purchased to perform domestic service for the merchant's family. Fong Quong filed a writ of habeas corpus, claiming that the girl was his child and had been wrongfully taken from him. However, the child testified in court that her mother had sold her in China, and once she was in San Francisco, brokers had sold her to Fong Quong. When Judge Frank J. Murasky asked her where she wanted to go, she said, " 'I want to go to the mission because she,' pointing to mother, 'is not my mother and I want to go to school.' " The judge granted custody to the Methodist mission.[32] In most cases, it appears that the court took a child's testimony at face value. Although the truth is difficult to discern in many of these cases because the children were obviously influenced by the adults around them, some children may have lied to authorities on their own volition in order to escape an undesirable living situation either at home or in the missions. No doubt a few astute youths learned to say what was necessary in order to influence the decision of the court and ultimately exercise their own desires.

Missionaries sometimes stretched legal boundaries in order to rescue the children from potentially dangerous environments. When the Presbyterian mission home rescued Ah Fah, Tong Dock protested the removal of the girl to the mission. The police agreed to keep the girl in jail for the night rather than allow her to go to the mission. Donaldina Cameron applied for guardianship the next morning. Tong Duck immediately countered by serving a writ on the chief of police to surrender the child. The police released Ah Fah, but federal authorities intervened by arresting Tong Dock for holding the child in involuntary servitude; authorities also seized custody of the girl as a witness against him. The federal authorities then turned the girl over to the mission home for temporary care. Tong Dock filed a writ of habeas corpus to force an earlier hearing. Cameron claimed to have received the summons late and therefore appeared in court an hour late and without Ah Fah. The judge, angry over the delay, declared Cameron in contempt of court.[33] Cameron insisted that it was necessary at times "to break the *letter* though not the *spirit* of the law when we rescued a Chinese child."[34] Cameron often carried out rescues similar to Ah Fah's, essentially kidnapping some children from their legal guardians and later applying for letters of guardianship in order to secure the mission's legal custody of the child. Cameron believed that any delay in the rescue would give the slave owners time to conceal the child. Missionaries acted in what they perceived to be the best interest of the children by first seeking to remove them from potentially life-threatening situations before the opportunity disappeared. Adults fought for physical possession of the children to achieve their own agendas.

Some parents teamed with missionaries in an attempt to regain custody of their children. In 1914 Yoke Wan filed a petition against Lee Git and Mar Shee to regain custody of her four-year-old daughter. As a prostitute in a Chinatown brothel, Yoke Wan had given birth to a baby girl. However, her owner had forced her to sell the baby to a Chinese couple when the baby was only three days old. Yoke Wan eventually married out of bondage and later sought refuge from this miserable marriage at the Presbyterian mission home. With the assistance of the missionaries, Yoke Wan hoped to regain custody of her child. In a series of more than forty court hearings lasting over a year and a half, the mother battled for the right to raise her own child while the foster parents tried to maintain custody of their adopted girl. Accusations flew as both parties attacked the character and parenting abilities of the other. A court order temporarily removed the child from her foster parents' custody into the hands of the missionaries. Yoke Wan, reunited with her long-lost daughter, arranged to take a photograph with her baby. Further court hearings and additional evidence refuted the mother's claims to custody. Dr. Emma La Fontaine, the physician who had attended the birth of the baby, testified that Yoke Wan willingly turned the baby over to the foster parents. Testimony from Reverend Fathers Thomas Cullen and Edward Brady of St. Mary's Paulist Church and from Joseph Cunningham of the Pacific Gas and Electric Company affirmed the good reputation of the foster parents. The court eventually dismissed Yoke Wan's petition, declaring her unfit for motherhood and affirming the guardianship rights of Mar Shee and Lee Git. Despite the mother's appeals, the state supreme court later upheld the decision.[35]

In rare cases, some guardians willingly relinquished their guardianship rights to missionaries, often out of a legitimate concern for a child's future. After noticing a seven-year-old girl struggling on crutches in Chinatown, Margarita Lake inquired into the girl's situation. She learned that Wong King Que had been hurt in a fall several years before; her hip had failed to set properly and had begun to decay. A doctor examined the girl and recommended immediate medical treatment. The fearful child hesitated, but her concerned parents desperately hoped to secure medical treatment for their daughter. The father offered her $1.00 to go with the white woman to the mission home. In September 1897 the parents of Wong King Que willingly granted guardianship of their daughter to Lake. Carefully negotiating the terms of the arrangement, the parents requested medical treatment, food, clothing, and education for their child while also retaining full visitation rights. The mother followed Lake and Wong King Que to the mission home and watched intently as missionaries clothed and bathed the ill child. Over the next year, Wong King Que endured three painful operations. At the children's hospital, Que had her leg amputated by white doctors. In October 1898, she wrote the following letter to Lake: "I got the doll and things you sent me and many thanks for them. Bring me out that dress you brought out before. My sour [sic] is nearly well. I am up walking now. Come out and see me Thursday if you can. If you do bring me out some cloth to make my doll a dress."[36] Despite the best efforts of her parents, the doctors, and the missionaries, Wong King Que contracted erysipelas, a bacterial skin infection, and died.

The cases of Yoke Wan and Wong King Que illustrate the cooperation between Chinese community members and missionaries to assist the children of Chinatown. As individual Chinese families turned to the missions and the courts for assistance, Chinese community leaders often forged alliances with white law-enforcement officers, reformers, journalists, and photographers in an effort to eliminate crime, protect Chinese families, and promote an alternate image of Chinese American family life that conformed to American middle-class notions of normative domesticity. Prostitution, domestic slavery, and crime all represented threats to that ideal image. The Chinese elite generally discouraged aberrations from a two-parent Chinese family model as a threat to the future of Chinese America.

BIRACIAL CHILDREN

The presence of biracial children in Chinatown often came to the attention of the courts, as these cases aroused fear over the slave trafficking of white children. San Francisco's *Morning Call* frequently cited examples of white babies recovered from dens of vice in Chinatown. In 1885 the newspaper reported that the SPCC had identified at least fifty white children who had been sold to Chinese men and women in the city. The organization further commented that "outgoing passengers for China have been seen carrying children of suspiciously white complexion and golden hair, and the possible extent of the heinous traffic in the past is indeterminable."[37] In 1886 the *Morning Call* detailed the suspicious story of a three-year-old baby of "Scandinavian parentage" recovered from a Chinese brothel on Jackson Street. Detectives discovered the blonde-haired child dressed in Chinese clothing and disguised with a fake queue. Despite the intense objections of the baby's Chinese parents, the officers removed the child to the headquarters of the SPCC.[38] In their annual report, the SPCC claimed to have recovered twenty-four additional white babies in Chinatown. The officers of the society had conducted a raid to locate and rescue these children from their suspected Chinese captors, removing the children to various charitable institutions in the city.[39] Whether these children represented conclusive evidence of the Chinese trafficking of white slave children, the offspring of interracial unions, or legitimate adoptions on the part of Chinese families appeared irrelevant to the authorities. Most of the time, rumors of white children in Chinatown proved to be more hysteria than reality. Nevertheless, private institutions like the SPCC and local law enforcement increasingly used their authority to intervene in family affairs in an attempt to protect the sexual morality and integrity of the white family by enforcing a segregated ideal of domesticity.[40]

Guardianship disputes involving biracial children proved especially contentious. Such cases not only aroused concern over the safety of the child but also raised questions about parental fitness. The primary question was whether it was appropriate for Chinese parents to raise a partially white child. A number of interesting cases appear in San Francisco's newspapers in the early twentieth century. The case of Ho Lin perhaps best illustrates efforts of reformers to police racialized domestic boundaries. In early January 1903, the police received a tip that a young girl named Ho Lin and disguised as a Chinese child was actually a white child sold by her parents into slavery. Detective George McMahon of the San Francisco Police Department and Frank J. Kane of the Pacific Humane Society stormed into the Chinese theater on Washington Street and seized Ho Lin. A Chinese actor, Ho Kin, and his actress wife, Ngan Yow, followed the officers to the prison, angrily protesting the seizure of the child and insisting that Ho Lin was their foster child.[41] The little girl sobbed and cried out "Mamma, Mamma!" as the matron of the city prison tried to assuage her fears. Although dressed in Chinese clothing, the girl's blue eyes and coppery brown hair attracted the attention of authorities and led Judge James V. Coffey to issue the writ that allowed Kane and McMahon to seize the child in the first place. Ho Kin desperately attempted to procure the release of Ho Lin on bail, but the bond clerks refused to allow it.[42] Prison officials sent the terrified child to the Chambers Chinese mission under the care of Rev. John and Naomi Sitton until the case could be decided in court.

The local newspapers watched the developing story with intense interest and closely questioned Ho Kin about the case. Ho Kin contended that Ho Lin was the child of a white woman in New York who had died when the baby was only seventeen days old. Josie Low, a half-white/half-Chinese woman who was a friend of the baby's mother, took care of the child after the mother's death. Unable to care for a baby and her own three children, Josie Low agreed to allow Ho Kin and his wife to adopt Ho Lin and raise her as their own. When reporters questioned Ho Kin as to why he had dressed the child in Chinese clothing and darkened her hair, he answered, "I wanted to make her look like my own child. I want to have her given back to me, but I do not understand the American law."[43] Ho Kin's act of dressing Ho Lin in Chinese clothing was also perhaps an effort to protect her from the suspicions of outsiders and prevent a public scandal such as the one that unfolded.

In the ensuing court battle, medical experts on both sides offered conflicting "scientific" testimony about the parentage of the child. Doctors analyzed her height, the color of her skin, eyes, and hair, the shape of her nose, and the diameter of her head in an effort to determine her race. Dr. William Barbat testified that he could not "see one characteristic of a Chinese about this little girl."[44] Dr. Albert J. Elliott disagreed, however, insisting that the "large square-shaped chest, eyebrows, almond eyes, texture of skin and hair, and shape of the hands were indisputable evidence that some Chinese blood flowed in Ah Lin's veins."[45] Dr. Vilva of the U.S. Chinese Bureau testified that he had seen interracial Chinese children with blonde hair and blue eyes. Vilva concluded that it could be impossible to tell whether a child was partially Chinese based only on physical appearance.[46]

Clearly the state intervention in the Ho Lin case reflected the anti-Chinese sentiment prevalent in California and the fear of the unassimilability of Chinese families. Anti-Chinese readers may have interpreted Ho Kin's decision to dress Ho Lin in Chinese clothing as his inability to conform to American cultural conventions and an unwillingness to recognize the girl's white heritage. Yet, in the eyes of some whites, Ho Kin had committed an even worse offense than simply failing to assimilate. The white public viewed the act of dressing Ho Lin in Chinese dress not only as a rejection of American cultural values but also as a clear attempt to assimilate a white child into Chinese culture. The primary objection was that Ho Lin's foster parents were not white and were therefore not fit to care for a white, or partially white, child.[47] The extensive examination of Ho Lin's physical features in an attempt to reveal the degree of her Chinese heritage also aroused fears that the Chinese *would* fully assimilate into American society—even to the point of marrying white women and producing mixed-race children.[48] Maintaining the segregated boundaries of the family thus proved an essential function of the court in these cases.

The Ho Lin case came to a rather abrupt end in January 1903. Confused (and probably annoyed) by the conflicting testimony, the judge ultimately returned Ho Lin to the custody of her foster parents and insisted that he had no jurisdiction in the matter since Ho Kin and Ngan Yow were residents of

New York.[49] Judge Coffey admitted that he had no doubt that the girl was partially Chinese and had been adopted by Ho Kin and Ngan Yow. He thus returned the child to their custody. For Ho Lin, the terrifying ordeal was finally over. Police had arrested her, missionaries had bathed and clothed her, and doctors had thoroughly examined her body in a fruitless attempt to determine her racial identity. Police, child-welfare officers, and reporters had delved deep into the personal lives of Ho Kin and Ngan Yow to scrutinize and challenge their parental rights. The *San Francisco Chronicle* seemed sympathetic to Ho Lin's ordeal, noting that the child had been forcibly removed from her people and now would return to Chinatown "to be Ah Lin the remainder of her days."[50] The reporter from the *Examiner*, however, was enraged by the judge's decision.

> Even the respectable Chinese are protesting against the delivery of this little girl into the hands of [Ho Kin and Ngan Yow]. These Chinese say that the fate of this child is as certain as it is horrible, and they fear that she will never again be seen by the eyes of her own people. She will be immured in the very depths of the lowest kennels of the Chinese quarter, and she will die as hundreds of others are dying—in misery, despair and the agony that shrieks to echoless walls, and ears as deaf to her pitiful cries as are those insensate walls of her living tomb. Apparently there is no hope for little Ah Lin, the white Chinese slave. The law has allowed it, and the court has awarded it.[51]

The division in the Chinese community over Ho Lin's fate suggests that some Chinese may have recognized that the outcome of this case would have an impact on the public perception of the Chinese American community. Their objection no doubt was formed partly out of concern for the safety of the child and partly out of a desire to promote a positive image of Chinese America through a normative model of domesticity. Ho Lin became a physical symbol of decades of racial tensions and anxieties between Chinese and white Americans.

THE MISSION METHOD

After the guardianship issues had been settled and a child was securely in the care of the missions, reformers began the process of reeducating their charges. Chinese assistants worked as interpreters in the homes and assisted

Rescued Chinese slave girls living at the Methodist mission home. Ethel, Josephine, and Margaret are in the back row, left to right; Maude, Siu, Helen, Gene, and Marie are in the front row, left to right. (1993.033:50–ALB, ca. 1906; courtesy of the Bancroft Library, University of California, Berkeley)

in the schools to help ease the transition for the women and children. Older girls served as mentors for the increasing numbers of younger children who came into the missions. Education at the missions included religious and domestic training as well as traditional schooling. In the Methodist mission, the children typically rose at 6:00 A.M. and dressed for breakfast by 6:30 A.M. Mission home life consisted of daily routines of singing and prayers, lessons in English, and domestic chores such as washing, sewing, cooking, and cleaning. Missionaries also attempted to provide education in Chinese language and history to foster an understanding of the children's own native culture. The monotony of schoolwork and chores in the mission homes was broken by holidays and occasional outings to places such as Golden Gate Park.[52]

The Methodists and Presbyterians encouraged the children to retain their Chinese cultural heritage while adopting American habits of domesticity. Photographs of the mission girls show them in both Chinese and Western clothing engaging in a variety of domestic activities. Donaldina Cameron of the Presbyterian mission told reporters in 1901 that the children wore Chinese clothing and learned to read and write Chinese because the goal was to make them useful members of the Chinese American community. The reporter also noted that the goal was to make them good wives for respectable Chinese men.[53] The missions thus attempted to enforce a segregated, American middle-class ideal of domesticity while encouraging their charges to at least partially retain their Chinese cultural identity. Beginning in the late nineteenth century, reformers such as Jane Addams encouraged immigrants to retain their native dress, language, food, holidays, and folklore in an effort to avoid forcing their pupils to choose between two cultures and to help with their assimilation.[54] The work of missionaries such as Donaldina Cameron at the Presbyterian mission followed in this vein.

The population of the missions seemed to continually grow. By 1900 the Methodist mission was home to thirteen women and girls, six of whom were sixteen or younger. The youngest residents were two six-year-old girls. That same year, the census reported that the Presbyterian mission home housed thirty-six women and girls. Seventeen of the residents were sixteen and under, while seven were under age ten.[55] By 1915 the Presbyterian mission home was so crowded that the managers opened the Tooker Home in East Oakland to accommodate many of the younger children from San Francisco. In the 1920s Dr. Charles R. Shepherd, a Baptist medical missionary, opened the Chung Mei Home for orphaned Chinese boys in Oakland.[56]

THE BATTLE AGAINST VICE

The growing number of two-parent families in the late nineteenth century increasingly demanded efforts to eliminate crime in Chinatown. Chinatown merchants and business owners also objected to the existence of prostitution in Chinatown, as it adversely impacted the success of their businesses. The intent to protect their families from violence and immorality, combined with a desire to attract more tourism (and therefore business) to Chinatown, influenced Chinatown officials to campaign against tongs and prostitutes.[57] Editorials in the Chung Sai Yat Po insisted on the eradication of prostitution and the mui tsai system. The Chinese consulate, Chinese Six Companies, Chinese Society of English Education, Chinese Students' Alliance, Chinese American Citizens Alliance, and Chinese Cadet Corps also fought to break the power of the tongs and end prostitution in Chinatown.[58] Some individuals risked their lives to stop the trafficking of women into America. Members of the Chinese Society of English Education, composed of prominent Chinatown merchants and professional men, hired attorneys and actively assisted immigration authorities in attempting to prevent the landing of prostitutes. After the society interfered with the landing of alleged prostitute Kan Kam Oi in 1897, tong leaders determined to take coercive action against the society's members. A letter specifically addressed to six members of the society insisted that unless the individuals abandoned their efforts to prevent the landing of Chinese prostitutes, the members would not live more than one month. Several days later, placards appeared on billboards in Chinatown announcing that the tongs had hired assassins, or highbinders, to execute the society members. With the assistance of local police and hired bodyguards, the society members managed to thwart the efforts of the assassins. This incident, and the publicity produced by the *San Francisco Call*, encouraged San Franciscans to draft a petition to President William McKinley demanding more decisive action against Chinese slavery.[59] The battle raged for years as the slave dealers, well equipped with money and lawyers, continued to resist all efforts to suppress the lucrative trade. In 1898 a rash of kidnapping cases inspired a representative of the Chinese consul in San Francisco to appeal directly to the chief of police for aid in capturing the highbinders responsible for the disappearance of several women and young girls in the city.[60] Chinese community leaders turned to the police and legislators for assistance in battling crime in Chinatown.

Coinciding with this controversy over forced prostitution, white female reformers began to launch campaigns that attacked the double standard of sexual behavior. In the late nineteenth and early twentieth centuries, middle-class efforts to police female adolescent sexuality in the United States resulted in purity campaigns that demanded specific government action. Progressive reformers no longer viewed women as simply victims but looked to environmental factors to explain the increased sexual immorality of working-class youth. California women campaigned against laws that punished women more harshly than men for sexual transgressions. Prior to 1889, California's age of consent was ten years old. The state's Woman's Christian Temperance Union lobbied for a bill to increase the age of consent to eighteen. In 1897 the state legislature settled on sixteen as the age of consent.[61] Ironically, as historian Mary Odem argues, rather than empowering young women to resist sexual exploitation, the laws resulting from the social-purity campaigns "merely perpetuated the stigma and supported the punishment of working-class females who engaged in unorthodox sexual behavior."[62] However, the efforts of both American and Chinese reformers in San Francisco proved crucial in establishing the legal framework necessary to protect Chinese children from a transnational system of sexual exploitation and physical abuse.

Newspaper reports of the persistence of prostitution and child domestic servitude fanned the flames of public anxiety and furthered the desire to suppress vice in Chinatown. As white-slavery hysteria gripped the nation, cities across the country formed vice commissions to investigate the problem of prostitution in their communities. In February 1901 the California state assembly committee investigated rumors of corruption and graft in the San Francisco Police Department. The Fisk Investigative Committee, under the leadership of Assemblyman Joseph R. Knowland, accused Mayor James D. Phelan and Chief of Police William P. Sullivan Jr. of failing to enforce the laws against gambling and prostitution in Chinatown and making little effort to remove minors from houses of ill repute.[63]

Missionaries and ministers publicly condemned the political corruption in sermons that ended in a denunciation of law-enforcement and city officials for failing to protect Chinese women and children. The Reverend Frank C. Baker of the First Methodist Episcopal Church implicated the mayor, the chief of police, and the Police Commission in the perpetuation of Chinese sexual slavery.[64] Margarita Lake and Donaldina Cameron both accused police of ignoring criminal activity in Chinatown. Lake and Cameron testified that the police only took action when specifically called upon. The missionaries and child-protective societies further testified to police efforts in thwarting their rescue missions.[65] Missionaries and reformers used the stories of these Chinese children not only as evidence of the corruption of the San Francisco Police Department but also as part of a broader effort to eliminate graft and reform local government.

The campaign against white slavery gained momentum in the early twentieth century as reformers publicized the results of federal, state, and local investigations. In 1909 a Senate commission, popularly known as the Dillingham Commission, reflected growing nativism by largely blaming foreigners for the growth of the white slave trade in America. The official report reflected national anxiety about the sexual danger of the new immigrant.[66] In San Francisco, concerns about public health culminated in a 1911 decision by the Board of Public Health to segregate prostitution to a specific district and to certify the health of these prostitutes in the Municipal Clinic. After a brief experiment in legalized and regulated prostitution, public complaints from social-purity advocates, who preferred to eliminate prostitution altogether, and threats of a boycott of the upcoming Panama-Pacific International Exposition eventually forced the mayor to abandon the clinic in 1913. That same year, the state legislature passed the Redlight Injunction and Abatement Act, which declared brothels public nuisances and allowed citizens to sue the owners of houses of prostitution. In 1917 police forced all prostitutes out of the buildings in San Francisco's Barbary Coast. The adoption of abolitionist policies drove prostitution underground and led to its dispersal throughout the city.[67] Although the rescue efforts of missionaries and legal attempts to eliminate prostitution did greatly reduce the visibility of the sex trade in the city, Chinese brothels remained a fixture in San Francisco for some time afterward. Stories of the plight of Chinese slave girls remained a popular genre that continued to serve the purposes of both reformers and anti-Chinese politicians into the 1920s.

CHINESE BOYS AND THE CRIMINAL JUSTICE SYSTEM

Anti-Chinese San Franciscans attributed the overall growth of crime in the city to the presence of Chinese immigrants. The prevalence of numerous opium dens and gambling halls in Chinatown further contributed to Chinatown's sordid reputation. Police mug-shot books from the late nineteenth and early twentieth centuries recorded a large number of Chinese criminals. Although much of modern historical research focuses on the delinquency of Chinatown's girls, young Chinese boys also sometimes found themselves in trouble with the law. Temporarily free from parental supervision and the societal constraints of their homeland, some young immigrant boys chose to engage in criminal activity. Immigrant children in urban settings frequently joined gangs or resorted to small-scale crime as a means of coping with poverty, familial conflicts, and cultural dislocation. Selma Cantor Berrol has noted that immigrant children or second-generation children constituted half of the population of New York City's juvenile reformatories and houses of refuge in 1850. Recently arrived immigrants were frequently most at risk.[68] Throughout the 1870s, Chinese boys often appeared in the police records in San Francisco as perpetrators of petty theft and other small crimes. A few became adult members of the notorious tongs and profited from the illicit business of the criminal underworld in Chinatown. Most boys, however, were only temporarily sidetracked by minor transgressions of the law.

At this point, it is impossible to provide an accurate statistical comparison of Chinese juvenile criminals compared to other immigrant groups or even compared to adult offenders in San Francisco. The majority of nineteenth-century police and court records for San Francisco were lost in the 1906 earthquake and fires. Although only a few incomplete police mug-shot books and records remain, these records can provide some insight into the nature of juvenile delinquency in early Chinatown. The surviving San Francisco police records of 1876, for example, reveal a number of Chinese youth arrested for petit larceny and burglary.[69] Boys as young as fourteen served time in county and state correctional facilities, often confined with adult offenders. The sentences for such crimes varied from ten days in the county jail to four years in the state prison. A small number of the arrested Chinese children were committed to the San Francisco Industrial School for juvenile offenders. The length of the sentence and the location of confinement no doubt depended on the severity of the crime, the will of the judge, and the history of prior offenses. Ah Lin began his criminal career at age thirteen and operated under a number of aliases, including Ah Hoy, Ah Loy, Ah Sam, Yee Ah Sam, and Louis Sing. He was arrested three times for petit larceny and twice for burglary or attempted burglary, serving sentences ranging from thirty days in the county jail to four years in the state prison. Although the documentary evidence is limited, Ah Lin's life of crime is no doubt typical of the cycle of delinquency that many Chinese juveniles found themselves unable to break.[70]

The surviving remnants of police records seem to indicate that the Chinese committed a disproportionate number of crimes in early Chinatown. Nineteenth-century census data also support this assumption. In 1880 census enumerators determined that 4 percent of the inmates at the city prison were Chinese. For the fiscal year 1879–80, 11 percent of the prisoners at the city's House of Correction were Chinese. Yet, the Chinese comprised only about 9 percent of the city population according to the 1880 census.[71] That same year, Chinese inmates constituted 18 percent of the prison population at San Quentin. The vast majority were adult criminals; however, eleven (4 percent) of the Chinese prisoners were children under age sixteen.[72] The absence of a stable family life may partially account for the higher crime rate among Chinese immigrants; however, when one considers that this was the period of intense anti-Chinese sentiment in California and just two years before the passage of the Chinese Exclusion Act, the question of selective enforcement of laws emerges.

Discriminatory laws and selective enforcement had been a reality since the mid-nineteenth century. Many of the city ordinances discussed in previous chapters were designed primarily to target and harass the Chinese population. For example, in 1882 the *Morning Call* reported the arrest of several Chinese men for sleeping in hallways in what constituted a violation of the Cubic Air Ordinance. Three of the offenders were children under fourteen, and therefore they were only sentenced to twenty-four hours in jail. The remainder, however, were adults sentenced to ten days in jail.[73] City officials created the Cubic Air Ordinance to regulate the number of people living in a building with the knowledge that Chinese men frequently lived in communal settings with large numbers of individuals housed in a single dwelling. Although this law clearly related to the health and safety of the entire community, law-enforcement officials primarily used it against the Chinese community as part of a larger effort to encourage the departure of Chinese immigrants from San Francisco. A study conducted by Walter Beach in 1932 suggested that the crimes attributed to Chinese in California between 1900 and 1921 were predominately offenses against public policy and morals or health and safety rather than crimes against persons or property. Law-enforcement officials most frequently arrested Chinese for violations of gaming, lottery, vagrancy, or immigration laws or for possession of narcotics, especially opium. According to Beach's research, crimes against persons and property constituted less than 2 percent of all the crimes attributed to the Chinese in the first two decades of the twentieth century. Furthermore, crime attributed to Chinese youth was also extremely low, with less than 3 percent of the arrests of Chinese criminals involving teenagers between the ages of fifteen and nineteen.[74] Thus, publicized incidents of crime among the Chinese reveal as much about the biases of the judicial system as they do about the nature of crime in Chinatown itself.

By 1900 the number of Chinese criminals seemed to be in decline. Chinese inmates constituted only 4 percent of the prison population of San Quentin and Folsom combined. This number was just 1 percent above the total Chinese population for California.[75] Although the total number of Chinese criminals appeared to have greatly declined after 1900, tong violence in San Francisco's Chinatown became the subject of public scrutiny. At the same time that merchants and leaders were trying to improve Chinatown's image and destroy the power of the tongs, the media increasingly focused on vice in Chinatown. Bloody tong murders made headline news in San Francisco.

Tong violence posed a very real threat to the safety and security of the Chinese community. Whereas Beach looked at the overall arrest statistics for Chinese in California, Kevin Mullen's 2005 research, focused specifically on the city of San Francisco, reveals high rates of violence among the Chinese. Mullen argues that from 1870 to 1930, the Chinese accounted for 19.9 percent of the homicides in San Francisco, or more than three times their representation in the city. The statistics also reveal that convicted Chinese murderers were twice as likely to be hanged or receive a life sentence in San Francisco. Although he does not discount the possibility that anti-Chinese sentiment accounted for the higher rate of capital punishment, Mullen argues that the premeditated nature of the murders (occurring in the form of robberies, extortions, or ownership disputes) probably accounts for the severe sentences.[76] Murders committed in the "heat of passion" were less frequent, although such incidents did occur and young Chinese sometimes were the victims. In 1911 police discovered sixteen-year-old Chun Ah Lee dead in her apartment with her throat slashed from ear to ear. Evidence of a struggle convinced authorities that Leong Soon, Chun Ah Lee's husband, had killed her in a fit of jealousy. Friends and family of the couple had reported that Leong Soon had "complained of her actions in paying attentions to other men." This act of domestic violence ended tragically for the child bride.[77]

Mullen argues that although the overall percentage of murders committed by Chinese declined over time, the homicide rate for Chinese continued to dramatically rise after the turn of the century. An upsurge in tong violence, coupled with an overall decline in the Chinese population in San Francisco, can help account for the dramatic increase in the Chinese homicide rate.[78] The brutal nature of these killings, and their media coverage, intensified public fears of crime in Chinatown at the same time that Chinese merchants were attempting to attract the business of white tourists. In an effort to improve the image of Chinatown, the Chinese Six Companies and groups of prominent merchants requested that law enforcement put more pressure on the tongs. Although the San Francisco Police Department created the Chinatown Squad as early as 1877 to prevent crime in Chinatown, actual enforcement of the laws varied greatly. The police officers of the Chinatown Squad conducted legally questionable raids, using axes to break into gambling dens and intimidate gang leaders. Despite the effective hard-line enforcement tactics, accusations of police corruption and collusion with tong leaders challenged the credibility of the Chinatown Squad.[79] The 1901 results of a grand jury investigation and a state assembly investigation committee confirmed the continued existence of graft in the San Francisco Police Department and led to public demand for stronger law enforcement in Chinatown.[80] Chinese community leaders sought law-enforcement assistance in protecting Chinese women and children from tong violence.

Despite general disdain for the adult male Chinese criminal, there was a tendency among whites to view immigrant boys as redeemable. In the increasingly accepted view of children as malleable, reformers tended to believe that young children might be reformed and assimilated. The literature of the Methodist and Presbyterian Chinese missions and articles in the popular press reflected this idea.[81] Mainstream books, newspapers, and popular periodicals describing Chinatown also reflected an Orientalized image of Chinese childhood, coupled with a belief in the redemptive potential of Chinese children. An article in *Scribner's Monthly* in 1876 noted that "the grown-up children, the boys and girls of nine and thereabouts, are decidedly uninteresting, being nothing more than a needless addition to the hoodlum ranks of San Francisco; but the *nune-mun-chi* (baby) is quite an attractive little atom. . . . [T]he prevailing dinginess of the Chinese quarter is considerably relieved by the gaudy costumes of the children."[82] The author relies on conventional stereotypes of the vice of Chinatown and contrasts these with the idea that younger Chinese children bear none of the stain or corruption of their older counterparts. The fear of youthful depravity, coupled with a belief in the ability to redeem and reform children, inspired major changes in the juvenile justice system of nineteenth-century California.

INDUSTRIAL SCHOOLS AND THE JUVENILE COURT

Concern over the welfare of child offenders began in the early nineteenth century. In 1824 reformers in New York City established the first juvenile reformatory. The founders of the New York House of Refuge intended to reform criminal, vagrant, neglected, and unruly children.[83] The institutional movement spread throughout the country, and efforts to reform delinquents in San Francisco began as early as the 1850s. Reformers grew increasingly alarmed with the negative effects of imprisoning minors with adult criminals. In 1858 San Francisco established the Industrial School, which was based on the penitentiary model that sought to reform troubled youth through isolation in institutions. Divided into three stories, the school housed inmates on the second and third floors. The children slept on metal bunks in cells that measured 5 ½ feet by 7 ½ feet and shared toilet and bathing facilities with the other inmates who lived on the floor. The children marched to and from their daily activities and adhered to other strict rules that regulated their conduct.[84] The vast majority of the youth committed to the institution had been convicted of "leading an idle and dissolute life." The president of the Industrial School Department, Nathan Porter, insisted that the school's purpose was to reform young boys by teaching them useful trades and occupations. Inmates learned to make clothing, boots, and shoes, washed and ironed clothes, and grew their own vegetables.[85] This regimen would also help to instill discipline and prevent children from turning to a life of crime.

The Industrial School offered its reform program to all children, regardless of race. Between 1859 and 1889, Chinese children never constituted more than 16 percent of the school's population in any given year and typically composed less than 1 percent of the total student body.[86] In 1863–64 the school reported eighteen Chinese girls and one Chinese boy, totaling 17 percent of the school's total population. The next year, the Industrial School housed seventeen Chinese children, or about 14 percent of the school's population. Thirteen of these children were girls. These figures suggest that prior to the establishment of the Chinese mission homes, the Industrial School had sheltered Chinese girls arrested for prostitution.[87] However, after 1866 the Chinese inmates of the school were predominately male. The Chinese children experienced the same disciplined regimen as their white counterparts.

Ironically, children committed to the Industrial School may have faced conditions far worse than any they had encountered at home. During the school's first year of operation (1859–60), the chief of police reported thirty-four arrests of children who had escaped from school grounds.[88] Although some of these escapes may have been multiple attempts by the same children, the high number seems to indicate the level of discontent with conditions at the school. In an effort to limit the opportunity for escape, the administration denied inmates access to shoes and socks and later built a twelve-foot-high fence around the perimeter of the building.[89] School officials tended to downplay the incidents, defensively reporting that the escapes could be attributed to "the whim of the moment," and that on at least one occasion, seven children had only temporarily run off to see some elephants that they had heard about. School officials noted that the boys generally returned on their own within a few days.[90] Still, these escape attempts represent tangible evidence of inmate discontent with conditions in the school.

An official investigation of the San Francisco Industrial School in 1869 revealed the extent of the cruelty children faced in the institution. Responding to reports from local newspapers, the board of managers of the Industrial School launched an investigation of the school superintendent, Colonel Joseph Wood. The investigators found Wood guilty of embezzlement of funds, theft of state property, and numerous instances of physical abuse of the children under his care. Inmates and staff testified that misbehaving boys were sometimes committed to solitary confinement, fed only bread and water, bucked, gagged, and/or whipped.[91] Following the investigation, the new administration insisted that they had replaced all cruelty and harshness with "a system of kindness." School officials also decided that a separation of the sexes would facilitate efforts at reform, so the Sisters of Mercy formed the Magdalen Asylum to house wayward and delinquent girls. Although physically separated from the boys' school, the girls officially remained under the authority of Industrial School administrators.[92] Despite the changes in administration, inmates continued to express frustration over their commitment to the institution.

Some inmates legally challenged their confinement in the Industrial School. In 1872 Frederick H. Adams, an attorney for a sixteen-year-old Chinese boy named Ah Peen, questioned the constitutionality of the boy's imprisonment in the Industrial School. Although he had committed no crime, the boy had been arrested by police for "leading an idle and dissolute life." Adams, relying on a precedent set by the Illinois Supreme Court, challenged the authority of police court judges by claiming that the courts had denied Peen due process and the right to a trial by jury prior to his imprisonment in the Industrial School. The California Supreme Court, however, denied the claim, arguing that the intent of the court was not to punish or imprison Peen but to isolate and reform him. The state reserved the right to intervene on behalf of such children under the doctrine of *parens patriae* (the legal concept that empowers the government to assume guardianship of orphaned or neglected children). The court remanded Ah Peen to the custody of the superintendent of the Industrial School.[93] Although some children such as Ah Peen questioned the authority of the Industrial School, the courts effectively upheld the authority of the state over orphaned, abandoned, or otherwise neglected minors.

Despite the changes in administration in the early 1870s, criticism from outsiders and a general lack of resources continued to plague the Industrial School staff. Challenges from the juvenile inmates also remained a problem. By the late 1880s, the state legislature had approved the creation of the Whittier State School and the Preston School of Industry to reform and train youthful offenders. The legislature also created a separate school, the California School for Girls, for female juvenile offenders. The opening of these schools eventually forced the closure of the San Francisco Industrial School in 1892.[94]

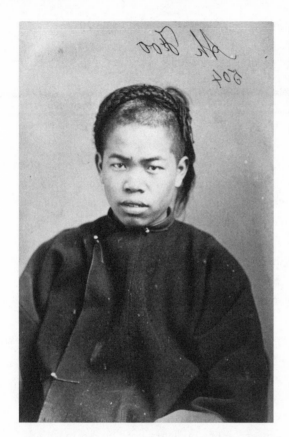

A youthful Chinese offender (Photograph 110, Delos Woodruff's Album of Chinese Prisoners, San Francisco, ca. 1872 to 1880s; vault #185:39, California Historical Society, FN-36603)

The records of the Whittier and Preston reform schools indicate the presence of a small number of Chinese inmates. Because these schools accepted children from all over the state, the percentage of Chinese children remained generally less than 1 percent. An interesting case from the inmate registers illustrates the types of crimes for which the courts committed Chinese boys to the institutions. On July 6, 1900, a judge committed San Francisco native Yet Chew to the Preston School of Industry for grand larceny. The sixteen-year-old boy apparently stole his employer's diamonds while working as a cook for Mrs. Nelhi Phinney on Van Ness Avenue. Yet Chew denied guilt and testified that a friend had actually stolen the diamonds and pawned them. However, police apparently discovered a pawn ticket in Yet Chew's room, implicating him in the crime. Although Judge William P. Lawlor of the San Francisco Superior Court sentenced Yet Chew to four years at Preston, school officials ordered his discharge after only two and a half years, probably as a reward for good behavior.[95] The majority of boys committed to these institutions served time for similar types of property offenses.

Despite the existence of the Industrial School and later juvenile reformatories, the courts by necessity continued to confine some violent youth offenders to the state prison or the county jail. Children convicted of property crimes also sometimes ended up in the state prison. In 1874 a San Francisco judge sentenced fourteen-year-old Ah Quong to serve three years at San Quentin for burglary. San Quentin housed eleven Chinese boys under age sixteen in 1880.[96] The number of children imprisoned with adults had declined by the start of the twentieth century. However, as late as 1900, census enumerators listed two Chinese boys as inmates of the county jail.[97]

Reformers increasingly argued for a different approach to the treatment of children in the court system. Society generally accepted a view of criminals as conditioned in part by biology and in part by living conditions. In this nature-and-nurture model, reformers argued that the best approach to criminal justice was to prevent the creation of criminals through an emphasis on sobriety, thrift, industry, and education during childhood. Progressives tended to argue that urbanization and industrialization disrupted family lives and made it more difficult for working-class parents to raise their children in safe, moral conditions. The appeal of city life proved particularly tempting to youth. In 1911 officials of the San Francisco Juvenile Court noted that trouble for a boy "usually begins by his remaining out late nights; he gets in with the 'gang'; he smokes cigarettes; drinks a little; hangs around the street corners and the cheap theatres; in the morning he over-sleeps and is late at his work; soon he loses his job, and then he goes on the 'bum.' "[98] Court officials argued that girls, on the other hand, more frequently fell victim to temptations of "immorality" as a result of low wages in the factories and the appeal of urban commercialized amusements, such as dance halls and cafés.[99] Progressives believed that the influence of immigrant cultures also posed a threat to American families. Juvenile justice reformers pushed for the segregation of youth and adult criminals, private and informal court hearings, and the removal of delinquents from corrupting influences. The general juvenile justice philosophy increasingly evolved into an emphasis on assistance and guidance rather than criminal punishment for youthful offenders. A professional class of juvenile justice administrators and civil servants emerged to address the unique needs of these offenders.[100]

By the late nineteenth century, increasing frustration with the failures of reform schools and efforts to protect abused and neglected children encouraged movements against child labor and in support of compulsory education and juvenile court legislation. The creation of the first juvenile court in Chicago in 1899 provided the model for juvenile justice in cities across the nation. In 1903 California adopted the Juvenile Court Law, which provided separate court hearings for minors; authorized judges to appoint probation officers for children; prohibited the confinement of children in the same institution, room, yard, or enclosure with adult criminals; and allowed courts to commit children to societies that provided for neglected, dependent, or delinquent children. Although San Francisco had already taken many of these steps in the treatment of juvenile offenders, the creation of the juvenile court in San Francisco emerged from the 1903 law. Judge Murasky served as the first juvenile court judge.[101] Law enforcement increasingly referred youthful offenders to the juvenile court. Chinese children, and other immigrant and native-born youth, had to answer to Judge Murasky for their offenses.

Judge Murasky believed that the purpose of the juvenile court was "to exert the influence of a careful parent."[102] San Francisco city officials authorized the construction of a Juvenile Detention Home to provide temporary detainment facilities for wards of the juvenile court while separating and removing them from adult criminals. Probation officers investigated the child's home life, personal acquaintances, leisure activities, school attendance, and work record. Court officials blamed juvenile delinquency primarily on negative environmental influences and personal associations. Native-born Anglo-Americans frequently associated immigrant families (and Chinese children specifically) with disease and moral corruption. By 1913 the San Francisco Police no longer arrested children who committed minor offenses. Instead, city probation officers handled the matter by simply visiting the child and parents in the home and attempting to directly deal with the issue. When possible, Judge Murasky avoided removing the child from the home, preferring instead to reform the family by encouraging "habits of cleanliness, sobriety, and industry." The court increasingly committed children to a state institution such as Preston or Whittier only as a last resort.[103]

The juvenile court intervened in family affairs when necessary to protect the welfare of the child. Although as a general policy the judges avoided removal of juvenile offenders from their family, in a few extreme cases of child abuse or neglect, removal remained the best option to ensure the safety and rehabilitation of the child. The majority of the children who came before the juvenile court stood accused of minor crimes such as petit larceny or simply "wayward or incorrigible" behavior. In 1913 Chong Joe Quong stole twenty dollars from his mother's purse and ran away from his home on Grant Avenue in San Francisco. The boy, listed in the newspaper as under the age of ten, ran away to Oakland, where he and a friend rented a boat and went for a joy ride on Lake Merritt. The Oakland police attempted to track him down.[104] Frustrated families sometimes appealed to the juvenile court to resolve irreconcilable family disputes. Historians of the Progressive Era have noted that immigrant parents tended to turn to the juvenile court for assistance with wayward children and for resolving generational conflicts.[105] The evidence presented here indicates that Chinese parents, distraught over the delinquency of their children, also began to turn to the justice system and missions for assistance. This may seem especially ironic, given the history of anti-Chinese laws and the courts' tendency to side with white missionaries in guardianship disputes involving Chinese children. Yet, as we have seen in previous chapters, the Chinese frequently appealed to the courts for assistance in battling exclusion and segregation. It seems reasonable to assume that individual Chinese would also turn to the courts for help resolving difficult family matters.

Some parents sought state intervention when traditional methods of parenting failed. Ignoring curfews and creating havoc, Elmer Wok Wai recalled numerous encounters with the Chinatown Squad in his youth: "They used to catch me and take me to the police station and pretend to ring for the patrol wagon—holding down the telephone receiver all the while. Then in a few minutes, as of course that wagon didn't come, they would give me a kick and let me go."[106] His frustrated father, angered over the boy's frequent transgressions and attempts to run away from home, finally took him to an orphan asylum on Christmas Eve. The children were playing with games and toys and enjoying the festivities of the holiday. When his father asked him if he wanted to stay, the boy responded in the affirmative. However, Wai quickly recognized his father's deception when the home returned to its normal daily routine. Limited and poor-quality food, coupled with a daily regimen of prayers, reduced Wai to tears. His father arrived at the end of the month and, feeling sorry for Wai, took him home again. However, Wai did not immediately reform his delinquent behavior. When the boy again ran away from home, his father found him and took him before Judge Murasky of the juvenile court, who insisted that Wai return to his father's home. Despite the best efforts of his father and Judge Murasky, Wai continued his life of crime, eventually becoming a tong member and serving time in San Quentin for committing murder at the age of sixteen.[107]

Cases of juvenile incorrigibility often reveal the frustrations and echo the concerns of many immigrant Chinese parents struggling to control the behavior of the second generation. In 1903 fourteen-year-old Ah Sam was seized by the California SPCC at the request of his parents, who insisted that the boy was out of control. Sam stayed out late at nights and refused to obey his mother and father. When Officer McMurray from the SPCC arrived at the family home, Sam threatened to kill himself. McMurray thwarted the attempt and took the boy before Police Judge Alfred Fritz. The parents intended to place Sam at the Boys' and Girls' Aid Society, but they relented after he begged to be returned home. The frustrated parents agreed to give the boy another chance.[108] The court offered a recourse when generational conflicts proved irreconcilable.

A few parents blamed their children's behavior on the negative influence of Americanization. Chum Shee, the widowed mother of thirteen-year-old Lee Kee Cheong, appealed to the Oakland court in her efforts to control her son. Since his father's death in the San Francisco earthquake, the boy had begun to smoke cigarettes and opium, drink, and run away from home. Chum Shee told the judge that she believed that contact with white boys had led to the corruption of her son. Judge Melville deemed the boy incorrigible and sent him to the Preston School in Ione. Lee Kee Cheong expressed his discontent with the court's decision by kicking and screaming as officers dragged him from the courtroom.[109] A similar case from Los Angeles also serves to illustrate the point of some parents that Americanization could have negative consequences. In May 1904 Wong Fon Sue, a merchant in Los Angeles's Chinatown, had his son, Wong Fong Sue, arrested for incorrigibility. The *Los Angeles Express* followed the case closely and reported that the father objected to his son's adoption of an American hairstyle and clothes. However, Wong Fon Sue, through an interpreter, told juvenile court judge Wilbur that his problem was that his son stayed out late at night, gambled, and was unwilling to help support the family, which included six other children. No doubt hoping to gain sympathy from the white judge, the boy argued that he disobeyed his father because his father wanted him to work in a gambling den. The judge apparently agreed with the father that the child was in need of reform and ordered Wong Fong Sue committed to the reform school at Whittier on May 20, 1904.[110] Although both Chum Shee and Wong Fon Sue partially blamed American culture for the behavior of their sons, they appealed to the American juvenile justice system to reform their children.

Split-household immigrant families may have more frequently turned to the courts and the state to assist in rearing especially difficult children. In 1913 Soon Lee's father had him committed to the Preston School of Industry for smoking opium. Soon Lee's case file noted that his mother remained with two children at the family home in China, while his father was raising the boy and his brother in San Francisco. The difficulties of child rearing were further exacerbated by the split-household model and the pressures it created for the parent raising the children alone in America. When all else failed, the records indicate, some Chinese parents relied on the courts to assist in the child-rearing process. However, as immigrant parents increasingly relied on the assistance of missions and the courts in the reformation of wayward children, they gradually transferred their parental authority to the state. This was the essential irony of the Progressive reforms that were intended to strengthen the family and the home.[111]

CONCLUSION

As previous chapters have demonstrated, by 1900 the vast majority of children in San Francisco's Chinatown lived in two-parent families and spent the majority of their day in school. Ironically, this is also the period of the most fantastic journalistic accounts detailing lurid cases of prostitution, child slavery, and crime in Chinatown. The image of vice in Chinatown obscured middle-class Chinese American family life. Unfortunately, crime and vice were a reality for poor, working-class children in Chinatown. Adolescent girls, either willingly or forced, participated in the sex trade in San Francisco. Boys turned to petty theft or more serious crimes under the influence of powerful Chinatown tongs. Although crime was a fact of life, the cases highlighted by reporters and the individual stories presented in this chapter were mostly exceptional accounts that deviated from the standard and exceedingly private narrative of family life in Chinatown. Journalists and entrepreneurs, seeking to profit from the public's fascination with scandal, marketed an image of Chinatown's vice to the paying public.

Chinese children were especially vulnerable to exploitation. Although reformers' efforts to assist Chinese children were clearly influenced by their desire to hasten the Americanization and Christianization of Chinese families, the missionaries were also instrumental in assisting relatively helpless

Chinese children escape the clutches of an oppressive system of exploitation. The images of an innocent and malleable Chinese childhood that the missionaries promoted stood in stark contrast to the images of deviant Chinese domesticity promoted by anti-Chinese writers. Regardless of their inherent attitude of cultural superiority, these missionaries proved important allies of the children of Chinatown.[112] Chinese community leaders, concerned with the political and economic repercussions of crime in Chinatown and its impact on their own children, demanded that law enforcement suppress the trafficking of prostitutes and insisted on an end to tong violence. Chinese parents, distraught and frustrated over the delinquent behavior of their children, sometimes found an ally in the missions and juvenile court system. White and Chinese missionaries, social reformers, law-enforcement officers, and community leaders often worked together to eliminate vice in the community. Chinese children also found a voice through the missions and courts and attempted to use the system to secure their futures. It is important to recognize that the effort to eliminate child abuse and sexual assault in early Chinatown in order to create a safer environment for Chinese children was a collaborative endeavor on the part of white and Chinese reformers, informants, interpreters, and community leaders. The next chapter explores how images of Chinese childhood and the children themselves would come to play a key role in the campaign to clean up Chinatown's image.

6   CHILDREN OF THE NEW CHINATOWN

In a 1902 article in the *San Francisco Chronicle* titled "How to Show Your Eastern Cousins through Chinatown," the reporter painted contrasting images of the children in Chinatown, beginning with a description of the following scene at Fish Alley: "[L]ittle groups of grotesquely decorated children scurry about among the horrid odors and heaps of decaying fruits, vegetables and fish. . . . And a howling mob of cats and dogs are fighting and chasing one another, the children and themselves in a sort of wild dance among the heaps of refuse."[1] In this bit of imagery, the reporter relies on stereotypes of a dirty and disease-ridden Chinatown, popularized and perpetuated by anti-Chinese politicians. The writer compares the heathen children to animals, inherently corrupted by their race and further soiled by an environment of filth. The children in this example clearly represent a threat to the moral and physical safety and security of American homes. However, as the author continues on his tour of Chinatown, he offers a more favorable account of Chinese childhood found near Pacific and Dupont Streets. In that area lived "a Christianized family of Chinese who love to do 'stunts' for the edification of the tourist." The family's "four little yellow tots, with silken pigtails hanging down their backs, will sing their Sunday-school songs for you, while fond papa will bring out for your inspection his newest, tiny baby, that has just been baptized."[2]

The writer uses the words "Christianized" and "family" here to separate these children from the wild mob playing down the street. In the tradition of missionary tracts, the reporter offers contrasting images of civilized and Christian, versus savage and heathen, Chinese children in an attempt to appeal to the tourist's desire to see both the good and the bad of Chinatown. The author illustrates the cleansing power of Christianity in part by contrasting these children with their neatly ordered "silken pigtails running down their backs" with the dirty mob of children playing among the refuse. Unlike the rowdy, idle, and unsupervised children playing in the back alleys, these children are accompanied by their parents and participating in wholesome family entertainment in a manner that closely models American middle-class ideals of domesticity. This 1902 article clearly delineates two of the common public perceptions of childhood in San Francisco's Chinatown. However, both images are illusory and fail to capture completely the reality of Chinese American childhoods. At the same time, this article reflects the emergence of Chinatown as a major tourist destination and Chinese children as a key attraction in the tourist trade.

The Chinese American community had a vested interest in promoting a new image of Chinatown that countered the picture of disease and vice heralded in the press. This chapter will examine how images of childhood proved essential to improving the reputation of Chinatown and encouraging tourism. At the same time, the children themselves grappled with a reality far removed from popular perception. These children created a dual identity as both Chinese and American. The 1906 earthquake and the 1911 Chinese Revolution sparked profound changes in Chinatown life. Although their parents made important decisions about the future of Chinatown and its inhabitants, the children ultimately defined what it meant to be Chinese American.

ETHNIC SLUMMING AND THE EMERGENCE
OF A TOURIST CHINATOWN

The dominant stereotypes of Chinese Americans in the late nineteenth century focused on the vice and corruption of Chinatown's predominately adult male inhabitants. As we have discussed in previous chapters, anti-Chinese propaganda generally depicted the Chinese as sinister, plotting tricksters who represented a social, moral, and political threat to white society. Portrayed as members of a corrupt and backward civilization, the Chinese seemed unable or unwilling to assimilate into the American mainstream. City officials declared Chinatown a public nuisance, and writers depicted Chinatown as a corrupt place inhabited by Chinese criminals, gamblers, and opium addicts. Photographer Arnold Genthe published this description of San Francisco's early Chinatown: "In the dark alleys and courtyards rickety staircases led up to tenement hovels where derelicts of the underworld found cover. The most sinister of these was the 'Devil's Kitchen,' an evil-smelling courtyard where drug addicts and suspicious characters of all sorts cooked on charcoal burners the scraps of food they had picked up in the streets, and came out only at night to squat on doorsills or to pursue their insidious ways."[3] Frequent references to gambling or opium dens reduced the Chinese to animals confined to filthy, earthen hovels. These images stood in stark contrast to the American middle-class ideal of cleanliness and purity. Fears of the filth and disease of the Chinese quarter culminated in numerous investigations and laws instituted by city officials in the late nineteenth century. Newspaper reports warned San Francisco's citizens of the inherent dangers emanating from the city's Chinese inhabitants.

Despite, or perhaps because of, the warnings, visitors flocked to Chinatown beginning in the late nineteenth century in an effort to catch a glimpse of the lurid Chinese underworld. Ethnic slumming became a popular pastime and a way to experience other cultures without directly embracing them. Early Chinatown tour books promised that visitors could safely explore the maze of underground opium dens in Chinatown by employing the services of a guide. White guides led tourists through dark alleys and underground passages to view Chinese prostitutes, gamblers, and opium fiends. Chinese men and women participated in the staging of these scenes in return for a small profit.[4] Genthe became friends with an old opium addict who made a living by smoking opium for tourists. Tour guides would bring visitors to his living quarters and announce, "If we are fortunate you will see a rare sight—a Chinaman smoking opium."[5] After observing the old man laying on a pile of rags and puffing away on his pipe, the visitors would depart satisfied that they had observed a genuine scene of "Oriental depravity," and the guides would pay him a few nickels for his effort. Although visitors rarely witnessed actual scenes of vice, as participants in these manufactured dramas they helped to perpetuate an image of an inherently depraved Chinese population.

Some white authors provided images of Chinese childhood that countered these preconceived notions of Chinatown. In 1876 B. E. Lloyd described the children in San Francisco's Chinatown: "The children all have a remarkably intelligent look; their bright black eyes have an expressiveness that is never seen in adult Chinamen. Their young intellects are free, not yet hampered by that scholastic training that enslaves the mind in the ever-narrowing limits of custom, and begets that stolid and unimpressionable look of unconcern, that is most repulsive in the countenance of the adult Chinese."[6] Although Lloyd paints a foreboding picture of adult Chinese, his description of Chinese children reveals the faith that many whites held in the malleability of youth. Lloyd imagines the children of Chinatown as capable of more than their fathers if removed from their corrupt environment. A number of white photographers, artists, and writers attempted to capture this more idealistic vision of Chinese youth around the late nineteenth and early twentieth centuries.

Works of fiction revealed this more optimistic view of Chinese childhood, as well as the continued pervasiveness of anti-Chinese stereotypes. In 1904 Jessie Juliet Knox created a book of short stories about Chinese children for white youth. Knox was an author of children's stories and the daughter of a Methodist Episcopal minister. After moving to San Jose, Knox became a prominent writer and lecturer noted for her sympathetic treatment of the California Chinese. Her book, *Little Almond Blossoms*, includes a number of short stories detailing the adventures of fictional Chinese children in San Francisco's Chinatown. In "The Little Highbinder," Knox recounts the story of a little boy, Sing Lee, who aspired to be a highbinder. The boy overheard a conversation between his father and other members of the Hip Sing tong. The tong determined to kill a man named Chong Sing, who had proven to be unfaithful to the tong by telling tong secrets to "a white devil." Sing Lee remembers that Chong Sing spoke kindly to him and often brought him candy. Sing Lee formed his own little band of highbinders and chose to inform Chong Sing of the tong's plan to kill him. The story concludes: "The little highbinder did not kill any one that day. . . . Never mind! He would kill some one next week, or 'to-mollow.' Some one who was bad—who did not bring candy."[7] Knox focused on the reforming potential of the Chinese child. Unlike his father, Sing Lee had the choice to either revert to the corrupt criminal ways of his heritage or become something more. The story of "The Little Highbinder" clearly reflected the opinions of social reformers and missionaries who insisted on the assimilability of Chinese children and believed in the power of reform. Although the story relies on stereotypes of a vice-ridden Chinatown full of tong members and aspiring gangsters, missionaries believed that with proper education and removal from the corrupting influences of Chinatown, Chinese children like Sing Lee could be saved from an otherwise inevitable fate.

Missionaries published a number of novels for both adults and children that detailed the lives of fictional Chinese children. The expressed purpose of these novels was to encourage the evangelization of the Chinese American community through the conversion of Chinese children. However, another unintended consequence of these stories was to garner sympathy and understanding for Chinese American children and, by extension, for the entire Chinese American community. In *Ti: A Story of Chinatown*, Mary Bamford presents an unusually sympathetic and well-researched portrayal of the life of a Chinese American boy. Ti and his father live in a fishing village on the shores of San Francisco Bay. One day, immigration officials arrive to examine the documents of the Chinese in the village, hoping to find fraudulent certificates. Bamford demonstrates the state of perpetual fear that existed in Chinese American communities as a result of exclusionary immigration laws. After satisfying the requests of the immigration officials, Ti and his father temporarily move in with Ti's aunt and uncle in the city. At this point, the story appeals to some of the stereotypes of a dirty, diseased, and superstitious Chinese community, as Ti's cousins contract diphtheria and die. Ti's parents believe that the illness was a result of an earlier transgression against a Chinese god. Ti's distraught aunt and uncle beg his father to allow the boy to stay in the city so that they can raise him as their own son. Bamford appeals to the parental instincts of the reader as she describes the deep grief and agony of Ah Cheng, Ti's aunt, as she tries to cope with the loss of her children. An American missionary woman tries to help the family through their grief by introducing them to stories of Jesus Christ. The uncle eventually reluctantly agrees to allow the boy to attend mission school. As Ti grows stronger in his Christian convictions, he refuses to worship idols and provide offerings at the family altar. Ti endures beatings for his disobedience and suffers numerous crises of faith. Bamford's descriptions of the trials of Ti reflect biblical themes of temptation, sin, and salvation.

Although Bamford's story ultimately varies little from others in its genre, her multidimensional Chinese characters succeed in arousing the sympathy and support of her audience. In the tradition of missionary literature, Bamford frequently uses the imagery of light and darkness to contrast a Christian and heathen life. The American teacher "thought of the light burning before the ancestral tablet in Ti's home, and in many other homes. And as she held the little boy's hand, she prayed in her heart that though he lived in darkness, yet that he might learn the truth."[8] Bamford also portrays heathen Chinese, as represented by Ti's uncle, as suspicious of missionaries, addicted to opium and gambling, and clinging to idol worship and superstitions. However, Ti eventually vows to become a missionary to Chinese children, and the American teacher in the story remarks: "The poor little Chinese children! Often the parents won't believe us teachers when we tell them of Jesus and his love, but sometimes they will believe their children when they carry home the gospel we have taught them. Oh, if only there were more teachers to tell the story to the poor little Chinese children! Dear Lord, send forth more laborers into this, thine harvest!"[9] The story ends with the typical testament to the reforming potential of Chinese children and a challenge to the Christian reader to take up the duty of evangelization. Yet Bamford allows her Chinese characters to express real emotion, and in so doing she encourages her readers to identify with the Chinese as human beings. The accompanying sketches further foster a connection to a tangible image of Chinese childhood. It is Bamford's ability to breathe life into her fictional Chinese boy that is most important. Missionary literature impacted middle-class views of Chinatown. Stories such as Ti's, no matter how fictional, had the potential to appeal to the heart of the reader. This new, intimate, and more human view of Chinese American family life existed simultaneously with anti-Chinese images of deviant domesticity in Chinatown.

The line between fiction and reality blurred as visitors hoped to catch glimpses of Chinatown's "little highbinders" or a real-life Ti. Chinese children seemed capable of rescue and redemption, and their presence in Chinatown appealed to white visitors. In 1896 Theodore Wores offered this description of Chinatown: "What delights the eye often offends the nose; and a worse combination of evil smells can hardly be imagined than those one meets in this crowded and filthy quarter. Its picturesqueness, however, is its redeeming feature; and the prettiest things that greet the eye are the bright-eyed and quaintly clad little children."[10] Although Wores relied on conventional stereotypes of Chinatown, he offered a contrasting image of Chinese children as potential redeemers of the race. In the early twentieth century, Will Irwin similarly described the children of Chinatown as "the pride, joy, beauty and chief delight of the Quarter . . . [t]iny, yellow flowers of the world."[11] Irwin described the adoration that the children elicited from tourists and Chinatown residents. Irwin insisted that four o'clock was the "children's hour," the time when the children left the schoolhouse and played in the streets of Chinatown. The presence of the children, according to Irwin, "showed Chinatown at its sweetest and most gracious." This image of innocent Chinese children stands in stark contrast to his description of Chinese merchants as cruel, cold-blooded, and barbaric.[12] Irwin generally treats his Chinese subjects with respect and admiration. Yet, his account is not exempt from the taint of the earlier anti-Chinese rhetoric. Irwin's description of the

"A Holiday" (Arnold Genthe, photographer; courtesy of
the California Historical Society, FN-02301)

Chinese quarter is a tribute to the pre-earthquake Chinatown. His text accompanied a book of photographs produced by Genthe. White writers, artists, and photographers increasingly recognized the marketing potential of producing images of Chinese childhood for the tourist trade.

Although Genthe was not the first photographer to capitalize on images of Chinese children, he was by far the most prolific and the most renowned photographer of early Chinatown. He traveled to the United States in 1895 as a tutor to the son of a wealthy German family, staying with the family in their home in San Francisco. Entranced by the city, and especially by the people of Chinatown, Genthe attempted to photograph the scenes that he witnessed. He described his efforts to carefully set up his camera and patiently wait to surreptitiously capture images of passing Chinese. Genthe took over 200 photographs of early Chinatown, many of which capture the innocent, natural expressions of Chinese youth. A large majority of his photographs feature children out on the streets on festival days. One photograph shows two children dressed in their finest clothes and standing on the sidewalk, apparently watching the holiday festivities in the street. The boy holds tightly onto a balloon with his left hand while leaning his head to the right slightly to catch a glimpse of the activities. The young girl stands behind him covering her ears, most likely from the sounds of the firecrackers, and stares in the direction of the photographer.[13] Genthe would later market these images as scenes of ordinary Chinatown life even though the photographs show children celebrating the amusements of an extraordinary day. He found it easiest to photograph these children on holidays, when families emerged from the privacy of their homes to celebrate in public. Genthe believed that the large crowd in the streets also helped to conceal his presence. Although Genthe liked to perpetuate an image of himself as covertly capturing photographs of real Chinese family life, the children and their parents often seemed very aware of his presence. Some stared defiantly back at the camera, others stopped and posed, and many turned away to avoid the photographer. Still, Genthe's images of quaintly attired children proved extremely popular and inspired many imitators.[14]

Lesser-known photographers and artists also flocked to Chinatown in the late nineteenth and early twentieth centuries in an effort to capture images of Chinese youth. Isaiah West Taber, Laura Adams Armer, Louis Stellman, and Mervyn Silberstein produced images of Chinatown and Chinese children for public consumption. Theodore Wores, Ernest Clifford Peixotto, Mary Davison, Hortense Schulze, and Esther Hunt convinced Chinese parents to allow them to sketch and paint pictures of their children. Festive, brightly clad, and smiling images of Chinese youth softened and countered anti-Chinese depictions of Chinatown. The image of a bachelor community seemed to dissolve with the prolific reproduction of images of Chinese youth. Although not all of these photographers and artists considered the Chinese as their intellectual or moral equals, their depictions of Chinatown's children fostered a more acceptable view of Chinese America. Whereas some whites saw the Orientalization and commodification of images of Chinatown as a means of reinforcing the racial hierarchy, others sought to prove the equality of the races and express a common sense of humanity through shared visions of middle-class domesticity. These images helped white and Chinese neighbors find common ground in their shared conception of the innocence and purity of childhood.

Chinese American entrepreneurs saw the value in redirecting tourist interest into a new ideal of Chinatown in an effort to counter earlier anti-Chinese images of Chinatown. As early as 1904, the Chinese Six Companies, Chinese Native Sons, Chinese Students' Alliance, Chinese Cadet Corps, and Chinese consul general petitioned the San Francisco police to stop tour guides from promoting or manufacturing scenes of Chinese depravity for the benefit of tourists. Specifically, Chinese American community leaders objected to tour guides who entertained visitors by visiting brothels and opium dens, therefore perpetuating misconceptions of Chinese American life. These community leaders requested that police shut down the brothels and opium dens and admonish the tour guides.[15] The Chinese Students' Alliance, Native Sons, and Cadet Corps further took matters into their own hands by raiding the house of a noted opium smoker. The mob demolished his windows and insisted that he avoid smoking opium in the presence of visitors. The *San Francisco Chronicle* explained the situation: "Incensed at having the vices and not the virtues of the Celestials exposed to the public, there is a determined effort being made by the better class of Chinese to stop this kind of sightseeing in Chinatown."[16] In response to the demands of the Chinese American community, the Board of Police Commissioners adopted a resolution that promised to revoke the license of any guide caught escorting tourists to places where "lewd, immoral and indecent practices are exhibited or to any place where opium is smoked for exhibition purposes."[17] Although such exhibitions no doubt continued, the Chinese American community increasingly sought to eliminate vice and improve public perception of Chinatown.

The immense public fascination with Chinese children provided an opportunity to turn public attention away from Chinatown's darker side. Chinese families expressed pride in their children, and community leaders encouraged a limited number of positive public displays of middle-class family life. Chinese babies received a great deal of attention from both Chinese and white society. Grinning fathers proudly paraded their infants about town. Mothers or servants carried babies on their backs in a carrying tie and lulled them to sleep by singing songs.[18] In March 1898 over 200 Chinese children participated in a Chinese baby show at the San Francisco Mining Fair. Parents dressed their children in new clothes and proudly displayed the babies before the white judges. Parents also consented to allow newspaper illustrators to sketch pictures of the prize-winning children. Participants and organizers deemed the event an overall success, as a similar event drew nearly 3,000 observers the following year at the Mechanics' Pavilion.[19] The publicity generated by this event helped to call attention to family life in Chinatown and offered an alternate image of the bachelor society.

THE 1906 EARTHQUAKE AND THE NEW CHINATOWN

The 1906 earthquake presented many challenges for Chinese American families and later provided the opportunity to physically rebuild the image of Chinatown. The memories of the event were seared into the consciousness of everyone who lived through the experience. Most people were asleep when the shaking began at 5:12 in the morning on April 18, 1906. Fathers, mothers, and children raced out into the streets to see what was happening. Fifteen-year-old Hugh Liang managed his deceased father's store with the assistance of his cousin. The pair were asleep in the basement of the store when Liang was awakened by the trembling of the earthquake and falling plaster: "I quickly dressed and ran into the street, the building across from our place collapsed. The streets were buckling and people were running around shouting 'aih yah, dai loong jen, aih yah dai loong jen' (the earth dragon is wriggling). Later the fire came, people watched in horror as it came closer to Chinatown."[20] Abandoned by his cousin, Liang managed to escape to the Presidio and later stowed away on a cargo boat to Napa. People loaded up all available wagons with their belongings and fled Chinatown. Wagons were scarce, and poorer families and children like Liang fled to the Presidio by foot. Pardee Lowe's father managed to bribe an Italian scavenger who had a wagon to drive the family to the Embarcadero, where ferries were helping people flee the city.[21]

In the midst of the chaos of the earthquake and fires, Nam-Art Soo Hoo, the first ordained Chinese pastor of the Presbyterian church in Chinatown, determined to assist his local community. He divided the family and neighbors into five different groups, with an English-speaking member in charge of each group. The goal was to get safely across the bay to Oakland. He charged his fourteen-year-old daughter with the supervision of her younger brother and sister; a bound-foot neighbor and her two small children also joined them. The younger sister recalled how they found themselves separated from the larger group: "We saw many people crushed and mangled, and tried to extricate them. There were many houses with one or two sides gone—but the furniture inside still there, before being consumed by the fire, like open doll-houses—but there was the *terrible* feeling of being lost and forgotten, for it was three days before we were able to get on a ferry boat to cross the Bay." The children finally reunited with their parents at a refugee camp in Oakland.[22] Some immediately escaped the Chinese quarter; others waited until forced out by soldiers.

The fires that followed the earthquake were even more damaging, resulting in the complete destruction of homes and businesses in Chinatown and an unknown number of dead. The earthquake and fires temporarily scattered families and disrupted the Chinese community. Over 20,000 Chinese fled the city, seeking refuge in outlying communities such as Oakland, San Jose, Richmond, Fresno, Stockton, Marysville, Napa, Vallejo, Courtland, Walnut Grove, and Sacramento. Some built new lives in these towns, while others slowly returned to San Francisco to rebuild their homes and businesses.[23] Chinese community leaders faced the daunting task of rebuilding Chinatown during a period of immense upheaval in Chinese and Chinese American history.

Some white citizens attempted to impede Chinese efforts to rebuild. However, the Chinese American community successfully resisted anti-Chinese efforts to permanently remove Chinatown to the outskirts of the city. A leading Chinatown merchant, Look Tin Eli, rebuilt his store to reflect the Orientalized tastes of tourists. The newly reconstructed Sing Chong Bazaar stood as a gateway to Chinatown on the corner of California and Grant Streets. Look Tin Eli hoped that the large pagoda-shaped structure, with bright red, green, and gold colors, would attract tourists to the new Chinatown. Soon, other Chinese and white property owners began to replicate the Oriental style of the Sing Chong Bazaar. Look Tin Eli insisted that "San Francisco's new Chinatown is so much more beautiful, artistic, and so much more emphatically Oriental, that the old Chinatown, the destruction of which great writers and artists have wept over for two years, is not worthy to be mentioned in the same breath."[24] Look Tin Eli and his imitators helped to transform Chinatown into a visible construction of white Americans' imaginative, idealized Chinatown.[25] This process of reconstructing the image of Chinatown was already in place prior to 1906, but the earthquake and fires provided the opportunity to literally rebuild Chinatown. The new Chinatown was deemed cleaner, safer, and more modern than its predecessor.

SELLING CHINESE CHILDHOOD

Following the earthquake and fires, both Chinese and white entrepreneurs recognized the appeal of Chinatown's children to middle-class pocketbooks and redoubled their efforts to market images of Chinese childhood and family life. Photographers and artists profited from selling compelling images of Chinese children to a public captivated by the mysteries of Chinatown. Despite their abundance, these images represented a far-from-accurate portrayal of childhood in Chinatown. Arnold Genthe found a new market for his photographs following the earthquake. Genthe spent some time reworking the photographs he had taken before the earthquake in order to market them as images of "old Chinatown." John Kuo Wei Tchen analyzed over 100 photographs taken by Genthe and discovered that many of these images endured extensive touch-ups in the hands of the photographer. Genthe apparently converted English signs into Chinese and removed evidence of white people in the photos in an attempt to make the subject appear more exotic. Tchen concludes that "Genthe tried to portray a mythical, purely Chinese 'Canton of the West'" and sold these photos to his upper-class white patrons as "authentic" images of an irretrievable past, a Chinatown lost.[26]

Esther Hunt's paintings and chalkware busts of Chinese children also found widespread acceptance among middle-class white shoppers, even as they reflect the Orientalizing trend of Genthe. As a student at Mark Hopkins Institute of Art in 1901, Hunt began to explore San Francisco's Chinatown. Hunt found the children of Chinatown particularly inspiring and often persuaded Chinese parents to let their children serve as models.[27] Hunt's paintings and busts show children in holiday clothing surrounded by Chinese scenery and props. Hunt accented the children with Chinese lilies and cherry blossoms. The children in her paintings carry parasols, fans, incense, or bowls of Chinese food and play with firecrackers and kites. The chalkware busts frequently represent female children wearing elaborate headdresses. These children are often posed with heads tilted meekly downward and to the side, wearing pensive or expressionless faces. Hunt's work follows in the tradition of Genthe and other artists and photographers who focused on a mysterious and foreign Chinatown.

Other photographers and artists recognized a profitable industry in the reproduction of postcards for tourists. The souvenir picture postcard became popular in Europe after the Paris Exposition in 1889. Following the 1893 Chicago Exposition, private publishers began to produce postcards in the United States. Postcard collecting became widespread in Europe by the early twentieth century, and the postcard craze hit America by 1905. The picture postcard remained a popular collectible until World War I. At the peak of the postcard frenzy in 1913, Americans sent 968 million postcards in a single year. Prior to the passage of the 1909 Payne Aldrich Tariff, the vast majority of postcards were imported from Germany. Several San Francisco postcard publishers that specialized in images of Chinatown manufactured their cards in Germany. Goeggel & Weidner, Richard Behrendt, and the Pacific Novelty & Company all advertised their cards as made in Germany. Britton & Rey were among the earliest San Francisco postcard publishers to begin printing views of Chinatown, and they printed their images exclusively in the United States. Edward H. Mitchell, another early San Francisco postcard publisher, also published his cards in America. Mitchell attempted to capitalize on American patriotism by advertising his cards as "Made in America" or "Made in the United States." Mitchell published a wide variety of postcard views of the West Coast, Hawaii, Japan, and the Philippines. Mitchell's views of San Francisco, and especially of Chinatown, remain highly collectible today. Mitchell eventually dominated the industry in San Francisco, buying out many of his competitors.[28]

Images of the ethnic "other" became a highly collectible genre of post-cards. Photographs and caricatures of Indians, blacks, Japanese, and Chinese proliferated as publishing companies manufactured more cards to meet the demand. The racist nature of these cards illustrates the widespread accep-tance of attitudes of Anglo-American cultural superiority in early twentieth-century American society. American Indians appeared as legendary and ro-mantic images of a noble and vanishing race. Postcards often portrayed stereotypes of lazy, ignorant, violent, or savage blacks. Cartoon postcards exaggerated and distorted the facial features of black Americans through large lips, unkempt hair, elongated limbs, and big white teeth. Japanese and

"Chinese Children in Holiday Attire" (Britton & Rey, San Francisco;
postcard from author's collection)

Chinese Americans appeared as exotic and foreign. These stereotypical depictions of the "other" helped to dehumanize ethnic Americans by turning
them from subjects to objects.[29]

Postcard producers featured ethnic children in a more favorable light,
reflecting the late nineteenth-century belief in the innocence and purity of
childhood. Some photographers preferred action shots that featured children
at play or in amusing situations. However, most postcard photographers
carefully posed the children in an effort to create an idealized view of childhood innocence. The smiling faces of Chinese children proved especially
endearing and irresistible to tourists. Images of Chinese childhood helped to
promote a familial image of Chinese Americans that sharply contrasted with
the dominant anti-Chinese stereotypes that continued to deny the existence
of Chinese families and children. Still, Orientalized postcards turned Chinese
children into commodities to be collected by predominately white, middle-
class Americans.

Although produced by a wide array of photographers and manufacturers,
postcards featuring Chinese children appear remarkably similar in appear-

ance. They all generally include groups of Chinese children under about age ten. In most cases, the artists deliberately posed the children, lining them up against a wall, a fence, or another appropriate backdrop. Photographers sometimes carefully arranged the children by height, and at other times they lined the children up in no apparent order. The children in these posed shots often appear bewildered and perhaps confused by the varied instructions of the photographer. More candid shots, especially of children at play, captured the children laughing. However, even in these rare instances of spontaneity, the photographer has disrupted the play and asked the children to look at the camera long enough to take the picture. In one Britton & Rey postcard created in 1905, five Chinese children play in and around a wicker basket. Although obviously actively engaged, the children all appear in a state of suspended animation, as the photographer clearly distracted them long enough to take the picture.[30]

Some postcard photographers chose not to pose the shots at all but simply to attempt to capture men, women, and children walking about the streets. These images are similar in style to Genthe's early photographs. The subjects ignore the camera and continue about their business. This fact suggests that Chinese men and women were less willing to have their picture taken and that the photographs of children were taken without their parents' knowledge and consent. An account of the life of Elmer Wok Wai seems to confirm the latter. Wai grew up in San Francisco's early Chinatown and remembered that photographers would ask him and his friends to pose: "[I]n doorways, on balconies, before the joss house, they would stand us up and snap, snap with cameras—and my God! Those picture were put on postcards and went all over the world."[31] Although Wai was extremely pleased with the appearance of his photograph at the newsstand of the St. Francis Hotel, his godmother objected to the distribution of the boy's photograph as embarrassing to the family. In rare cases, families apparently posed willingly for the camera.[32]

In a vast majority of postcards, the children are elaborately dressed in brightly colored, decorative, and distinctively Chinese holiday attire. Children in Western clothes or more common Chinese clothing rarely appear in the postcards, and when they do the photographer often tries to subtly blend them into the picture. The children appear as quaint and foreign, similar to the Chinese-made objects that adorn their person. The viewer's eye is drawn toward the children's elaborate Chinese headdresses, hats, bracelets, embroidered shoes, and handkerchiefs. The children often carry fans, flowers, dolls,

and balloons. The photographers and artists also sought to add to the Oriental character of the cards by purposefully posing the children in front of storefronts with Chinese decor, signs, or bulletins. When unavailable, the publisher simply added these embellishments to the final image. A holiday card produced by Richard Behrendt poses two Chinese children in between two New Year's narcissus plants. Chinese accessories and props help to further exoticize the children.[33]

Following in the tradition of Genthe, some postcard publishers went to great lengths to embellish the original images. Photographer Mervyn Silberstein, working in Chinatown beginning in the 1920s, "adjusted" his photographs and advertised them as "Chinee-Graphs! Distinctively Oriental-

Colorful-Attractive, The Ideal Gift for Every Occasion." Silberstein's Chinee-Graphs exclusively featured Chinese children. The photographer captured his subjects on the street during the Chinese New Year festival. Like Genthe, Silberstein retouched the images in his studio, erasing English words, adding Chinese characters, and highlighting the Chinese designs of the children's clothing. Silberstein postcards continued in circulation until the 1950s.[34]

William Henry Jackson, a photographer of the Detroit Photographic Company (known as the Detroit Publishing Company after 1905), also carefully staged and embellished a series of postcards featuring Chinese children. The Detroit Photographic Company, though not a San Francisco–based company, produced numerous images of Chinese American children and marketed them in cities with major Chinatowns. Jackson produced a series of postcards from a single photo shoot. Positioned on the roof of an unknown building in an unknown city, the children posed in their holiday attire and stood next to signs bearing Chinese calligraphy. Jackson also took a number of photographs of the children walking in front of the camera. In the actual production of the postcard, Jackson isolated and cropped individual children from the photographs. The publisher then pasted the isolated image onto a white background and embellished the original black-and-white image with bright colors. The finished postcard highlighted the Chinese designs of the children's clothing and included cute or descriptive captions. One image of two seated girls included the caption, "A Bit of Gossip." The title erroneously suggests to the viewer that the photographer spontaneously captured the children engaged in a private conversation. The original series of photographs reveal the staged nature of the actual photo shoot, and the "Chinese" flourishes serve only to further isolate and detach Chinese children from mainstream American society.[35]

The captions on the cards also often had an Orientalizing and a dehumanizing effect. Publishers at the Detroit Photographic Company labeled a 1901 postcard of a young Chinese girl "Demure and Shy." The downward tilt of the girl's head and eyes seems to affirm that assertion. Such captions only furthered the stereotype of the passive and meek Asian female. Most cards include simple captions that describe the individuals as "a group of Chinese children" or "Chinese girls." The identity of the children remain unknown. Similar studies of ethnic postcards conclude that the anonymity of ethnic subjects helps to dehumanize the subject.[36] This was undoubtedly one of the consequences of the mass production of these nearly identical images of Chinese American children. Ironically, at the same time that these post-

"Chinese" (William Henry Jackson, photographer; circa 1901, LC-D4-9050, Detroit Publishing Company Collection; courtesy of the Library of Congress, Washington, D.C.)

"Troubles of His Own" (Detroit Photographic Company; postcard from author's collection)

cards distanced Chinese children from American society, the production of these images countered the invisibility of Chinese family life as perpetuated by anti-Chinese rhetoric. In a sense, then, the creation and distribution of these postcards helped increase the visibility and humanize the Chinese American community for white audiences. The actual reactions of the individuals who purchased, sent, and received the postcards were unquestionably more varied and nuanced.

Postcards featuring Chinese children, made available for purchase in many local shops and newsstands in Chinatowns across the West Coast, apparently had widespread popular appeal. Visitors sent postcards from San Francisco and Oakland to friends in small towns and big cities in California, Nebraska, Missouri, Massachusetts, Pennsylvania, and New York. Some of these cards ended up overseas in places such as Liverpool, England, or Paris, France. Sightseers sent the cards to family and friends as mementos of the experiences of their trip. Others used the cards simply to send messages. One gentleman sent a postcard featuring Chinese women and children to St. Joseph, Missouri. He wrote: "Just to let you know that in my hurry in leaving I forgot to mail you my check. Will do so on my return." Another man sent a postcard featuring two Chinese girls and a Chinese boy to inform friends that his family had moved once again: "Dear Bess and George, Back Again in the same little cottage we left 6 months ago." Such ordinary messages written on postcards demonstrate the increasingly widespread acceptance and popularity of Orientalized images of Chinatown.[37]

The messages written on postcards featuring Chinese children remain generally positive. In 1909 Colonel George Armistead sent a postcard with the images of fourteen Chinese children on it to Miss Gallagher in Liverpool, England. Armistead wrote: "Here is quite a nice assortment of little Chinese tots for you."[38] Another tourist sent a postcard of Chinese children playing in and around a giant basket. The writer remarked: "I choose the one away back in the basket." Grace Locke Davis sent a card featuring a Chinese boy in a wagon to Felix Sandder. Davis wrote: "Here's a little boy with a push mobile come to call on you from San Francisco." In each of these three postcards, the writers selectively chose their favorite child and in a sense took possession of them as their own. Through the purchase of these postcards, the senders seemed to be purchasing a sense of ownership over the children of Chinatown, which partially reflects an attitude of cultural superiority.[39] However, these images and their reception prove much more positive than earlier anti-Chinese depictions of Chinatown. By selecting and buying the

"A Group of Chinese Children" (Britton & Rey, San Francisco, ca. 1905;
postcard from author's collection)

postcards, these visitors in a sense were purchasing a stake in the new
Chinatown. By sending these images and sentiments to friends and relatives
around the world, the writers were effectively assisting in the campaign to
promote this alternate image of Chinatown. Meanwhile, the lives of the real
children captured in the photographs remain obscured by their commodified
representations.

Many writers used the images to point out distinctions between white
middle-class Americans and the children of Chinatown. A postcard sent from
Oakland, California, to Miss Emma Johonnett in Pittsfield, Maine, in 1907
bore the image of five Chinese boys and girls. Although the photograph
featured one boy dressed exclusively in Western attire, the writer chose to
focus on the distinctive clothing of the other four. In reference to the women
and children of Chinatown the writer remarked, "Their dresses are very rich
of silk and alpaca principally. The little caps the babies wear have ridiculous
little ears lined with fur stitching up on top." In 1909 an adult member of the
Campbell family made similar comments on a postcard featuring women
and children. The writer, sending the card to an obviously younger child,
asked, "What do you think of these little children in their play clothes? And
what do you think of the way the ladies are dressed would you like your

昇昌

金山 正卑 昇昌公司

SING CHONG COMPANY
CHINATOWN
SAN FRANCISCO

Chinese and Japanese Bazaar

mama, me and Ellen and Helen to dress so?" The intent of both writers was apparently to share this cute image of the quaintly dressed Chinese women and children. In so doing, however, the writers clearly set the subjects apart from their own conceptions of style and dress. Although the messages on the postcards appear to positively promote a common vision of childhood innocence, by calling attention to the distinctive clothing of the Chinese women and children, the writers define them as distinct from white Americans.[40]

Other writers were more explicit in separating Chinatown's children from white America. A few days after the 1906 San Francisco earthquake, Dora Hansen sent a humorous note on a postcard featuring Chinese children to a friend in Germany. The writer inscribed new identities on each of the Chi-

nese children by labeling them as "My bro.," "Myself," and "My Sister."
Hansen then noted, "This is our photograph taken just a few moments
before the earthquake, we look a little different now." Perhaps the writer was
remarking on how much older and wiser the earthquake had made her
family, destroying, in a way, their childhood innocence. The use of these
ethnic children, clearly distinct in clothing and physical features, serves Hansen's seemingly humorous intent in further contrasting her family's pre- and
postearthquake appearance and in effect separating Chinese children from
American families. Another woman, visiting San Francisco during the 1915
Panama-Pacific International Exposition, sent a postcard of Chinese children
to a child in West Virginia. The writer remarked, "There are lots of little boys
& girls here like these, but they are not as sweet & dear as little American
girls." In contrasting the appearance and manner of the Chinese children
with white children and refusing to recognize Chinese children as "American," the writer is effectively denying American-born Chinese children their
status as American citizens.

Chinese American entrepreneurs also produced Orientalized postcards in
an effort to promote their businesses and profit from the new tourist industry. By the early twentieth century, Look Tin Eli was a prominent member of
the San Francisco business community as a secretary of the Chinese Chamber of Commerce, the president of the Canton Bank, and an officer of the
Sing Chong Company Bazaar. The Sing Chong Company catered to Chinatown tourists through their large assortment of "Oriental arts and antiques."
Customers also received souvenir postcards to remember their visit. One
postcard features a smiling young Chinese girl festively dressed and adorned
with an elaborate headdress, fan, handkerchief, and platform shoes. The
company's name appears in both English and Chinese in the corners of the
postcard. In this manner, images of an Orientalized Chinese American childhood proved crucial not only in promoting Look Tin Eli's business but also in
promoting a tourist-friendly image of Chinatown.[41]

Other Chinatown promoters recognized the economic and social benefits
of these more acceptable images of Chinatown. A 1909 tourist guidebook of
San Francisco's Chinatown, compiled with the support of Chinatown's leading merchants, attempted to dispel myths about danger and disease while
constructing an alternate vision of Chinatown. The book disputed stories
of rat eating, bubonic plague, underground opium dens, and white slavery in Chinatown. The writers promoted a positive image of childhood in
Chinatown by highlighting safe and clean mission schools: "American ladies

teach Chinese Mission Schools in San Francisco in absolute safety—and have for FORTY YEARS. Visit the schools and see for yourself what a dangerous occupation this is!"[42] The guide also directed visitors to several must-see sights that included local Chinese children: "Some Sights You Mustn't Miss. . . . See the PUBLIC SCHOOL CHILDREN march down Clay Street (Powell to Stockton) at 12 o'clock noon, on any school day."[43] The Chinese American community began to encourage tourists to see Chinatown as a place to visit with the whole family. The schoolchildren became, by default, a sort of tourist attraction.

In 1915 an executive committee of white and Chinese American community leaders in San Francisco proposed a carnival to encourage tourism in Chinatown, and the Woman Citizens League, the Chinese Chamber of Commerce, the Chinese Six Companies, and the Chinese Native Sons of the Golden West offered Ferris wheels, parades, merry-go-rounds, bands, dances, and shows in an effort to attract visitors to Chinatown. A flyer distributed throughout Chinatown encouraged merchants and property owners to "Boost for Chinatown." Chinese children again proved essential to the Chinatown tourist industry. The executive committee encouraged parents to bring their babies to the baby show to compete for prizes. This event had the dual effect of generating profits for Chinatown's merchants and encouraging visitors to explore the "new" Chinatown.[44]

Individual entrepreneurs also recognized the financial rewards of interest in the new respectable image of Chinatown. Wong Sun Yue met white missionary Ella May Clemens in a refugee camp following the 1906 earthquake. Despite continued prejudice against interracial marriages, the two fell in love and wed. Shortly thereafter, the newlyweds opened a curio shop in Chinatown, catering to tourists. Advertising in the 1909 Chinatown guidebook, the couple urged tourists to visit "Pompeii in America," a refugee house filled with relics from the 1906 earthquake and fire.[45] Their unusual enterprise and status as one of Chinatown's few interracial marriages generated publicity in the local press. The couple also offered daily tours of Chinatown. In 1915 Mrs. Clemens Wong compiled a guidebook and directed public attention to respectable Chinatown by noting the many missions, churches, and schools. Children proved crucial to this image of Chinatown, and Clemens Wong makes this point by concluding the guide with a photograph of "Baby Ah Yoke at the Tea Garden." The photograph portrays a young Chinese girl, richly adorned and grinning attractively for the camera. Above the photograph, Clemens Wong included a flag of the new Republic of China.

The image of the traditionally dressed Baby Ah Yoke, coupled with an image of the flag representing a New China, suggests the interesting mixture of old and new on display in Chinatown. This presents a "something-for-everyone" approach to advertising by guaranteeing that the visitor would see the Chinatown that she or he desires. However, Clemens Wong eliminated all references to opium, gambling, and prostitution, choosing to focus tourist attention instead on a romanticized vision of old Chinatown. At the same time, she directed visitors to sites such as the various temples and churches, the Chinese Public School, the mission homes, the Canton Bank, and the Chinese Chamber of Commerce to illustrate the development of a new and respectable Chinese American community. The guidebook received the official endorsement of Police Commissioner Jesse B. Cook and the Chinese consul general in San Francisco.[46]

Some Chinese families took advantage of tourists' specific fascination with Chinese American family life by making arrangements with local tourist guides to perform for visitors for a small fee. Guides promised visitors the opportunity to witness a glimpse of "real" Chinese American family life. A widowed mother of four daughters invited visitors into her home and offered to show her bound feet for a fee. This type of display proved highly controversial within the Chinese American community. Still, some families found the tourist industry a way to earn a little extra income. Winding through back alleys and dark cellars, the guide would lead tourists to "singing children" who would sing Western and Chinese songs for paying tourists. Mother and father provided musical accompaniment for the children. The Pacific Novelty Company published at least two postcards featuring such singing children. The actual identity of the children remains unknown. In a sense, then, they remain only caricatured images produced for the pleasure of white audiences. However, this family's success in benefiting financially from tourists' curiosity about Chinese family life reveals their effort to take some ownership of the images and to control their own lives. Tourist guidebooks often describe the family as "Christianized Chinese" in order to separate them from the mass of "heathen Chinese children." The Western attire of the children suggests that their parents sought to set them apart from the Orientalized stereotypes of Chinese children. The family was fighting their own battle against the dominant images of an exotic Chinatown, even as they profited from the traveler's attraction to it.[47] By putting their children on display, these families recognized a way to benefit financially from the curiosity of foreigners. These staged performances also had

The Singing Children 4434

"The Singing Children" (Pacific Novelty Company, San Francisco; postcard from author's collection)

the effect of advertising Chinese family life and countering the image of a bachelor community.

In some ways, the commodification of images of Chinese childhood and family life ensured the protection and privacy of real Chinese family life from the intrusion of curious outsiders. Still, some visitors recognized the staged performances of family life as shams and longed to see a "real" Chinese family. Tour guides attempted to assuage the frustrations of unsatisfied customers by encouraging them to peer into the doors and windows of private homes and try to catch a glimpse of family life as they walked through Chinatown's alleys. Most Chinese parents resented the intrusion of tourists into the private realm. Some families hung signs on their doors: "Chinese Family—Respectable—Please Do Not Ring Bell."[48] However, many families responded indignantly to these improprieties by simply slamming doors in the visitors' faces.[49] In 1905 a Chinese American girl named Bessie Ah Tye told a white reporter: "The tourists see all that is lowest and basest in Chinatown; they see only what the guides show them. The best side—the real home life of the better classes—is too sacred a thing for display and, because unseen on the surface, it is overlooked."[50] Some Chinese resented the tourists and those within their community who made a living by catering to them. Although as a boy, Elmer Wok Wai was proud of the postcard images that photographers had produced of him, as he became a teenager, he resented the presence of tourists in Chinatown and considered the activities of certain Chinese families to be scandalous and shameful to China. Wai and his gang forced a family to move away by stoning them for earning a living by showing the wife's bound feet to tourists. When a Chinese "fortune-teller" set up a fake joss house and opium den in his basement, Wai's gang lit a string of firecrackers and threw them into the room full of tourists. This type of harassment forced the man out of business.[51] Yet, the production of photographic images, drawings, paintings, ceramics, and staged performances of Chinese childhood offered a safe, public venue for outsiders to experience "genuine" Chinese American family life. In some ways, this public performance protected and preserved the sanctity of actual Chinese homes.[52]

White photographers and artists, together with Chinese American entrepreneurs, successfully countered earlier anti-Chinese stereotypes of Chinatown. The images that these photographers and artists produced of Chinese children stood in opposition to the image of a vice-ridden and diseased Chinatown occupied by inherently corrupt Chinese. Although only imaginary constructions of their real-life counterparts, these Chinese children entered the homes of American families and found some acceptance in white society. However, the new caricature of Chinese childhood, which featured these children in traditional Chinese clothing and accoutrements, perpetuated an image of a forever foreign, static, and still largely unassimilable Chinese American community.

THE 1911 CHINESE REVOLUTION

Few images of Chinese childhood accurately reflected the reality of Chinese American family life. The images produced by artists, photographers, and writers often perpetuated an impression of a static Chinatown, caught somewhere between the past and the present. However, life in Chinatown

was constantly evolving. Individual children and their families found themselves continually adapting to small familial crises and major historical events. As active participants in a transpacific culture, Chinese children growing up in early twentieth-century San Francisco witnessed profound changes in both Chinese and American society.

The 1911 Chinese Revolution further spurred the changes already under way in Chinatown as families adapted to the Westernizing and modernizing forces inspired by the revolution. Chinese children proved more than passive observers and often played a prominent role in facilitating change. The success of the revolution depended on the support of overseas Chinese communities like the one in San Francisco. Many children remembered the exciting events surrounding the revolution. Wong Wing Ton was twelve years old in 1910. He remembered sitting in Portsmouth Square, listening to a speech by Dr. Sun Yat-sen, who ultimately led the revolution and became the founder of the Republic of China. Women and children sat on the grassy lawn, listening as the man waved and shouted his revolutionary rhetoric. "I was young, but felt the vibrations when he talked to a spellbound audience," Wong Wing Ton remembered.[53] Sun Yat-sen stayed with Lily King Gee Won's family in January and February 1910. Security was strict. In order for a visitor to gain access to the house, he or she had to know secret codes and hand signals. Lily and her sisters enjoyed practicing the secret codes and signals until their mother ordered them to stop playing. According to Lily, the girls were primarily responsible for delivering food to the room and watching for suspicious people loitering in front of the house: "I was not really very good at this assignment because I had always been such an active child that I found it hard to concentrate on one task for long. Besides there were so many passersby I didn't know whom to watch for. However, since I was instructed to keep watch, I frequently looked outside the window to see if anyone was coming up the stairs or if anyone was loitering near the entrance."[54] Children participated in the revolution by waving flags, marching in parades, or raising funds to support Sun Yat-sen's work. Families actively sought to modernize Chinatown while reforming China.[55]

At least one white photographer attempted to capture these revolutionary changes in Chinatown and record its impact on the children. Following the earthquake of 1906, Louis Stellman photographed a far different and less alien Chinatown than the one photographed by his predecessors. Stellman's portraits are rarely posed and tend to show children in action and frequently at play. One photograph is particularly captivating in its candid view of Chinese boys playing tug-of-war in the street. Stellman photographed the boys (who were dressed in Western-style clothing) laughing, running, and struggling to hold on to the rope. This amusing photograph captured a much more realistic portrayal of childhood in Chinatown than many of the more static, posed, or deliberately manipulated images of an earlier generation. However, Stellman's lens was far from unbiased. In Stellman's opinion, the 1906 earthquake seemed to cleanse Chinatown of filth and vice, while the 1911 revolution represented a Westernizing influence. Stellman offered an image of the new Chinatown as a modern, Chinese American community. His images portrayed children in Western dress, waving American flags,

Tug of war (Chinese: Children: Stellman Collection, #10, 880; courtesy of the California History Room, California State Library, Sacramento)

and playing with American toys. Stellman's Chinatown was full of families and smiling children engaged in everyday activities. The leading Chinatown newspapers welcomed Stellman's more egalitarian vision of the Chinese in American society.[56] Stellman's photographs serve as evidence of the fluidity and evolution of Chinese family life in America during the era of the Chinese Revolution.

There is little doubt that the Chinese Revolution impacted Chinatown life. Coinciding with changes in the political structure of China and the resulting transformations within Chinese American society, Chinese family life in San Francisco grew in size and importance. Inspired by revolutionary ideals, as well as Western and Christian influences, the Chinese American community embraced a number of reforms intended to modernize Chinatown. Men cut their queues, women unbound their feet, and many individuals abandoned Chinese clothing in favor of Western styles.[57] The second generation increasingly participated in American culture by reading American newspapers, books, and magazines; listening to American music; eating American food; and wearing American clothes. Yet, no matter how much they acculturated to American society, they still remained outcasts in the eyes of many whites.[58]

Historian Yong Chen has argued that although the dramatic transformations in the appearance of Chinatown could be interpreted as conscious efforts at assimilation, for most Chinese Americans, these changes had more to do with a renewed China. Strong transpacific ties allowed Chinese Americans to see themselves as both Chinese and American.[59] However, members of the Chinese American community recognized the political value of emphasizing the Americanization of Chinatown. As we have seen, anti-Chinese propaganda perpetuated images of Chinese deviant domesticity and targeted Chinese children specifically as unassimilable purveyors of Chinese corruption. White and Chinese entrepreneurs countered this image and recognized the social and economic value of an Orientalized image of Chinatown.

By the 1920s, however, many leaders in the Chinese American community increasingly resisted attempts to exoticize Chinatown not only by emphasizing its two-parent, middle-class families but by highlighting the degree of Americanization of its children. In 1922 newspaper editor Ng Poon Chew argued that Chinatown's children were thoroughly Americanized in their manners and speech: "There is nothing Chinese about them except their complexion which is only skin-deep." He insisted that the children were well-educated and patriotic American citizens. Chew described the complete transformation of Chinatown:

> As one strolls along the streets of Chinatown one sees no longer the sight of Chinese children garbed with the pleasing raiments of the Orient, in the colors of the rainbow with their skull caps bright and colorful, chattering in the speech of their fathers, playing the games which were played by their forebears centuries before in the valley of the Yangtse. But he will see Oriental children, with closely clipped hair, in smart American clothes, and many in khaki uniform of the Boy Scouts, playing American games, mostly delighting in parading with wooden guns carrying the Stars and Stripes in martial array, singing "Dixie Land" and "Marching through Georgia." The Chinese children in their every-day speech prefer English to the Chinese language. They are masters of the American's slang, and their vocabulary in that line of expression is surprisingly large.[60]

Chew's image of Chinese family life stood in stark opposition to anti-Chinese propaganda, which emphasized the unassimilability of the Chinese immigrant. However, he also rejected the Orientalized images of Chinatown's children, which consistently dressed them in the "pleasing rainments of the Orient." Like Stellman, Chew preferred an image that celebrated the Americanness of the Chinese American community. Middle-class American families could relate to his references to the "Boy Scouts," "the Stars and Stripes," "Dixie Land," and "Marching through Georgia." Chew attempted to transcend racial boundaries by appealing to the shared values of all middle-class Americans.

The Chinese American Citizens' Alliance (CACA) also responded to harmful stereotypes by highlighting the Americanization of their children. The passage of the Immigration Act of 1924 elicited an angry response from American-born Chinese. Lawmakers intended to prevent the immigration of unassimilable people, especially the "new immigrants" from eastern and southern Europe. However, the law also denied admission to "aliens ineligible for citizenship," which essentially barred immigration from all Asian countries. The CACA argued that the unequal sex ratio of Chinese in America severely hampered the ability of Chinese American men to find Chinese wives in America. Thus, American-born Chinese often looked for wives in China. The act specifically impacted American-born Chinese by denying entry to their China-born wives. In a 1926 pamphlet, CACA members expressed their outrage and staked their claim to their rights as American citizens by demonstrating the degree of Americanization of their families: "These children, born and reared here, speak the English language, were educated or are being educated in our public schools and colleges, wear the American dress, follow American customs, live in homes as typically American as do Caucasian children, and being surrounded by the same environment as Caucasian children, grow up with the same ideas and follow the same pursuits as Caucasians and are in every respect true Americans, loyal to their country and an asset to the State."[61] The CACA eventually succeeded in winning a 1930 amendment that allowed women married to American citizens before 1924 to reunite with their husbands. By highlighting the Americanization of their children and appealing to the shared cultural values of middle-class American families, the CACA found an effective argument in the battle against exclusion.[62]

Caroline Chew, the daughter of Ng Poon Chew, similarly attempted to dispel popular myths and construct an alternate image of Chinese American family life by appealing to American middle-class conceptions of domesticity. In 1926 she completed her master's thesis at Mills College, describing the development of Chinese family life in both China and America. Chew intended to counter the images produced by writers and film producers who "have thrown a bizarre light on it, giving the general impression that it is a round of trap doors, secret passages, opium dens, and the like." Chew insisted that Chinese American family life was just as "normal and placid" as American family life. Chew also congratulated Chinese families for their adaptability and willingness to assimilate. Still, Chew warned against a complete abandonment of Chinese customs, suggesting that Chinese families fuse their own customs with "the best in American customs."[63] This new image of Chinese American families positioned Chinese children as legitimate inheritors of American rights and freedoms. Yet, it was the children themselves who struggled to create a place for themselves on the boundaries of two cultures. Segregation and continued racial hostilities in San Francisco contributed to a feeling of isolation from mainstream American society. These children selectively adopted American and Chinese traditions as they attempted to define themselves as Chinese American.

WHAT DOES IT MEAN TO BE CHINESE AMERICAN?

Increasingly, American-born Chinese children demanded their rights as Americans and staked their claims in American society. Chinese children were extremely important, not just as pawns in the games of adults, but in their efforts at challenging exclusion and segregation in their daily lives and thereby laying the foundations for a Chinese American community. Despite the internal conflicts created by living on the margins of two worlds, Chinese American children created a world uniquely their own. Fred Wing remembered his childhood as a time of watching movies about cowboys and eating french fries, T-bone steaks, and pork buns at Chinese-owned restaurants.[64] Organizations such as the YMCA, the YWCA, the Boy Scouts, and the public and mission schools attempted to inculcate American values into the children they served. Still, these children spoke Cantonese at home, ate Chinese food, attended Chinese school, and celebrated Chinese holidays. Pardee Lowe remembered the decorum and daily rituals of Chinese family life with some resentment while fondly recalling Chinese holidays: "At home our lives were a round of polite Oriental salutations and formal bowings and scrapings. For the most part, all this bored us, and we longed to escape from it and do as our American school friends did. But that was not so during our great New Year's feast. This was one thing on the Chinese side of our existence that appealed to us children."[65] Lowe explained that as a child, the New Year's festivities appealed to him because of the numerous gifts and abundant food. American-born Chinese children enjoyed the worst and the best of both worlds. These children forged a Chinese American identity based on their common experiences.

As American-born Chinese children embraced and rejected aspects of American and Chinese culture, conflict and tension with their parents inevitably increased. Families experienced the usual generational conflicts heightened by the divide that separated many immigrant parents from their American-born children. Chinese American society had undergone its own revolution of cultural ideals. The Chinese Revolution challenged the status quo and turned the old order upside down. Reformers advocated an end to foot binding, rejected arranged marriages, and promoted education for women. Dramatic social and political changes also characterized American society in the 1920s. Women and youth celebrated their newfound freedoms as Victorian social barriers collapsed. Although both American and Chinese culture agreed that women's primary place remained in the home, women achieved a greater sense of freedom with the removal of many of the old restrictions. Parents listened to the ideas of Chinese reformers, who suggested alternate child-rearing strategies while promoting education and equality for women. Girls especially enjoyed greater social freedom, although this freedom did not come without conflict.

Parents raised under more traditional cultural values often resisted the efforts of their children to participate in American culture. George Lem came to America in 1875 as a child immigrant. In 1924 Catharine Holt from the Survey of Race Relations asked Lem to comment on his American-born children:

> The children here have no respect for the old people. It is not so in China, there they respect the old people. But here, if you are old, they think you ought to die. When the boy is twenty-one, he says, "I am twenty-one, I will do as I please." And when the girl is eighteen, she says, "I am eighteen and I can do as I please." The father will want to advise and will say, "I think it is better this way," but the young people will say, "I want to do this way and I am going to do this." . . . There is too much liberty. I believe in liberty, but I think in some ways there is too much among the young people.[66]

Tensions were further exacerbated by changing roles in the family structure. American-born children frequently served as cultural mediators for their parents. Educated in American schools, Chinese American children understood more English than their parents and helped with interpretation and translation when necessary. Chinese immigrant children helped to socialize their parents, and this role reversal upset the traditional balance of power within immigrant families. Children began to question parental authority and rely on outside authority figures as role models. This resulted in inevitable conflict between the first and second generations.[67]

Some Chinese American youth resented the severe restrictions on their freedom and sometimes compared their lives to the seemingly carefree lives of middle-class white children. Esther Wong felt cheated out of her childhood and blamed her father and the labor he demanded of the children. She recalled that her father pushed her to work hard in the family-owned clothing factory and denied her the opportunity to play. He taught them Chinese in the mornings, and at age eleven she began grammar school. She worked from 3:00 P.M. to 9:00 P.M. in the factory every day except Sunday. When she was twelve, her father gave her more responsibility in the factory, appointing her to supervise the work of twenty-five men. The money she earned from grammar school to high school went to support the family.[68] Chinese high school students frequently noted that their Euroamerican peers did not attend language school or work after school. Many children resented their Chinese heritage, as it seemed to demand too much from them and offered little in return.

While some children acquiesced to the demands of their parents, others openly rebelled against authority. Edwin K. Wong worked in the family laundry business and after school as a domestic. He resented his father's demands that he sacrifice an education to earn money to send back to China: "We lived in a room on top of the laundry. The atmosphere is not created to get an education. My father won't help me. He wanted to make money to go back to the old country."[69] Wong eventually ran away to live in Berkeley and continue his high school education. Few children were so bold in their efforts to resist their parents. The breaking point for many came over the issue of dating and marriage.

As the children grew older, conflict often erupted with regard to courting rituals. Some parents flatly refused to allow their daughters to date. As Esther Wong commented in the 1920s: "I was brought up in the very strictest Chinese way. I have never been to a dance, never had a caller that I received, although some have come, never had what is called 'fun' in my life. Father did not believe in it."[70] As Chinese youth adopted American dating rituals, their parents felt that the children were completely rejecting their Chinese heritage. Concern over the more liberalized attitude toward sexuality in the 1920s transcended racial barriers as most middle-class Americans feared the effect of the new sexual morality on their children. However, this issue added to the already tense relationship between immigrant parents and their American-born children.

The independence expressed by American-born children frustrated many traditional-minded Chinese parents, who preferred that their sons marry China-born girls instead. In 1924 Chin Cheung, though American-born himself, candidly told an interviewer his feelings about American-born Chinese girls and expressed his desire that his son seek a China-born wife. He insisted that American-born girls were too independent, as evidenced by their desire to go out in the evening, dance, and spend money. He insisted that China-born girls had more respect for their husbands and were better caregivers for the children.[71] In spite of the desires of their parents, Chinese youth often chose their own romantic partners in an act of rebellion.

A few children took drastic measures to make their voices heard. In 1917 a fifteen-year-old Oakland girl, Elsie Chan, expressed her frustration over her parents' attempts to force her into an arranged marriage with a Chinese shopkeeper. Chan unsuccessfully attempted to strangle herself with a cord. Police recovered a suicide note that Chan intended for her true love, a Chinese youth named William. The *Oakland Tribune* detailed the contents of the note: "Sorry to say that I could get no chance to see you before I died, as my mother forces me to marry, but I didn't obey her about it. I really intended to marry you, and I will follow you any time if I can. I am just worrying about my mother forcing me to marry, and that makes me die."[72] Luckily, the girl's mother discovered the child in time to prevent the suicide. Police accompanied Chan to the hospital. Although she fully recovered, her future and the outcome of the arranged marriage remain unknown. By the 1920s, the practice of arranged marriages was in decline.

Interracial relationships were also a cause for concern among the Chinese American community. The prohibitions against miscegenation were not only legal but cultural. White and Chinese adults worried about the potential of race degradation.[73] Such relationships remained taboo in the eyes of both Chinese American and white society for years to come. Despite the prohibitions against interracial relationships, some Chinese youth could not deny their feelings for their white classmates. In the early 1920s, Edward L. C., a Chinese high school student interviewed by members of the Survey of Race Relations, struggled with his feelings for a white girl named Elizabeth Pedrotti. "I have the peculiar feelings when I meet her—what is it? It is a question which every young man must ask himself. It is their own devotion to answer. As for myself I know that I can't have her."[74] Although Edward L. C. dared not challenge legal and cultural boundaries against such relationships, he still rebelled against the Chinese idea of arranged marriage. "My parent[s] planned to have me marry in China—but my idea of marriage is that one should not marry until he wants to marry."[75] His candid answers no doubt reflected the feelings of many American-born Chinese adolescents.

Second-generation Chinese American youth struggled with their parents over generational conflicts at the same time that they faced segregation and exclusion from the larger society. Many children recalled painful memories of enduring name-calling. Chinese boys also resented the tendency of whites to label all Chinese as "Charlie" or "John."[76] Many Chinese children and teens also encountered segregation in public recreational centers, theaters, and social clubs. Chinese boys and girls played on segregated basketball, track-and-field, tennis, baseball, volleyball, and soccer teams. Chinese children were typically allowed only limited access to recreational facilities. In most cases, local officials completely denied Chinese children the right to play on courts and fields used by white teams.[77] As a youth, David Young and a friend bought tickets to a show in a San Francisco theater. The boys were hoping to see some friends performing on stage. He recalled that the theater employees required them to sit upstairs even though the lower floor seats were only half full. Young and his friend left their seats, demanded their money back, and fled the theater, determined to never return again.[78]

Increasingly, second-generation Chinese American youth resented the limited employment opportunities available to them. At age thirteen, Pardee Lowe wanted to find a job, and he told his father he intended to be an office boy in an American business firm. His father suggested that they might not hire him. He applied at ten different firms: "Everywhere I was greeted with perturbation, amusement, pity or irritation—and always with identically the same answer. 'Sorry,' they invariably said, 'the position has just been filled.' My jaunty self-confidence soon wilted." Ultimately unsuccessful and completely disillusioned, he returned to school.[79]

Chinese girls faced limitations based on both their race and sex and struggled to overcome barriers both within and outside their own community. Working-class girls found it difficult to find employment outside of the factory system. By the 1920s, young merchant-class Chinese girls challenged the conventions of Chinese American society by working outside the home. At age fourteen, Rose Ow went to work selling tickets in a theater. Shortly thereafter, she went to work in a restaurant in the American section of town. At Tait's Café, Ow passed out candy and biscuits to the customers. However, some members of the Chinese American community were suspicious of a Chinese girl outside of Chinatown. She remembered men following her to work to see where she was going and people gossiping about her. In 1915 she began working as a dancer at the café, earning substantially more money. Like a dutiful Chinese daughter, she continued to turn her money over to her father, even though she was afraid to tell him where it had come from. She eventually made a career out of dancing.[80] Other girls resented the "China doll" image that employers expected young Chinese women to portray, passing out mints or filling water glasses in hotels and restaurants. Their purpose was to improve the aesthetic appeal of the establishment.[81] Still, Rose Ow relished the social and economic freedoms afforded by her job as she pushed the boundaries of acceptable behavior and aroused the concern of Chinese adults.

Chinese children in America also struggled with a dual identity as both Chinese and American. When interviewers asked Edward L. C. whether he felt more connection with China or with America, he replied that both sides seemed to hold equal pull: "One [is] the land of freedom which was my birthplace—my home—the other, my parents' home, my race's abode and my motherland."[82] However, he acknowledged that some Americans continued to resent the presence of the Chinese in America. When the interviewer asked him if he ever wished that he was white, Edward L. C.'s answer expressed his anxiety and confusion: "[It] is a very hard question to answer yet my conscience seems to say to me—why is it necessary to say anything— you have nothing to regret being a Chinese and member of the Mandarin race. My conscience says so but my heart seems to say—I am American. If you were me, what would you say?"[83] This open-ended statement expressed the frustration of many American-born Chinese who felt that they stood on the margins of two worlds, never fully accepted by either Chinese or American society. They struggled to define a place for themselves in both cultures. In the end, they created a uniquely Chinese American identity that their immigrant parents and white peers could not fully understand.

CONCLUSION

Chinese children played a key role in efforts to rebuild the image of Chinatown. The Chinese community and white writers, artists, and photographers offered constructions of childhood in Chinatown that countered the images of deviant domesticity heralded by anti-Chinese politicians. By marketing an image of Chinatown as a family community and highlighting cases of "legitimate" family life in Chinatown, the Chinese elite discovered a way of combating the stereotypes of a diseased, vice-ridden, and morally corrupt Chinatown. Chinese merchants and community leaders attempted to construct images of a family society at the same time that they worked to suppress organized crime in Chinatown to secure the safety of these families. Chinese and white photographers, artists, and entrepreneurs found a profitable market in Orientalized visions of Chinatown and images of Chinese childhood through the production and sale of photographs, postcards, paintings, and ceramics. However, this new image of Chinatown succeeded in stereotyping Chinese children as forever foreign, unassimilable, and separate from American society. Thus, even as the effort to improve the image of Chinatown proved successful, it contributed to the creation of new stereotypes that only further obscured the real problems of Chinese children and erected more obstacles to their full acceptance into American society. Some Chinese American community leaders recognized the value, at least publicly, of emphasizing their children's Americanness over their Chineseness in an effort to resist the negative repercussions of the new exoticized image of Chinatown.

Many Chinese Americans continued to financially profit from the static, Orientalized, tourist version of old Chinatown even as profound local and global changes altered Chinese American history. Frank J. Taylor lamented the emergence of modern Chinatown in his 1929 travel article, "San Francisco's New Chinese City." Taylor noted the presence of Chinese Boy Scouts, Girl Scouts, and basketball and football teams parading with the American flag in Chinatown and feared the inevitable loss of the old, traditional, and uniquely Oriental Chinatown. A Chinese merchant, however, reassured him that the Chinatown that he remembered would not change much. Taylor recorded the businessman's words: "Chinese merchants never change the stores. Maybe change upstairs where the family lives. But Chinese too good businessman to change Chinatown much. Chinatown always be what visitors like so much."[84] Although Taylor's decision to transcribe the Chinese man's words in broken English for "authenticity" detracts somewhat from the readability of the statement, the true meaning of the merchant's words are not lost on the reader. As a businessman, the merchant recognized the marketing value and profit potential of the tourist vision of Chinatown.

However, he assured the white reporter of a fact that the Chinese American community had always understood: behind the superficial façade of the tourist Chinatown, real Chinese American family life would continue to adapt and evolve with each succeeding generation.

Chinese youth grew up in a reality that did not fit neatly into the stereotypes produced by society. Children growing up in Chinatown in the early twentieth century witnessed profound changes in both American and Chinese history. The 1906 San Francisco earthquake and the 1911 Chinese Revolution ushered in dramatic transformations in Chinese American society. Chinese children struggled with the difficulties common to second-generation immigrant children as they challenged the seemingly overrestrictive rules of their parents. However, as the children of Chinese immigrants, they felt the burden of the added societal barriers created by over fifty years of anti-Chinese hostility. Even as they rebelled against the Chinese heritage of their parents' generation, institutionalized exclusion, segregation, and racism prevented them from fully embracing their American identity. These children struggled to create new identities as Chinese Americans in a society dominated by whites who still resented their Chineseness and rejected their Americanness. Chinese children growing up during the World War II period would continue the struggle.

CONCLUSION

CONSTRUCTING THE FUTURE

This book chronicles the various ways that the children of early Chinatown found themselves caught in political and societal battles over immigration restriction, segregation, cultural identity, crime and violence, child labor, and other momentous personal and communal crises. Through it all, a medley of adults—ranging from Chinese parents and community leaders to white reformers, missionaries, politicians, journalists, and anti-Chinese activists—evaluated and framed the conditions of Chinese children in order to reach their own particular objectives, directly influencing the children's day-to-day lives in the process. While the adults advocated, quarreled, and maneuvered, the children struggled with the consequences of constantly changing perceptions and daily confronted the harsh realities of life in a segregated urban, ethnic enclave.

Over time, Chinese community leaders realized that their children (and middle-class Chinese families in particular) were crucial to the effort of creating a socially acceptable image of Chinese America.[1] Although the Chinese in America maintained strong ties to China and were proud of their Chinese heritage, by the early twentieth century some members of the Chinese American elite recognized the necessity of at least publicly emphasizing their Americanness over their Chineseness in conscious effort to gain acceptance in a hostile society. By emphasizing their shared class values, the Chinese merchant class hoped that their middle-class status and family values would stand up against the anti-Chinese claims regarding the general unassimilability of the Chinese. Especially by the 1920s, some local leaders highlighted the Christianized and Americanized families of Chinatown and appealed to the shared middle-class values of their white counterparts.

At the same time that parents pointed to the academic success and Americanization of their children as a defense against the attacks of anti-Chinese politicians, the children felt the pressure to live up to these images in an effort to legitimate their claim to American citizenship.[2] Children growing up in early Chinatown struggled to develop their own sense of American identity. Participation in organizations such as the Boy Scouts and the Bluebirds fostered a sense of belonging and community, even as the segregated structure of these groups mirrored the segregated boundaries of society. Chinese American children felt compelled to succeed in school, and many attempted to transcend economic barriers by pursuing higher education and/or professional occupations. These status-oriented goals reflected, in part, their desire to demonstrate their success as a means of legitimating their status as Americans. Although the second generation by birth was legally entitled to the privileges of American citizenship, decades of inequities in American policy toward the Chinese in America prevented the full realization of their rights as citizens. These problems plagued future generations of Chinatown's children.

San Francisco's Chinese community witnessed the expansion of a second generation in the 1930s, even as Chinese exclusion continued to limit the number of immigrants allowed to enter the United States. The ratio of Chinese men to women in San Francisco fell dramatically, from approximately six to one in 1900 to three to one by 1930.[3] Although the 1924 National Origins Act prohibited "aliens ineligible for citizenship" from entering the country, the courts determined that wives of Chinese merchants could join their husbands in the United States. A 1930 amendment also allowed women married to American citizens before 1924 to reunite with their husbands.[4] By 1940, 51 percent of Chinese in the United States were American-born. However, Chinese families remained largely confined to the crowded and dilapidated tenements of San Francisco's Chinatown throughout the Great Depression and the World War II era. Infant deaths in Chinatown were twice the city rate, and tuberculosis, pneumonia, and bronchitis debilitated many Chinatown residents. The efforts of Chinese American social workers to improve conditions for families culminated in the construction of the Chinese Playground in 1927 and the opening of the Chinese Health Center in 1934. Community activists also lobbied for public-housing reforms. Legalized segregation prevented Chinese families and youth from moving out of

Chinatown and pursuing professional occupations. Some American-born Chinese children began to look to a future in China.[5]

China's role as an Allied power during World War II cast Chinese American families in a more favorable light, dismantled segregation, and hastened the repeal of Chinese exclusion in 1943. As families reunited and new families formed, the Chinese American community in San Francisco was no longer a bachelor society. Postwar economic growth and more liberal immigration policies benefited Chinese American families. The expansion of war industries and the restriction against racial discrimination in defense-industry employment provided job opportunities for Chinese Americans in San Francisco during World War II. Some Chinese men continued their employment in white-collar jobs after the war. Returning Chinese American veterans took advantage of the GI Bill to pursue higher education and professional careers. Many Chinese American families enjoyed the affluence of the postwar era and abandoned Chinatown's ghettos to create new lives in suburbia. Their white neighbors resisted the "invasion" by filing lawsuits to prevent the integration of their neighborhoods. Segregation began to crumble, however, with the Supreme Court's 1948 *Shelley v. Kraemer* decision invalidating racially restrictive covenants. The enforcement of the Fair Housing Act in the 1960s helped to hasten the process of residential integration.[6]

After the Chinese Communist Party defeated the Nationalists in 1949 and the U.S. government sought to eliminate the communist threat at home, Chinese families in the United States increasingly felt the need to at least publicly distance themselves from their Chinese heritage. Anticommunist hysteria led government officials to suspect the loyalty of Chinese Americans. The Federal Bureau of Investigation began to search for communist sympathizers in the Chinese American community. Many Chinese families publicly denied any communist association, renounced their connections to China, and sought acceptance from white America. Chinese children growing up in American suburbs attended predominately white schools, played with white children, and spoke mostly English. Chinese American families adopted white, middle-class values and attempted to distance themselves from Chinatown and the negative stereotypes associated with it. For a short period of time, Chinatowns throughout the United States began to shrink in size. Yet class divisions divided the Chinese American community, as less educated manual workers remained confined to the urban, ethnic enclave.[7]

The arrival of a new influx of working-class immigrants and their children in the 1960s helped to repopulate San Francisco's Chinatown. The loosening of immigration restrictions with the 1965 Immigration Act led to a dramatic increase in the Chinese American population. Post-1965 Chinese immigrants included a vast array of individuals with disparate socioeconomic, educational, and occupational backgrounds. The 1965 act focused on family reunification and therefore encouraged the immigration of family members of U.S. citizens and permanent residents. The new immigration policy also gave preferences to skilled workers and professionals. Later revisions to the law made exceptions to allow the admittance of refugees fleeing wars or natural disasters in their homeland. Chinese refugees from Southeast Asia primarily settled in urban ghettoes, while middle-class professionals from the People's Republic of China, Taiwan, and Hong Kong flocked to affluent American suburbs. Children from these diverse regions struggled with their own unique set of adjustment issues.[8]

Demographic changes in the Chinese American population have contributed to the image of Chinese children as model minorities. In opposition to claims of racism by civil rights reformers in the 1960s, conservatives pointed to the relative success of Chinese American families and used the image of Chinese children as model minorities to resist the claims of other racial groups. From the 1960s to today, Chinese Americans as a whole have steadily improved their socioeconomic position. According to the 2000 federal census, the Chinese American population is highly educated and has a higher median household income than the general population. Seventy-seven percent of Chinese Americans twenty-five years and older have earned at least a high school diploma, compared to 80 percent of the general population. The $51,444 median household income for Chinese Americans far exceeds the $41,994 for the general population. The percentage of Chinese Americans living below the poverty level (13 percent) closely aligns with national figures (12 percent).[9] According to these figures, many Chinese Americans appear to have achieved the American dream. The model-minority stereotype celebrates the achievement of Chinese Americans by emphasizing their academic and economic success in comparison to other minorities. However, this image obscures the realities of centuries of racism and segregation. Min Zhou and Jennifer Lee argue that "the model minority stereotype serves to buttress the myth that the United States is a country devoid of racism, and one that accords equal opportunity for all who take the initiative to work hard to get ahead. The image functions to blame those who lag behind and are not making it for their failure to work hard, their inability to delay gratification, and their inferior culture. Not only does the image thwart other racial/ethnic minorities' demands for social justice, it also pits minority groups against each other."[10] This stereotype plagues Chinese American children. Some parents encourage their children to work twice as hard as other children in order to achieve academic and socioeconomic success. American-born Chinese sometimes attempt to distance themselves from recent immigrants and other racial minorities. According to sociologist Nazli Kibria, the unintended consequence is to ironically affirm "the stereotype of themselves as a model minority, in an effort to ease their own path of integration into American society."[11] American society continues to construct and reconstruct images of Chinese children that only further obscure the realities of their daily lives. This subterfuge makes it increasingly difficult to create solutions to the problems faced by urban, ethnic, and low-income youth. Popular culture and the media rarely portray Asian American students who do not fit the model-minority image. This approach minimizes the problems that plague Chinese children in Chinatown today.[12]

Although most Chinese American families today live in suburbs and by all measures have achieved success, many immigrant and Chinese children in San Francisco's Chinatown continue to live in poverty conditions in crowded substandard housing with inadequate access to health care and other necessary resources. A clear division exists between uptown and downtown Chinese. By 1990 children under age fifteen constituted 14 percent of Chinatown's population. The rising cost of housing has driven a large number of families out of the city. Parents who stay in San Francisco work two to three jobs and go into debt to survive in the city.[13] No longer confined to Chinatown, large concentrations of Chinese Americans live in the city's outlying neighborhoods, such as Bayview Hunters Point, Excelsior, Oceanview, Merced Ingleside, Portola, Richmond, Sunset, and Visitacion Valley. According to the 2000 federal census, only 61 percent of Chinese Americans twenty-five years and older living in San Francisco have attained a high school degree or higher (Table 10). When this figure is compared to the 81 percent for the total population in San Francisco, the disparity becomes more pronounced. The median household income for Chinese Americans in San Francisco was $47,877 in 2000, below the $55,221 for the general city population. Eleven percent of Chinese Americans in San Francisco were living in poverty, equivalent to the percentage for the total city population. These figures include the entire Chinese American population in San Francisco; a breakdown by neighborhood reveals even deeper levels of poverty for Chinatown itself. In 2000 only 36 percent of Chinatown's population over age

TABLE 10 : Demographics of Modern Chinese Americans

	CHINESE AMERICANS IN UNITED STATES	CHINESE AMERICANS IN SAN FRANCISCO	CHINESE AMERICANS IN SAN FRANCISCO'S CHINATOWN
High school diploma or higher	77%	61%	36%
Median household income	$51,444	$47,877	$17,886
Individuals living below poverty level	13%	11%	21%

Sources: Mayor's Office of Community Development, Mayor's Office of Housing, San Francisco Redevelopment Agency, "City and County of San Francisco, Five-Year Consolidated Plan, July 1, 2005–June 30, 2010," San Francisco, California, 2005, <http://www.sfgov.org/site/uploadedfiles/mocd/2005-2010ConsolidatedPlanv15 .pdf> (May 19, 2008), 26, 35, 38, 41; U.S. Bureau of the Census, Census 2000, <www.factfinder.census.gov> (April 23, 2008).

twenty-five had attained a high school degree or higher. The median house-hold income in Chinatown was $17,886. Twenty-one percent of individuals in Chinatown lived below the poverty level.[14] A close look at the lives of Chinese children growing up in urban ghettoes reveals a far different reality from the lives of their suburban counterparts. Chinatown's children have been historically invisible, and unfortunately they remain largely invisible to this day. The model-minority myth obscures the reality of life for Chinese youth in San Francisco's Chinatown.

Many Chinese immigrant families in San Francisco's Chinatown are struggling to adapt to American culture and create a stable home life for their children. Low-income and immigrant families face overcrowded and unsanitary conditions in Single Room Occupancy apartments. Limited privacy hinders the ability of children to focus on schoolwork. Immigrant parents often work two jobs to provide enough income to support their families. Unfortunately, this leaves them with little time to help their children with homework or problems at school. In addition, language barriers often require children to serve as translators for their parents and take on adult responsibilities. This role reversal continues to upset family dynamics and create intergenerational conflicts, just as it did among previous generations of Chinese immigrant families.

The issue of child labor is no longer a major concern in San Francisco's

Chinatown. Compulsory attendance laws require parents to send their children to school. Modern child-labor laws also severely restrict and regulate the employment of children. Although some Chinese American children help their entrepreneur parents in the day-to-day operations of the family business, parents increasingly encourage their children to focus on school and view academic achievement as the path to improving the family's socio-economic position.[15] Chinese parents push their children to perform well in school, attend college, and pursue advanced professional degrees. Today, the children of Chinatown spend their entire childhood and adolescence in school. Parents also enroll their children in after-school activities designed to enhance academic performance. Perhaps even more than their historical counterparts, Chinese children are compelled to excel and take on the delicate task of balancing their familial responsibilities with their own academic responsibilities. Schoolteachers, administrators, and after-school program coordinators have become even more important in the lives of Chinese children.

Access to quality education remains the crucial issue facing all of San Francisco's children. Despite the advances in civil rights legislation, segregation continues to be a controversial issue in the San Francisco Unified School District. Governor Earl Warren officially ended legal, or de jure, segregation in California schools in 1947. However, de facto segregation, resulting from school boundaries, neighborhood patterns, and housing discrimination, continued to pose a problem in California's cities. Matters became much more complicated in the 1970s, when the Chinese American community in San Francisco resisted plans to forcibly integrate the schools by busing children to schools outside of Chinatown. Some Chinese parents expressed concern that integration would negatively impact the education of their children and harm Chinese cultural life. Families boycotted the public schools and sent their children to the "Freedom Schools" opened by the Chinese American community in response to the busing issue. Chinatown officials denied that antiblack sentiment fueled the decision to resist integration and insisted that they stood opposed to decades of institutional racism. The Chinese American community argued that their primary complaint was that the public schools failed to meet the educational needs of Chinese children.[16]

Although the boycott eventually ended and Chinatown's Freedom Schools closed, the debate over integration continued. A lawsuit filed by the National Association for the Advancement of Colored People in the 1970s resulted in a 1983 settlement in which the school district prohibited regular schools from admitting more than 45 percent of students from any one ethnic group. The court order also required a minimum of four ethnic groups per school. By the early 1980s, Lowell High School, a college preparatory school in San Francisco, had won numerous awards from both the state of California and the U.S. Department of Education for academic excellence. Lowell's merit-based admission policy was selective and competitive, based on high academic standards. In order to conform to the 1983 admission standards established by the courts, Lowell High School in 1993 set higher admission requirements for Chinese students, who represented a large portion of the student body. A group of Chinese parents, angered by the restrictive polices, filed a class-action lawsuit against the California Board of Education and the San Francisco Unified School District, arguing that admission criteria should be based on merit rather than race. Their settlement in the 1999 *Ho v. San Francisco Unified School District* eliminated race as a factor in school admissions. Although school district officials have attempted to use other factors—such as poverty, mother's education, English-language skills, home language, and academic performance—to integrate the schools, the result has been gradual resegregation.[17]

The *Ho* decision has only further divided the Chinese American community, with a number of critics arguing that conservatives are once again pitting minority groups against each other in an anti-integration and anti–affirmative action campaign. Chinese American students in San Francisco consistently outperform their African American and Latino peers on standardized tests. While Chinese students represent 31 percent of the district's student population, they constitute only 9 percent of the dropout rate. African Americans and Latinos, on the other hand, comprise 56 percent of dropouts even though they constitute only 35 percent of the student body. The widening achievement gap between white and Chinese students on the one side, and African American, Latino, and Pacific Islander students on the other, is presently of great concern.[18] Today, the advocacy group Chinese for Affirmative Action argues that race needs to be added as an additional diversity factor to ensure the desegregation of San Francisco's schools. The group also teams with community organizations such as Coleman Advocates for Children and Youth to fight for the needs of children suffering from the impact of the achievement gap.[19] Both of these organizations insist that the goal must be to provide all students with quality education through an equitable distribution of resources and highly qualified and experienced teachers.

Chinese for Affirmative Action also advocates for the needs of English-language learners (ELLS). Although Chinese American students consistently perform better than other ethnic groups in San Francisco, ELLS generally score poorly on standardized tests. Yet, the type of support schools should provide to ELLS remains a highly controversial topic. In 1968 Congress created the Bilingual Education Act providing support to ELLS by offering immigrants education in their first language. However, the program was voluntary, and not all school districts adopted bilingual programs. In the 1974 *Lau v. Nichols* decision, the U.S. Supreme Court agreed with the claims of Chinese parents in San Francisco that the schools failed to properly educate students with limited English proficiency. The court seemed to call for support for ELLS through the creation of bilingual education programs. However, the implementation of such programs was largely inconsistent and the results controversial. In 1998 California voters approved Proposition 227, eliminating bilingual education and promoting English-immersion programs instead. Congress replaced the Bilingual Education Act with the No Child Left Behind (NCLB) legislation in 2001, which also advocated English-language immersion over bilingual education.[20] The purpose of NCLB is to close the achievement gap. Yet, critics argue that NCLB sets impossibly high standards, while failing to provide access to necessary resources to ensure student success. Most schools do not provide sufficient support to ELLS, who are less likely to graduate from high school than native English speakers. Others perform poorly on standardized tests and fail to receive the necessary support to succeed academically. Chinese American students nationwide represent the largest population of Asian ethnic ELLS. The Asian American Legal Defense and Education Fund argues that bilingual programs are much more effective than English-only approaches in ensuring the academic success of students. Furthermore, they argue that school districts must establish multiple forms of assessment to measure student achievement, employ qualified bilingual education specialists, expand interpretation and translation services to enable parental involvement, and disaggregate data to reveal student needs based on ethnicity, class, and native language.[21]

Despite the attacks on bilingual education, the San Francisco Unified School District (SFUSD) remains committed to the spirit of *Lau v. Nichols* through its continuation of multilingual programs. After the passage of Proposition 227 in 1998, the San Francisco Board of Education unanimously voted to uphold the right to equal access to education for all students by continuing bilingual language programs. Since then, the SFUSD has made great strides in improving the education of ELLS. During the 2006–7 school year, 36 percent of the ELLS in San Francisco were native Cantonese speakers. Presently, the SFUSD operates the Chinese Education Center for newly arrived Cantonese- and Mandarin-speaking children in kindergarten through fifth grade. Older Chinese child immigrants may attend newcomer programs at Francisco Middle School and Newcomer High School. Students receive intensive English-language development and bilingual instruction for one year before being reassigned to their designated schools. The children of Chinatown usually attend John Yehall Chin, Garfield, Gordon Lau, Jean Parker, Spring Valley, or Yick Wo Elementary Schools. At Gordon Lau, located in the heart of China-town on the original site of the first Chinese public school, over 70 percent of the students in 2007 were ELLS. The parents of Chinese students attending Gordon Lau may choose from two different programs: the Cantonese Bilingual Program or the General Education Program. The Cantonese Bilingual Program teaches grade-level content in both English and Cantonese, while gradually decreasing Cantonese instruction as the child's English proficiency increases. The General Education Program offers English-only instruction, with native language support as needed. Eighteen San Francisco public schools offer Cantonese Bilingual Programs. Four schools also offer Cantonese Two-Way Immersion Programs, while two offer Mandarin Two-Way Immersion Programs. In the Two-Way Immersion Bilingual Program, Chinese students develop bilingual and biliterate competency in both English and Cantonese or English and Mandarin. Only one school, Alice Fong Yu, offers the Cantonese Total Immersion Program, which is specifically designed to teach fluent English speakers Cantonese by providing instruction in both English and Cantonese.[22] Although the schools have come a long way in assisting ELLS, language barriers still prevent parents from full involvement in their children's education. Nearly 30 percent of the students in San Francisco are ELLS. The No Child Left Behind Act requires that school districts involve limited-English-proficiency parents in their children's education by ensuring their access to programs and activities through translation of materials and oral interpretation. The San Francisco Unified School District has taken important steps in that direction by employing Chinese interpreters, but many parents still feel disconnected from their child's education and largely unaware of the available services. Presently, the school district is working on a new plan to address the communication gap, establish consistency across bilingual programs, and recruit additional bilingual teachers.[23]

Chinese students living in inner cities face additional school-related challenges in the form of high parental expectations, drug use, racial tensions, school violence, and suicidal thoughts. Parental pressure for academic success leads to heightened stress levels for Chinese American students. Chinese parents set strict limits on their children's activities and pressure them to excel academically as a way of bringing honor to the family. Chinese immigrant youth living in Chinatown ghettos often struggle with adjustment issues, economic disadvantages, and language barriers that may limit their academic success. Chinese children's identities become tied to their academic achievement. Intergenerational tensions often escalate as children grow older and declare their independence. Research conducted by the SFUSD in conjunction with the California Department of Education has revealed that middle school and high school students in San Francisco face a variety of dangerous situations in their daily lives. The results of the 2005 Youth Risk Behavior Survey revealed the extent of drug use, violence, and suicide among San Francisco high school students. Overall, San Francisco students, and Chinese students in particular, were less likely to use drugs and were less frequently the victims and perpetrators of violence than high school students nationwide. However, Chinese students did experience rates of attempted suicide above the national average for high school students. Chinese students sometimes turn to suicide as a means of escaping from school and familial pressures. Limited access to mental-health resources prevent many youth from obtaining the professional help that they need, a situation that remains a major cause of concern.[24]

Street crime involving Chinese American children has become an increasingly visible issue over the past three decades. Chinese American youth are both the victims and the perpetrators of crime. Youth gangs in Chinatown emerged in the 1950s and 1960s. These gangs engaged in rebellious activities but rarely committed serious crimes. The growth in the size and number of gangs paralleled the changes in American immigration policy that resulted in an influx of Chinese immigrant families from Hong Kong and China. Growing up in conditions of poverty and faced with severe anti-immigrant hostility, many Chinese youth turned to gangs as a means of defending themselves from verbal and physical abuse. In the late 1960s and 1970s, Chinese gangs engaged in more serious criminal activities, ranging from extortion and robbery to violent crimes. These more modern gangs included both adult and teenage members. Chinese tongs, annoyed that the activities of the youth were threatening the tourist industry, forged agreements with the gangs. The tongs provided members of the youth gangs with housing, food, and money in exchange for their services as guards, lookouts, and debt collectors. Tongs helped to finance gangs, although the arrangements remained permeable and the gangs largely retained their independence.[25]

Violent competitions for control of Chinatown culminated in gang warfare in the schools, streets, and nightclubs during the 1970s. Gang members began to carry weapons and sought to kill members of opposing gangs. These tensions erupted in 1977, leading to a gang shootout at the Golden Dragon restaurant. Members of the Joe Boys (Chung Yee) gang opened fire on the Wah Ching and Hop Sing boys eating in the restaurant. The incident resulted in the deaths of five bystanders. Following the massacre, the San Francisco Gang Task Force was formed to control the situation in Chinatown. Increased police surveillance and enforcement eliminated or drove the gangs temporarily underground. In the 1980s and 1990s, new generations of Chinese gangs emerged in Chinatown and found financial rewards in assault, extortion, and the protection of gambling houses and brothels. Law-enforcement officials have also linked Chinese gangs to international groups involved in the trafficking of drugs and the smuggling of illegal immigrants, although the full extent of the gangs' involvement remains unknown. Today, many of San Francisco's Chinese gangs include American-born Chinese, China-born Chinese, or ethnic Chinese refugees from Vietnam. There is some speculation that since the mid-1990s, many of these gangs have formed alliances with powerful triads in China, Hong Kong, and Taiwan who are actively recruiting Chinese youth in San Francisco as part of their international crime ring; however, the evidence remains sketchy and controversial.[26]

The persistence of the model-minority image has largely concealed the problems of violence among inner-city Chinese youth and prevented thorough research into the issue of Chinese juvenile delinquency. In San Francisco Chinese youth have the lowest arrest rates compared to other groups, including white, black, and Latino youth. Among Asian–Pacific Islander youth, however, Chinese youth represent one-third to one-half of all arrests. Peer delinquency, prior arrest, victimization, poor parental supervision, and harsh or inconsistent discipline are risk factors associated with delinquency, substance abuse, and violence. Low socioeconomic status, poor school performance, and negative attitudes about school also increase the risk for youth crime. However, it is also important to consider how cultural factors, such as second-generation status, individualism, acculturation, and intergenerational/intercultural conflicts, specifically increase the risk factors for Chinese Americans. Working-class parents, laboring long hours for low pay, often have little time to spend with their children. Chinese parents tend to blame themselves for their children's involvement in gangs, insisting that the solution is increased supervision and stricter control over their children's selection of friends. Chinese gang members told researchers that their primary reasons for joining a gang were to secure money and protection while enjoying the excitement, friendships, and power that comes from being a gang member. In a way, the gang forms a pseudo family that provides companionship and protection.[27]

Community advocates have founded a number of nonprofit and charitable organizations in an effort to improve the quality of life for children and families in San Francisco's Chinatown. These organizations offer resources to assist families in overcoming structural barriers and fight the influences of poverty, crime, and linguistic and social isolation. Families also receive assistance in dealing with cultural and generational conflicts.[28] Community Educational Services (CES) was formed in 1969 to assist immigrant youth in San Francisco. In 2004 CES merged with the Chinatown Beacon Center, which provides after-school programs for Chinese children. Today, the two organizations work together to offer arts and cultural programs, health and wellness support, tutoring and mentoring, and other enrichment opportunities for the children of Chinatown. Through a close partnership with local schools, CES and the Chinatown Beacon Center focus on empowerment strategies for youth.[29] The Chinatown Community Development Center (CDC), organized in 1977, continues to sponsor neighborhood projects to improve the streets, alleyways, and public transportation systems while also building new community centers and playgrounds. Chinatown CDC also advocates for affordable and clean housing for Chinatown's residents. Chinese youth play important leadership roles in the Chinatown CDC, especially through the Adopt-An-Alleyway project, which works to keep local alleyways graffiti and litter free.[30] In 2004 the Chinatown Families Economic Self-Sufficiency Coalition was formed to assist Chinese immigrant families in achieving self-sufficiency through job training and good employment. The coalition has identified a number of problems facing Chinese immigrant families, including limited access to affordable child care, quality health and dental care, decent housing, and vocational English-as-a-second-language courses. The coalition consists of representatives from various organizations, including the Wu Yee Children's Services, Asian Women's Resource Center, Chinese for Affirmative Action, Cameron House, and Kai Ming Head Start.[31] Individually, many of these groups also provide family counseling, domestic violence intervention, after-school programs for children, and services for youth at risk of becoming part of the juvenile justice system. The Community Youth Center works specifically with Asian youth in San Francisco to address problems of juvenile delinquency, gang violence, academic difficulties, substance abuse, and economic hardships.[32] The efforts of these organizations are essential to improving the conditions faced by Chinese children living in modern Chinatown.

TO UNDERSTAND THE CHALLENGES faced by Chinese American children today, it is necessary to look at the struggle of Chinese children growing up in San Francisco's early Chinatown. As this book has illustrated, barriers of immigration restriction and segregation posed formidable obstacles to Chinese American family formation. Still, Chinese men and women resisted these societal limitations and formed a variety of traditional and nontraditional families in San Francisco. In the late nineteenth and early twentieth centuries, images of Chinese American children proved significant to the larger debate over the "Chinese question," as various groups constructed and reconstructed images of childhood and family life in Chinatown. As adults debated their future, Chinese children coped with the daily realities of life on the margins of two worlds. The children of Chinatown struggled at home, at work, at school, and in the missions and court system to establish a place for themselves in America. In the process, these pioneering children helped to break down barriers of exclusion and segregation while creating a uniquely Chinese American identity.

Their battle, however, is far from over. Although the past and present efforts of Chinatown families have created more opportunities for Chinese children, Chinese youth growing up in modern Chinatown continue to struggle to overcome barriers that prevent the full realization of their dreams. The barriers imposed by institutional racism and segregation cannot be overcome in a few generations. Immigrant families still often lack access to the essential resources needed to survive and thrive in their new environment. Immigrant and American-born Chinese children need access to language-learning support, decent housing, and affordable child- and health-care services. Working-class parents labor hard to earn a living wage to support their families. These problems are not limited to Chinese American families in San Francisco; children of all ethnicities growing up in working-class, urban environments fight against these obstacles. African American and Latino youth, and English-language learners in particular, face severe inequities created by centuries of institutionalized racism and are at present the children most at risk. Although concerned citizens have created organizations in their own neighborhoods and cities to assist families and children, the problems will not be addressed until we, as members of a larger national community, recognize the right of every family in the United States to quality education and job-training programs, decent housing, translation assistance, health-care services, mental-health counseling, affordable child care, and a living wage. The story of the children of Chinatown is not just the story of a small minority group fighting to survive in America; rather, their story, extending from the 1850s to the modern day, reflects the larger American narrative of the struggle to live up to the ideal of equality and overcome the barriers imposed by racism.

NOTES

ABBREVIATIONS

AASL   Asian American Studies Library, University of California, Berkeley

BANC   The Bancroft Library, University of California, Berkeley

BLG   Burton/Lake/Garton Family Papers, Coll. 301, Special Collections and University Archives, Knight Library, University of Oregon

CAF   Chinese Arrival Files, San Francisco, Records of the U.S. Immigration and Naturalization Service, RG 85, National Archives, Pacific Region, San Bruno, California

CHR   California History Room, California State Library, Sacramento, California

CSA   California State Archives, Sacramento, California

INS   Records of the Immigration and Naturalization Service, Series A: Subject Correspondence Files, Part 1, Asian Immigration and Exclusion, 1906–13, National Archives, Pacific Region, San Bruno, California

OT   *Oakland Tribune*

SF Call   *San Francisco Call*

SF Chron   *San Francisco Chronicle*

SFCMR   San Francisco Chinese Mortuary Records, vols. 1–5, National Archives and Records Administration, Pacific Region, San Bruno, California

SF Exam   *San Francisco Examiner*

SFHC   San Francisco History Center, San Francisco Public Library, San Francisco, California

SFMC   *San Francisco Morning Call*

SFTS   San Francisco Theological Seminary, San Anselmo, California

SRR   Survey of Race Relations Collection, Hoover Institution on War, Revolution, and Peace, Stanford University

1   Defining childhood creates a number of problems. Nineteenth-century Americans often classified employed minors as adults. The various child-labor, compulsory-education, and child-welfare laws of the era failed to agree on a defining age for the beginning and end of childhood. The development and evolution of the professional fields of child psychology and pediatrics has further complicated definitions of childhood. Even modern scholars of childhood history vary greatly in their classification schemes. I have chosen to focus on individuals age sixteen and below in an effort to remain consistent with the definition of "child" established by many of California's early child-welfare laws. Chinese and American systems for determining age differed. Chinese parents declared a child one year old at birth, and with each passing New Year, an additional year was added. In most of the cases in this study, the method used to determine age was unclear. Therefore, I took the age reported in immigration files, census records, newspaper reports, and other documents at face value. I have also included all children within the given age range (birth to sixteen), regardless of whether or not they were employed or living independently of their parents. Whenever possible, I will distinguish between immigrant Chinese children and American-born Chinese children. In general, however, I refer to both groups as "Chinese American" in an effort to acknowledge their role in the formation of a Chinese American community. The term "exclusion" also requires definition. I generally use the term to refer to the 1882 Exclusion Act, which denied the right of Chinese male laborers to enter the country. However, I also use the term in a broader context to describe the exclusion of Chinese children from full participation in white society.

2   In *Contagious Divides*, Nayan Shah argues that "the lives of Chinese men and women were depicted as contrary to respectable domesticity and an ominous threat to ideal visions of American morality and family life" (12). For a full discussion of this, see chapter 3, "Perversity, Contamination, and the Dangers of Queer Domesticity," in *Contagious Divides*.

3   Morrison G. Wong, "The Chinese American Family," 287–92; Glenn with Yap, "Chinese American Families," 279–81.

4   U.S. Department of the Interior, *The Public School System of San Francisco*, 14–15.

5   U.S. Census Bureau, *Eighth Census of the United States, 1860*; U.S. Census Bureau, *Ninth Census of the United States, 1870*; U.S. Census Bureau, *Tenth Census of the United States, 1880*; U.S. Census Bureau, *Twelfth Census of the United States, 1900*; U.S. Census Bureau, *Thirteenth Census of the United States, 1910*; U.S. Census Bureau, *Fourteenth Census of the United States, 1920*.

6   Peggy Pascoe insists on the agency of women and girls "rescued" by Chinatown missionaries by highlighting the ways in which they utilized the missions to their own advantage. Linda Gordon argues that the child welfare reforms of the Progressive era emerged not only from the determined efforts of middle-class reformers but also from the demands of the poor and working-class. Pascoe,

Relations of Rescue, 86–87, 98; and Gordon, "Family Violence, Feminism, and Social Control," 195.

7 For studies of the dilemmas of second-generation Chinese Americans, see Yung, *Unbound Feet*; and Chan, "Race, Ethnic Culture, and Gender in the Construction of Identities."

8 West and Petrick, *Small Worlds*, 2.

9 Calvert, *Children in the House*; Berrol, *Growing Up American*; Wilma King, *Stolen Childhood*; Clement, *Growing Pains*; Schwartz, *Born in Bondage*; Illick, *American Childhoods*. The first work devoted to Asian American children was published in 2004; see Tong, *Asian American Children*.

10 Chan, "Against All Odds"; Yong Chen, "Invisible Historical Players"; Hirata, "Free, Indentured, Enslaved"; Hirata, "Chinese Immigrant Women"; Ling, "Chinese Merchant Wives in the United States, 1840–1945"; Ling, "Growing Up in 'Hop Alley'"; Ling, *Surviving on the Gold Mountain*; Pascoe, "Gender Systems in Conflict"; Pascoe, *Relations of Rescue*; Yung, *Unbound Feet*. Other important works that address women and children in Chinatown include Beesley, "From Chinese to Chinese American"; Gee, "Housewives, Men's Villages, and Sexual Respectability"; Peffer, "Forbidden Families"; Tong, *Unsubmissive Women*; and Shah, *Contagious Divides*.

11 Yong Chen, "Invisible Historical Players," 25.

CHAPTER ONE

1 Lee Him, file 9234/41, box 4, CAF.

2 Salyer, *Laws Harsh as Tigers*, 20.

3 Tong, *The Chinese Americans*, 21–23.

4 Yong Chen has challenged the traditional view of Chinese emigration as a flight from poverty, instead proposing that Guangdong's economic vitality and its unique ties to the West in part explain the phenomena. As a port city, Canton served as a vital link that provided global news and information. The prosperity of the region's market-oriented economy and its ties to Western countries encouraged individuals to pursue opportunities away from home. In most of the cases that I examined, individuals came primarily to escape poverty at home. Yong Chen, *Chinese San Francisco*, 12–13.

5 Lee Chew, "The Life Story of a Chinaman," 179.

6 Valerie Lau, "An Oral History," 1, student paper, vertical file, AASL.

7 Mak, *In Search of a New Life*, 23–24.

8 Tong, *The Chinese Americans*, 26.

9 Upon hearing that she was to be sold, Chun escaped from her mistress and, with the help of some friendly Chinese men, found her way to the Methodist Mission Home. "Chan Fung Chün was born in Canton City, China," [ca. 1900], BLG.

10 Hirata, "Free, Indentured, Enslaved," 9; Tong, *Unsubmissive Women*, 43–44.

11 Nee and Nee, *Longtime Californ'*, 84; Yung, *Unbound Feet*, 39.

12 Yan Phou Lee, *When I Was a Boy in China*, 95–96.

13   Huie Kin, *Reminiscences*, 21.

14   Minnick, *Samfow*, 8–9; Tong, *The Chinese Americans*, 29; Janice L. Woo, "Interview with Ben Woo," December 2, 1976, 2, Asian American Oral History Composite, BANC.

15   Berrol, *Growing Up American*, 1.

16   Yan Phou Lee, *When I Was a Boy in China*, 104; Lee Chew, "The Life Story of a Chinaman," 179.

17   *In Memory of Dr. Fong F. Sec*, 4.

18   Huie Kin, *Reminiscences*, 23.

19   Esther Luke, "An Oral History of Ling Wah Chu," 1974, 4, student paper, vertical file, AASL.

20   Lau, "An Oral History," 13, AASL.

21   Lee Chew, "The Life Story of a Chinaman," 179.

22   Wen Bing Chung, "Reminiscences of a Pioneer Student," 33.

23   Mrs. J. S. Look, "Life History as a Social Document," Major Document 182, 1, SRR.

24   Evans, "Steamer from China," 212–15.

25   *In Memory of Dr. Fong F. Sec*, 4.

26   Davis, *Chinese Immigration*, 6.

27   Geary, "The Other Side of the Chinese Question," 458.

28   Mrs. S. L. Baldwin, "A Memorial from Representative Chinamen in America to His Excellency U. S. Grant," 37–38.

29   Peffer, "Forbidden Families," 28–29, 42; Erika Lee, *At America's Gates*, 41.

30   Salyer, *Laws Harsh as Tigers*, 14.

31   Tong, *The Chinese Americans*, 42–43; Aubitz, "Tracing Early Chinese Immigration into the United States," 38.

32   Erika Lee, *At America's Gates*, 124.

33   Miner's views were no doubt colored by her earlier experience with immigration officials in San Francisco. In September 1901, Miner had accompanied two Chinese students from China. Problems with the students' paperwork resulted in a delay of sixteen months in their admission to the United States. Miner, "Chinese Students and the Exclusion Laws," 977. See also Salyer, *Laws Harsh as Tigers*, 149–50; "Students Cause Ho Yow Trouble," *SF Call*, September 27, 1902; "Bars Are Let Down for Two Young Chinese," *SF Call*, January 13, 1903.

34   "Pacific Mail Dock," *Hong Kong Telegraph*, October 2, 1909, microfilm reel 12/248–251, Detention Shed, San Francisco, case file 522270/21, INS.

35   *Chinese World*, January 22, 1910; quoted in Lai, "Island of Immortals," 91.

36   Chea Ham, file 9277/16, box 258, CAF.

37   Lai, "Island of Immortals," 90–91.

38   H. K. Wong, *Gum Sahn Yun*, 156.

39   Lai, "Island of Immortals," 94–95; Lai, Lim, and Yung, *Island*, 80; Bamford, *Angel Island*, 16; "Interview with Detainee at Angel Island," HOC-DOI Project San Francisco, vertical file, 3–5, AASL.

40   Huie, "A Community of Voices," 4.

41 Trauner, "The Chinese as Medical Scapegoats in San Francisco, 1870–1905," 75–76; Erika Lee, *At America's Gates*, 84–87, 211–12.

42 Shah, *Contagious Divides*, 183–93; Erika Lee, *At America's Gates*, 82–83; Lai, "Island of Immortals," 93–94.

43 Statements by Ida K. Greenlee's group of Chinese students, case file 52753/13B (1913), microfilm reel 21, INS. Translated by Stephanie Chen Wu.

44 Erika Lee, "Exclusion Acts," 77–89; Erika Lee, *At America's Gates*.

45 Grittner, *White Slavery*, 65, 130; Rosen, *The Lost Sisterhood*, 6, 123, 138; Stout, *Chinese Immigration and the Physiological Causes of the Decay of a Nation*, 20–26; Cott, *Public Vows*, 136–38; Salyer, *Laws Harsh as Tigers*, 147.

46 Gee, "Housewives, Men's Villages, and Sexual Respectability," 102.

47 Donovan, *White Slave Crusades*, 21.

48 Lai Ah Kew, file 10134/3539, box 124, CAF.

49 Boyer, *Urban Masses and Moral Order in America*, 18; Rosen, *The Lost Sisterhood*, 8.

50 Lai Ah Kew, file 10134/3539, box 124, CAF.

51 Healy and Chew, *A Statement for Non-Exclusion*, 128–29; Erika Lee, *At America's Gates*, 90.

52 Erika Lee, "Exclusion Acts," 78–82; Erika Lee, *At America's Gates*, 94–95.

53 Chun Ah Ngon, file October 23, 1885/180, box 1, CAF.

54 McClain, *In Search of Equality*, 156–57, 163–65; Chan, *Asian Americans*, 92; Salyer, *Laws Harsh as Tigers*, 20.

55 Erika Lee, *At America's Gates*, 209–11.

56 Fong Sun Moon, file 10385/37, box 402, CAF.

57 I found no evidence that female children were asked to disrobe to authenticate age. Shah states that medical officers only asked women to disrobe if they suspected disease. Shah, *Contagious Divides*, 185.

58 From 1873 to 1898, immigration officials defined a child as an individual under age fifteen. Between 1899 and 1917, the definition of a child changed to anyone under age fourteen. From 1918 to 1920, the numbers include all individuals under age sixteen. *Annual Report of the Superintendent of Immigration, June 30, 1892*, 42–43; *Annual Reports of the Commissioner-General of Immigration, 1896–1920*; Ferenczi and Wilcox, *International Migrations*, 444–49.

59 McKeown, "Transnational Chinese Families and Chinese Exclusion, 1875–1943."

60 Immigration officials admitted 91 percent of Chinese children under age ten, 84 percent of children between eleven and fourteen, and 79 percent of children age fifteen to sixteen. This information is based on a sample of the Chinese Arrival Files of 320 Chinese child applicants to the Port of San Francisco from 1885 to 1920. The total number of files for children (sixteen and under) is at present unknown. Sucheng Chan has also noted that the Chinese Arrival Investigation Case Files, from which my sample is based, is not a complete representation of all of the Chinese who applied for admittance. See Chan, "Against All Odds," 59.

61 Tang, "Chinese Women Immigrants and the Two-Edged Sword of Habeas Corpus," 49. The data in this paragraph is in part based on a sample of 320 Chinese Immigration Arrival Files of children age sixteen and under from the 1880–99

period (Records of the U.S. Immigration and Naturalization Service, Record Group 85, Chinese Arrival Files, San Francisco).

62 Lum Ah Yung, file 9234/47, box 4, CAF.

63 Chan Toi Leen, Chan Ngau Kew, Chan Ah Hoo, Chan Ah Ngan, file 5-22-85, CAF.

64 Salyer, *Laws Harsh as Tigers*, 79.

65 Bennie Lum, file 9588/223, box 38, CAF.

66 Erika Lee, "Exclusion Acts," 84; Erika Lee, *At America's Gates*, 91, 99.

67 Salyer, *Laws Harsh as Tigers*, 210.

68 Fong Bow, file 10329/63, box 322, CAF.

69 Chew Gim, file 10308/114, box 2979, CAF.

70 Based on *Annual Reports of the Commissioner-General of Immigration, 1904–1920*. Merchant figures were derived by adding the categories of "returning merchants" and "Section 6 merchants" or "other merchants." No data is available for the year 1906. Adam McKeown has shown that from 1907 to 1924, only 3.1 percent of wives of merchants were denied admission, compared to 16.5 percent of children of merchants. McKeown, "Transnational Chinese Families and Chinese Exclusion."

71 Department of Labor, Bureau of Immigration, *Treaty, Laws, and Rules Governing the Admission of Chinese*, 29.

72 Cheong Cum Yee, file 13043/3-24, box 749, CAF.

73 "Memorandum for the Assistant Secretary from the Commissioner-General of the Department of Commerce and Labor, Bureau of Immigration and Naturalization," September 10, 1907, microfilm reel 22, Status of Adopted Chinese Minors, case file 52903/42, INS.

74 Letter from the Office of the Solicitor, Department of Commerce and Labor to the Secretary of Commerce and Labor, October 8, 1907, microfilm reel 22, Status of Adopted Chinese Minors, case file 52903/42, INS.

75 Letter from Daniel J. O'Keefe, the Commissioner-General at the Bureau of Immigration and Naturalization, Washington to the Inspector in Charge, Seattle, Washington, March 12, 1909, microfilm reel 22, Status of Adopted Chinese Minors, case file 52903/42, INS.

76 *Laws, Treaty, and Regulations Relating to the Exclusion of Chinese*, 35.

77 "Amendments to the Regulations Governing the Admission of Chinese," Department of Commerce and Labor, Office of the Secretary, Washington, D.C., February 26, 1907, microfilm reel 21, Chinese Students—Mrs. Greenlee, case file 52753/13B (1913), INS; Salyer, *Laws Harsh as Tigers*, 166.

78 Department of Labor, Bureau of Immigration, *Treaty, Laws, and Rules Governing the Admission of Chinese*, 43.

79 Channing Kwan, file 10259/267, box 234, CAF.

80 Au Kai Yung, file 12796/02-20, box 707, CAF.

81 Transcript of stenographer's notes of the June 6, 1911, visit of the Downtown Association of San Francisco to Angel Island Immigration Station, microfilm reel 24, Witness Examination—Alleged Mistreatment, Angel Island, case file 52961/24D, INS.

82 Leo Bergholz, Consul General, Canton, China, "Precis of Investigations Upon Which Section 6 Certificates Have Been Refused to the Following Chinese," November 2, 1909, microfilm reel 21, Chinese Students—Mrs. Greenlee, case file 52753/13B, INS.

83 Leo Bergholz, Consul-General, Canton, China, to Secretary of the State, Washington, D.C., February 1, 1910, microfilm reel 21, Students—Mrs. Greenlee, case file 52753/13B, INS; Department of Commerce and Labor, Bureau of Immigration and Naturalization, Washington, D.C., Letter to the Secretary of State, March 19, 1910, 2, microfilm reel 21, Chinese Students—Mrs. Greenlee, case file 52753/13B, INS.

84 Based on *Annual Reports of the Commissioner-General of Immigration, 1906–1920.*

85 "Chinese Youths Tell Troubles," *SF Call,* February 11, 1906.

86 Hsu, "Gold Mountain Dreams and Paper Son Schemes," 52–54.

87 Lai, Lim, and Yung, *Island,* 47–48; "Interview with Detainee at Angel Island," August 29, 1970, 1, HOC-DOI Project San Francisco, vertical file, AASL.

88 "Chinese Lads as Smugglers," *SF Call,* November 27, 1902.

89 "Slaves Sold for Spot Cash," *SF Call,* April 14, 1896.

90 Yu, "Rediscovered Voices," 134–35; Erika Lee, *At America's Gates,* 198–200.

91 Tang, "Chinese Women Immigrants and the Two-Edged Sword of Habeas Corpus," 49.

92 Tong, *Unsubmissive Women,* 56–57.

93 Leong Lai Yook (Lowe Lai Yuet), file 9273/414, box 17, CAF.

94 Carol Green Wilson, *Chinatown Quest,* 85–86.

95 Erika Lee, *At America's Gates,* 68; Salyer, *Laws Harsh as Tigers,* 114, 143, 156.

96 Dong Fong, file 13608/7-7, box 815, CAF.

97 Fong Jom, file 14586/30-6, box 963, CAF.

98 Fritz, "A Nineteenth-Century 'Habeas Corpus Mill,'" 348–50; Chan, *Asian Americans,* 92; Salyer, *Laws Harsh as Tigers,* xvi–xvii; Lai, "Island of Immortals," 89; Erika Lee, *At America's Gates,* 125.

99 Yu, "Rediscovered Voices," 126.

100 Erika Lee, *At America's Gates,* 57.

101 Ibid., 129.

102 Ng Poon Chew, *The Treatment of the Exempt Classes,* 10.

103 Letter from the Chinese Consolidated Benevolent Association to the President of the United States, February 9, 1909, microfilm reel 13, 141–74; Delay in Chinese Cases—San Francisco, case file 52363/14, INS.

104 Letter from Lee Yung See and Others, Chinese Association San Francisco to the Self Government Society, *On Nga Po,* 13 April 1910, microfilm reel 23, Bogus Section Six Cases—Chinese Exclusion Laws, case file 52961/23, INS.

105 Statement from the Chinese Chamber of Commerce and the Six Companies to the San Francisco Chamber of Commerce, 1911, microfilm reel 24, Witness Examination—Alleged Mistreatment, Angel Island, case file 52961/24A, 3, INS; Transcript of Stenographers Notes of the June 6th, 1911 Visit of the Downtown

Association of San Francisco Committee Visit to Angel Island Immigration Station, microfilm reel 24, Witness Examination—Alleged Mistreatment, Angel Island, case file 52961/24D, INS.

106 Complaint by Ida Greenlee, Seattle, Washington, 1912, attached to Memorandum for the Secretary from Commissioner General Daniel J. O'Keefe, May 12, 1913, microfilm reel 21, Students—Mrs. Greenlee, case file 52753/13B, INS; Inspector Lauritz Lorenzen, Letter to the Chinese Inspector in Charge, Angel Island, June 24, 1912, microfilm reel 21, Students—Mrs. Greenlee, case file 52753/13B, INS.

107 Complaint by Ida Greenlee, Seattle, Washington, 1912.

108 Series of statements written by the boys in Chinese, microfilm reel 21, Students—Mrs. Greenlee, case file 52753/13B, INS. Translated by Stephanie Chen Wu.

109 Letter from Inspector Phillips B. Jones to Commissioner of Immigration, August 31, 1912, microfilm reel 21, Students—Mrs. Greenlee, case file 52753/13B, INS.

110 Letter from Ida Greenlee to Mr. Nagel, the Secretary of the Department of Commerce and Labor, September 9, 1912, microfilm reel 21, Students—Mrs. Greenlee, case file 52753/13B, INS.

111 Department of Labor, Bureau of Immigration, *Treaty, Laws, and Rules Governing the Admission of Chinese, 1914*, 44.

112 Yee Bo, one of the students brought to San Francisco by Greenlee in 1912, was working in a local restaurant five years after his arrival in the United States. Immigration officials discovered other alleged students engaged in manual labor. Yee Bo, file 11048/14236, box 612, CAF. Refer to this box to locate other Greenlee students later found laboring. For similar stories, see also Mak, *In Search of a New Life*, 30.

113 Fong Wing Look and Fong Sou Nam, file 14462/5-19, box 939, CAF.

114 Letter from Chinese Chamber of Commerce and Six Companies to San Francisco Chamber of Commerce, microfilm reel 24, Witness Examination—Alleged Mistreatment, Angel Island, case file 52961/24A, 3, INS; Ng Poon Chew, *The Treatment of the Exempt Classes*, 10.

115 "How the Lord Saved Ah Lou," October 18, 1898, Letters to Mrs. Kate Lake, BLG.

116 Letter from the United Parlor, Native Sons of the Golden State, San Francisco to W. B. Wilson, Secretary of Labor, Washington, D.C., 29 December 1915, microfilm reel 27, Entry of Chinese as Minor Sons of Merchants—Application of Chinese Exclusion Act, case file 53620/203A, 3–4, INS. The Native Sons of the Golden State later became the Chinese American Citizens Alliance. See Yong Chen, *Chinese San Francisco*, 208.

CHAPTER TWO

1 "How a Chinese Family Lives," *SF Chron*, January 18, 1903.

2 Ibid.

3 *Report of the Special Committee of the Board of Supervisors*, 9.

4 Shah, *Contagious Divides*, 13, 77, 83.

5 *Report of the Special Committee of the Board of Supervisors*, 59.

6 Chinese Exclusion Convention, *For the Re-Enactment of the Chinese Exclusion Law*, 4.

7 For a discussion of attitudes about Chinese and white relationships in New York City, see Lui, *The Chinatown Trunk Mystery*.

8 Illick, *American Childhoods*, 60–62; Clement, *Growing Pains*, 36–39, 57.

9 Morrison G. Wong, "The Chinese American Family," 286; Ling, *Surviving on the Gold Mountain*, 85.

10 U.S. Census Bureau, *Ninth Census of the United States, 1870*.

11 Peffer, "Forbidden Families," 28–29, 42.

12 By 1910 children in San Francisco age fourteen and under constituted 18.9 percent of the population and children nineteen and under 26.7 percent. Nationally, these figures were 32.1 percent and 42 percent, respectively. Children were comparatively rare even in 1910 San Francisco. The Chinese represented only 2.4 percent of the total San Francisco population. U.S. Department of the Interior, Bureau of Education, *The Public School System of San Francisco, California*, 12–15.

13 Based on my study of the 1870, 1880, 1900, 1910, and 1920 manuscript census data from San Francisco, Sacramento City, and Oakland City. I excluded data from Brooklyn Township in Alameda County, which would have inflated the numbers slightly for Oakland.

14 Census data has proved to be fraught with a number of problems, especially with regard to the Chinese. According to historian Yong Chen, official records consistently underestimated the Chinese American population. Some individuals may have been counted twice and some not at all. See Yong Chen, *Chinese San Francisco*, 53. However, Sucheng Chan has recently argued that the manuscript censuses are "among the most important sources of historical information that we have about the Chinese in the United States during the latter half of the nineteenth century and the first half of the twentieth." Chan, "Against All Odds," 68–69.

15 The data in this chapter is derived from my tally of the 1860, 1870, 1880, 1900, 1910, and 1920 manuscript census records for San Francisco County. For purposes of this chapter, I counted all Chinese children under age sixteen living in the boundaries of San Francisco County. Please note that errors may have occurred in the process of tallying the results. Although I checked the figures multiple times, the difficulty of reading the census taker's handwriting and the tedious nature of the work may have caused me to occasionally overlook a child or misinterpret the census records.

16 Morrison G. Wong, "The Chinese American Family," 287–92; Glenn with Yap, "Chinese-American Families," 279–81.

17 This is the theory adopted by Lucie Cheng Hirata in her study of Chinese prostitutes in San Francisco. See Hirata, "Free, Indentured, Enslaved," 21.

18 The 1900 census specifically listed these women as wives. In 1870 the relationships were not clearly defined. Based on the ages of these women, I made the assumption that they were wives of the male head of household.

19 According to Judy Yung's research, in 1910 thirty households included three generations. Thirty-seven households included a mother-in-law. Yung, *Unbound Feet*, 78.

20 Morris, "The Chinaman as He Is" (post-1868), MSS 71/206, 89, BANC.

21 Osumi, "Asians and California's Anti-Miscegenation Laws," 2; Shah, *Contagious Divides*, 98–99.

22 It may be impossible to identify all such individuals in the census because of variations in enumerators' classifications of such families. In addition, the families themselves may have offered differing answers to the question of race.

23 Tong, "Introduction," 7.

24 Data collected from the 1870, 1880, 1900, 1910, and 1920 manuscript census data from the cities of Sacramento and Oakland. I excluded data from Brooklyn Township in Alameda County.

25 Knox, "A Chinese Horace Greeley," 3–4.

26 Data extracted from vital statistics published in the *San Francisco Municipal Reports, 1901–1917*, CHR. Data missing for the years 1903–5.

27 Larson, *Sweet Bamboo*, 39–40; Minnick, *Samfow*, 250.

28 Chun Yuet Kum, file 9569/664, box 36, CAF.

29 Many of the Chinese Arrival Files kept by the Immigration Bureau included copies of birth certificates. A number of physicians' names appeared on the birth certificates, and some doctors testified as witnesses to the child's birth in order to facilitate the child's readmission into the country following a trip to China. See, for example, Jung Ah So, file 10261/6181, box 235, and Lee Got Chun, file 10308/28668, box 297, CAF.

30 Caroline Chew, "Development of Chinese Family Life in America," 31–32; Murray, *Plant Wizard*, 8; Lai, "Mon Quong Fong: Octogenarian Pioneer," Him Mark Lai Files, carton 121:15, 1, AASL; "A Chinese Christening," *SFMC*, May 11, 1882; Sui Sin Far, "Chinatown Boys and Girls," 226; Minnick, *Samfow*, 250.

31 "Chinese Break Ancient Rule," *SF Exam*, October 4, 1914; " 'Red Egg Feast' for Baby Chinese Girl," *SF Exam*, October 5, 1914.

32 Bennie Lum, file 9588/223, box 38, CAF.

33 "Sacrament Given to Chinese Girl," *SF Call*, June 29, 1908.

34 Yan Phou Lee, *When I Was a Boy in China*, 8–9.

35 Lowe, *Father and Glorious Descendent*, 19–20; "Low Fat Yuen Happy Boy Twins in Family," *SF Call*, March 9, 1913.

36 Saari, *Legacies of Childhood*, 8, 78–79.

37 Kline, "The Making of Children's Culture," 98; Griswold, *Family and Divorce in California, 1850–1890*, 146–48, 152.

38 "Child Life in Chinatown," 9.

39 Saari, *Legacies of Childhood*, 8, 78–79.

40 Betty Lee Sung, *The Story of the Chinese in America*, 169.

41 "The Life Story of Edward L. C. as Written by Himself," Minor Documents No. 443, 4, SRR.

42 Ling, "Chinese Merchant Wives in the United States," 80; Mark and Chih, *A Place Called Chinese America*, 70.

43 "Story of a Chinese College Girl," Major Document No. 54, 3, SRR. Identified as Esther Wong by Judy Yung in *Unbound Voices*, 297.

44 Jane Kwong Lee, "Chinese Women in San Francisco," 1; Yung, *Unbound Feet*, 6–7, 19; "Smallest Chinese Feet in America," *SF Call*, March 20, 1898.

45 "Torturing Helpless Children," *SF Call*, July 18, 1897.

46 "Foot Binding Crusade to Be Inaugurated," *SF Call*, May 19, 1899.

47 Nancy Cott's research on the history of marriage in America and Christopher Lasch's essays examining women and domesticity help to explain the response of American reformers to the Chinese practice of foot binding. Cott has argued, in her book *Public Vows*, that American society consistently responded with hostility to practices deemed contrary to the Christian, monogamous morality. Cott cited the example of the Page Act as evidence of white society's efforts to restrict "heathen" practices of prostitution, polygamy, and concubinage as affronts to political liberty and freedom. Lasch has argued in a series of essays that the nineteenth-century cult of domesticity, while emphasizing the home as a refuge from outside influences, also represented a rebellion against patriarchal authority. Middle-class women used their newfound moral authority to justify their increasing work outside the confines of the home. Thus foot binding represented an affront to these middle-class values and visions of America. Cott, *Public Vows*, 136–38; Lasch, "The Sexual Division of Labor," 95–98.

48 "Interview with Rose Ow," September 9, 1970, Phil Choy and Him Mark Lai, Him Mark Lai Files, 2000/80, carton 121:40, 6, AASL.

49 Yung argues that the influences of Chinese nationalism, Christianity, and acculturation into American life encouraged resistance against traditional gender roles and relations. Yung, "The Social Awakening of Chinese American Women," 83, 88; Yung, *Unbound Feet*, 6.

50 Saari, *Legacies of Childhood*, 41.

51 Nee and Nee, *Longtime Californ'*, 89.

52 "How the Chinese Children of San Francisco Play 'Horse' and Other Games," *SF Call*, April 4, 1897.

53 Lloyd, *Lights and Shades in San Francisco*, 225–26; *A Short Story About Chinatown*, 15; "How the Chinese Children of San Francisco Play 'Horse' and Other Games"; Lowe, *Father and Glorious Descendent*, 48.

54 "China Boys Enemies of Mrs. Gould's Sister," *SF Call*, March 1, 1909.

55 Davison, "The Babies of Chinatown," 608.

56 "Chinese Girl Killed by Falling from Roof," *SF Chron*, December 22, 1905; "Little Celestial Falls to Her Death," *SF Exam*, December 22, 1905; "Esther Woo," December 21, 1905, SFCMR.

57 Goodman, *Choosing Sides*, 14; McGerr, *A Fierce Discontent*, 102, 111–12.

58 *San Francisco Municipal Reports for the Fiscal Year 1911–1912*, 1092, CHR; Chudacoff, *How Old Are You?*, 76; Roberta J. Park, "Sport and Recreation among Chinese American Communities," 451–52; Goodman, *Choosing Sides*, 18.

59   Macleod, *Building Character in the American Boy*, 39, 47–49, 171, 182, 212, 253.

60   Chinn, "A Historian's Reflections on Chinese-American Life in San Francisco," 28–31, BANC; Moonbeam Tong Lee, *Growing Up in Chinatown*, 47–51.

61   Peiss, *Cheap Amusements*, 5–7; Odem, *Delinquent Daughters*, 1–3.

62   "The Life Story of Edward L. C.," 4–5; Franks, "Chinese Americans and American Sports," 137, 140–41; "Historical Sketch: Fiftieth Anniversary Chinese YMCA," 10–19, SFTS; Roberta J. Park, "Sport and Recreation among Chinese American Communities," 448; Huang, "YWCA Clay Street Center: Historical Sketch," YWCA Clay Street Center 50th Anniversary program brochure, November 4, 1966, 1, AASL.

63   Formanek-Brunell, "Sugar and Spite," 108.

64   "Letter from Fong Sun Chow," SFTS.

65   Larson, *Sweet Bamboo*, 84.

66   Wores, "The Children of Chinatown in San Francisco," 575–77; "Chinese Lantern Feast," 334; "Interview with Rose Ow," 6, AASL; "Celebrate Feast of Seven Angels," *SF Call*, August 2, 1908; "Chinese Damsels Observe Holiday," *SF Call*, August 3, 1908; Erlin, "Girls Day in Chinatown," *SF Call*, August 16, 1908, Magazine Section.

67   Larson, *Sweet Bamboo*, 81–85; "Interview with Rose Ow," 7, AASL.

68   "Holiday in the Chinese Quarter," 145; Chinn, Lai, and Choy, *A History of the Chinese in California*, 76–77; Perkins, *Encyclopedia of China*, 227.

69   Fun, "Alice Sue Fun, World Traveler," 268; see also Sui Sin Far, "The Chinese Woman in America," 60, 64.

70   Saari, *Legacies of Childhood*, 13–14; McLeod, *Pigtails and Gold Dust*, 268–69; Yan Phou Lee, *When I Was a Boy in China*, 9–10.

71   "A Chinese Christening," SFMC, May 11, 1882.

72   McLeod, *Pigtails and Gold Dust*, 263–64.

73   "Effie Lai," *Bitter Melon*, 67.

74   *San Francisco Municipal Reports for the Fiscal Year 1876–77*, 398, CHR; Trauner, "The Chinese as Medical Scapegoats in San Francisco," 73–79; Martin, *Chinatown's Angry Angel*, 78; Chan, *Asian Americans*, 57; *Report of the Joint Special Committee to Investigate Chinese Immigration*, 127–31; Shah, *Contagious Divides*, 1, 120–57.

75   It should be noted, however, that the report for the following year showed a dramatic increase in the death rate for Chinese children under seventeen—41 per 1,000 compared to 25.1 per 1,000 in the white population. This figure, however, appears to be skewed based on the fact that the population figures that health officials used for Chinese children dropped dramatically from 1,286 in 1873–74 to 855 in 1874–75. It seems highly unlikely that the population of Chinese children declined by 431 persons in the span of a year. The health officer depended on the school census for these figures but admitted that "there appears to be an error somewhere." I have determined that the 1873–74 figures are probably more accurate when compared to my calculations of the numbers of children reported in the 1870 census. *San Francisco Municipal Reports for the Fiscal Year 1873–74*, 353, CHR.

76 Report of the Joint Special Committee to Investigate Chinese Immigration, 645.

77 SFCMR.

78 Charles R. King, "Infant Mortality," 427; Meckel, Save the Babies, 41–42.

79 According to the "San Francisco Chinese Mortuary Records," the most common causes of death for the period 1870–79 were inanition, variola, and stillborn; for 1880–89, inanition, pneumonia, and stillborn; for 1890–99, pneumonia, bronchitis, and gastroenteritis; for 1900–1909, broncho pneumonia, tubercular meningitis, and premature birth; and for 1910–18, inanition, pneumonia, and broncho pneumonia. During the 1870s a number of deaths were listed as unknown causes. According to the 1872–73 health officer's report, this was because only Chinese physicians tended to the patients, and they often did not fill out a mortuary certificate. San Francisco Municipal Reports for the Fiscal Year 1872–73, 335, CHR.

80 Meckel, Save the Babies, 178–79.

81 San Francisco Municipal Reports for the Fiscal Year 1912–13, 678, CHR. As early as 1897, however, the Bureau of Food Inspection was conducting daily inspections of the milk sold in the city, and milk vendors had to acquire permits from the Health Department. See San Francisco Municipal Reports for the Fiscal Year 1896–97, 879–80, CHR.

82 Calculations based on vital statistics of births and deaths provided in San Francisco Municipal Reports, 1912–1917, CHR. Birth and death rates were inconsistently reported in the San Francisco Municipal Reports prior to 1912. Infant mortality rates in San Francisco remained lower than in major cities such as New York. For example, in 1900 the infant mortality rate in San Francisco was 136.2, while in New York City it was 183.1. During the 1914–15 fiscal year, San Francisco's infant mortality rate was 80.1; the infant mortality rate in New York City for 1915 was 96.2. Meckel, Save the Babies, 90, 106; San Francisco Municipal Reports for the Fiscal Year 1914–15, 676, 728, CHR.

83 McGerr, A Fierce Discontent, 101.

84 Meckel, Save the Babies, 5–6, 131–32, 220.

85 Shah, Contagious Divides, 105–7, 111.

86 "Annual Report" (1898?), California WHMS Annual Reports, 1–3, BLG.

87 Eighth Annual Report of the Occidental Branch of the Woman's Foreign Missionary Society, 41, BANC.

88 Ibid., 25.

89 Ibid., 37.

90 Mink, The Wages of Motherhood, 88–91.

91 Carol Green Wilson, Borrowed Babies, 1–5.

92 Shah, Contagious Divides, 219–20.

93 Yung, Unbound Feet, 97.

94 "No More Bicycling for Lee Kee Joke," SF Call, July 10, 1905; "Woman's Nerve and Strong Arm Save Chinese Boy from Death," SF Call, July 9, 1902; "Truck Hits Boy," OT, February 13, 1913.

95 Thirteenth Annual Report of the Occidental Branch of the Woman's Foreign Missionary Society, 65, BANC.

96   "The Fire Record," *SFMC*, May 22, 1885.

97   Jue Lin Ong's name also appears in the newspaper as Chew Lan Ong, and Jue Do Hong appears as Gin Do Hing. "Journeys from China to Wreak Vengeance on an Innocent Boy," *SF Call*, July 30, 1901; "Sentenced to Be Hanged," *SF Call*, May 1, 1904; "Dies on the Scaffold Proclaiming Innocence," *SF Call*, July 23, 1904.

98   *Report of the Joint Special Committee to Investigate Chinese Immigration*, 329, 331.

99   Densmore, *The Chinese in California*, 84; see also John L. Meares, city health officer, commenting on the lack of compassion of the Chinese toward the sick (*Report of the Joint Special Committee to Investigation Chinese Immigration*, 130–31, 139). Dr. Stout defends the Chinese practice on page 647. "Alone in a Chamber of Death," *SF Call*, July 18, 1897; "Slowly Died in a Living Grave," *SF Call*, July 19, 1897.

100 McLeod, *Pigtails and Gold Dust*, 269.

101 Trauner, "The Chinese as Medical Scapegoats," 82–84.

102 "Story of a Chinese College Girl," Major Document No. 54, 3–4, SRR; Griggs, *Chinaman's Chance*, 17.

103 For a good secondary source on Chinese death rituals, see Chung and Wegars, *Chinese American Death Rituals*.

104 Griggs, *Chinaman's Chance*, 14–17.

105 McGerr, *A Fierce Discontent*, 80, 101–2.

CHAPTER THREE

1   Negative nos. 10, 818 and 10, 859, Stellman Photograph Collection, CHR.

2   Based on Shumsky's population and labor force figures. Shumsky, *The Evolution of Political Protest*, 81.

3   According to my calculations, the number of Chinese children sixteen and under employed in San Francisco was 1,081. The percentage of Chinese children working as child laborers was calculated using my figures from the 1870 census data and Shumsky's figures for the total labor force and Chinese labor force in 1870. Shumsky, *The Evolution of Political Protest*, 81.

4   National child-labor numbers based on statistics provided in Clement, *Growing Pains*, 146. Figures for San Francisco Chinese children based on my survey of the 1870 manuscript censuses. Throughout this chapter, I generally look at children age sixteen and under. Here, however, I have calculated the statistics for children age ten to fifteen in San Francisco in order to compare with the national statistics of working children.

5   These figures were derived by subtracting the number of children whose occupations are listed as "at home," "at school," "none," or "unknown." That number is then divided by the total number of male or female Chinese children. U.S. Census Bureau, *Ninth Census of the United States, 1870*.

6   Dudden, *Serving Women*, 1.

7   Catharine Holt, "Interview with Mr. George Lem," August 4, 1924, Major Document No. 298, 2, SRR.

8   Dudden, *Serving Women*, 226.

9   Huie Kin, *Reminiscences*, 31–34.

10 "Americanized Chinese Boy" and "Chinese Boy Wishes Position," *SF Call*, May 14, 1905.

11 Lee Chew, "The Life Story of a Chinaman," 180.

12 Huie Kin, *Reminiscences*, 28.

13 Kathleen Wong, "Quan Laan Fan: An Oral History," student paper, 1974, vertical file, 5, AASL.

14 *Report of the Chinese Mission to the California Conference of the Methodist Episcopal Church, 1889*, 15.

15 Letter from Laura Lee to Margarita Lake, November 15, 1897, BLG.

16 Ibid.

17 Letter from Marie Chan to Margarita Lake, June 29, 1910, BLG.

18 Ong, "An Ethnic Trade," 95, 105.

19 Yong Chen, *Chinese San Francisco*, 65.

20 Ong, "An Ethnic Trade," 103; Siu, *The Chinese Laundryman*, 77–79.

21 Mak, *In Search of a New Life*, 24, 56.

22 Tygiel, *Workingmen in San Francisco*, 21, 23.

23 Morris, "The Chinaman as He Is" (post-1868), MSS 71/206, 51, BANC.

24 Yung, *Unbound Feet*, 26.

25 *Thirteenth Annual Report of the Occidental Branch of the Woman's Foreign Missionary Society*, 65, BANC.

26 Kathleen Wong, "Quan Laan Fan: An Oral History," 6, AASL.

27 Won, "Recollections of Dr. Sun Yat-Sen's Stay at Our Home in San Francisco," 70. See also Alice Sue Fun's account of balancing American school, Chinese school, and sewing at home. Fun, "Alice Sue Fun, World Traveler," 268–69.

28 Mears, *Resident Orientals on the American Pacific Coast*, 262–64.

29 Chinn, "A Historian's Reflections on Chinese American Life in San Francisco, 1919–1991," 254–56, BANC.

30 Based on my study of Chinese children in the 1870, 1880, 1900, 1910, and 1920 manuscript census data of San Francisco, Sacramento City, and Oakland City.

31 Gratton and Moen, "Immigration, Culture, and Child Labor in the United States," 378–79, 386, 388–90.

32 Ibid., 390.

33 Yong Chen, *Chinese San Francisco*, 65.

34 "Memorial on Chinatown," in *Chinatown Declared a Nuisance*, 13.

35 For a full discussion of this topic, see Shah, *Contagious Divides*, 63–64, 87–90.

36 Henshaw, "California Housekeepers and Chinese Servants," 739.

37 *Report of the Joint Special Committee to Investigate Chinese Immigration*, 138–39.

38 Densmore, *The Chinese in California*, 41.

39 Siu, *The Chinese Laundryman*, 66.

40 Ibid., 51.

41 Chan, *Asian Americans*, 94–95.

42 "Chinese Laundries," *SF Call*, January 18, 1897.

43   "Report of Cigar Factory Inspector," *San Francisco Municipal Reports for the Fiscal Year 1897–98*, 259–62, CHR.

44   U.S. Census Bureau, *Ninth Census of the United States, 1870*; U.S. Census Bureau, *Tenth Census of the United States, 1880*; U.S. Census Bureau, *Twelfth Census of the United States, 1900*.

45   Morris, "The Chinaman as He Is," 52.

46   Whitney, *The Chinese and the Chinese Question*, 113.

47   Chinn, Lai, and Choy, *A History of the Chinese in California*, 13–14; Sandmeyer, *The Anti-Chinese Movement in California*, 27–29.

48   Aarim-Heriot, *Chinese Immigrants, African Americans, and Racial Anxiety*, 68.

49   Workingmen's Party of California, *An Address from the Workingmen of San Francisco to Their Brothers throughout the Pacific Coast*, 4.

50   Chinese Exclusion Convention, *For the Re-Enactment of the Chinese Exclusion Law*, 7.

51   White working women also agitated against the immigration of Chinese laborers as a threat to the domestic sphere and the economic opportunities of white families. See Holden, "Gender, Protest, and the Anti-Chinese Movement," 294–302.

52   Gibson spent ten years as a missionary in China before returning to San Francisco to begin a mission to the Chinese on the Pacific Coast. *Report of the Joint Special Committee to Investigate Chinese Immigration*, 396–98.

53   Ibid., 817–19.

54   Ibid., 819, 821; U.S. Census Bureau, *Ninth Census of the United States, 1870*. William Jessup and his match factory were located in the Eleventh Ward, First District, San Francisco, California (164).

55   Henry Pearson Gratton, *As a Chinaman Saw Us*, 280–81.

56   Lee Chew, "The Life Story of a Chinaman," 184–85.

57   Frank Wu has located the nineteenth-century origins of the "model minority" myth in the efforts of southern plantation owners, northern industrialists, railroad barons, and labor brokers to recruit a cheap labor force. Historian K. Scott Wong has also noted that during the late nineteenth and early twentieth centuries, the Chinese elite responded to anti-Chinese attacks in part by "denigrating other immigrant and minority groups." Wu, *Yellow*, 59–63; K. Scott Wong, "Chinatown," 8.

58   "Appendix F, Constitution and By-laws of the Anti-Chinese Union of San Francisco," *Report of the Joint Special Committee*, 1170.

59   Jack Chen, *The Chinese of America*, 109.

60   Coolidge, *Chinese Immigration*, 370.

61   Chinn, Lai, and Choy, *A History of the Chinese in California*, 52; Jack Chen, *The Chinese of America*, 109.

62   In 1876 a Chinese boy named Ah Jim was arrested and charged with assault and battery for defending himself against an attack by three white hoodlums. The judge, however, dismissed the charge, recognizing that the boy acted in self-defense. "Ah Jim Set Free," *San Francisco Daily Morning Call*, June 2, 1876.

63 Shumsky, *The Evolution of Political Protest*, 13–17; Tygiel, *Workingmen in San Francisco*, 55.

64 Holt, "Interview with Mr. George Lem," 2, SRR.

65 Lee Baung Keen, Lee Die Churn, and Lee Baung Hoong, file 8-24-85, box 1, CAF.

66 H. K. Wong, *Gum Sahn Yun*, 181–82.

67 Shinn, "Charities for Children in San Francisco," 89; "Laws Relating to Charities, Paupers, Vagrants, and Minors," in Jenness, *The Charities of San Francisco: A Directory*, 65–66.

68 "An Act to Regulate the Hours of Labor and Employment of Minors, Approved February 8, 1889," in Jenness, *The Charities of San Francisco: A Directory*, 69–70.

69 "A Dangerous Practice," *San Francisco Daily Morning Call*, October 16, 1875; "Fatal Use of Kerosene," *San Francisco Daily Morning Call*, 18 October 1875; "Ah Sam," October 17, 1875, SFCMR.

70 *Fifteenth Annual Report of the Occidental Board of the Woman's Foreign Missionary Society*, 43, BANC.

71 "Three Chinese Women of San Francisco," 174.

72 "Kum Ying Says She Was Sold," *SF Call*, June 1, 1901, 9.

73 Illick, *American Childhoods*, 58–61.

74 Zelizer, "From Useful to Useless: Moral Conflict over Child Labor," 90.

75 Trattner, *Crusade for the Children*, 41, 107, 146–47; Hindman, *Child Labor*, 50.

76 Ellis, "Social and Philanthropic Work among Orientals," 32–34.

77 "Women in Fight for Chinese Girl," *OT*, October 5, 1912; "Seek Possession of Chinese Girl," *OT*, November 19, 1912; "Miss Carrie Davis Loses Fight for Little Helen Lau," *OT*, November 20, 1912.

78 "Oakland," *OT*, August 1, 1925.

79 *Child Labor Law*, 1–9; "Children Must Attend School," *SF Call*, May 18, 1905.

80 Illick, *American Childhoods*, 96–97.

81 Trattner, *Crusade for the Children*, 159.

82 U.S. Census Bureau, *Ninth Census of the United States, 1870*; U.S. Census Bureau, *Twelfth Census of the United States, 1900*; U.S. Census Bureau, *Fourteenth Census of the United States, 1920*.

83 Hindman, *Child Labor*, 206.

84 Ellis, "Social and Philanthropic Work among Orientals," 32–34.

85 Major Document 148, SRR.

86 My figures are based on a tally of the occupations of the primary wage earner in two-parent families in the 1870 and 1920 census. Although I mostly examined the occupation of the male head of household, I also recorded the occupation of the wife when her occupation was not listed or recorded as "none." I have adopted Judy Yung's classification scheme as set forth in *Unbound Feet*. Yung specifically examined the occupations of Chinese male heads with at least one female present in the household. According to Yung's research on the 1900 census, 43 percent worked in agriculture, domestic/personal service, or artisan/manufacturing positions. Fifty-six percent worked in professional or trade occupations. By 1920 the number of men working in these categories had increased to 67 percent,

while the number working in agriculture, domestic/personal service, or artisan/
manufacturing positions had declined to 33 percent. Included in the category of
domestic and personal service are cooks, janitors, laborers, porters, servants,
seaman, and waiters. Agricultural workers included farmers, fishermen, and
cannery workers. The category of artisan/manufacturer included cigar makers,
garment manufacturers, jewelers, machinists, shoemakers, and tailors. Yung
identifies trade or clerical occupations as agents, bankers, boarding housekeepers,
bookkeepers, brothel keepers, clerks, labor contractors, laundrymen, managers,
merchants, grocers, peddlers, restaurateurs, salesmen, and teamsters. Professional occupations include actors, dentists, interpreters, journalists, physicians,
and druggists. Although my data set is more narrowly defined than Yung's—I
examine only men who are married and living with a wife and children—our data
for 1920 closely corresponds. I generally use the term "working-class" to refer to
those families whose heads of household were employed in the categories of
domestic and personal service, agriculture, or artisan/manufacturer. I refer to
"merchant-class" as those employed in trade/clerical or professional service.
Yung, *Unbound Feet*, 301.

87 Lai, "Mon Quong Fong: Octogenarian Pioneer," Him Mark Lai Files, carton
121:15, 1, AASL; Yu, "A History of San Francisco Chinatown Housing," 98; Won,
"Recollections of Dr. Sun Yat-Sen's Stay at Our Home in San Francisco," 75.

88 Gillenkirk and Motlow, *Bitter Melon*, 67–68; Ling, "Growing Up in 'Hop Alley,'"
66; Chinn, "A Historian's Reflections on Chinese American Life in San Francisco,
1919–1991," 18, BANC.

89 Tong, "Introduction," 8–9.

90 Brian Gratton and Jon Moen argue that working-class children's labor was less a
necessity to survival than a luxury that afforded families extra income to bolster
their standard of living. Gratton and Moen, "Immigration, Culture, and Child
Labor in the United States, 1880–1920," 363.

91 Moonbeam Tong Lee, *Growing Up in Chinatown*, 3–5.

92 *California Juvenile Court Law, 1919*, 22.

CHAPTER FOUR

1 U.S. Congress, *Statistical Review of Immigration, 1820–1910*, 84.

2 Berrol, *Growing Up American*, 31–33, 37.

3 Aarim-Heriot, *Chinese Immigrants, African Americans, and Racial Anxiety*, 10.

4 The best source on this topic is Low, *The Unimpressible Race*, 6, 10, 13–17, 20–22.
See also Wollenberg, *All Deliberate Speed*, 10–14; Dolson, "The Administration of
the San Francisco Public Schools," 120–22; Ferrier, *Ninety Years of Education in
California*, 102; Swett, *History of the Public School System of California*, 205; Kuo,
"Excluded, Segregated, and Forgotten," 34; and Hendrick, *The Education of Non-
Whites in California*, 16.

5 Wollenberg, *All Deliberate Speed*, 22–25, 33.

6 Chang, *The Chinese in America*, 176–77; Low, *The Unimpressible Race*, 49–50; Ferrier, *Ninety Years of Education in California*, 103, 118.

7 "To the Honorable the Senate and Assembly of the State of California," 1, Miscellaneous Selections: Chinese/Chinese American Communities, BANC.

8 Kerr, *The Chinese Question Analyzed*, 16.

9 Densmore, *The Chinese in California*, 27

10 *Report of the Special Committee of the Board of Supervisors*, 58–61.

11 "Mongolian Children: Shall They Be Admitted to Our Public Schools?," *San Francisco Daily Record Union*, January 16, 1885.

12 Wollenberg, "An Exercise in Segregation," 24; Chang, *The Chinese in America*, 176–77.

13 Misspellings in original. Tape, "A Letter from Mrs. Tape," 174.

14 Circular 86, Office of the Superintendent of Common Schools, April 1, 1886, Series 2: Administration, 1874–1994, Sub-series A, Superintendent of Schools, Part 1: Circulars and Bulletins, boxes 5–19, San Francisco Unified School District Records, SFHC.

15 Perman, *The Struggle for Mastery*, 264–69.

16 Johnsen, "Equal Rights and the 'Heathen "Chinee," ' " 58, 61, 67–68.

17 Beck, "The Other Children," 142–43.

18 Based on the enumerators' classification of children as students. Children who worked or attended school part-time may not have been listed as students. The actual number of students is probably greatly underreported. U.S. Census Bureau, *Ninth Census of the United States, 1870*; U.S. Census Bureau, *Twelfth Census of the United States, 1900*.

19 Nee and Nee, *Longtime Californ'*, 73.

20 Kuo, "Excluded, Segregated, and Forgotten," 40; Low expresses confusion over the exact date of this incident. It is possible that this occurred in 1905. See Low, *The Unimpressible Race*, 84, 221.

21 "Must Attend Chinese School," *SF Call*, November 30, 1902.

22 "Must Attend Chinese School," *SF Call*, November 30, 1902; "Race Question in the Schools," *SF Call*, December 6, 1902.

23 Kuo, "Excluded, Segregated, and Forgotten," 37.

24 "Chinese Ask for Justice," *SF Call*, May 15, 1903, 4.

25 Kuo, "Excluded, Segregated, and Forgotten," 39; Chan, *Asian Americans*, 59.

26 Letter from the Chinese Consolidated Benevolent Association to the President of the United States, February 9, 1909, microfilm reel 13, 141–74, Delay in Chinese Cases—San Francisco, case file 52363/14, 1909, INS.

27 Chan, "Race, Ethnic Culture, and Gender," 153.

28 Lee and Ow, "Chinese Historical Society of America Talk," April 9, 1974, Him Mark Lai Files, 2000/80, carton 121:40, 2, AASL.

29 C. H. Burnett, "Life History and Social Document of David Young," Seattle, August 29, 1924, Major Document No. 272, 2–3, SRR.

30 Ibid.

31   *Thirteenth Annual Report of the Occidental Branch*, 71, BANC.

32   *Third Annual Report of the California Branch of the Woman's Foreign Missionary Society*, 9, SFTS.

33   Yung, *Unbound Feet*, 6–8, 52–54, 126–27; Yung, "The Social Awakening of Chinese American Women," 82, 88–91.

34   *The Unity of Three*, 17.

35   Yuk Ying Lee, "Education of Chinese Women," 106.

36   "A Bevy of Chinese High School Girls," *SF Call*, July 2, 1905.

37   Yung, *Unbound Feet*, 126–27.

38   Moonbeam Tong Lee, *Growing Up in Chinatown*, 2–4.

39   Yong Chen, *Chinese San Francisco, 1850–1943*, 169.

40   Wollenberg, *All Deliberate Speed*, 34.

41   *Sixth Annual Report of the Occidental Branch of the Woman's Foreign Missionary Society*, 13, SFTS.

42   *The Annual Report of the Woman's Union Mission, 1880*, 3–4, BANC.

43   Morris, "The Chinaman as He Is," 33–34.

44   Martin, *Chinatown's Angry Angel*, 159; Mrs. Clemens Wong, *Chinatown*, 35.

45   *Report of the Presbyterian Mission to the Chinese in California*, 4, BANC.

46   Fred H. Hackett, "Only One in the World," *SF Call*, August 23, 1896.

47   Ibid.

48   Shepherd, "Educational Work in the Chinese Community," 21–24.

49   "Education of Youthful Mongolians," *SF Call*, January 23, 1898.

50   Berrol, *Growing Up American*, 31, 44; Clement, *Growing Pains*, 87–90.

51   "A Visit to the Chinese School," *Alta*, August 21, 1867.

52   U.S. Department of the Interior, *The Public School System of San Francisco, California*, 220–21, 545–47.

53   Ibid., 200–201.

54   Barlow, "The Images of the Chinese, Japanese, and Koreans," 139, 142, 147.

55   Dunn, *Civics*, 37.

56   Cora M. Older, "Teaching English to the Little Yellow Men," *San Francisco Evening Bulletin*, April 4, 1896.

57   U.S. Department of the Interior, *The Public School System of San Francisco, California*, 538.

58   H. K. Wong, *Gum Sahn Yun*, 167–68.

59   "Story of a Chinese College Girl," August 1, 1924, Major Document No. 54, 4–5, SRR; Yung, *Unbound Voices*, 297–98.

60   H. K. Wong, *Gum Sahn Yun*, 183; Chang, *The Chinese in America*, 178; Low, *The Unimpressible Race*, 109–10.

61   C. H. Burnett, "Life History and Social Document of Andrew Kan," Seattle, Washington, August 22, 1924, Major Document No. 178, 2, SRR. For accounts of hostilities between whites and Chinese, see also Lee and Ow, "Chinese Historical Society of America Talk," 1, AASL; "Summary of Interview with J. P. Wong, Age 76," July 16, 1977, H. M. Lai, Philip Fong, Him Mark Lai Files, 2000/80, carton 121:45, 2, AASL.

62 H. K. Wong, *Gum Sahn Yun*, 168.

63 Wong was later acquitted. "Boy Is Slain by Chinese Gunman," *SF Call*, February 21, 1912; "Wong Shee Named as Boy's Slayer," *SF Call*, February 3, 1912.

64 "Chinese, 11, Stabbed Battling Italian Lads," *SF Call*, January 23, 1918.

65 Chinn, "A Historian's Reflections on Chinese American Life in San Francisco, 1919–1991," 38, BANC.

66 Yong Chen, *Chinese San Francisco, 1850–1943*, 169.

67 Lai, "Retention of the Chinese Heritage," 10–11.

68 "Chinese School Is Established Here," *SF Call*, February 1, 1909; "Imperial Chinese School Opened in San Francisco," *SF Call*, February 9, 1909; Liang Qinggui, "The Report Transmitting the Register of Schools," 50; Lai, "Retention of the Chinese Heritage," 12–13.

69 Shepherd, "Educational Work in the Chinese Community," 25.

70 Moonbeam Tong Lee, *Growing Up in Chinatown*, 36–38.

71 Lai, "Retention of the Chinese Heritage," 10; Moonbeam Tong Lee, *Growing Up in Chinatown*, 36–39.

72 Moonbeam Tong Lee, *Growing Up in Chinatown*, 39–41. Pardee Lowe remembered similar methods of cheating utilized by his peers at the Chinese School in East Belleville. See Lowe, *Father and Glorious Descendent*, 108.

73 Moonbeam Tong Lee, *Growing Up in Chinatown*, 39–42.

74 Choy and Lai, "Summary of Interview with Dr. James Hall," August 23, 1970, Him Mark Lai Files, 2000/80, carton 121:19, 2, AASL. See also "The Life Story of Edward L. C. as Written by Himself," Minor Document No. 443, 3, SRR.

75 Berrol, *Immigrants at School*, 53, 128; Berrol, "Immigrant Children at School, 1880–1940," 54–56.

76 "A Visit to the Chinese School," 1.

77 *The Unity of Three*, 16.

78 "Education of Youthful Mongolians."

79 "Christmas Entertainments of the Occidental Board Mission Schools," 10, SFTS.

80 Primary Register, Presbyterian Church, San Francisco Chinatown, 1918–1924, BANC FILM 2766, BANC.

81 "Graduating Exercises of the Oriental Public School, San Francisco," St. Mary's Hall, June 9, 1910, California State Library, Sutro Branch.

82 "Education of Youthful Mongolians."

83 Berrol, *Immigrants at School*, 127–28. Pardee Lowe remembered the children receiving weekly baths in the school bathrooms from his teacher at the public school in East Belleville. Lowe, *Father and Glorious Descendent*, 131; "Rescue Work of the Occidental Board," 11, SFTS.

84 "Report of the Medical Inspection of Schools," *San Francisco Municipal Reports for the Fiscal Year 1910–11*, 188–89, CHR.

85 *Twenty-Fifth Annual Report of the Woman's Occidental Board of Foreign Missions*, 74–75, SFTS.

86 Herman, "Neighbors on the Golden Mountain," 351, 391, 396–99; Mink, *The Wages of Motherhood*, 80.

87 State Commission of Immigration and Housing of California, *Heroes of Freedom*, 8–12.

88 *Fifteenth Annual Report of the Occidental Board*, 50, BANC.

89 Ibid.

90 Lasch, "Life in the Therapeutic State," 176–77.

91 State Commission of Immigration and Housing of California, *Heroes of Freedom*, 6–9; State Commission of Immigration and Housing of California, *A Manual for Home Teachers*, 7.

92 Donovan, *White Slave Crusades*, 64.

93 State Commission of Immigration and Housing of California, *Heroes of Freedom*, 6–9; State Commission of Immigration and Housing of California, *A Manual for Home Teachers*, 7.

94 Mink, *The Wages of Motherhood*, 85.

95 U.S. Department of the Interior, *The Public School System of San Francisco, California*, 546–47.

96 Herman, "Neighbors on the Golden Mountain," 509.

97 "Education of Youthful Mongolians."

98 Correspondence between Jennie Cilker and A. L. Kroeber, file 1912, C-Misc, box 21, CU-23, Records of the University of California, Berkeley, Department of Anthropology, BANC; Correspondence between A. L. Kroeber and Phoebe Hearst, File Hearst, Phoebe, file 1912, C-Misc, box 21, CU-23, Records of the University of California, Berkeley, Department of Anthropology, BANC; Correspondence between C. C. Newhall and A. L. Kroeber, File N-Misc, box 22, CU-23, Records of the University of California, Berkeley, Department of Anthropology, BANC.

99 Older, "Teaching English to the Little Yellow Men."

100 Laughlin, "Chinese Children in American Schools," 500–503.

101 Greenwell, "Oakland Public Schools, Lincoln School," Letter to Professor C. E. Hugh, UC Berkeley, November 13, 1924, Minor Document No. 356, 2, SRR.

102 "Oriental Pupils Talk English Quicker When Segregated," *OT*, October 4, 1925.

103 Mary Bo-Tze Lee, "Problems of the Segregated School for Asiatics in San Francisco," 14.

104 Ibid., 18–19.

105 In contrasting Chinese laborers with African American and Irish workers, capitalists declared the Chinese a more reliable and hard-working labor force. Wu, *Yellow*, 59–63; K. Scott Wong, "Chinatown," 8.

106 Timothy P. Fong, *The Contemporary Asian American Experience*, 60–61; Chan, *Asian Americans*, 167–69.

CHAPTER FIVE

1 Boyer, *Urban Masses and Moral Order in America*, 71; Langum, *Crossing the Line*, 15–16.

2 Langum, *Crossing the Line*, 15–18; Grittner, *White Slavery*, 47, 67.

3 Asbury, *The Barbary Coast*, 151.

4   *Report of the Joint Special Committee to Investigate Chinese Immigration*, 146.

5   My data is based on a count of all Chinese children sixteen and under in the San Francisco 1870 census. According to Lucie Cheng Hirata's research, the majority of children in Chinatown in 1860 lived in brothels. By 1880, however, more children lived outside of brothels than inside of them. Hirata noted that in 1870, about seventeen children under age fifteen were listed as prostitutes in the U.S. census, and 254 children lived in brothels that year. My numbers are higher because I included children age sixteen and under. Hirata, "Free, Indentured, Enslaved," 21–23.

6   *Report of the Joint Special Committee to Investigate Chinese Immigration*, 192, 221; Hirata, "Free, Indentured, Enslaved," 13–14, 18, 21; Tong, *Unsubmissive Women*, 75; Asbury, *The Barbary Coast*, 148; Yung, *Unbound Feet*, 28–29.

7   Griggs, *Chinaman's Chance*, 27–30; Yung, *Unbound Feet*, 29; Hirata, "Free, Indentured, Enslaved," 13–14.

8   "The Board of Health: Resolutions of Condemnation Adopted," in *Chinatown Declared a Nuisance*, 4–5.

9   Rosen, *The Lost Sisterhood*, 8.

10 Donovan, *White Slave Crusades*, 43, 48, 52, 127–29.

11 See Shah, *Contagious Divides*.

12 *Report of the Joint Special Committee to Investigate Chinese Immigration*, 651–52.

13 Rosen, *The Lost Sisterhood*, 9.

14 Tong, *Unsubmissive Women*, 116–18, 176.

15 Nee and Nee, *Longtime Californ'*, 84–85.

16 "Her Back Was Burnt with Irons," *SF Call*, July 23, 1897; "Scourged with Fire and Knife," *SF Call*, July 24, 1897.

17 Shinn, "Charities for Children in San Francisco," 88–89; Jenness, *The Charities of San Francisco*, 65–67; Nunn and Cleary, "From the Mexican California Frontier to Arnold-Kennick," 6; Schackelford, "To Shield Them from Temptation," 501–2, 504–6.

18 Schackelford, "To Shield Them from Temptation," 409–10.

19 Shinn, "Poverty and Charity in San Francisco," 541–42; Boyer, *Urban Masses and Moral Order in Urban America*, 89–90, 144–46.

20 Shinn, "Charities for Children in San Francisco," 90–91.

21 Mink, *The Wages of Motherhood*, 12.

22 The Pacific Society for the Suppression of Vice organized in 1893 to fight against "all kinds of vice, including illicit literature, obscene pictures and books, the sale of morphine, cocaine, opium, tobacco and liquors to minors, lottery tickets, etc." Jenness, *The Charities of San Francisco*, 45–47.

23 Letter from Ah Oye, Pacific Grove, February 22, 1902, Rescue Documents, BLG.

24 Letter from Ah Oye, March 1902, Rescue Documents, BLG.

25 Carol Green Wilson, *Chinatown Quest*, 35–36.

26 "Obeying Her Owner the Girl Fought Her Rescuers," *SF Exam*, January 15, 1901.

27 "Rescue of Child Slave Girl from a Chinese Den Frustrated by White Watchman," *SF Exam*, March 2, 1901, 2.

28 "A Real Missionary," *SF Chron*, May 5, 1901, 27.

29 "Fight For a Slave Girl," *SF Call*, July 9, 1895, 4; "Federal Law for Ah Soo," *SF Call*, July 10, 1895, 8.

30 "Court Awards Little Chinese Girl to Mother," *SF Call*, March 11, 1902; Staley, "Contested Childhoods," 45–46. Staley argues that Kane may have preferred family-based care as opposed to the older model of institutional care. Indeed, this was an issue of great debate among reformers in the early twentieth century. The National Conference of Charities and Correction argued against orphanages and advocated an early form of foster care, emphasizing the importance of maintaining family-based care for orphans. Adherents for both public and private models of child welfare policy were represented at the 1909 White House Conference on the Care of Dependent Children. Preference for home care as opposed to institutional care clearly dominated the proceedings. Goodwin, *Gender and the Politics of Welfare Reform*, 24, 36–37.

31 The California Society for the Prevention of Cruelty to Children, *Thirteenth Annual Report, 1889*, 15.

32 "Rescued from a Life of Bondage," *SF Chron*, October 5, 1902.

33 "Judge Wants No Tardiness," *SF Chron*, December 19, 1902; Ah Fah ultimately ended up in the Mission Home at her own choosing. *Thirtieth Annual Report of the Woman's Occidental Board of Foreign Missions*, 53, SFTS.

34 Martin, *Chinatown's Angry Angel*, 86.

35 "Hidden Chinese Girl Found for Mother," *SF Exam*, January 29, 1914; "Chinese Slave Girl in Fight for Child," *SF Exam*, April 9, 1914; "Coffey to Settle Chinese Child Case," *SF Exam*, April 10, 1914; "Court Fight Opens for Chinese Child," *SF Exam*, May 9, 1914; Carol Green Wilson, *Chinatown Quest*, 50–53.

36 To Wong Fong Mann & Wife, September 1, 1897, BLG; Wong King Que, Letter of Guardianship, San Francisco, September 3, 1897, BLG; C. W. Kinsey, "The Story of Little Ah Kue" (New York: Woman's Home Missionary Society of the Methodist Episcopal Church), scrapbook 2, BLG; Letter from Ah Kue to Margarita Lake, October 17, 1898, BLG.

37 "The Bartered Babies," *SFMC*, February 3, 1885.

38 "A Baby Slave," *SFMC*, February 18, 1886.

39 "Friends of the Little Ones," *SFMC*, January 14, 1886.

40 Mary Ting Yi Lui has examined interracial relationships in New York's early Chinatown. Lui finds that the New York SPCC promoted an image of Chinese sexual depravity and warned parents against allowing their children to visit Chinese businesses. The New York SPCC actively investigated cases of alleged relationships between Chinese men and white girls. On numerous occasions, officers of the New York SPCC accompanied New York police officers in raids in Chinatown to locate and rescue female minors from dens of vice. Social reformers were especially concerned with policing the activities of working-class girls. The actions of the SPCC in New York and California suggest that the organization, with the assistance of the local courts, intended to enforce the

racialized boundaries of Chinese marriage and family life. Lui, *The Chinatown Trunk Mystery*, 68–71, 95.

41 "Take Baby-Girl from Chinatown," *SF Call*, January 9, 1903.

42 "Chinese Owners of White Child," *SF Exam*, January 9, 1903.

43 "Little Ah Lin Is Surely All White," *SF Exam*, January 13, 1903; "Claims to Be of Chinese Descent," *Chung Sai Yat Po*, January 14, 1903.

44 "Trying to Prove Ah Lin Is White," *SF Exam*, January 15, 1903.

45 "Experts Testify in Ah Lin Case," *SF Call*, January 15, 1903.

46 "Trying to Prove Ah Lin Is White."

47 Linda Gordon details a similar story in her book, *The Great Arizona Orphan Abduction*. Gordon examines the hostility encountered by Mexican foster parents in Arizona who attempted to adopt Irish Catholic orphans from New York in 1904. Gordon argues that the Anglo community established their dominance over the Mexican community by attacking their parental fitness. As in the Ho Lin case, the central objection was to the race of the foster parents. Gordon, *The Great Arizona Orphan Abduction*, 302–3.

48 This is a point made by Mary Ting Yi Lui in her examination of the Elsie Sigel murder case. Lui argues that New Yorkers feared that the interracial relationship between Sigel and Leon Ling represented the ability of the Chinese to fully assimilate into American life. Lui, *The Chinatown Trunk Mystery*, 12.

49 "Returns Pretty Ah Lin to Her Foster Parents," *SF Call*, January 20, 1903.

50 "Mongol Actor Keeps Ah Lin," *SF Chron*, January 20, 1903; "Return of the Pearl," *Chung Sai Yat Po*, January 20, 1903.

51 "Back to a Chinese Master," *SF Exam*, January 20, 1903.

52 Mason, "Social Christianity, American Feminism, and Chinese Prostitutes," 206; "Rescue Work of the Occidental Board," 11, SFTS; Martin, *Chinatown's Angry Angel*, 61–63; "Rules of Inmates," Summer [1903?], BLG; WHMS Annual Report, October 1900–September 1901, BLG.

53 "A Real Missionary," *SF Chron*, May 5, 1901.

54 Donovan, *White Slave Crusades*, 64.

55 U.S. Census Bureau, *Twelfth Census of the United States*, 1900.

56 Carol Green Wilson, *Chinatown Quest*, 102, 109.

57 Light, "From Vice District to Tourist Attraction," 378–79, 388–90.

58 The editor of *Chung Sai Yat Po* was a Christianized Chinese American named Ng Poon Chew. Chew's wife, Chun Fah, was once a *mui tsai* in Chinatown but was rescued by officers of the SPCC and raised by the missionaries of the Presbyterian Mission. For her full story, see Mason, "Social Christianity, American Feminism and Chinese Prostitutes," 211–12; Yung, *Unbound Feet*, 75; and Tong, *Unsubmissive Women*, 67–68.

59 Asbury, *The Barbary Coast*, 139–40; "Dying Day of Six Men Is at Hand," *SF Call*, August 1, 1897; "Six More Men Are Doomed," *SF Call*, August 2, 1897; "Suggesting a Remedy," *SF Call*, August 12, 1897.

60 "Want the Kidnappers Arrested," *SF Call*, April 1, 1898.

61 Odem, *Delinquent Daughters*, 3–5, 8–9; Rosen, *The Lost Sisterhood*, 55; Gullet, "City Mothers, City Daughters, and the Dance Hall Girls," 149–55.

62 Odem, *Delinquent Daughters*, 188.

63 Asbury, *The Barbary Coast*, 135; "Transcript of the Evidence Taken and Proceeding Had before the Assembly Committee of the Legislature," 385, 389–90, 395, CSA; "Grave but Uncorroborated Accusations Are Made against Chief Sullivan and Captain Wittman," *SF Call*, February 10, 1901; "Missionaries Describe to Investigators the Horrors of the Chinese Slave Trade," *SF Call*, February 12, 1901; "Local Police Officials Are Charged with Inactivity," *SF Call*, February 22, 1901.

64 " 'Slavery Must Be Stamped Out!,' " *SF Exam*, February 18, 1901; "Pulpits Ring with Denunciation of Officials Too Weak to Battle with the Wiles of Oriental Vice," *SF Exam*, February 11, 1901.

65 "The Grand Jury's Report," *San Francisco Star*, May 4, 1901.

66 U.S. Congress, *Importing Women for Immoral Purposes*, 23.

67 Shumsky and Springer, "San Francisco's Zone of Prostitution," 77–85; Shumsky, "Vice Responds to Reform, San Francisco, 1910–1914," 34, 44; Rosen, *The Lost Sisterhood*, 9, 16–17.

68 Berrol, *Growing Up American*, 96–99.

69 The data presented in this paragraph is based on the information recorded in the one remaining and largely incomplete 1875/1876 police criminal photo key in the SFHC.

70 Ah Lin apparently continued his criminal career, as the record book also referenced page 4779, presumably of another record book. The SFPL only had this one record book from this time period in their collection. 1035, 1129, 1256, Police Criminal Photos, Chinese, Number 3, Key, box 13 of 25, SFHC.

71 "House of Correction Report," *San Francisco Municipal Reports for the Fiscal Year 1879–80*, 304, CHR; U.S. Census Bureau, *Tenth Census of the United States, 1880*.

72 The 1880 census lists 1,495 inmates in San Quentin, 264 of whom were Chinese. U.S. Census Bureau, *Tenth Census of the United States, 1880*.

73 "Another Horde of Mongolian Criminals in Court," *SFMC*, May 11, 1882.

74 Beach, *Oriental Crime in California*, 55–60, 83, 92–93.

75 In 1900 there were fifty-five Chinese inmates in San Quentin and thirty-four Chinese prisoners in Folsom. The total number of inmates in these two institutions was 2,145. U.S. Census Bureau, *Twelfth Census of the United States, 1900*; Gibson and Jung, "Historical Census Statistics on Population Totals by Race."

76 Mullen, *Dangerous Strangers*, 63, 66, 69, 72–74.

77 "Chinese Girl Wife Is Found Slain," *SF Call*, March 8, 1911.

78 Mullen, *Dangerous Strangers*, 77–78.

79 Ibid., 75–81.

80 "Transcript of the Evidence Taken and Proceeding Had before the Assembly Committee of the Legislature," 385, 389–90, 395–402, CSA; "The Grand Jury's Report."

81 Bellingham, "The 'Unspeakable Blessing,' " 305.

82 "John Chinaman in San Francisco," 866.

83 Grossberg, "Changing Conceptions of Child Welfare in the United States," 16–17.

84 Macallair, "The San Francisco Industrial School and the Origins of Juvenile Justice in California," 3, 16, 21.

85 Ibid., 17; "Report of the Industrial School Department," *San Francisco Municipal Reports for the Fiscal Year 1864–5*, 276, CHR; "Report of the Industrial School Department," *San Francisco Municipal Reports for the Fiscal Year 1867–8*, 348, CHR.

86 "Report of the Industrial School Department," *San Francisco Municipal Reports, 1859–1889*, CHR. Includes children eighteen years and under listed as born in China and/or of Chinese race. Original reports did not always list whether inmates were boys or girls.

87 These children's nativity is listed as China. It remains unclear whether or not American-born Chinese would be listed as natives of California or included in the category of China-born. It is possible, therefore, that the number of Chinese children (both China-born and American-born) in the institution could have been higher. "Report of the Industrial School Department," *San Francisco Municipal Reports for the Fiscal Year 1864–65*, 259, 264, CHR; "Industrial School Report," *San Francisco Municipal Reports for the Fiscal Year 1863–64*, 233, CHR.

88 "Chief of Police's Report," *San Francisco Municipal Reports for the Fiscal Year 1859–60*, 44, CHR.

89 Macallair, "The San Francisco Industrial School and the Origins of Juvenile Justice in California," 22–23.

90 "Report of the Industrial School Department," *San Francisco Municipal Reports for the Fiscal Year 1859–60*, 79–80, CHR.

91 "The Industrial School," *Daily Alta California*, July 8, 1869; "The Industrial School," *Daily Alta California*, August 4, 1869.

92 "Report of the Industrial School Department," *San Francisco Municipal Reports for the Fiscal Year 1869–70*, 373, CHR.

93 Macallair, "The San Francisco Industrial School and the Origins of Juvenile Justice in California," 41–44; Nunn and Cleary, "From the Mexican California Frontier to Arnold-Kennick," 9; *Ex Parte Ah Peen*, 51 Cal. 280 (1876).

94 Nunn and Cleary, "From the Mexican California Frontier to Arnold-Kennick," 8–9.

95 Yet Chew, case file no. 0428, Preston School of Industry Inmate Register (1900–1905), Youth Authority Records, 1872–1993, CSA.

96 San Quentin State Prison Inmate Commitment Papers, 1867–1900, Department of Corrections Records, CSA; U.S. Census Bureau, *Tenth Census of the United States, 1880*.

97 U.S. Census Bureau, *Twelfth Census of the United States, 1900*.

98 *The Juvenile Court of the City and County of San Francisco*, 30–31.

99 Ibid., 31.

100 Willrich, *City of Courts*, 73–74, 138; Odem, *Delinquent Daughters*, 105; Platt, *The Child Savers*, 25, 43–45, 54–55, 137.

101 Schackelford, "To Shield Them from Temptation," 254, 577, 580; "New Court Is

for Children," *SF Chron*, April 30, 1903; Nunn and Cleary, "From the Mexican California Frontier to Arnold-Kennick," 10–14.

102 *The Juvenile Court of the City and County of San Francisco*, 8.

103 Ibid., 16, 30–31; *Annual Report: San Francisco Juvenile Court for the Year 1916*, 6; "Report of Juvenile Detention Home," *San Francisco Municipal Reports for the Fiscal Year 1915–16*, 940, 944, CHR; Odem, *Delinquent Daughters*, 105.

104 "Chinese Boy Leaves Home; Is Joy-Rider," *OT*, October 19, 1913. The paper lists him as only six years old.

105 Willrich, *City of Courts*, 220. See also Clapp, *Mothers of All Children*, 66; Odem, *Delinquent Daughters*, 159.

106 Griggs, *Chinaman's Chance*, 37.

107 Elmer Wok Wai was sixteen or seventeen when he shot Ah Hing in Monterey on March 3, 1915. Accounts of his age differ from record to record. He was tried by a jury in Monterey, found guilty of first-degree murder, and sentenced to San Quentin at age seventeen. The 1920 census lists "Wok Wai" in San Quentin, age twenty-one and working as a cook in the officers' residence. He served sixteen years in state prison. Griggs, *Chinaman's Chance*, 37–38, 58, 73, 105; U.S. Census Bureau, *Fourteenth Census of the United States, 1920*; Wok Wai, Inmate #29606, San Quentin Inmate Register, MF 1:9, CSA; Wok Wai, Inmate #29606, Inmate Case File, F3750:252, CSA.

108 "Chinese Boy Attempts to Commit Suicide," *SF Call*, January 1, 1903.

109 "White Boys Corrupt a Chinese Youth," *SF Call*, November 27, 1902.

110 Wong Fong Sue, case file no. 1825, 1904, Whittier Inmate Register, Youth Authority Records, 1872–1993, CSA.

111 Lasch, "Life in the Therapeutic State," 176–77.

112 Historian Peggy Pascoe has extensively examined the Presbyterian Chinese Mission Home and concluded that Victorian women reformers in San Francisco's Chinatown often portrayed female prostitutes and children as powerless victims. These images reflected an assumption of Anglo-Saxon superiority that tended to ignore the female victimization and male domination that existed in their own American Victorian culture. However, Pascoe admits that much research has shown that many of these Chinese women were the victims of "exploitative sexual and labor practices." Pascoe contends that despite the ideological limitations of these mission workers, their efforts to resist the exploitation of women should be acknowledged. Pascoe, *Relations of Rescue*, 53–55.

CHAPTER SIX

1 "How to Show Your Eastern Cousins through Chinatown," *SF Chron*, October 19, 1902.

2 Ibid.

3 Genthe, *As I Remember*, 33.

4 Light, "From Vice District to Tourist Attraction," 378–79, 388–90; Asbury, *The*

Barbary Coast, 136. For a discussion of slumming expeditions in New York City, see also Lui, *The Chinatown Trunk Mystery*, 38–39.

5 Genthe, *As I Remember*, 36.

6 Lloyd, *Lights and Shades in San Francisco*, 220.

7 Knox, *Little Almond Blossoms*, 35–36.

8 Bamford, *Ti*, 50.

9 Ibid., 93.

10 Wores, "The Children of Chinatown in San Francisco," 575–77.

11 Genthe and Irwin, *Old Chinatown*, 63–64.

12 Ibid., 113.

13 Genthe, "A Holiday (Some Children—Another Rose)," 1895–1906, SF: China-town: Genthe No. 2: FN 2301, CHS.

14 Tchen, *Genthe's Photographs of San Francisco's Old Chinatown*, 3, 10–13.

15 "Asks That Police Enforce Opium Laws," *SF Chron*, September 21, 1904; "Call a Halt on the Guides," *SF Chron*, September 24, 1904.

16 "Mob Attacks House of an Opium Smoker," *SF Chron*, September 24, 1904.

17 "Call a Halt on the Guides," *SF Chron*, September 24, 1904.

18 "How the Chinese Children of San Francisco Play 'Horse' and Other Games," *SF Call*, April 4, 1897.

19 "Oriental Babies Have an Inning," *SF Chron*, March 4, 1898; "Household Gods Were There," *SF Call*, March 4, 1898; "Chinese Baby Show at the Fair Proved a Brilliant Spectacle," *SF Call*, September 24, 1899.

20 H. K. Wong, *Gum Sahn Yun*, 187–88.

21 Lowe, *Father and Glorious Descendant*, 29.

22 Mrs. William Z. L. Sung, "A Pioneer Chinese Family," 289.

23 "Interview with Rose Ow," 1, AASL; Edwar Lee, "Growing Up in Chinatown," Address at the Chinese Historical Society, San Francisco, January 25, 1975, vertical file, 1, AASL; Pan, "The Impact of the 1906 Earthquake on San Francisco's Chinatown," 61–62.

24 Look Tin Eli, "Our New Oriental City."

25 Rast, "The Cultural Politics of Tourism in San Francisco's Chinatown," 53–54; Cocks, *Doing the Town*, 200–201.

26 Tchen, *Genthe's Photographs of San Francisco's Old Chinatown*, 14–15.

27 Yick, *Esther Hunt*, 15, 19.

28 Vaule, *As We Were*, 47; Miller and Miller, *Picture Postcards in the United States*, 15, 22, 26, 28, 155–56.

29 Miller and Miller, *Picture Postcards in the United States*, 126–30; Brooke Baldwin, "On the Verso," 15, 17, 22; Mellinger, "Postcards from the Edge of the Color Line," 415, 419, 422, 430; Rydell, "Souvenirs of Imperialism," 55; Albers, "Symbols, Souvenirs, and Sentiments," 65–66, 72.

30 Unless otherwise cited, most of the postcards discussed in this section are from my own collection.

31 Griggs, *Chinaman's Chance*, 49.

32 Yick, *Esther Hunt*, 15, 19.

33 Albers makes a similar point with regard to postcards featuring Native Americans. Albers, "Symbols, Souvenirs, and Sentiments," 67, 70, 76.

34 Mervyn Silberstein, "Chinee-Graphs!" post-1910, San Francisco Chinatown: Silberstein: 23250, CHS.

35 William Henry Jackson, photographer, "Chinese Subjects," ca. 1901, The Detroit Publishing Company Collection, Library of Congress. See Albers for a similar discussion of modifications to postcards featuring American Indians. Albers, "Symbols, Souvenirs, and Sentiments," 70.

36 Albers, "Symbols, Souvenirs, and Sentiments," 69–70.

37 Brooke Baldwin has argued that the ubiquitous use of postcards featuring racist stereotypes of African Americans demonstrates the deep-rooted racism in American society. Brooke Baldwin, "On the Verso," 17. Wayne Mellinger makes a similar point in "Postcards from the Edge of the Color Line," 428.

38 "Group of Chinese Children," San Francisco Chinatown (ante-1910): SF Chinatown (ii): postcards: 23273 (verso), CHS.

39 See also Albers, "Symbols, Souvenirs, and Sentiments," 72.

40 Baldwin explains that postcards depicting blacks as "slow-witted, lazy beasts of burden" and associating them with agricultural products denied them their humanity. Similarly, postcards of Chinese children that focus on the exotic nature of their dress deny American-born Chinese children their status as Americans. Brooke Baldwin, "On the Verso," 22.

41 "Chinese Bazaars Are Radiant with New Goods," *OT*, September 11, 1910.

42 *San Francisco's Chinatown: An Aid to Tourists*, 12, BANC.

43 Ibid., 6.

44 "Chinatown Grand Pageant and Carnival," August 1915, Posters: No. 34, CHS.

45 *San Francisco's Chinatown: An Aid to Tourists*, 2, BANC.

46 Mrs. Clemens Wong, *Chinatown*, 1915, PAM 9740, CHS.

47 Griggs, *Chinaman's Chance*, 47, 52; Carey, *By the Golden Gate or San Francisco*, 166–68.

48 Lowe, *Father and Glorious Descendant*, 38.

49 "How to Show Your Eastern Cousins through Chinatown."

50 "A Bevy of Chinese High School Girls," *SF Call*, July 2, 1905.

51 Griggs, *Chinaman's Chance*, 52.

52 Rast, "The Cultural Politics of Tourism in San Francisco's Chinatown," 45, 50–54.

53 H. K. Wong, *Gum Sahn Yun*, 157–58.

54 Won, "Recollections of Dr. Sun Yat-Sen's Stay at Our Home in San Francisco," 72–77. The Tongmenghui advocated the education of women and their participation in the revolution. Lily King Gee Won remained active in the movement, following the revolution to China. Yung, *Unbound Feet*, 98–99.

55 Won, "Recollections of Dr. Sun Yat-Sen's Stay at Our Home in San Francisco," 78–79; Ross, *Caught in a Tornado*, 9–11, 20.

56 Anthony W. Lee, *Picturing Chinatown*, 165, 187, 190; Shehong Chen, *Being Chinese, Becoming Chinese American*, 94.

57 "Interview with Rose Ow," 6.

58 Tong, "Introduction," 10–11.

59 Yong Chen, *Chinese San Francisco*, 182, 264.

60 Ng Poon Chew, "Chinese Are Riding on Waves of Changing Sea of Modernism," *SF Chron*, Magazine Section, January 18, 1922.

61 Chinese American Citizens' Alliance, "Admission of Wives of American Citizens of Oriental Ancestry (1926)," 133.

62 Zhao, *Remaking Chinese America*, 17, 21, 24.

63 Caroline Chew, "Development of Chinese Family Life in America," 1, 42.

64 H. K. Wong, *Gum Sahn Yun*, 112.

65 Lowe, *Father and Glorious Descendant*, 67–68.

66 Catherine Holt, "Interview with Mr. George Lem," August 4, 1924, Major Document No. 298, 3, SRR.

67 Chan, "Race, Ethnic Culture, and Gender in the Construction of Identities among Second-Generation Chinese Americans," 128; Yung, *Unbound Feet*, 6, 115–16.

68 "Story of a Chinese College Girl," Major Document No. 54, 1–2, SRR.

69 Deanna Wong, "Working for a Better Future," 1988, student paper, vertical file, 5–6, AASL.

70 "Story of a Chinese College Girl," Major Document No. 54, 8, SRR. Identified as Esther Wong by Judy Yung in *Unbound Voices*, 297.

71 C. H. Burnett, "Life History as a Social Document of Mr. Chin Cheung," August 21, 1924, Major Document No. 187, 4–5, SRR.

72 "Chinese Girl, in Love Net, Tries Suicide," *OT*, June 8, 1917.

73 Gladys M. Leonard, "Life History of a Chinese," Minor Document No. 384, 3, SRR.

74 "The Life Story of Edward L. C. as Written by Himself," Minor Document No. 443, 8, SRR.

75 Ibid., 7.

76 C. H. Burnett, "Life History as a Social Document of Mr. Chin Cheung," 3, SRR.

77 Chinn, "A Historian's Reflections on Chinese-American Life," 33–34, BANC.

78 C. H. Burnett, "Life History and Social Document of David Young," August 29, 1924, Major Document No. 272, 7–8, SRR.

79 Lowe, *Father and Glorious Descendant*, 143–46.

80 Lee and Ow, "Chinese Historical Society of America Talk," 4, AASL; "Interview with Rose Ow," September 9, 1970, Phil Choy and Him Mark Lai, Him Mark Lai Files, 2000/80, carton 121:40, 1–2, AASL.

81 Ellis, "Social and Philanthropic Work among Orientals," 35.

82 "The Life Story of Edward L. C. as Written by Himself," Minor Document No. 443, 5, SRR.

83 Ibid., 9.

84 Taylor, "San Francisco's New Chinese City," 54.

1   Historian K. Scott Wong has noted that the Chinese elite responded to anti-Chinese attacks with three defensive strategies: "they denied the charges and paraded the 'virtues' of Chinese history and culture; they sought equal treatment with other groups in America based on class similarities; and finally, they defended the presence of the Chinese in America by comparing them favorably to others or by denigrating other immigrant and minority groups." K. Scott Wong, "Chinatown," 8. Nayan Shah also argues that the Chinese American community in the 1930s and 1940s developed a strategy of highlighting those individuals who had adopted middle-class norms. Shah, *Contagious Divides*, 13–15, 77, 83. I argue that Chinese Americans had adopted this strategy even earlier—in the late nineteenth century—and that the presence of children was especially crucial to this strategy.

2   Lisa Sun-Hee Park in her examination of the lives of modern children of Asian immigrant entrepreneurs has argued that through the pursuit of high-status careers and other displays of conspicuous consumption, these children offer evidence of their attainment of the American dream. They feel the burden of proving their Americanism through patriotism and economic mobility. Lisa Sun-Hee Park, *Consuming Citizenship*, 12–15, 24, 112.

3   Yung, *Unbound Feet*, 296.

4   Zhao, *Remaking Chinese America*, 17, 21, 24.

5   Glenn with Yap, "Chinese American Families," 282; Chun, "Shifting Ethnic Identity and Consciousness," 114–17; Shah, *Contagious Divides*, 226–30; Yu, "A History of San Francisco Chinatown Housing," 101–3.

6   Kwong and Miscevic, *Chinese America*, 206, 316–18; Glenn with Yap, "Chinese American Families," 284–85; Zhao, *Remaking Chinese America*, 2–3; Shah, *Contagious Divides*, 247–48.

7   Chun, "Shifting Ethnic Identity and Consciousness," 120–25.

8   Kwong and Miscevic, *Chinese America*, 232, 316–18; Kibria, *Becoming Asian American*, 10; Timothy P. Fong, *The Contemporary Asian American Experience*, 90–91; Glenn with Yap, "Chinese American Families," 284–85; Fong and Browne, "United States Immigration Policy and Chinese Children and Families," 194–95.

9   U.S. Census Bureau, *Census 2000*.

10 Zhou and Lee, "Introduction," 18.

11 Kibria, *Becoming Asian American*, 53, 88, 206.

12 Hune and Chan, "Educating Asian Pacific Americans," 143.

13 Coleman Advocates for Children and Youth, "Families Struggle to Stay," 4–6; Ong and Umemoto, "Life and Work in the Inner City," 238.

14 Mayor's Office of Community Development, "City and County of San Francisco, Five Year Consolidated Plan, July 1, 2005–June 30, 2010," 26, 35, 38, 41; U.S. Census Bureau, *Census 2000*.

15 Lisa Sun-Hee Park, "Ensuring Upward Mobility," 125.

16 Wollenberg, *All Deliberate Speed*, 26–27, 108, 161–62; Lum, "The Creation and Demise of San Francisco Chinatown Freedom Schools," 57, 60–61, 63, 69.

17 San Francisco Unified School District, "Lowell High School History"; Leslie Fulbright and Heather Knight, "With More Choice Has Come Resegregation," *SF Chron*, May 29, 2006; Timothy P. Fong, *The Contemporary Asian American Experience*, 95; Kwong and Miscevic, *Chinese America*, 387–88.

18 San Francisco Unified School District, "Accountability Report Card 2006–2007," 4; San Francisco Unified School District, "Academic Plan for Student Achievement, 2007–2008 School Year," 7.

19 Chinese for Affirmative Action, "School Integration and Asian Americans," 1, 3; Coleman Advocates for Children and Youth, "An Agenda for Education Equity," 2, 7; Christina Wong, Chinese for Affirmative Action, interview.

20 Timothy P. Fong, *The Contemporary Asian American Experience*, 89–91.

21 Redondo and others, "Left in the Margins," 1, 3, 7–13.

22 San Francisco Unified School District, "School Accountability Report Card School Year 2006–07"; San Francisco Unified School District, "School Accountability Report Card School Year 2006–07"; San Francisco Unified School District, "Gordon J. Lau Elementary School Profile"; San Francisco Unified School District, "Alternative Program Placement Form"; San Francisco Unified School District, "Enrollment Guide, 2008–2009"; Helen Joe-Lew, SFUSD Multilingual Programs, interview; Marlene Callejas, Principal Gordon Lau Elementary School, interview.

23 Chinese for Affirmative Action, "Lost without Translation," 3; Helen Joe-Lew, SFUSD Multilingual Programs, interview; Christina Wong, Chinese for Affirmative Action, interview.

24 Melvin N. Wilson and others, "Ethnic Minority Families and the Majority Educational System," 269–70; Fong and Browne, "United States Immigration Policy and Chinese Children and Families," 197–99; Timothy P. Fong, *The Contemporary Asian American Experience*, 89–91, 93–101; ETR Associates, "2005 Youth Risk Behavior Survey High School Level Summary Report," 13–31.

25 Toy, "A Short History of Asian Gangs in San Francisco," 651–58; Chin, *Chinatown Gangs*, 7; Huston, *Tongs, Gangs, and Triads*, 102–3.

26 Toy, "A Short History of Asian Gangs in San Francisco," 658–65; Isaacs, "Twice Burned"; Chin, *Chinatown Gangs*, 7, 18–19, 161–63; Huston, *Tongs, Gangs, and Triads*, 116; Bill Lee, *Chinese Playground*, 143–73.

27 Le and Wallen, "Youth Delinquency," 15–16; Le and others, "Not Invisible," 5, 11, 46; U.S. Department of Health and Human Services, "Youth Violence"; Chin, *Chinatown Gangs*, 108, 123; Zhang, "Chinese Gangs," 227, 230–31, 234–35.

28 Zhou, "Social Capital in Chinatown," 333.

29 Ben Wong, Deputy Director Community Education Services, interview; Community Educational Services, <http://www.cessf.org/>; Chinatown Beacon Center, <http://www.chinatownbeacon.org/cbc/>.

30 Chinatown Community Development Center, <http://www.chinatowncdc.org>.

31 National Economic Development and Law Center, "Chinatown Families Economic Self-Sufficiency Coalition," 1, 19, 43.

32 Community Youth Center, <http://www.cysf.org/outreach.php>.

BIBLIOGRAPHY

ARCHIVAL COLLECTIONS

Berkeley, Calif.
    Asian American Studies Library, University of California, Berkeley
        Angel Island Oral History Project, 1975–90
        Him Mark Lai Files
        HOC-DOI Project San Francisco, Vertical File
        Judy Yung Files
        Miscellaneous Papers, Vertical File
    Bancroft Library, University of California, Berkeley
        Angel Island Interviews
        Asian American Oral History Composite
        Thomas W. Chinn, "A Historian's Reflections on Chinese American Life in San Francisco, 1919–1991" (interviews conducted by Ruth Teiser in 1990 and 1991)
        George B. Morris, "The Chinaman as He Is"
        Primary Register, Presbyterian Church, San Francisco Chinatown
        Records of the University of California, Berkeley, Department of Anthropology
        Roy D. Graves Pictorial Collection
        San Francisco Chinese Community and Earthquake Damage Photographs
        "To the Honorable the Senate and Assembly of the State of California," San Francisco, 1878
Davis, California
    Special Collections, University of California, Davis
        Chinatown Declared a Nuisance. San Francisco, 1880.
Eugene, Ore.
    Special Collections and University Archives, Knight Library, University of Oregon
        Burton/Lake/Garton Family Papers, Coll. 301
Palo Alto, Calif.
    Hoover Institution on War, Revolution, and Peace, Stanford University
        Survey of Race Relations Collection
    Special Collections and University Archives, Stanford University
        Mildred Martin Papers

Sacramento, Calif.

California History Room, California State Library

San Francisco Municipal Reports, 1859–1917

Stellman Photograph Collection

California State Archives

Common School Reports

Preston School of Industry Inmate Registers, 1900–1905, 1911–12, 1912–14

San Quentin Inmate Register, MF 1:9

San Quentin State Prison Inmate Commitment Papers, 1867–1900, Department of Corrections Records

"Transcript of the Evidence Taken and Proceeding Had Before the Assembly Committee of the Legislature of the State of California, Sitting at San Francisco, California, Commencing Tuesday, Feb. 6, 1901"

Whittier Inmate Register, Youth Authority Records, 1872–1993

San Anselmo, Calif.

San Francisco Theological Seminary

"Historical Sketch: Fiftieth Anniversary Chinese YMCA, San Francisco, 1911–1961"

San Bruno, Calif.

National Archives, Pacific Region

Records of the U.S. Immigration and Naturalization Service, Record Group 85, Chinese Arrival Files, San Francisco

Records of the U.S. Immigration and Naturalization Service, Series A: Subject Correspondence Files, Part 1, Asian Immigration and Exclusion, 1906–13 (microform)

San Francisco Chinese Mortuary Records, 1870–1933, vols. 1–5 (unnumbered microfilm)

San Francisco, Calif.

California Historical Society

Arnold Genthe Photograph Collection

"Chinatown Grand Pageant and Carnival," August 1915, Posters: No. 34

"Group of Chinese Children," San Francisco Chinatown (ante-1910): SF Chinatown (ii): postcards: 23273 (verso)

Silberstein Photograph Collection

California State Library, Sutro Branch

"Graduating Exercises of the Oriental Public School, San Francisco," St. Mary's Hall, June 9, 1910

San Francisco History Center, San Francisco Public Library San Francisco Unified School District Records

Police Criminal Photos, Chinese, Number 3, Key, 2875–76

Washington, D.C.

Library of Congress

Detroit Publishing Company Collection

NEWSPAPERS

Alta (San Francisco)

Chung Sai Yat Po (San Francisco)

Daily Alta California (San Francisco)

Oakland Tribune

San Francisco Call

San Francisco Chronicle

San Francisco Daily Morning Call

San Francisco Daily Record Union

San Francisco Evening Bulletin

San Francisco Examiner

San Francisco Morning Call

San Francisco Star

San Francisco Sunday Examiner
 & Chronicle

AUTHOR INTERVIEWS

Callejas, Marlene. Principal, Gordon Lau Elementary School. Interview, August 29, 2008.

Joe-Lew, Helen. San Francisco Unified School District Multilingual Programs. Interview, September 4, 2008.

Wong, Ben. Deputy director, Community Education Services. Interview, September 4, 2008.

Wong, Christina. Chinese for Affirmative Action. Interview, September 9, 2008.

PUBLISHED MATERIALS

Aarim-Heriot, Najia. *Chinese Immigrants, African Americans, and Racial Anxiety in the United States, 1848–82*. Urbana: University of Illinois Press, 2003.

Albers, Patricia C. "Symbols, Souvenirs, and Sentiments: Postcard Imagery of Plains Indians, 1898–1918." In *Delivering Views: Distant Cultures in Early Postcards*, edited by Christraud M. Geary and Virginia-Lee Webb, 65–89. Washington, D.C.: Smithsonian Institution Press, 1998.

Annual Report: San Francisco Juvenile Court for the Year 1916 and Report of the San Francisco Juvenile Detention Home for the Fiscal Year Ending June 30, 1917. San Francisco, 1917.

Annual Report of the Superintendent of Immigration to the Secretary of the Treasury for the Fiscal Year Ended June 30, 1892. Washington, D.C.: Government Printing Office, 1892.

The Annual Report of the Woman's Union Mission of San Francisco to Chinese Women and Children for the Year Ending Dec. 31, 1880. San Francisco: George Spaulding & Co, 1881.

Annual Reports of the Commissioner-General of Immigration. Washington, D.C.: Government Printing Office, 1896–1920.

Asbury, Herbert. *The Barbary Coast*. New York: Alfred A. Knopf, 1933. Reprint, New York: Ballantine Books, 1973.

Aubitz, Shawn. "Tracing Early Chinese Immigration into the United States: The Use of I.N.S. Documents." *Amerasia Journal* 14, no. 2 (1988): 37–46.

Baldwin, Brooke. "On the Verso: Postcard Messages as a Key to Popular Prejudices." *Journal of Popular Culture* 22, no. 3 (Winter 1988): 15–28.

Baldwin, Mrs. S. L. "A Memorial from Representative Chinamen in America to His Excellency U. S. Grant." In *Must the Chinese Go? An Examination of the Chinese Question*. 3rd ed. New York: H. B. Elkins, 1890. Reprint, San Francisco: R and E Research Associates, 1970.

Bamford, Mary. *Angel Island: The Ellis Island of the West*. Chicago: The Woman's American Baptist Home Mission Society, 1917.

———. *Ti: A Story of Chinatown*. Chicago: David C. Cook Publishing Company, 1899.

Barlow, Janelle Mary Schlimgen. "The Images of the Chinese, Japanese, and Koreans in American Secondary School World History Textbooks, 1900–1970." Ph.D. diss., University of California, Berkeley, 1973.

Beach, Walter G. *Oriental Crime in California: A Study of Offenses Committed by Orientals in That State, 1900–1927*. Stanford: Stanford University Press, 1932. Reprint, New York: AMS Press, 1971.

Beck, Nicholas Patrick. "The Other Children: Minority Education in California Public Schools from Statehood to 1890." Ed.D. diss., University of California, Los Angeles, 1975.

Beesley, David. "From Chinese to Chinese American: Chinese Women and Families in a Sierra Nevada County." *California History* 67, no. 3 (September 1988): 168–79.

Bellingham, Bruce. "The 'Unspeakable Blessing': Street Children, Reform Rhetoric, and Misery in Early Industrial Capitalism." *Politics and Society* 12, no. 3 (1983): 303–30.

Berrol, Selma Cantor. *Growing Up American: Immigrant Children in America Then and Now*. New York: Twayne Publishers, 1995.

———. "Immigrant Children at School, 1880–1940: A Child's Eye View." In *Small Worlds: Children and Adolescents in America, 1850–1950*, edited by Elliot West and Paula Petrik, 42–60. Lawrence: University Press of Kansas, 1992.

Boyer, Paul. *Urban Masses and Moral Order in America, 1820–1920*. Cambridge, Mass.: Harvard University Press, 1978.

California Juvenile Court Law, 1919. Sacramento: California State Printing Office, 1920.

The California Society for the Prevention of Cruelty to Children. *Thirteenth Annual Report for the Year Ending December 31, 1889*. San Francisco: Geo. Spaulding & Co., 1890.

Calvert, Karin. *Children in the House: The Material Culture of Early Childhood, 1600–1900*. Boston: Northeastern University Press, 1992.

Carey, Joseph. *By the Golden Gate or San Francisco the Queen City of the Pacific Coast; With Scenes and Incidents Characteristic of Its Life*. Albany, N.Y.: The Albany Diocesan Press, 1902.

Chan, Sucheng. "Against All Odds: Chinese Female Migration and Family Formation on American Soil during the Early Twentieth Century." In *Chinese American Transnationalism: The Flow of People, Resources, and Ideas between China and America during the Exclusion Era*, edited by Sucheng Chan, 34–135. Philadelphia: Temple University Press, 2006.

———. *Asian Americans: An Interpretive History*. New York: Twayne Publishers, 1991.

———. "Race, Ethnic Culture, and Gender in the Construction of Identities among Second-Generation Chinese Americans, 1880s–1930s." In *Claiming America:*

Constructing Chinese American Identities during the Exclusion Era, edited by K. Scott Wong and Sucheng Chan, 127–64. Philadelphia: Temple University Press, 1998.

Chang, Iris. *The Chinese in America: A Narrative History*. New York: Viking Penguin, 2003.

Chen, Jack. *The Chinese of America*. San Francisco: Harper & Row, 1980.

Chen, Shehong. *Being Chinese, Becoming Chinese American*. Urbana: University of Illinois Press, 2002.

Chen, Yong. *Chinese San Francisco, 1850–1943: A Trans-Pacific Community*. Stanford: Stanford University Press, 2000.

——. "Invisible Historical Players: Uncovering the Meanings and Experiences of Children in Early Asian American History." In *Asian American Children: A Historical Handbook and Guide*, edited by Benson Tong, 25–45. Westport, Conn.: Greenwood Press, 2004.

Chew, Caroline. "Development of Chinese Family Life in America: As Observed in San Francisco's 'Chinatown.'" Master's thesis, Mills College, 1926.

Chew, Ng Poon. *The Treatment of the Exempt Classes of Chinese in the United States*. San Francisco, 1908.

Child Labor Law. [Sacramento] Bureau of Labor Statistics, State of California, [1909?].

"Child Life in Chinatown." *The Wave* 15, no. 29 (January–December 1896): 8–9.

Chin, Ko-lin. *Chinatown Gangs: Extortion, Enterprise, and Ethnicity*. New York: Oxford University Press, 1996.

Chinatown Beacon Center. <http://www.chinatownbeacon.org/cbc/> (accessed September 4, 2008).

Chinatown Community Development Center. <http://www.chinatowncdc.org> (accessed May 19, 2008).

Chinese American Citizens' Alliance. "Admission of Wives of American Citizens of Oriental Ancestry (1926)." In *Chinese American Voices: From the Gold Rush to the Present*, edited by Judy Yung, Gordon H. Chang, and Him Mark Lai, 129–37. Berkeley: University of California Press, 2006.

Chinese Exclusion Convention. *For the Re-Enactment of the Chinese Exclusion Law*. San Francisco: The Star Press, ca. 1901.

Chinese for Affirmative Action. "Lost without Translation: Language Barriers Faced by Limited-English Proficient Parents with Children in the San Francisco Unified School District." November 2006. <http://www.caasf.org/PDFs/Lost%20With out%20 Translation%20%5BCAA%5D.pdf> (accessed May 19, 2008).

——. "School Integration and Asian Americans." September 2007. <http://www.caasf .org/PDFs/AALDEF—CAA—School—Integration—Fact—Sheets—090607.pdf> (accessed May 19, 2008).

"Chinese Lantern Feast." *Harper's Weekly*, April 28, 1877.

Chinn, Thomas W., H. Mark Lai, and Philip P. Choy, eds. *A History of the Chinese in California: A Syllabus*. San Francisco: Chinese Historical Society of America, 1969. Reprint, 1973.

"Christmas Entertainments of the Occidental Board Mission Schools." *Far West* 11, no. 4 (February 1911): 10.

Chudacoff, Howard P. *How Old Are You? Age Consciousness in American Culture.* Princeton: Princeton University Press, 1989.

Chun, Gloria Heyung. "Shifting Ethnic Identity and Consciousness: U.S.-Born Chinese American Youth in the 1930s and 1950s." In *Asian American Youth: Culture, Identity, and Ethnicity*, edited by Jennifer Lee and Min Zhou, 113–28. New York: Routledge, 2004.

Chung, Sue Fawn, and Priscilla Wegars, eds. *Chinese American Death Rituals: Respecting the Ancestors.* Lanham, Md.: AltaMira Press, 2005.

Chung, Wen Bing. "Reminiscences of a Pioneer Student (1923)." In *Chinese American Voices: From the Gold Rush to the Present*, edited by Judy Yung, Gordon H. Chang, and Him Mark Lai, 30–38. Berkeley: University of California, 2006.

Clapp, Elizabeth J. *Mothers of All Children: Women Reformers and the Rise of Juvenile Courts in Progressive Era America.* University Park: Pennsylvania State University Press, 1998.

Clement, Priscilla Ferguson. *Growing Pains: Children in the Industrial Age, 1850–1890.* New York: Twayne Publishers, 1997.

Cocks, Catherine. *Doing the Town: The Rise of Urban Tourism in the United States, 1850–1915.* Berkeley: University of California Press, 2001.

Coleman Advocates for Children and Youth. "An Agenda for Education Equity." Presented by the Education Equity Committee and Y-MAC, April 24, 2007. <http://www.colemanadvocates.org/includes/downloads/tionplatform 04.24.07public.pdf> (accessed May 19, 2008).

———. "Families Struggle to Stay: Why Families Are Leaving San Francisco and What Can Be Done." March 1, 2006. <http://www.colemanadvocates.org/includes/ downloads/amiliesstruggletostaypg111.pdf> (accessed May 19, 2008).

Community Educational Services. <http://www.cessf.org/> (accessed September 4, 2008).

Community Youth Center. <http://www.cysf.org/outreach.php> (accessed June 20, 2008).

Coolidge, Mary Roberts. *Chinese Immigration.* New York: Henry Holt and Company, 1909.

Cott, Nancy F. *Public Vows: A History of Marriage and the Nation.* Cambridge, Mass.: Harvard University Press, 2000.

Davis, Horace. *Chinese Immigration: Speech of Hon. Horace Davis, of California, in the House of Representatives, June 8, 1878.* Washington, D.C., 1878.

Davison, Mary. "The Babies of Chinatown." *Cosmopolitan* 28, no. 6 (April 1900): 605–12.

Densmore, G. B. *The Chinese in California.* San Francisco: Pettit & Russ, 1880.

Dolson, Lee Stephen, Jr. "The Administration of the San Francisco Public Schools, 1847 to 1947." Ph.D. diss., University of California, Berkeley, 1964.

Donovan, Brian. *White Slave Crusades: Race, Gender, and Anti-Vice Activism, 1887–1917.* Urbana: University of Illinois Press, 2006.

Dudden, Faye E. *Serving Women: Household Service in Nineteenth-Century America.* Middletown, Conn.: Wesleyan University Press, 1983.

Dunn, Arthur William. *Civics: The Community and the Citizen*. Sacramento: California State Printing Department, 1910.

Eighth Annual Report of the Occidental Branch of the Woman's Foreign Missionary Society of the Presbyterian Church of the Pacific Coast. Philadelphia: Presbyterian Journal Company, 1881.

Ellis, Sarah. "Social and Philanthropic Work among Orientals." In *Oriental Mission Work on the Pacific Coast of the United States of America*, 29–38. New York: Home Missions Council and Council of Women for Home Missions, 1920.

"English Learners, Instructional Settings and Services, 2006–07. San Francisco Unified School District. Gordon J. Lau Elementary School." California Department of Education Demographics Unit. <http://data1.cde.ca.gov/dataquest/> (accessed May 19, 2008).

ETR Associates. "2005 Youth Risk Behavior Survey High School Level Summary Report." San Francisco Unified School District. January 2006. <http://www.healthi ersf.org/Statistics/docs/YRBSReport2005HS—Final.pdf> (accessed May 19, 2008).

Evans, Albert S. "Steamer from China." In *More San Francisco Memoirs, 1852–1899: The Ripening Years*, edited by Malcom E. Barker, 206–17. San Francisco: Londonborn Publications, 1996.

Ferenczi, Imre, and Walter F. Wilcox, eds. *International Migrations*. Vol. 1, *Statistics*. New York: National Bureau of Economic Research, Inc., 1929.

Ferrier, William Warren. *Ninety Years of Education in California, 1846–1936: A Presentation of Educational Movements and Their Outcome in Education Today*. Berkeley: Sather Gate Book Shop, 1937.

Fifteenth Annual Report of the Occidental Board of the Woman's Foreign Missionary Society of the Presbyterian Church of the Pacific Coast. San Francisco: The Occident Printing House, 1888.

Fong, Rowena, and Colette Browne. "United States Immigration Policy and Chinese Children and Families." In *Children of Color: Research, Health, and Policy Issues*, edited by Hiram E. Fitzgerald, Barry M. Lester, and Barry S. Zuckerman, 187–203. New York: Garland Publishing, Inc., 1999.

Fong, Timothy P. *The Contemporary Asian American Experience: Beyond the Model Minority*. 2nd ed. Upper Saddle River, N.J.: Prentice Hall, 2002.

Foo, Lora Jo. *Asian American Women: Issues, Concerns, and Responsive Human and Civil Rights Advocacy*. New York: iUniverse Inc., 2003.

Formanek-Brunell, Miriam. "Sugar and Spite: The Politics of Doll Play in Nineteenth-Century America." In *Small Worlds: Children and Adolescents in America, 1850–1950*, edited by Elliott West and Paula Petrik, 107–24. Lawrence: University Press of Kansas, 1992.

Franks, Joel S. "Chinese Americans and American Sports, 1880–1940." *Chinese America: History and Perspectives* 10 (January 1996): 133–48.

Fritz, Christian G. "A Nineteenth-Century 'Habeas Corpus Mill': The Chinese before the Federal Courts in California." *American Journal of Legal History* 32, no. 4 (October 1988): 347–72.

Fun, Alice Sue. "Alice Sue Fun, World Traveler: 'A Rebel at Heart.'" In *Unbound Voices: A Documentary History of Chinese Women in San Francisco*, edited by Judy Yung, 264–72. Berkeley: University of California Press, 1999.

Geary, T. J. "The Other Side of the Chinese Question." *Harper's Weekly*, May 13, 1893.

Gee, Jennifer. "Housewives, Men's Villages, and Sexual Respectability: Gender and the Interrogation of Asian Women at the Angel Island Immigration Station." In *Asian/Pacific Islander American Women: A Historical Anthology*, edited by Shirley Hune and Gail M. Nomura, 90–105. New York: New York University Press, 2003.

Genthe, Arnold. *As I Remember*. New York: Reynal & Hitchcock, 1936.

Genthe, Arnold, and Will Irwin. *Old Chinatown: A Book of Pictures*. New York: Mitchell Kennerly, 1912.

Gibson, Campbell, and Kay Jung. "Historical Census Statistics on Population Totals by Race, 1790 to 1900, by Hispanic Origin, 1970 to 1990, for the United States, Regions, Divisions and States." Working Paper Series No. 56. Washington, D.C.: Population Division, U.S. Census Bureau, 2002. <www.census.gov/population/www/documentation/twps0056.html> (accessed August 2, 2006).

Gillenkirk, Jeff, and James Motlow. *Bitter Melon: Inside America's Last Rural Chinese Town*. 3rd ed. Berkeley: Heyday Books, 1997.

Glenn, Evelyn Nakano, with Stacey G. H. Yap. "Chinese American Families." In *Asian Americans: Experiences and Perspectives*, edited by Timothy P. Fong and Larry H. Shinagawa, 277–92. Upper Saddle River, N.J.: Prentice Hall, 2000.

Goodman, Cary. *Choosing Sides: Playground and Street Life on the Lower East Side*. New York: Schocken Books, 1979.

Goodwin, Joanne L. *Gender and the Politics of Welfare Reform: Mothers' Pensions in Chicago, 1911–1929*. Chicago: University of Chicago Press, 1997.

Gordon, Linda. "Family Violence, Feminism, and Social Control." In *Women, the State, and Welfare*, edited by Linda Gordon, 178–98. Madison: University of Wisconsin Press, 1990.

———. *The Great Arizona Orphan Abduction*. Cambridge, Mass.: Harvard University Press, 2002.

Gratton, Brian, and Jon Moen. "Immigration, Culture, and Child Labor in the United States, 1880–1920." *Journal of Interdisciplinary History* 34, no. 3 (Winter 2004): 355–91.

Gratton, Henry Pearson, ed. *As a Chinaman Saw Us: Passages from His Letters to a Friend at Home*. New York: D. Appleton and Company, 1906.

Griggs, Veta. *Chinaman's Chance: The Life Story of Elmer Wok Wai*. Jericho, N.Y.: Exposition Press, 1969.

Griswold, Robert L. *Family and Divorce in California, 1850–1890: Victorian Illusions and Everyday Realities*. Albany, N.Y.: State University of New York Press, 1982.

Grittner, Frederick K. *White Slavery: Myth, Ideology, and American Law*. New York: Garland Publishing, Inc., 1990.

Grossberg, Michael. "Changing Conceptions of Child Welfare in the United States, 1820–1935." In *A Century of Juvenile Justice*, edited by Margaret K. Rosenheim and others, 3–41. Chicago: University of Chicago Press, 2002.

Gullet, Gayle. "City Mothers, City Daughters, and the Dance Hall Girls: The Limits of Female Political Power in San Francisco, 1913." In *Women and the Structure of Society: Selected Research from the Fifth Berkshire Conference on the History of Women*, edited by Barbara J. Harris and JoAnn K. McNamara, 149–59. Durham, N.C.: Duke University Press, 1984.

Healy, Patrick J., and Ng Poon Chew. *A Statement for Non-Exclusion*. San Francisco, 1905.

Hendrick, Irving G. *The Education of Non-Whites in California, 1849–1970*. San Francisco: R & E Research Associates, 1977.

Henshaw, Sarah E. "California Housekeepers and Chinese Servants." *Scribner's Monthly* 12, no. 5, 1876, 736–42.

Herman, David George. "Neighbors on the Golden Mountain: The Americanization of Immigrants in California; Public Instruction as an Agency of Ethnic Assimilation, 1850–1935." Ph.D. diss., University of California, Berkeley, 1971.

Hindman, Hugh D. *Child Labor: An American History*. Armonk, N.Y.: M. E. Sharpe, 2002.

Hirata, Lucie Cheng. "Chinese Immigrant Women in Nineteenth-Century California." In *Women of America: A History*, edited by Carol Ruth Berkin and Mary Beth Norton, 223–41. Boston: Houghton Mifflin Company, 1979.

———. "Free, Indentured, Enslaved: Chinese Prostitutes in Nineteenth-Century America." *Signs* 5, no. 1, Women in Latin America issue (Autumn 1979): 3–29.

Holden, Margaret K. "Gender, Protest, and the Anti-Chinese Movement." In *Major Problems in the History of the American West*. 2nd ed. Edited by Clyde A. Milner II, Anne M. Butler, and David Rich Lewis, 294–302. Boston: Houghton Mifflin Company, 1997.

"Holiday in the Chinese Quarter." *Overland Monthly* 2, no. 2 (February 1869): 145.

Hsu, Madeline. "Gold Mountain Dreams and Paper Son Schemes: Chinese Immigration under Exclusion." *Chinese America: History and Perspectives* 11 (January 1997): 46–60.

Huie, Chris. "A Community of Voices: Studying the Poetry at Angel Island Immigration Station." *Passages: The Newsletter of the Angel Island Immigration Station Foundation* 7, no. 3 (Summer 2004): 3–5.

Huie Kin. *Reminiscences*. Peiping, China: San Yu Press, 1932.

Hune, Shirley, and Kenyon S. Chan. "Educating Asian Pacific Americans: Struggles and Progress." In *Asian Americans: Experiences and Perspectives*, edited by Timothy Fong and Larry H. Shinagawa, 141–68. Upper Saddle River, N.J.: Prentice-Hall, Inc., 2000.

Huston, Peter. *Tongs, Gangs, and Triads: Chinese Crime Groups in North America*. San Jose, Calif.: Authors Choice Press, 2001.

Illick, Joseph E. *American Childhoods*. Philadelphia: University of Pennsylvania Press, 2002.

In Memory of Dr. Fong F. Sec. Hong Kong: Caritas Printing Training Centre, 1966.

Isaacs, Matt. "Twice Burned." *San Francisco Weekly*, June 14, 2000. <http://www.sf weekly.com/2000-06-14/news/twice-burned/1> (accessed May 26, 2008).

Jenness, C. K. *The Charities of San Francisco: A Directory*. San Francisco: Book Room Print, 1894.

"John Chinaman in San Francisco." *Scribner's Monthly* 12, no. 6, October 1876, 862–72.

Johnsen, Leigh Dana. "Equal Rights and the 'Heathen "Chinee"': Black Activism in San Francisco, 1865–1875." *Western Historical Quarterly* 11, no. 1 (January 1980): 57–68.

The Juvenile Court of the City and County of San Francisco. San Francisco: Foster & Short, Printers, 1911.

Kerr, John G. *The Chinese Question Analyzed: A Lecture Delivered in the Hall of the Young Men's Christian Association*. November 13, 1877. San Francisco, 1877.

Kibria, Nazli. *Becoming Asian American: Second-Generation Chinese and Korean American Identities*. Baltimore: Johns Hopkins University Press, 2002.

King, Charles R. "Infant Mortality." In *Childhood in America*, edited by Paula S. Fass and Mary Ann Mason, 427–31. New York: New York University Press, 2000.

King, Wilma. *Stolen Childhood: Slave Youth in Nineteenth-Century America*. Bloomington: Indiana University Press, 1995.

Kline, Stephen. "The Making of Children's Culture." In *The Children's Culture Reader*, edited by Henry Jenkins, 95–109. New York: New York University Press, 1998.

Knox, Jessie Juliet. "A Chinese Horace Greeley." *Oakland Tribune Magazine*, December 3, 1922. Reprinted in *Bulletin, Chinese Historical Society of America* 6, no. 4 (April 1971): 3–4.

———. *Little Almond Blossoms: A Book of Chinese Stories for Children*. Boston: Little, Brown, and Company, 1904.

Kuo, Joyce. "Excluded, Segregated, and Forgotten: A Historical View of the Discrimination against Chinese Americans in Public Schools." *Chinese America: History and Perspectives* 14 (January 2000): 32–48.

Kwong, Peter, and Dusanka Miscevic. *Chinese America: The Untold Story of America's Oldest New Community*. New York: The New Press, 2005.

Lai, Him Mark. "Island of Immortals: Chinese Immigrants and the Angel Island Immigration Station." *California History* 57, no. 1 (Spring 1978): 88–103.

———. "Retention of the Chinese Heritage: Chinese Schools in America before World War II." *Chinese America: History and Perspectives* 14 (January 2000): 10–31.

Lai, Him Mark, Genny Lim, and Judy Yung. *Island: Poetry and History of Chinese Immigrants on Angel Island, 1910–1940*. 4th printing. Seattle: University of Washington Press, 1999.

Langum, David J. *Crossing the Line: Legislating Morality and the Mann Act*. Chicago: University of Chicago Press, 1994.

Larson, Louise Leung. *Sweet Bamboo: A Memoir of a Chinese American Family*. Berkeley: University of California Press, 1989.

Lasch, Christopher. "Life in the Therapeutic State." In *Women and the Common Life: Love, Marriage, and Feminism*, edited by Elisabeth Lasch-Quinn, 161–86. New York: W. W. Norton & Company, 1997.

———. "The Sexual Division of Labor, the Decline of Civic Culture, and the Rise of the Suburbs." In *Women and the Common Life: Love, Marriage, and Feminism*, edited by Elisabeth Lasch-Quinn, 93–120. New York: W. W. Norton & Company, 1997.

Laughlin, Rev. John Hood. "Chinese Children in American Schools." *Overland Monthly* 57, no. 2 (February 1911): 500–507.

Laws, Treaty, and Regulations Relating to the Exclusion of Chinese. Washington, D.C.: Government Printing Office, 1900.

Le, Thao N., and others. "Not Invisible: Asian Pacific Islander Juvenile Arrests in San Francisco County." Oakland: Asian Pacific Islander Youth Violence Prevention Center, National Council on Crime and Delinquency, 2001.

Le, Thao N., and Judy L. Wallen. "Youth Delinquency: Self-Reported Rates and Risk Factors of Cambodian, Chinese, Lao/Mien, and Vietnamese Youth." *AAPI Nexus* 4, no. 2 (Summer/Fall 2006): 15–44.

Lee, Anthony W. *Picturing Chinatown: Art and Orientalism in San Francisco*. Berkeley: University of California Press, 2001.

Lee, Bill. *Chinese Playground: A Memoir*. San Francisco: Rhapsody Press, 1999.

Lee, Erika. *At America's Gates: Chinese Immigration during the Exclusion Era, 1882–1943*. Chapel Hill: University of North Carolina Press, 2003.

———. "Exclusion Acts: Chinese Women during the Chinese Exclusion Era, 1882–1943." In *Asian/Pacific Islander American Women: A Historical Anthology*, edited by Shirley Hune and Gail M. Nomura, 77–89. New York: New York University Press, 2003.

Lee, Jane Kwong. "Chinese Women in San Francisco." *Chinese Digest*, June 1938. Reprinted in *Bulletin, Chinese Historical Society of America* 6, no. 2 (February 1971): 1–3.

Lee, Mary Bo-Tze. "Problems of the Segregated School for Asiatics in San Francisco." Master's thesis, University of California, Berkeley, 1921.

Lee, Moonbeam Tong. *Growing Up in Chinatown: The Life and Work of Edwar Lee*. [San Francisco?]: Fong Brothers Printing, 1987.

Lee, Yan Phou. *When I Was a Boy in China*. London: Blackie & Son, 1887.

Lee, Yuk Ying. "Education of Chinese Women." *Chinese America: History and Perspectives* 2 (January 1988): 103–7. Reprinted from *The Dragon Student*. San Francisco: Chinese Students' Alliance of America, 1905.

Lee Chew. "The Life Story of a Chinaman." In *The Life Stories of Undistinguished Americans as Told by Themselves*, edited by Hamilton Holt, 174–85. New York: Routledge, 2000.

"Letter from Fong Sun Chow." February 9, 1893. *Occidental Leaves*. San Francisco: Woman's Occidental Board of Foreign Missions, 1893.

Liang Qinggui. "The Report Transmitting the Register of Schools of Overseas Chinese in North America to the Ministry of Education, Second Year of the Xuantong Reign Era [1910]." Translated by Him Mark Lai and Ellen Yeung. *Chinese America: History and Perspectives* 14 (January 2000): 49–53.

Light, Ivan. "From Vice District to Tourist Attraction: The Moral Career of American Chinatowns, 1880–1940." *Pacific Historical Review* 43, no. 3 (August 1974): 378–90.

Ling, Huping. "Chinese Merchant Wives in the United States, 1840–1945." In *Origins and Destinations: 41 Essays on Chinese America*, 79–92. Los Angeles: Chinese Historical Society of Southern California and UCLA Asian American Studies Center, 1994.

———. "Growing Up in 'Hop Alley': Chinese American Youth in St. Louis during the Early Twentieth Century." In *Asian American Children: A Historical Handbook and Guide*, edited by Benson Tong, 65–81. Westport, Conn.: Greenwood Press, 2004.

——. *Surviving on the Gold Mountain: A History of Chinese American Women and Their Lives*. Albany: State University of New York Press, 1998.

Lloyd, B. E. *Lights and Shades in San Francisco*. San Francisco: A. L. Bancroft & Company, 1876. Reprint, Berkeley: Berkeley Hills Books, 1999.

Look Tin Eli. "Our New Oriental City—Veritable Fairy Palaces Filled with the Choicest Treasures of the Orient." In *San Francisco: The Metropolis of the West*. San Francisco: Western Press Association, 1910.

Low, Victor. *The Unimpressible Race: A Century of Educational Struggle by the Chinese in San Francisco*. San Francisco: East/West Publishing Co., 1982.

Lowe, Pardee. *Father and Glorious Descendent*. Boston: Little, Brown and Company, 1943.

Lui, Mary Ting Yi. *The Chinatown Trunk Mystery: Murder, Miscegenation, and Other Dangerous Encounters in Turn-of-the-Century New York City*. Princeton: Princeton University Press, 2005.

Lum, Philip A. "The Creation and Demise of San Francisco Chinatown Freedom Schools: One Response to Desegregation." *Amerasia Journal* 5, no. 1 (1978): 57–73.

Macallair, Daniel. "The San Francisco Industrial School and the Origins of Juvenile Justice in California: A Glance at the Great Reformation." *UC Davis Journal of Juvenile Law and Policy* 7, no. 1 (Winter 2003): 1–60.

Macleod, David I. *Building Character in the American Boy: The Boy Scouts, YMCA, and Their Forerunners, 1870–1920*. Madison: University of Wisconsin Press, 1983.

Mak, Clara Yim-tong. "In Search of a New Life: The Story of the Chinese Immigrant Laundrymen in San Francisco, 1900–1950." Master's thesis, Holy Names College, 1975.

Mark, Diane Mei Lin, and Ginger Chih. *A Place Called Chinese America*. Rev. printing. Dubuque, Iowa: Kendall/Hunt Publishing Company, 1985.

Martin, Mildred Crowl. *Chinatown's Angry Angel: The Story of Donaldina Cameron*. Palo Alto, Calif.: Pacific Books, 1977.

Mason, Sarah Refo. "Social Christianity, American Feminism, and Chinese Prostitutes: The History of the Presbyterian Mission Home, San Francisco, 1874–1935." In *Women and Chinese Patriarchy: Submission, Servitude, and Escape*, edited by Maria Jaschok and Suzanne Miers, 198–220. London: Hong Kong University Press, 1994.

Mayor's Office of Community Development, Mayor's Office of Housing, San Francisco Redevelopment Agency. "City and County of San Francisco, Five-Year Consolidated Plan, July 1, 2005–June 30, 2010." San Francisco, Calif., 2005. <http://www.sfgov.org/site/uploadedfiles/mocd/20052010ConsolidatedPlanv15.pdf> (accessed May 19, 2008).

McClain, Charles J. *In Search of Equality: The Chinese Struggle against Discrimination in Nineteenth-Century America*. Berkeley: University of California Press, 1994.

McGerr, Michael. *A Fierce Discontent: The Rise and Fall of the Progressive Movement in America*. Oxford: Oxford University Press, 2003.

McKeown, Adam. "Transnational Chinese Families and Chinese Exclusion, 1875–1943." *Journal of American Ethnic History* 18, no. 2 (Winter 1999): 73–110. Expanded

Academic ASAP, Thomson Gale, University of California, Davis (CDL), <http://find.galegroup.com/itx/infomar.do?&contentSet=IAC-Documents&type=r> (accessed July 3, 2006).

McLeod, Alexander. *Pigtails and Gold Dust*. Caldwell, Idaho: The Caxton Printers, Ltd., 1948.

Mears, Eliot Grinnell. *Resident Orientals on the American Pacific Coast: Their Legal and Economic Status*. Chicago: University of Chicago Press, 1928.

Meckel, Richard A. *Save the Babies: American Public Health Reform and the Prevention of Infant Mortality, 1850–1929*. Baltimore: Johns Hopkins University Press, 1990.

Mellinger, Wayne Martin. "Postcards from the Edge of the Color Line: Images of African Americans in Popular Culture, 1893–1917." *Symbolic Interaction* 15, no. 4 (November 1992): 413–33.

Miller, George and Dorothy. *Picture Postcards in the United States, 1893–1918*. New York: Clarkson N. Potter, Inc., Publisher, 1976.

Miner, Luella. "Chinese Students and the Exclusion Laws." *Independent*, April 24, 1902.

Mink, Gwendolyn. *The Wages of Motherhood: Inequality in the Welfare State, 1917–1942*. Ithaca: Cornell University Press, 1995.

Minnick, Sylvia Sun. *Samfow: The San Joaquin Chinese Legacy*. Fresno, Calif.: Panorama West Publishing, 1988.

Mullen, Kevin J. *Dangerous Strangers: Minority Newcomers and Criminal Violence in the Urban West, 1850–2000*. New York: Pallgrave Macmillan, 2005.

Murray, Marian. *Plant Wizard: The Life of Lue Gim Gong*. London: Crowell-Collier Press, 1970.

National Economic Development and Law Center. "Chinatown Families Economic Self-Sufficiency Coalition: Building Bridges to Help Chinese Families Reach Economic Self-Sufficiency." Final Report, November 21, 2005. <http://www.insightcced.org/uploads///publications/wd/Building%20Bridges%20Helping%20Chinese.pdf> (accessed May 19, 2008).

Nee, Victor G., and Brett de Bary Nee. *Longtime Californ': A Documentary Study of an American Chinatown*. Stanford: Stanford University Press, 1986.

Nunn, Diane, and Christine Cleary. "From the Mexican California Frontier to Arnold-Kennick: Highlights in the Evolution of the California Juvenile Court, 1850–1961." *Journal of the Center for Families, Children, and the Courts* 5 (2004): 3–34.

Odem, Mary. *Delinquent Daughters: Protecting and Policing Adolescent Female Sexuality in the United States, 1885–1920*. Chapel Hill: University of North Carolina Press, 1995.

Ong, Paul. "An Ethnic Trade: The Chinese Laundries in Early California." *Journal of Ethnic Studies* 8, no. 4 (Winter 1981): 95–113.

Ong, Paul, and Karen Umemoto. "Life and Work in the Inner City." In *Contemporary Asian America: A Multidisciplinary Reader*, edited by Min Zhou and James V. Gatewood, 233–53. New York: New York University Press, 2000.

Osumi, Megumi Dick. "Asians and California's Anti-Miscegenation Laws." In *Asian and Pacific American Experiences: Women's Perspectives*, edited by Nobuya Tsuchida, 2–8. Minneapolis: Asian/Pacific American Learning Resource Center and General College, University of Minnesota, 1982.

Pan, Ying Zi. "The Impact of the 1906 Earthquake on San Francisco's Chinatown." Ph.D. diss., Brigham Young University, 1991.

Park, Lisa Sun-Hee. *Consuming Citizenship: Children of Asian Immigrant Entrepreneurs*. Stanford: Stanford University Press, 2005.

———. "Ensuring Upward Mobility: Obligations of Children of Immigrant Entrepreneurs." In *Asian American Children: A Historical Handbook and Guide*, edited by Benson Tong, 123–35. Westport, Conn.: Greenwood Press, 2004.

Park, Roberta J. "Sport and Recreation among Chinese American Communities of the Pacific Coast from Time of Arrival to the 'Quiet Decade' of the 1950s." *Journal of Sport History* 27, no. 3 (Fall 2000): 445–70.

Pascoe, Peggy. "Gender Systems in Conflict: The Marriages of Mission-Educated Chinese American Women, 1874–1939." In *Unequal Sisters*, edited by Ellen Carol DuBois and Vicki L. Ruiz, 123–40. New York: Routledge, 1990.

———. *Relations of Rescue: The Search for Female Moral Authority in the American West, 1874–1939*. New York: Oxford University Press, 1990.

Peffer, George Anthony. "Forbidden Families: Emigration Experiences of Chinese Women under the Page Law, 1875–1882." *Journal of American Ethnic History* 6, no. 1 (Fall 1986): 28–46.

Peiss, Kathy. *Cheap Amusements: Working Women and Leisure in Turn-of-the-Century New York*. Philadelphia: Temple University Press, 1986.

Perkins, Dorothy. *Encyclopedia of China: The Essential Reference to China, Its History and Culture*. New York: Roundtable Press, 1999.

Perman, Michael. *The Struggle for Mastery: Disfranchisement in the South, 1888–1908*. Chapel Hill: University of North Carolina Press, 2001.

Platt, Anthony M. *The Child Savers: The Invention of Delinquency*. Chicago: University of Chicago Press, 1969.

Rast, Raymond W. "The Cultural Politics of Tourism in San Francisco's Chinatown, 1882–1917." *Pacific Historical Review* 76, no. 1 (February 2007): 29–60.

Redondo, Brian, and others. "Left in the Margins: Asian American Students and the No Child Left Behind Act." New York: Asian American Legal Defense and Education Fund, 2008.

Report of the Chinese Mission to the California Conference of the Methodist Episcopal Church for the Year Ending August 31st, 1889. San Francisco: Cubery & Company, 1889.

Report of the Joint Special Committee to Investigate Chinese Immigration, United States Senate Forty-fourth Congress. Washington, D.C.: Government Printing Office, 1877. Reprint, New York: Arno Press, 1978.

Report of the Presbyterian Mission to the Chinese in California. San Francisco: George Spaulding & Co., 1881.

Report of the Special Committee of the Board of Supervisors of San Francisco on the Condition of the Chinese Quarter and the Chinese in San Francisco, July 1885. San Francisco: P. J. Thomas, 1885.

"Rescue Work of the Occidental Board." *Woman's Work: A Foreign Missions Magazine* 26, no. 1 (January 1911): 11.

Rosen, Ruth. *The Lost Sisterhood: Prostitution in America, 1900–1918*. Baltimore: Johns Hopkins University Press, 1982.

Ross, James R. *Caught in a Tornado: A Chinese American Woman Survives the Cultural Revolution*. Boston: Northeastern University Press, 1994.

Rydell, Robert W. "Souvenirs of Imperialism: World's Fair Postcards." In *Delivering Views: Distant Cultures in Early Postcards*, edited by Christraud M. Geary and Virginia-Lee Webb, 47–60. Washington, D.C.: Smithsonian Institution Press, 1998.

Saari, Jon L. *Legacies of Childhood: Growing Up Chinese in a Time of Crisis, 1890–1920*. Cambridge: Harvard University Press, 1990.

Salyer, Lucy E. *Laws Harsh as Tigers: Chinese Immigrants and the Shaping of Modern Immigration Law*. Chapel Hill: University of North Carolina Press, 1995.

Sandmeyer, Elmer Clarence. *The Anti-Chinese Movement in California*. Urbana: University of Illinois Press, 1991.

San Francisco's Chinatown: An Aid to Tourists and Others in Visiting China-Town. San Francisco, 1909.

San Francisco Unified School District. "Academic Plan for Student Achievement, 2007–2008 School Year." Gordon J. Lau Elementary School. April 13, 2007. <http://portal.sfusd.edu/data/AcademicPlans/acad-49000.pdf> (accessed May 19, 2008).

———. "Accountability Report Card 2006–2007." <http://orb.sfusd.edu/sarcs/darc/sfusd—darc.pdf> (accessed May 19, 2008).

———. "Alternative Program Placement Form." Multilingual Forms. <http://portal.sfusd.edu/data/multilingual/AlternativeProgPlmntForm.pdf> (accessed May 19, 2008).

———. "Enrollment Guide, 2008–2009." San Francisco: San Francisco Unified School District, 2007.

———. "Gordon J. Lau Elementary School Profile." <http://orb.sfusd.edu/profile/prfl-490.htm> (accessed May 19, 2008).

———. "Lowell High School History." <http://www.sfusd.edu/schwww/sch697/about/history/page2.html> (accessed May 19, 2008).

———. "School Accountability Report Card School Year 2006–07." Chinese Education Center. <http://orb.sfusd.edu/sarcs2/sarc-476.pdf> (accessed May 19, 2008).

———. "School Accountability Report Card School Year 2006–07." Gordon Lau Elementary School. <http://orb.sfusd.edu/sarcs2/sarc-490.pdf> (accessed May 19, 2008).

Schackelford, Ruth. "To Shield Them from Temptation: 'Child-saving' Institutions and the Children of the Underclass in San Francisco, 1850–1910." Ph.D. diss., Harvard University, 1991.

Schwartz, Marie Jenkins. *Born in Bondage: Growing Up Enslaved in the Antebellum South*. Cambridge, Mass.: Harvard University Press, 2000.

Shah, Nayan. *Contagious Divides: Epidemics and Race in San Francisco's Chinatown*. Berkeley: University of California Press, 2001.

Shepherd, Rev. Charles R. "Educational Work in the Chinese Community of San Francisco, Calif." In *Oriental Mission Work on the Pacific Coast of the United States of*

America, 21–29. New York: Home Missions Council and Council of Women for Home Missions, 1920.

Shinn, M. W. "Charities for Children in San Francisco." *Overland Monthly and Out West Magazine* 15, no. 85 (January 1890): 78–101.

———. "Poverty and Charity in San Francisco." *Overland Monthly and Out West Magazine* 14, no. 83 (November 1889): 535–47.

A Short Story about Chinatown. San Francisco: Dettmar & Co., 1903(?).

Shumsky, Neil Larry. *The Evolution of Political Protest and the Workingmen's Party of California*. Columbus: Ohio State University Press, 1991.

———. "Vice Responds to Reform, San Francisco, 1910–1914." *Journal of Urban History* 7, no. 1 (November 1980): 31–47.

Shumsky, Neil Larry, and Larry M. Springer. "San Francisco's Zone of Prostitution, 1880–1934." *Journal of Historical Geography* 7, no. 1 (1981): 71–89.

Siu, C. P. *The Chinese Laundryman: A Study of Social Isolation*. Edited by John Kuo Wei Tchen. New York: New York University Press, 1987.

Sixth Annual Report of the Occidental Branch of the Woman's Foreign Missionary Society of the Presbyterian Church. San Francisco: C. H. Street, Printer & Publisher, 1879.

Staley, Jeffrey L. "Contested Childhoods: The Pacific Society for the Suppression of Vice vs. the WHMS Methodist Oriental Home, 1900–1903." *Chinese America: History and Perspectives* 21 (January 2007): 43–54. Special Twentieth Anniversary Issue. Branching Out the Banyan Tree: A Changing Chinese America. Conference Proceedings, edited by Colleen Fong and Lorraine Dong.

State Commission of Immigration and Housing of California. *A Manual for Home Teachers*. Sacramento: California State Printing Office, 1919.

———. *Heroes of Freedom*. Sacramento: California State Printing Office, 1919.

Stout, Arthur B. *Chinese Immigration and the Physiological Causes of the Decay of a Nation*. San Francisco: Agnew & Deffebach, Printers, 1862.

Sui Sin Far. "Chinatown Boys and Girls." *Los Angeles Express*, October 15, 1909. Reprinted in *Sui Sin Far, Mrs. Spring Fragrance, and Other Writings*, edited by Amy Ling and Annette White-Parks, 226–28. Urbana: University of Illinois Press, 1995.

———. "The Chinese Woman in America." *Land of Sunshine* 6, no. 2 (January 1897): 59–64.

Sung, Betty Lee. *The Story of the Chinese in America*. New York: Collier Books, 1967.

Sung, Mrs. William Z. L. "A Pioneer Chinese Family." *The Life, Influence, and the Role of the Chinese in the United States, 1776–1960*. San Francisco: Chinese Historical Society of America, 1975.

Swett, John. *History of the Public School System of California*. San Francisco: A. L. Bancroft and Company, 1876.

Tang, Vincente. "Chinese Women Immigrants and the Two-Edged Sword of Habeas Corpus." In *The Chinese American Experience: Papers from the Second National Conference on Chinese American Studies, 1980*, edited by Genny Lim, 48–56. San Francisco: Chinese Historical Society of America and the Chinese Culture Foundation of San Francisco, 1984.

Tape, Mary. "A Letter from Mrs. Tape." April 8, 1885. In *Unbound Voices: A Documentary*

History of Chinese Women in San Francisco, edited by Judy Yung, 174–75. Berkeley: University of California Press, 1999.

Taylor, Frank J. "San Francisco's New Chinese City." *Travel Magazine*, March 1929, 18–21, 54.

Tchen, John Kuo Wei. *Genthe's Photographs of San Francisco's Old Chinatown*. New York: Dover Publications, Inc., 1984.

Third Annual Report of the California Branch of the Woman's Foreign Missionary Society of the Presbyterian Church of San Francisco. San Francisco: C. W. Gordon, Steam Book and Job Printers, 1876.

Thirteenth Annual Report of the Occidental Branch of the Woman's Foreign Missionary Society, of the Presbyterian Church of the Pacific Coast. San Francisco: The Occident Printing House, 1886.

Thirtieth Annual Report of the Woman's Occidental Board of Foreign Missions. San Francisco, 1903.

"Three Chinese Women of San Francisco." *Woman's Work: A Foreign Missions Magazine* 24, no. 8 (August 1909): 174–75.

Tong, Benson. *The Chinese Americans*. Westport, Conn.: Greenwood Press, 2000.

———. "Introduction: The Worldview of Asian American Children." In *Asian American Children: A Historical Handbook and Guide*, edited by Benson Tong, 3–23. Westport, Conn.: Greenwood Press, 2004.

———. *Unsubmissive Women: Chinese Prostitutes in Nineteenth-Century San Francisco*. Norman: University of Oklahoma Press, 1994.

———, ed. *Asian American Children: A Historical Handbook and Guide*. Westport, Conn.: Greenwood Press, 2004.

Toy, Calvin. "A Short History of Asian Gangs in San Francisco." *Justice Quarterly* 9, no. 4 (December 1992): 647–65.

Trattner, Walter I. *Crusade for the Children: A History of the National Child Labor Committee and Child Labor Reform in America*. Chicago: Quadrangle Books, 1970.

Trauner, Joan B. "The Chinese as Medical Scapegoats in San Francisco, 1870–1905." *California History* 57, no. 1 (Spring 1978): 70–87.

Twenty-Fifth Annual Report of the Woman's Occidental Board of Foreign Missions. San Francisco, 1898.

Tygiel, Jules. *Workingmen in San Francisco, 1880–1901*. New York: Garland Publishing Inc., 1992.

U.S. Census Bureau. *Census 2000*. <www.factfinder.census.gov> (accessed April 23, 2008).

———. *Population Schedules of the Eighth Census of the United States, 1860*. Microform. Washington, D.C.: National Archives and Records Service, 1967.

———. *Population Schedules of the Ninth Census of the United States, 1870*. Microform. Washington, D.C.: National Archives and Records Service, 1965.

———. *Population Schedules of the Tenth Census of the United States, 1880*. Microform. Washington, D.C.: National Archives and Records Service, 1965.

———. *Population Schedules of the Twelfth Census of the United States, 1900*. Microform. Washington, D.C.: National Archives and Records Service, 1981.

——. *Population Schedules of the Thirteenth Census of the United States, 1910.* Microform. Washington, D.C.: National Archives and Records Service, 1982.

——. *Population Schedules of the Fourteenth Census of the United States, 1920.* Microform. Washington, D.C.: National Archives and Records Administration, 1992.

U.S. Congress. Senate. *Importing Women for Immoral Purposes: A Partial Report from the Immigration Commission on the Importation and Harboring of Women for Immoral Purposes.* 61st Cong., 2nd sess. Senate Document No. 196. Washington, D.C.: Government Printing Office, 1909.

——. Senate. *Statistical Review of Immigration, 1820–1910.* 61st Cong., 3rd sess. Senate Document No. 756. Washington, D.C.: Government Printing Office, 1911.

U.S. Department of Health and Human Services. "Youth Violence: A Report of the Surgeon General." 2001. <http://www.surgeongeneral.gov/library/youthviolence/toc.html> (accessed May 19, 2008).

U.S. Department of the Interior. Bureau of Education. *The Public School System of San Francisco, California.* Washington, D.C.: Government Printing Office, 1917.

U.S. Department of Labor. Bureau of Immigration. *Treaty, Laws, and Rules Governing the Admission of Chinese.* Washington, D.C.: Government Printing Office, 1914.

——. *Treaty, Laws, and Rules Governing the Admission of Chinese.* Washington, D.C.: Government Printing Office, 1915.

The Unity of Three. Santa Cruz, Calif.: Asian American Student Alliance, 1977.

Vaule, Rosamond B. *As We Were: American Photographic Postcards, 1905–1930.* Boston: Davis R. Godine, Publisher, 2004.

West, Elliott, and Paula Petrik, eds. *Small Worlds: Children and Adolescents in America, 1850–1950.* Lawrence: University Press of Kansas, 1992.

Whitney, James A. *The Chinese and the Chinese Question.* 2nd ed. New York: Tibbals Book Company, 1888.

Willrich, Michael. *City of Courts: Socializing Justice in Progressive Era Chicago.* Cambridge: Cambridge University Press, 2003.

Wilson, Carol Green. *Borrowed Babies: The Story of the Babies Aid.* [San Francisco?], 1939.

——. *Chinatown Quest: The Life Adventures of Donaldina Cameron.* Rev. ed. Stanford: Stanford University Press, 1950.

Wilson, Melvin N., and others. "Ethnic Minority Families and the Majority Educational System: African American, Chinese American, Hispanic American, and Native American Families." In *Children of Color: Research, Health, and Policy Issues,* edited by Hiram E. Fitzgerald, Barry M. Lester, and Barry S. Zuckerman, 257–80. New York: Garland Publishing, Inc., 1999.

Wollenberg, Charles. *All Deliberate Speed: Segregation and Exclusion in California Schools, 1855–1975.* Berkeley: University of California Press, 1976.

Won, Lily King Gee. "Recollections of Dr. Sun Yat-sen's Stay at Our Home in San Francisco." Translated by Ellen Yeung. *Chinese America: History and Perspectives* 4 (January 1990): 67–82.

Wong, H. K. *Gum Sahn Yun: Gold Mountain Men.* San Francisco: Bechtel Publications, 1987.

Wong, K. Scott. "Chinatown: Conflicting Images, Contested Terrain." *Melus* 20, no. 1 (Spring 1995): 3–15.

Wong, Morrison G. "The Chinese American Family." In *Ethnic Families in America: Patterns and Variations*, 4th ed., edited by Charles H. Mindel, Robert W. Habenstein, and Roosevelt Wright Jr., 284–310. Upper Saddle River, N.J.: Prentice Hall, 1998.

Wong, Mrs. Clemens. *Chinatown*. San Francisco, 1915.

Wores, Theodore. "The Children of Chinatown in San Francisco." *St. Nicholas* 23, no. 7 (May 1896): 575–77.

Workingmen's Party of California. *An Address from the Workingmen of San Francisco to Their Brothers throughout the Pacific Coast*. San Francisco: Workingmen's Party of California, 1888.

Wu, Frank H. *Yellow: Race in America beyond Black and White*. New York: Basic Books, 2003.

Yick, Donna R. *Esther Hunt: A Collector's Guide*. San Francisco: Poco Books, 2005.

Yu, Connie Young. "A History of San Francisco Chinatown Housing." *Amerasia Journal* 8, no. 1 (Spring/Summer 1981): 93–109.

——. "Rediscovered Voices: Chinese Immigrants and Angel Island." *Amerasia Journal* 4, no. 2 (1977): 123–39.

Yung, Judy. "The Social Awakening of Chinese American Women as Reported in the Chung Sai Yat Po, 1900–1911." *Chinese America: History and Perspectives* 2 (January 1988): 80–102.

——. *Unbound Feet: A Social History of Chinese Women in San Francisco*. Berkeley: University of California Press, 1995.

——. *Unbound Voices: A Documentary History of Chinese Women in San Francisco*. Berkeley: University of California Press, 1999.

Zelizer, Viviana A. "From Useful to Useless: Moral Conflict over Child Labor." In *The Children's Culture Reader*, edited by Henry Jenkins, 81–94. New York: New York University Press, 1998.

Zhang, Sheldon X. "Chinese Gangs: Familial and Cultural Dynamics." In *Gangs in America III*, edited by C. Ronald Huff, 219–36. Thousand Oaks, Calif.: Sage Publications, 2002.

Zhao, Xiaojian. *Remaking Chinese America: Immigration, Family, and Community, 1940–1965*. New Brunswick, N.J.: Rutgers University Press, 2002.

Zhou, Min. "Social Capital in Chinatown: The Role of Community-Based Organizations and Families in the Adaptation of the Younger Generation." In *Contemporary Asian America: A Multidisciplinary Reader*, edited by Min Zhou and J. V. Gatewood, 315–35. New York: New York University Press, 2000.

INDEX

Accidents, 62, 73–74

Adams, Frederick H., 168

Addams, Jane, 135, 159

African Americans, 112–13, 116–17, 188

Age of consent laws, 160–61. *See also* Reformers

Aguilar, Jose, 129

Americanization, 55–60, 66, 67, 110–11, 132–38, 173–74. *See also* Families: adaptation to American culture

Americanization Day, 133–34

Amulets, 56–57, 67

Angel Island: construction of, 18–19; detention at, 19; medical exams at, 20–21, 22, 23, 37; interrogations at, 21–22, 24–31, 33–35, 38; exempt-class immigrants at, 22–23, 25–31; and illegal immigration, 32–35; criticisms of, 35–40. *See also* Immigration of Chinese children

Anti-Chinese movement: criticism of Chinese family life, 2–3, 15–17, 41, 42–45, 58, 74, 76, 114, 154–57, 176–81, 213; opposition to Chinese labor, 3, 15–17, 20–22, 41, 92–99, 108, 117; fear of disease, 3, 68–69, 93–94, 108, 110–11, 113–16, 143–44, 176–81, 213; opposition to Chinese immigration, 15–17, 20–22, 33, 41; opposition to Chinese prostitutes, 16–17, 20–22, 44, 141–45, 161–62, 174; fear of miscegenation, 44–45, 154–57; use of violence by, 98–99, 128–29; demand for segregation of schools,

110–17, 138–39; criticism of Chinese crime, 162, 163–64, 166, 174–75, 176–81, 213. *See also* Stereotypes of Chinatown; Stereotypes of Chinese Americans

Anti-Chinese Union of San Francisco, 98

Antimiscegenation laws, 44. *See also* Interracial families

Armer, Laura Adams, 183

Asian American Legal Defense and Education Fund, 223

Asian Women's Resource Center, 227–28

Associated Charities, 72

Au Kai Yung, 30

Babies' Aid Society, 73

Baby Hygiene Committee, 73

Baby shows, 185

Bachelor society, 1, 2–3, 15–17, 43–49, 76, 184–85. *See also* Families

Baker, Frank C., 161

Bamford, Mary, 180–81

Baptism, 57

Baptist Mission School, 120, 124–25

Barbat, William, 156

Baskin, (Mary?), 135

Batchelder, Captain, 100

Behrendt, Richard, 188

Beng, Ah, 110–11

Bergholz, Leo, 31

Bertillon system, 20, 23, 36

Bilingual Education Act, 223

Bluebirds, 64, 216

Bokee, Marian, 123

Condit, Ira, 72

Court cases: *In re Look Tin Sing*, 9, 23; Habeas corpus hearings, 18, 22–23, 35; *United States v. Wong Kim Ark*, 23; *Quock Ting v. United States*, 26; *United States v. Ju Toy*, 34, 35; *Yick Wo v. Hopkins*, 94–95; guardianship hearings, 102–3, 150–57; *Ward v. Flood*, 113; *Tape v. Hurley*, 115–16, 118; *Plessy v. Ferguson*, 116; *Wong Him v. Callahan*, 118–19; *Ex Parte Ah Peen*, 168; Juvenile court hearings, 170–74; *Shelley v. Kraemer*, 217; *Ho v. San Francisco Unified School District*, 222; *Lau v. Nichols*, 223

Crime, 159–74, 177–79, 213, 225–27. *See also* Violence

Cubic Air Ordinance, 164

Culbertson, Margaret, 148

Cullen, Thomas, 153

Cunningham, Joseph, 153

Davis, Carrie, 21–22, 102–3

Davis, Horace, 15

Davison, Mary, 183–84

Death, 13, 18, 62, 67–76, 100, 154, 164–65. *See also* Disease and illness

Densmore, G. B., 74, 94, 114–15

Densmore Investigation, 33

Detroit Photographic Company (Detroit Publishing Company), 192

Dillingham Commission, 161

Disease and illness, 13, 18, 19–20, 67–76, 74–75, 93–94, 143–44, 153–54. *See also* Stereotypes of Chinese Americans: as dirty/diseased

Domestic servants, 52–53, 79, 80, 82–88, 93, 100. *See also* Child labor, Chinese

Dong Fong, 34–35

Dong Ho, 149–50

Downtown Association of San Francisco, 37

Earthquake (1906), 32, 185–87

Education: and model-minority stereotype, 6, 136–39, 218–19, 226; and Americanization, 57–58, 110–11, 132–38; at mission schools, 110–11, 123–25, 134–35, 158–59; segregation of, 110–23, 137–39, 221–22; at Chinese Public School, 111, 113, 118, 119–20, 121, 122, 123, 125–29, 132–33, 135–36; at Chinese-language schools, 112, 129–31; and battle against segregation, 114–23, 137–39, 217, 221–25; advocated for young Chinese women, 121–23; enrollment of Chinese children, 127; and bilingual education, 223–24; and No Child Left Behind Act, 223; and Proposition 227, 223. *See also* Students, Chinese

Elliott, Albert J., 156

English-language learners, 222–24

Ethnic slumming, 177–78

Evans, Albert S., 14–15

Exclusion laws: Chinese Exclusion Act (1882), 5, 9, 17, 95; Page Act (1875), 9, 16–17, 47, 141, 142; fight against, 9, 35–37, 40–41, 206; circumventing, 13, 32–35; anti-Chinese push for, 15–17, 33, 41; and impact on family formation, 16–17, 23–24, 46–48; enforcement of, 17–40; and habeas corpus hearings, 18, 22–23, 35; and exempt classes, 25–32, 37–40. *See also* Immigration of Chinese children

Ex Parte Ah Peen, 168

Factory labor, 79–80, 89–91, 93–94, 97, 98, 104–5

Fah, Ah, 152

Families: split-household, 1, 2–3, 47, 49, 174; anti-Chinese attacks on, 2–3, 15–17, 41, 42–45, 58, 74, 76, 114, 154–57, 176–81, 213; and middle-class domesticity, 6, 55, 76, 106–7, 108–9, 115–16, 118–19, 199–201, 205–7, 212–14, 215–16, 217; and decision to emigrate, 10–12, 41; and poverty, 10–13, 67–69, 71–72,

102, 106–7, 108–9, 219–20, 227–29; and
paper sons or daughters, 13, 32–35, 41;
of merchants, 13–14, 22–23, 26–29, 35,
36–37, 41, 55, 106–7; and domestic
arrangements, 15–17, 43–44, 45–55, 76–
77, 106–7, 142; obstacles to establishment of, 16–17, 23–24, 46–47, 67–68,
76–77; and family economy, 24, 89–91,
91–92, 100–109; of native-born citizens,
26–29; and transpacific ties, 41, 123,
129–30, 201–7; Christianization of, 42,
55–56, 57, 64, 71–72, 110–11, 121–25, 157–
59, 174–75, 176–77; and child rearing,
43–47, 58–60, 100–107, 108–9, 189;
adaptation to American culture, 45–
60, 62–65, 66, 67, 76–77, 110–11, 115–16,
118–19, 121–23, 132–38, 157–59, 173–75,
176–77, 201–14, 216, 217; and rituals,
55–60, 65–67, 75–76; and Progressive
reformers, 62–64, 72–73, 100–105, 108–
9, 132–36, 171–75; and guardianship
hearings, 102–3, 150–57; and juvenile
delinquency, 171–75, 226–27; and 1906
earthquake, 185–87; and tourism, 176–
85, 187–201, 212–14; and Chinese Revolution, 201–5, 214; and generational
conflicts, 208–12, 214, 220, 225; and
reunification, 216
Family economy, 24, 89–91, 91–92,
100–109. *See also* Child labor,
Chinese
Feast of the Hungry Ghosts, 67
Felton, Katherine, 72
Festivals. *See* Holidays
Field, Edna R., 56
Filial piety, 58–59
First Chinese Baptist Church, 123
First Methodist Episcopal Church, 161
Fisk Investigative Committee, 161
Folklore and folk religion, 67
Folsom Prison, 164
Fong Bow, 27
Fong Quong, 151
Fong Sec, 13, 15

Fong Sou Nam, 39
Fong Sun Chow, 66
Fong Sun Moon, 23
Fong Wing Look, 39
Foo Tai, 42
Foot binding, 22, 59–60
Freedom Schools, 221
Fritz, Alfred, 173
Full moon celebration, 56–57

Gale, Zona, 42
Gambling, 13, 165, 173, 178, 226. *See also*
Crime
Games. *See* Recreation
Gardiner, Mrs., 84
Geary, Thomas J., 16
Genthe, Arnold, 177–78, 183, 187–88
Gentlemen's Agreement (United States–
Japan), 120
Gibson, Otis, 97
Girls: immigration of, 11–12, 14–15, 20–
22, 24–25, 28, 33–34, 39–40; and foot
binding, 22, 59–60; and gender roles,
46, 56, 59–60, 75, 208–9; numbers of,
47–48; in mostly female households,
49–51, 54; and recreation, 61–65; labor
of, 80–83, 85–88, 90, 101, 102–3, 141–46;
education of, 121–23, 157–59; in the
missions, 147–59; in the juvenile jus-
tice system, 167, 168, 170; stereotyped
as passive, 188, 192; and conflicts with
parents, 208–10; and courting and
marriage, 209–11; discrimination in
employment of, 211–12. *See also* Missionaries; *Mui tsai*; Prostitution
Goeggel & Wiedner, 188
Golden Dragon shooting, 226
Gold Mountain School (Academy of the
Great Qing Empire), 130
Grant, Ulysses S., 16
Greenlee, Ida K., 37–39
Greenwell, William, 137
Guai Ching, 75
Guangdong province, 10

Habeas corpus, 18, 22–23, 35, 150, 151, 152. *See also* Immigration of Chinese children; Exclusion laws

Hackett, Fred, 124–25

Hall, James, 131

Hearst, Phoebe, 136

Henshaw, Sarah, 93

Hoffman, Ogden, 22–23, 35

Ho Kin, 155–57

Holidays, 65–67, 132–33, 183, 207

Ho Lin, 155–57

Homework, 89–91, 104–5. *See also* Child labor, Chinese

Homicide. *See* Crime; Violence

Hookworm, 20, 38. *See also* Immigration of Chinese children: and medical exams

Hop Sing, 226

Hospitals, 20, 74, 75, 100, 153

Housing, 67–68, 69, 71–72, 106–7, 220

Ho v. San Francisco Unified School District, 222

Ho Yow, 101

Huie Kin, 12, 13, 84, 85

Huie Ngou, 13

Hung, Charley, 150

Hunt, Esther, 183–84, 187–88

Illiteracy rates, 112

Immigration Act of 1965, 218

Immigration of Chinese children: and challenges to exclusion, 9, 35–41, 206; as laborers, 10–11, 22; motives for, 10–12; and conditions of travel, 12–14; and illness and death, 13, 18; and illegal immigration, 13, 32–35; arrival in the United States, 14–15; anti-Chinese opposition to, 15–17, 20–22, 33, 41; and detention and examination, 17–40; and habeas corpus hearings, 18, 22–23, 35–36; and medical exams, 19–21, 22, 23, 36, 37; admittance rates, 24–25, 28, 31; and exempt classes, 25–32, 37–40; and literacy tests, 31; and depor-

tation, 39–40. *See also* Exclusion laws

Industrial schools, 166–70, 173, 174

Industrial Welfare Commission, 90

Infant mortality, 68–71. *See also* Death

In re Look Tin Sing, 9, 23

Interracial families, 44–45, 53–54, 154–57, 210–11, 254 (n. 40)

Irwin, Will, 181–82

Italians, 97, 112, 128–29, 137, 185

Jackson, William Henry, 192

Japanese, 54, 119–20, 139, 141, 188

Jeong, John, 118

Jessup, William H., 97

Joe Boys (Chung Yee), 226

Johnson, Hiram, 133

Jones, Anna, 39–40

Jones, P. B., 34

Jue Do Hong, 74

Jue Lin Ong, 74

Jung Ah Mook, 29

Jung Luen Piu, 29

Juvenile Court Law (1903), 171

Juvenile justice system, 162–74

Kai Ming Head Start, 227–28

Kan, Andrew, 128

Kane, Frank J., 150–51, 155, 254 (n. 30)

Kan Kam Oi, 160

Kearney, Denis, 99. *See also* Workingmen's Party

Keating-Owen Act, 104

Kerr, John G., 114

King, W. W., 23

Knights of St. Crispin, 98

Knowland, Joseph R., 161

Knox, Jessie Juliet, 179

Kroeber, Alfred L., 136

L. C., Edward, 59, 210–11, 212

Labor: anti-Chinese movement objects to Chinese, 3, 15–17, 20–22, 41, 92–99, 108, 117; immigration of Chinese, 10,